W9-CIG-669

SOULED AMERICAN

How Black Music Transformed White Culture

SOULED AMERICAN

How Black Music Transformed White Culture

· KEVIN PHINNEY ·

Billboard Books

an imprint of Watson-Guptill Publications
NEW YORK

Executive Editor: Bob Nirkind
Editor: Meryl Greenblatt
Interior Design: Jay Anning, Thumb Print
Cover Design: Bob O'Brien
Production Manager: Ellen Greene

First published in the United States in 2005 by Billboard Books
an imprint of Watson-Guptill Publications
a division of VNU Business Media, Inc.
770 Broadway, New York, New York 10003
www.wgpub.com

Library of Congress Control Number: 2005922306

ISBN: 0-8230-8404-3

Printed in the United States of America

First printing, 2005

1 2 3 4 5 6 7 8 9/13 12 11 10 09 08 07 06 05

To Ray Joseph,
for his abiding love and faith.

Contents

Acknowledgments

I want to thank those who stood by me in the many seasons it took to complete this project: First and foremost, David P. Hime, who assured me the idea would work; Bob Nirkind, the editor/contortionist who held my hand while kicking my ass every step of the way; and my gentle-but-wise second editor, Meryl Greenblatt. My gratitude also goes out to Phil Richardson and Michael Jones, Jesse Retherford, Jeremy Ellis, and the McCarleys—Linda and Bill—who provided shelter from the storm in a very real way.

I owe Terry Lickona, Gregg Geller, Marian Winik, my beloved confidante Kathy Cronkite, and our Austin writers group an enormous debt for helping me get started; Ed Ward, Kent Benjamin, Maxine O'Dell, Casey Monahan, Dave Laczko, Louis Black, David Fricke, Diane Holloway, Mark Murray, Rosemary Cullen, Betty Sue Flowers, Wendy Morgan, Ochame Haley, Bruno Kirby, Eric Morris, and Randy Haecker for their unflagging support and help with materials; and thanks to the staff of KGSR at Emmis Austin Radio, especially Jyl Hershman-Ross, Jimbo Kipping, Afton Castello, and my comrade in music journalism, Jody Denberg. A special acknowledgment to my radio co-host Kevin Connor, who provided support as only he could. I'd also like to thank my volunteer sounding board, which included Robert Dotson, Herb Watkins, Bill Ikard, Alan Hutcheson, and Dr. Larry Browning. Last, but far from least, I benefited beyond measure from the help provided by my secret weapon, Karen La Blanc of Rhino Records, who did more for me as a courtesy than most do for a paycheck.

Many thanks to my mother Margaret Craig and to all her children: Rick, Barbara, Karen, Jo-Ellen, Mary, and Vickie. I'm blessed and honored to be your brother. I also want to express my appreciation to the family of Catherine Bell, particularly my best friend since 1964, Don. I hope this redeems me as the white sheep of the family.

Certainly *Souled American* wouldn't have been much without the generous participation of my interview subjects. Particular thanks go to Paula Nelson for her help in scheduling time with her father, Willie, and Spencer Gibb, who arranged my interview with his uncle, Maurice Gibb, who passed away not long after our conversation. I'd also like to remember the late Ray Charles and the late Artie Shaw—each a singular talent, a man of his time, and no sufferer of fools.

During the past five years, I've been fortunate to connect with a number of kindred spirits, including my cherished friends in Tower of Power, Emilio and "Doc" Kupka; the most soulful voice still singing, Sam Moore; the bright and tight Rascals drummer Dino Danelli; and Monte Moir of the Time. In addition, I'm grateful to Ike Turner, Brian Wilson, session bassist Chuck Rainey, The Raiders' Mark Lindsay, Wilson Pickett, Boz Scaggs, June Pointer, Stewart Copeland, author Gerri Hershey, *Monterey Pop* documentarian D.A. Pennebaker, Tracy Chapman, U2's Larry Mullen, Jr., Tone Loc, Danny Glass of Royal Crown Revue, Kid Rock, Robert Randolph, and the Blind Boys of Alabama for their willingness to address the topics here for background material.

Let me now formally thank those who participated in the discussion: Dr. Horace Boyer, former Fats Waller guitarist Albert Casey, Walter Cronkite, Artie Shaw, Ray Charles, B.B. King, Casey Kasem, Buddy Guy, Eric Burdon, Little Richard, Mitch Ryder, Steve Cropper and Donald "Duck" Dunn (of Booker T. and the MG's), Mary Wilson (the Supremes), Levi Stubbs (the Four Tops), Melvin Franklin (the Temptations), Marlon Jackson (the Jackson 5), Cory Wells (Three Dog Night), Felix Cavaliere, Dino Danelli, and Gene Cornish (the Rascals), Mr. and Mrs. Sam Moore and the late Dave Prater (of Sam and Dave), producer Jerry Wexler, music journalist Ian Whitcomb, Sylvester Stewart/Sly Stone, John Fogerty, Bill Withers, Janis Joplin collaborator and confidante Sam Andrew, Willie Nelson, Billy Preston, Jimi Hendrix's drummers Mitch Mitchell and Buddy Miles, Joe Cocker, Donny Osmond, Bonnie Raitt, Emilio Castillio and Tower of Power, Asleep at the Wheel's Ray Benson, Chaka Khan, Harry Casey (the KC of Sunshine Band fame), Daryl Hall, Donna Summer, Michael McDonald, Donald Fagen and Walter Becker of Steely Dan, Philip Bailey of Earth, Wind and Fire, Maurice Gibb of the Bee Gees, the Time, *Austin City Limits* producer Terry Lickona, *Blues Brothers* and *Thriller* director John Landis, George Clinton, Alan Hunter and Martha Quinn of MTV, Nile Rodgers of Chic, David Byrne, Ziggy Marley, Double Trouble's Chris Layton, Sheila E., Vanilla Ice, Vernon Reid, Beck, Janet Jackson producer Jimmy Jam Harris, Lyle Lovett, Susan Tedeschi, television documentarian Ken Burns, and the journalists to whom I turned for guidance: Joe Nick Patoski, Dave Marsh, David Ritz, Michael Point, Peter Guralnick, and Paul Grein.

There are three people I never met who nonetheless had a profound impact on this book. One is Robert F. Kennedy, the senator from New York, who inspired me to look for the commonalities rather than the differences between us all; another is mythologist Joseph Campbell, whose work suggested that popular culture, of all things, could be considered a barometer of race relations captured in time, and finally, Leonard Bernstein, the ebullient composer/conductor. Bernstein was once quoted as saying, "Life without music is unthinkable. Music without life is academic. That is why my contact with music is a total embrace."

According to an informal poll I took while conducting interviews over the last five years, 99.999 percent of those listed above agree with the maestro.

Preface

"Listen: Race is too serious an issue to be discussed under the auspices of something as narrow as music, be it jazz, rock 'n' roll, or whatever . . . I would not violate the sanctity of the seriousness of the problem by discussing it in the framework of something as frivolous as entertainment."

Singer/songwriter Bill Withers on Souled American

"You ain't heard nothin' yet."

Entertainer Al Jolson

Bill Withers is not alone in believing that this book shouldn't exist. Alongside him are those who point to America's still-evident enclaves of bigotry as proof that music has done little to bridge the racial divide. Other skeptics have a different quarrel. They'll grant that it's possible to see the last four hundred years of music in this country as an ongoing conversation between the races, much of it during a time when any other exchange of ideas would have been unthinkable. Doubtless many of them consider this a black story, though, and as such ought to be told by a black scholar and not some white entertainment journalist.

When Bill Withers dismissed my carefully crafted arguments with one broad sweep of his hand, you can bet I had second thoughts. I wondered whether my own ethnic background (Irish, for the most part) might be more of an impediment to the book's success than my ability to conduct research or interviews. Friends shared their misgivings, too. One night over dinner with Sam Moore (of Sam and Dave fame), a joke went around the table that if a certain white writer got anything wrong about race in his book, he could count on becoming to music what Salman Rushdie represented to Muslim fundamentalists. Sam smiled at the quip, but he did not offer to hide me out.

Ultimately, I decided to tackle this book because its message would not leave me alone. And, after years of studying the voices gathered here—on records and in interviews—I reconfirmed the notions that set me on this journey in the first place. Rather than cling to the premise that "music has done more to break down barriers between the races than any enactment of law," as I so often stated in conversations, I challenged history and the accumulated wisdom of those in the music business to persuade me of the truth in my theory. Through trial and error, I found myself arriving at the same inescapable conclusion. The music that enriches our lives today—so much a part of our identities that we blare it from our cars to announce who we are; pipe it into our elevators, supermarkets, and offices to make intolerable environments bearable; and sing it at ballgames and play it at funerals as a show of unity—would not exist as it does without contributions from both races. More than sports, visual art, or literature, American music really is our creation together, and neither race can be removed from the equation without drastically changing the result.

Souled American: How Black Music Transformed White Culture began in the 1980s as a five-part newspaper series for the *Austin American-Statesman* on "crossover music"—specifically, the overnight resurgence of black hits at the top of the *Billboard* Top 40 listings. Performers exiled to the rhythm & blues (R&B) charts as a result of the backlash against the domination of disco in the late 1970s and early 1980s were finally selling enough records to again "cross over" into the terrain of Top 40 pop sales, that rarefied atmosphere where mainstream success and multimillion-dollar paychecks await. Sales of Michael Jackson's *Thriller*, Tina Turner's *Private Dancer*, and Prince's *Purple Rain* signified that R&B was no longer commercial kryptonite, and white artists returned to black-derived music for inspiration, leading to hits for the Smokey Robinson–influenced Boy George, the Philly soul duo Hall and Oates, and a young dance music devotee named Madonna.

That series was a snapshot in time. As the musicians, singers, producers, disc jockeys, and journalists share their stories here, a larger picture starts to emerge—a complex portrait of the dysfunctional American family in which one sibling is the fair-haired favorite while the other receives comparatively little attention and credit. With so much history and so many details in play, such a picture wouldn't have been revealed had these artists spoken only about their own projects of the moment, as is usually the case. The contributors included here have a profound grasp of their own career achievements, but each represents only a single fleck in the kaleidoscope of pop music. And although I hope to have assembled enough of the principals to describe a broad panorama over decades, I concede that other writers could listen to the same records, talk to another list of subjects, and draw different conclusions. I encourage them to do so.

I sketched out a book outline that opened with the birth of rock 'n' roll. Back when I started work on the newspaper series in 1984 for the *Austin American-Statesman*, I was one of the paper's entertainment writers. I approached our music columnist, Ed Ward, a fellow who had been with *Rolling Stone* in its counterculture years, and asked him what he thought of my idea. Ward agreed that the "project had merit, and didn't bat an eye a few days later when I asked him who sang "(Reach Out) I'll Be There." He could have said, "It's *only* one of the most famous Motown songs of all time, and if you don't know Motown, how can you know soul? And if you don't know soul, how the hell can you write this series?" Ed was the first of many patient tutors.

Interview subjects for the series included Little Richard, who insisted I call him at midnight in Los Angeles—2 A.M. local time—for our conversation. Invariably, he'd answer the phone in his over-the-top tenor: "This is Mister Penniman!!" I may have been groggy, but Richard remained hyperanimated, even though he was working 10-hour days on the set of *Down and Out in Beverly Hills* at the time. "You know I'm 56 years old," Richard confided, "and they got me runnin' 'round filmmin' like a crazy person!" The *Statesman* articles also involved members of the Jackson 5, Rascals, Temptations, Supremes, Four Tops, and Donna Summer, as well as Philip Bailey of Earth, Wind, & Fire and Harry Wayne Casey—"KC" of the Sunshine Band. There were also producers, disc jockeys, and journalists, including Jerry Wexler (Aretha Franklin's producer at Atlantic Records), radio personality Casey Kasem, and Dave Marsh, the well-known rock critic.

After nearly a year and a half spent collecting interviews—some quotes of which reappear here—the series was published as "The History of Crossover Soul" in the summer of 1985. Newspapers like the big concept, and when management feels there's something worth promoting, they'll approve a cardboard insert for the coin-operated metal boxes that sit on street corners and outside supermarkets. The inserts are called "rack cards," and in the ten years I wrote for the *Statesman*, the crossover series gave me my one and only rack card.

In 1990, I took an offer to write for *Premiere* magazine in Los Angeles as a cue to move west. There I had my first opportunity to interview Sam Moore. We met at the offices of Michael Jackson's publicist, where I showed Sam a grainy tenth-generation video of the 1967 tour of artists on the Stax/Volt label. It was their only international outing as a group and showcased the company's biggest stars—Booker T. and the MGs, Carla Thomas, Arthur Conley, Sam and Dave, and Otis Redding. Sam and Dave were burning on all cylinders, singing in tandem, in harmony, and in unison. With the MGs as the backing band, Carla sang "B-A-B-Y," Arthur filled "Sweet Soul Music" with joyous gusto, and the audience of white Europeans watched slack-jawed as Sam and Dave's hits tumbled out in rapid succession, from "Hold On, I'm Comin'," through "I Thank You," to the final showstopper, "Soul Man." After several nights of giving every last ounce of energy to top them, Otis complained backstage that he never wanted to follow Sam and Dave again. "Those motherfuckers," he groused, "make you work too damned hard."

At one point, I glanced from the TV to Sam and noticed his eyes filling with tears. He looked over to me and shook his head. "I've never seen any of this before," he whispered hoarsely. "Half the people up there are dead now." But there they were, and we both saw it: a perfectly captured moment where music transmutes into something more than demonstrable racial harmony. It was a kind of spell, an unblinking eyelock between two groups, each eager to grasp the other's experience. Over the course of my time at *Premiere* and later *The Hollywood Reporter*, I came to see how my theory of music-as-barometer of race relations might make sense. A CNN reporter friend asked me to help her interview the Bee Gees, and I fed her questions while posing as the producer of the shoot. At the same time, I began writing liner notes for CD reissues, including *The Very Best of Otis Redding*, and similar volumes on Wilson Pickett, the Spinners, and Tower of Power for Rhino Records. In mid-1992, after completing coverage of the Hollywood awards season, I returned to Austin, where I began a freelance career that led me to interviews with Boz Scaggs, former Supreme Mary Wilson, David Byrne, Ike Turner, and Robert Van Winkle, a.k.a. Vanilla Ice.

By the mid-1990s, my desk was crammed with transcripts and news clippings that I felt added up to more than random quotes about someone's new record, video, or movie project. They were pieces of a jigsaw puzzle waiting to be fit together. And they sat undisturbed until on a whim I began to reread *Rock of Ages*, an exhaustive overview of rock 'n' roll published by the editors of *Rolling Stone* and written in part by my friend Ed Ward.

A few pages in, my curiosity was piqued by a quote from Sam Phillips, a white producer of R&B records in Memphis in the 1950s. According to rock 'n' roll lore, Phillips is supposed to have told his secretary often, "If I could find a white man with the Negro sound and the Negro feel, I could make a billion dollars." When I discovered he made his now-famous remarks at Sun Records years *before* meeting Elvis Presley, it was as though I had uncovered one of the pillars of Pompeii jutting out of the ash, and I couldn't wait to find out what else had been buried in the passage of time. I started to consider just how many performers fit that description: not just Elvis, who was only the first and best of his kind, but the endless variety of those who followed in his wake—including the Rascals, Janis Joplin, Van Morrison, Bonnie Raitt, and Kid Rock. Conversely, there were those held in low regard, accused of expropriating elements associated with R&B, rock 'n' roll, or jazz solely for personal gain. Many of them ended their careers with fatter bank accounts than more legitimate practitioners on either side of the color line.

There was more than enough material for a book, but where to begin? The earliest purveyor of rock 'n' roll and R&B attitude (to my ears) is Louis Jordan. In his heyday, such music was called "jump blues," and Jordan's string of hits made him a jukebox and concert favorite throughout the 1940s and into the early 1950s. His best tracks were suggestive without succumbing to vulgarity and delivered with tongue so firmly in cheek you could almost hear the wink he left in the wax. His smooth handling of songs like "Caldonia," "Choo Choo Ch'Boogie," and "Is You Is, or Is You Ain't (My Baby)?" called me back to the Harlem Renaissance and Jordan's much-maligned predecessor, Cab Calloway, who was accused of dressing up in hepcat threads for an "Uncle Tom" routine in order to amuse white folks. One afternoon in a musty New Orleans record shop, I spied one of Cab's records on the wall—the zoot-suited Calloway in his Cotton Club prime, arms akimbo, calling "Hi-De-Hi-De-Hi-De-Ho." Opposite was another disc from the same period on which, covered in burned cork, knelt crooner Al Jolson, caught in his signature "Mammy" pose. Why is so much of our national identity caught up in playing to preconceived notions and stereotypes of one another, I wondered.

After *Rock of Ages*, I read anything linking race with music and tried to eavesdrop every time I heard the topic mentioned in a conversation. A record executive named Gregg Geller became an early advocate. I met him over the telephone in 1984 while researching my newspaper series, and we discussed a long-lost Sam Cooke performance he'd unearthed from the vaults of RCA Records. Cooke was shot to death during an alleged motel tryst in 1964, and while songs like "Another Saturday Night," and "(What a) Wonderful World" are familiar oldies radio fare, Sam had long since ceased to be a household name. But Geller went to bat for the concert's release on disc and, to this day, *Live at the Harlem Square Club* remains one of my favorite albums because it so captures the spirit of the time, the soul of the singer, and the adulation of the audience. (The filmmakers behind the 2001 *Ali* biopic apparently liked the record, too, since the first five minutes of the movie virtually re-create the opening of *Harlem Square Club*.) Geller and I continued to talk and apprise each other of new records and music books. When a new

Sam Cooke biography called *You Send Me* hit the shelves in 1995, I phoned Gregg to ask if he'd seen it. He hadn't. He asked in return if I knew about a just-published book on composer Stephen Foster and *Blacking Up*, an out-of-print exploration of minstrelsy. "That," he said, "is where you should really consider starting, because Foster was a white guy writing black music before the Civil War." His suggestion gnawed at me for weeks, as I tried to wrangle my way out of telling this story without delving into another hundred years' worth of music and history.

Geller's wisdom, already apparent, soon prevailed. His instinct seemed so irrefutable, I decided not to wait for something or someone else to prod me further. Every story has a beginning, and this one starts the day indentured Africans arrived on the shores of Colonial America, because that's when the races began to experience each other and occupy the same world.

To occupy is not to "share," though. These days, black existence in America only overlaps white experience in the mundane functions of everyday life—waiting in line at the bank, going to the movies, or supporting the kids at an after-school event. Thanks to the efforts of Rosa Parks, Martin Luther King, Jr., and countless others, blacks can now choose their own seats on a bus and eat undisturbed at a lunch counter. They can vote unchallenged and sue if they feel discriminated against in housing, education, or employment. But racism thrives. At the turn of the millennium, it thrives not only in East Texas, where white supremacists dragged a black man named James Byrd from the back of their truck until his body came apart in pieces on a dirt road. It also bubbles below the surface—in schoolyards and classrooms, on the job and in the marketplace. These days, the problem is not someone using a racial epithet—something that, while calculated to enrage, disappears into air as soon as it's spoken. In this era of political correctness, the "N" word is not the way racism does its damage. It's done surreptitiously, and is therefore more difficult to detect and uproot. Many whites discount these racist subtleties, but anyone trying to comprehend how alienated some blacks feel in our Anglocentric United States should spend an hour in a record store listening to rap. To paraphrase a saying so popular among today's motivational speakers, "if you want to understand what you're really sending out as communication, listen closely to the response you get." Rap is a reaction to existing circumstances, not some showbiz fabrication dreamed up by a marketing firm.

With bigotry alive and well everywhere we live, and black people aware that it is so, their experience sitting across the room anywhere in America is fundamentally different from a white person's. Our culture is littered with vestigial expressions of bigotry all but invisible to whites. And even when none are present, centuries of abuse have left many African Americans suspicious that any slight is directly attributable to race-related malice, which is an insidious poison of its own. Say, for example, that you're at a restaurant and your white waitress takes a meal order from the table seated after you, but has yet to even offer you drinks. Why? Discrimination becomes a handy explanation. Given incorrect change at the supermarket? Cut off while changing lanes? Prejudice, plain and simple. When these mishaps interrupt a white person's routine, the impulsive response is more apt to be a word like "asshole" than a word like "racist."

Misunderstanding also persists across the color line, where blacks are still too often regarded through the filters of a mythology that predates the plantation era. Many whites continue to typecast Africans and their American descendants as exotic—more in touch with their bodies and sexuality, and more susceptible to the "temptations of the flesh"—including flashy clothes, parties, games, food, and booze. Music, especially if listened to absently, reinforces these clichés: Think of "Stagger Lee" (a jealous rage that escalates into a knife fight), "Saturday Night Fish Fry" (a "rent party" wild enough to require police intervention), "Devil With the Blue Dress On" (dressing to kill), "Good Times" (Chic's homage to the roller disco craze), or R. Kelly's "Remix to Ignition," where the narrator ticks off the merits of getting drunk, slipping off to the after-party, and coaxing lady friends upstairs to the hotel room. "It's the freakin' weekend," he raps, "and I'm 'bout to have me some fun." Whites who buy into these stereotypes are inevitably left with two conflicting responses running concurrently: in one breath, whites seem to wonder why they can't loosen up and enjoy themselves as black people do, and in the next, they shake their heads in disgust at what they perceive to be a lackadaisical black work ethic. In the final analysis, we are all to one degree or another staring at fun house images of each other, neither side able to see the other free of distortions.

Souled American seeks to craft a better mirror than those we've been using. It's not often that fans of country, hip-hop, blues, rock 'n' roll, and jazz sit down to discuss the place of music in society, how one genre impacts another, or what music tells us about how we feel about ourselves and each other, and it's safe to say that each of the disparate parties has something to say that will surprise or enlighten. I've tried to gather as diverse a group of participants for this book as possible and attempted to guide their discussion into these issues. Sadly, the number whose reminiscences stretch before the Great Depression dwindles daily, and prior to that era, I have relied on research and the help of friends who directed me to Web sites, books, and the occasional video documentary. Not everyone I contacted wanted to cooperate. Publicists for some said they would grant an interview only after reading the manuscript (public relations doublespeak and tantamount to refusal), while others simply declined to return years of monthly phone calls. I wish they were here.

In trying to outline the similarities and differences between us, there's always the fear of accidental generalization. Blanket statements applied to race are, after all, the building blocks of prejudice. Intent has to account for something, though, and I believe that both the research and the absence of malice here speak for themselves. This is a book about discovering how we created this music together—unwittingly and unwillingly at times—but it is a story of both races. No one gets away clean, and no one receives all the glory. *Souled American* identifies patterns in our relationship that run concentrically over time, inflected differently as each new genre reflects our racial squabbles, brush fires, and full-scale wars. By using music as a barometer, we can monitor our progress toward racial harmony. The more frustrated we grow, the more raucous the sound.

Introduction

no one talks about polkas, marches, or bluegrass as "white music," but try a phrase like "black music" on the average person today and you can stand back and watch a kind of cultural Rorschach test response take place. The mere mention of "black music" automatically fires off a host of images—some flattering, others summoning secrets of the id we'd rather keep hidden, even from ourselves. To a jazz buff, black music may trigger visions of "cutting contests," those late-night duels where players vie for instrumental supremacy fueled only by nerve and virtuosity. Others might recall Motown's Golden Age, when beehived girls crooned in graceful precision. Today, through the critical mass of media exposure, black music has become synonymous with the powder keg that is hip-hop, where percussion and profanity join to glorify the male ego, the objectification of women, and materialism.

For the purposes of this discussion, "black music" refers to music generally considered of African American origin or derivation. There were also a few Garden-of-Gethsemane moments when I weighed using the words "African American," "Afro-American," "colored," "Negro," and of course, "Nigger." I never enter into their use casually. In most cases, the latter word appears only in song, in quotes, or to accurately portray a moment in time. "Nigger Heaven," for example, was show-business slang for a venue's balcony seats, where blacks were required to sit for a segregated show. To sidestep these words not only revises history, it downplays the obstacles civil rights activists faced in attempting to bring us together as one people.

Despite the forces at work to keep them separate, the bond between black influences and American music grows stronger every day. For evidence, consider the steady incursion of rhythm into what was once a melody-dominated discipline. Beginning with the introduction of ragtime, rhythm has been gaining ground against melody in popular music until even the most vapid music reaches for a percussive flourish to make it danceable, convey urgency, or create drama. Similarly, once jazz arrived on the national scene, simple rags seemed almost rudimentary by comparison. Bebop brings even more adventurous harmonic structures and sophistication; rock 'n' roll and rhythm and blues (R&B) consolidate those, and rap now seeks to elevate rhythm to a position of preeminence.

That's one advantage of hindsight. From the distance of a hundred years, it's easier to follow the flow of early jazz as it pumped out of New Orleans and into the extremities of America to saturate the population centers of Chicago, Kansas City, New York, and beyond. Stand back far enough, and it's possible to watch a slow turning in the grand wheel of time, as each succeeding generation makes its attempt to address the chasm between our cultures.

This book doesn't try to settle the question of what constitutes black music, or even whether such a thing exists. Rather, it asserts that African Americans are the unsung innovators of American music, while white artists tend to popularize and develop each trend to a creative and commercial end. There are occasional exceptions to the rule, but the main advances of music in American history—spirituals, ragtime, jazz, gospel, country, R&B, rock 'n' roll, and rap—all point to black antecedents combined with structural influences cribbed from European music traditions. The resultant music may indeed be equal parts black and white, but there's little question of who consistently reaps the greater financial reward.

We're far from reaching a consensus on these notions, though, and every new era in music is met by a new assortment of naysayers. Usually the factions will include at least one group of white moralists certain that this latest iteration is the long-dreaded call of Armageddon. A brochure distributed in the early days of rock 'n' roll is fairly typical: "Help save the youth of America!" it reads. "Don't let your children buy or listen to these Negro records. The screaming, idiotic words and savage music are undermining the morals of our white American youth." They say that this music has to be stopped in its tracks by shunning it and those who compose in its style, and if that doesn't work—well, a citizen's action group should be called up, because *something has got to be done*. In the film *This Is Elvis*, another detractor puts it in plain language: "We've set up a twenty-man committee to do away with this vulgar, animalistic nigger rock 'n' roll bop."

Numerous self-proclaimed champions of tradition, Judeo-Christian ethics, and "family values" speak out in these pages. Centuries ago, their predecessors decried any rhythmic music (which promoted dancing, the first stepping stone on the path to moral degeneration, which inevitably includes alcohol, sex, and disrepute) as "hypnotic" and a "pestilence." The music was an appeal to humanity's most base impulses, they warned, supplanting piety and respect for authority with Godless sensuality. Left unchecked, black music would eventually transform white America into a nation of swivel-hipped, jive-talking layabouts. This same fear has driven conservatives to try to suppress African American communication since the slave era. Plantation owners banned the use of the drum, spirituals were denounced as irreverent, ragtime and jazz were said to inspire delinquency, rock 'n' roll was considered "the devil's music," and Tipper Gore felt so threatened by Prince and 2 Live Crew (and white offenders ranging from Twisted Sister to Frank Zappa) that she rounded up a posse of congressional wives to tag records with a "Parental Advisory." Yet the more subversive black music appears, the more popular it becomes, and the failure of conservatives to keep the genie of their nightmares bottled up can be measured today in the multimillions, as rap and hip-hop (especially with the advent of such *white* artists as Eminem and Limp Bizkit) set sales records.

Moral watchdogs on the right are not the only ones pining for the glories of yesteryear. Left-of-center aesthetes complain that any new idea defiles tradition and pollutes that which was once so beautiful in its simplicity. The hisses and boos that greeted Bob Dylan in 1965 when he plugged in his guitar at the Newport Folk Festival may be the most famous example (and was rooted as much in fear of change as in elitism), and were echoed in the late 1960s when trumpet legend Miles Davis fused jazz with rock music on *Bitches Brew*. Such outcries against big band, free jazz, and rap found liberal blacks and whites united against music they considered beyond the parameters of "art." Their argument takes on racial overtones when acts in search of success are accused of "Tomming" (playing up their racial roles for profit) whenever they try to broaden their appeal. Other groups are slammed for contaminating once pristine music with their own idiosyncrasies. Of course, these troublemakers are in good company, since other nonconformists include Louis Armstrong, Charlie Parker, John Coltrane, Ornette Coleman, Sam Cooke, Ray Charles, Brian Wilson, the Beatles, Janis Joplin, Gram Parsons, Aretha Franklin, Leonard Bernstein, and Willie Nelson. Each of them understood that when art has its boundaries predetermined, creative minds long to roam free. Innovation is sacrificed for re-creation, and that's when an art form is in real danger of becoming a relic.

Accepting the premise that blacks have more often been the innovators while whites have been the ones to benefit from exploiting those innovations requires an acknowledgment that African Americans are more interested in discovering The Next Big Thing than in riding a fad past its relevance to daily life. Certainly there's no reason for black Americans to romanticize their experience here. This country hasn't provided any "good old days" for people of color. Before 1964, they were less than second-class citizens. Before the Civil War, they were slaves. Therefore, while white Americans are forever revisiting and romanticizing previous eras (witness the rebirth of 1950s rock with *American Graffiti* in the 1970s, *The Big Chill* revival of the 1980s, and the return of the 1970s and 1980s through radio's "classic rock" and "jammin' oldies" formats), black artists are constantly pushing forward. By the time the (white) majority wholly embraces a trend in music, it's in the form of a revival, itself a pastiche of the original radical movement.

In the jazz community today, those same issues are at the forefront of an ideological battle, with one side shouting that "traditional jazz" is the only true jazz while the other maintains that in order for the music to grow and remain viable, new voices and sounds must be permitted. Wynton Marsalis spearheads what the media has dubbed the "neoclassicist" movement. He and his allies claim that the pedigree of a jazz piece can be verified according to a series of musical identifiers; without that checklist completed, the music simply cannot be called jazz. His adversaries include such critics as Eric Neisenson, who counters that arbitrary rule making thwarts creativity and that many acknowledged jazz classics flunk Marsalis' litmus test for legitimacy. They say Marsalis wants to leave a revisionist version of jazz in his wake—one that ignores experimentation and discounts white contributions—as is clear from the interviews Marsalis and his ideological symbiant Stanley Crouch granted Ken Burns for his 2000 television documentary *JAZZ*. Rather than use the music as a metaphor for communication and building a bridge between the music and audiences of both colors, Marsalis and Crouch build an impressive monument to black ingenuity and perseverance. It's a valid enough approach, but one that often rings smug and exclusionary. And, with documentarian Ken Burns choosing them as his TV tour guides, *JAZZ* emerges stuffed to the rafters with tributes to Louis Armstrong and Duke Ellington and leaves only a few remaining minutes to explore the thirty years of jazz we've heard since the 1960s. But even if Marsalis is intentionally trying to downplay the Bix Beiderbeckes, Artie Shaws, and Jaco Pastoriuses, his motives remain understandable, since white Americans haven't exactly been shy to claim nearly every conceivable advancement of mankind since the founding of the republic. Marsalis apparently considers himself a sentry at the gates, determined that whites will not ransack the cultural Fort Knox that is jazz—at least not during his watch.

This book goes to the heart of these controversies by dividing its focus between the pivotal figures on both sides of the color line. In combination, their voices reveal how we created the music that has become the soundtrack of our lives and a cherished part of our common heritage. Moreover, these stories have a cumulative effect: they illustrate how we have treated each other on every step of our journey. Several related themes appear in the book as if on cue, among them the notions that we've spoken more honestly in song than in conversation about our interactions, and that music may be one of the great common denominators that constantly inform us about each other, bringing us together at concerts and dances and invisibly uniting us as we sit at home listening or watching music on TV. Nearly every one of the subjects interviewed was asked about whether music has been an effective tool in battling racism, and whether "soul" (as they define it) is tied solely to race. If there's a big "chicken-or-the-egg" question behind this book, here it is, and it's posed in a new context every few pages: are whites "stealing" music from blacks— whether by "borrowing" the melodic signatures that make a tune memorable, incorporating certain rhythmic identifiers (such as those which gave rise to ragtime, rock, and rap), or appropriating wholesale a creative idea simply for monetary gain? The answer varies from one decade (and one performer) to the next.

Since this is a book addressing the connections between race and music, let's start the conversation on the same terms: what exactly did Thomas Dartmouth "Daddy" Rice set loose in America in the mid-1800s when he bought a black man's rags, either learned or parodied his moves, and then sold tickets to see the prototypical black caricature he created? Whether a historical man or a fictional archetype, "Jim Crow" has been with us ever since. Granted, no citizen is immune from the jibes of a clever satirist (as set forth in the First Amendment), but Rice's supposed purchase goes beyond parody into a realm of thievery now argued in law as "intellectual property." To buy a coat or a pair of pants is one thing (and that is all Rice supposedly paid for), but to appropriate a person's individual and ethnic identity in order to ridicule his or her entire race ought to meet any court's standard of a swindle. But is it possible to steal from someone who is not free, when his or her possessions were the legal property of another? Concepts of what could be stolen were much simpler then, and it's unfair to label someone a thief by today's standards when the actions he or she undertook at the time were well within the limits of the law.

But if it *was* theft when Rice first "jumped Jim Crow," then the same principle applies to the white minstrels who corked their faces to mock blacks during vaudeville, and the same should be said for those who adopt racial stereotypes for profit today. Without corking up in blackface, the same kind of exploitation still thrives, and we can see the whole tableau play out on a regular basis—when Pat Boone scores a hit with a pale imitation of Little Richard . . . when Donny Osmond is pushed out in front of his brothers to compete with the Jackson 5 . . . when Vanilla Ice's hip-hop credentials prove a public relations fabrication . . . or when Kenny G drenches a Louis Armstrong classic in his own soprano sax meanderings.

The theft of black music might be an open-and-shut case if it weren't for two peculiarities: first, there's always been a segment of African Americans who relish watching white performers plying their own version of faux-black entertainment—whether or not they are deemed to have artistic merit by the critics. Consider this: at the peak of their popularity, the white radio actors who played Amos 'n' Andy were nearly as popular in segments of black society as with white audiences. Second is a far stranger phenomenon: that an increasing number of white artists appear so steeped in the nuances and underlying ethos of the black experience that they are accepted as authentic—including, among others, Van Morrison, Janis Joplin, Eric Clapton, Bonnie Raitt, and the Beastie Boys.

Admittedly, artists of all colors have been influenced by black (as well as other) ideas, and have synthesized them into a personal aesthetic, but there is a distinction between "woodshedding" (musician speak for solitary rehearsing to hone an individual style) and plundering a culture. There's no crime in whistling someone else's melody when you're in an elevator; it's actually flattery. What's criminal is latching onto a facet of social identity and recklessly distorting it without concern about the appearance or the result—so long as it makes money.

Current pop music trends send a mixed message about the direction in which we want to move as a society. The careers of the hottest-selling artists of the moment—including such varied performers as Eminem, Red Hot Chili Peppers, and Christina Aguilera—all owe a debt to black music, from the electronic beats percolating at the bottom end of their tracks to the wails of studio singers above, and to the endless variety of "remixes" that can turn a ballad into a dance floor workout. These are stars whose pictures adorn the bedroom walls and backpacks of today's teenagers, and their ubiquity speaks volumes about how deeply black music stylings permeate our culture. But the most famous, and by far the richest, are white.

This book examines black and white interaction through music from our first meeting to the present, but it does not offer solutions for the future. In fact, it repeatedly suggests that the ignition point sparking our most creative music results directly from an arrangement with proven inequities: more often than not, blacks innovate/create and whites popularize/exploit until, finally, the trend breaks through to mass acceptance.

Utilitarians could well argue that since this capitalist paradigm works, why fix it? Conservative commentators like Patrick Buchanan insist that we have already wandered too far down the path of apologizing for the way our forefathers built this country. According to the "melting pot" social model, hearts should swell with nationalistic pride that we all contributed to the common good. Certainly mistakes were made, they'd allow. Our ancestors may have owned slaves, but we know better now, and isn't it enough to have ended that heinous institution? From their vantage point, conservatives defend a kind of Norman Rockwell–John Phillip Sousa–Disneyland–Beach Boys America—a gauzy utopia where, because the Constitution guarantees liberty and justice for all, citizens cannot be disenfranchised. If you haven't gotten your share of the American dream, the only explanation can be indolence or what's been labeled a "victim mentality."

Hackles are raised when these folks admit that, sure, whites wrested this continent from the indigenous tribes settled here, breaking one treaty after another during the expansion westward. And the prosperity that helped bankroll those settlements came at the expense of African men and women who were enslaved here, while the railroads that consolidated white Protestant control of the nation's vast natural resources were built on the backbreaking labor of minorities from Asia, Ireland, and elsewhere. When challenged at the time, white clerics fell back on Biblical scripture to justify America's xenophobia, redefining their quest as an evangelical calling. Inflictions of misery were mitigated by the doctrine of manifest destiny, which required Christians to go forth and multiply "to establish dominion over the earth."

It's long been passé to disavow those shameful acts, and these days we congratulate ourselves for believing that we'd never vote against a man because of the color of his skin, or refuse to let him sit next to us on public transportation or at a restaurant. In truth, it's much like the child who gets caught with his hand in the cookie jar after nearly all the cookies are gone. He apologizes and vows never to repeat his sin, but makes no effort to replace the cookies he's taken. As a culture, whites are still stealing from blacks, only our excuse now is that we don't mean to steal, and we'd really much rather call it "sharing," if you don't mind. But shouldn't the decision to share be initiated by the owner rather than the borrower?

There are laws to protect melodies from being used without permission or compensation, but rhythms are a trickier concept. When the issues are clearcut, as they are when it comes to "sampling" (e.g., lifting a snippet of a preexisting track for use in another piece of music), the courts side with the creators. But while artists can own the drum tracks that appear on their records, it's tougher to prove ownership of basic components like beats or a rhythm sequence the way someone might claim ownership of a guitar riff or melodic hook. Clearly then, rap music is at a legal disadvantage, since so much of rap's appeal is in presenting listeners with new beat combinations. Black-inspired music is often more fluid and harder to transcribe, and that makes it tougher to defend on a proprietary basis, too. Black and white artists may have to resign themselves to the reality that they'll have to share the elements that no one owns. After all, no one patented the call-and-response pattern that anchors songs from "Please Please Me" (in which John Lennon sings, "Come on!" and Paul McCartney and George Harrison answer back, "Come on!") all the way back to "Swing Low, Sweet Chariot" and as recent as the Beck single, "Mixed Bizness?" No one owns the instrumental solo or the notion of playing guitar with a slide, or can say who gets credit for developing ragtime, blues, country, or jazz in this country.

"You could say black musicians are responsible for the blue or the crushed note," says Ian Whitcomb, anglophile and author of *After the Ball: Pop Music from Rag to Rock.* "But it's unclear how much of what we know as the blues music came from Africa anyway, because a lot of the structural antecedents are simply not in Africa; they never were. There are many of the same scales in Gypsy and Jewish music as in the blues. So that alone makes a tremendous case for the fact that white people—or Western Europeans if you prefer—had a great deal to do with the establishment if not the evolution of what we know as the blues today."

In the final analysis, the question of "Who owns this music?" is the kind of riddle that makes for a lively, albeit combustible, after-dinner diversion if no one remembered to bring a board game. Such conundrums offer no insight into the actual differences between black and white people living in 21st-century America, and, more to the point, they're worthless in helping one group of people respect the differences of another.

Besides, to see polite society's reaction, the emergence of every new music in America has been greeted with all the enthusiasm of a mansion gardener who's spied an errant weed drawing attention from his prize-winning roses. American music is nothing if not the tune of a struggling underclass: unwelcome among the well-bred, and often intentionally created to flout convention. When Limp Bizkit's Fred Durst roars, "I did it all for the nookie, the nookie, the nookie/so you can take that cookie and stick it up your ass," today it's not received much differently than when the Hepcats of Harlem paid tribute to "that funny Reefer Man" or turned street slang into songs about oral sex.

Highbrow contempt for the mongrel origins of American music and the erratic patterns of its growth remain the linchpin of why, after nearly 400 years, its power remains undiminished. And as long as human beings take sides, some will fall one way or another when they argue about what makes a piece of music resonate inside the listener. This book asserts that the real value in addressing the issue of origin and ownership is not to find out who gets billed for nearly 400 years of entertainment, but to discover what asking the question tells us about who we as Americans are together.

CHAPTER ONE

Of Massas
and Minstrels

Gold Coast slave ship bound for cotton fields
Sold in a market down in New Orleans. . .
    "Brown Sugar" by Mick Jagger and Keith Richards

I n the early days of the 17th century, Englishman Richard Jobson became one of the first Europeans to record his travels through Gambia. He was impressed enough with the natives' musical abilities to write, "There is without a doubt no people on the earth more naturally affected to the sounds of musicke [*sic*] than these people." Those few words, nearly 500 years old, are among the first on record about black music from a white man. Today, Jobson's words may be more memorable for what they describe than for their date of entry. His observation encapsulates all the marvel and mockery attributed to whites in their appreciation of the relationship between blacks and music, and the questions his comments implicitly raise remain center stage in a debate still raging on both sides of the color barrier: is the essence of American music really a matter of geographical origins in Africa and Western Europe, and can a white artist compose, sing, or play in black idioms without calling his or her own artistic legitimacy into question?

Though Jobson the explorer could scarcely have known it at the time, his vague compliment set these ideological battle lines in sharp relief. His infatuation is clear, but is it also tainted with Western European condescension? We get that he's fascinated by the Africans' embrace of their music, but doesn't his comment betray a germinus of racism between the lines? Doesn't he also suggest that blacks are "natural" musicians, entertaining to watch in their primitive simplicity? And when whites adopt black influences as their own and express them artistically despite being raised apart from African Americans, where do they lead us? Does their music nudge society toward racial harmony or naked profiteering and ridicule? Either way, the eavesdropping that Jobson and his party committed to paper has resulted in seismic consequences for both races. Whether his intentions were benign or covetous, Jobson did more than simply overhear the rudiments of today's music. His report is one flashpoint of a fuse that sizzles from one continent to another over hundreds of years, when black and white sounds recombine in increasingly volatile mixtures, giving rise to spirituals, ragtime, jazz, country, rhythm and blues (R&B), rock, and hip-hop.

Through it all, the issue of primary ignition remains unresolved: who owns this music, the most indigenous of American art forms? Can African American music be filtered through white sensibilities without something essential being lost or changed in the process? Memphis record producer Sam Phillips believed his discovery of Elvis Presley proved that "a white man with the Negro sound and the Negro feel" would tranform into his personal pot of gold, but the idea is hardly a new one. More than a hundred years earlier, white minstrel entertainers misappropriated black dances and instruments and mangled their styles for profit, largely from white audiences. In the 1850s, composer Stephen Foster found immortality through blackface (begun by white men who masqueraded as black onstage) and such original singalongs as "Camptown Races" and "Oh, Susanna" Generations before Elvis, the white creators of *Amos 'n' Andy* made a fortune in radio and television via their theatrical approximations of blackness. Time and again, America has shown its love for black culture—especially black music—but most often when presented by white artists. With a few notable exceptions, the cycle repeats like the proverbial broken record: blacks create and innovate, whites popularize and homogenize, until black imagination illuminates some new path to follow. The trail, and its signposts, are evident from the earliest exchanges between white Americans and black Africans.

WELCOME

In 1619, just a year before Jobson's expedition, Africans made their first appearance in the English colonies of the New World. Pocahontas' widower John Rolfe documents their arrival in Jamestown in an almost casual manner: "About the last of August," the tobacco grower writes, "came a Dutch man of war that sold us twenty Negars." As it turns out, the Africans were spoils of war captured from a Spanish vessel bound for the West Indies. The import of Africans accelerated steadily, and by midcentury they were a common sight in nearly every colonial settlement.

Of course, by the time Africans were introduced to the colonies, the practice of slavery itself was already eons old. As recently as 1501, black servants had accompanied the Spanish to the New World to chart the American Southwest, where most blacks either departed with their owners or had their cultural identities absorbed through intermarriage among a variety of Indian tribes from Texas to Central America. The English were late in entering the "human commodities" trade in the Americas, although ships' manifests indicate British vessels transported slaves from one non-American port to another as early as 1607. Still, the first Africans brought to these shores did not arrive as slaves for life. Like many of their European counterparts, they came as indentured servants who might earn independence and be free to participate in the social life of the colony, which meant purchasing land and even buying slaves of their own.

Since slaves' assets were skills rather than possessions, they understood their musicality was a valued commodity that could be traded for hard labor, prestige, or over time the kind of money it took to purchase freedom. Many rapidly mastered two portable and easy-to-maintain staples of colonial life, the fife and fiddle, perhaps because they bore similarities to instruments found in Africa. Early colonial newspapers are rife with accounts of musician slaves for sale or hire, and each servant's proficiency became an important bargaining point. Advertisements in such local newspapers as *The Virginia Gazette* routinely offered slave musicians for sale. "TO BE SOLD," read a 1766 posting, "A young healthy Negro fellow who has been used to wait on a gentleman and plays extremely well on the French horn."

Slaves were forbidden to make music referring to their capture or enslavement, and adaptability—the ability to improvise—became a crucial element of survival. Slaves learned quickly to mimic Western styles even though the instruments themselves were often unfamiliar. Much Western literature and folklore depicts Africa as a monolithic continent of drum-beating pagans, but, in reality, the many nations there teemed with instruments of endless shape, pitch, and variety. In West Africa alone, rudimentary versions of the xylophone, lute, and banjo were found in abundance—and the instruments were not employed solely for making music. Some served double duty as fashion accessory and had religious implications as well.

While it's a matter of record that slavers heard music in Africa, how much they understood of what they heard remains unclear. African drum music involves sophisticated percussion parts played on homemade instruments ranging widely in shape and size; some are no more than ten inches long, while others extend more than ten feet. They might be two or three inches in diameter or several feet wide. To describe these drums as "hand-crafted" does an injustice to the artisans who lavished skill and devotion on their creations. In certain regions, drum makers began the process by paying tribute to the living tree, including an offering of distilled spirits and an egg (a symbol of life) before the wood could be sacrificed to become a drum. Some drums were made from logs painstakingly hollowed out over a length of time; others were constructed by slicing a gourd or calabash in half and stretching an animal skin tightly over an exposed end. One slave trader who traveled the continent actually identified the instruments by their African names: one, a drum open at the lower end, was called the "tangtang" and another was called the "tabulu," or "talking drum."

Such talking drums, according to music historian Dr. Horace Boyer, are made out of an animal whose skin is pliable, and pressing the drum in different locations changes its pitch. But it was not the drum's musicality that made it an object of white dread. Slaveholders quickly learned that certain sounds made on the drum corresponded with African words. Real terror descended, Boyer says, when whites learned "there were *sentences* being created by these drums." By substituting drumbeats for words, he explains, slaves could tell each other, "Go . . . there. Come . . . here . . . now." This capacity to transmit mutually understood messages through the air over distance predated the telegraph by hundreds of years, and slavers readily grasped that if Africans could communicate with one another, then revolt was just that much more possible. The colonists dealt with drums swiftly. "The first law governing the African slave in the New World was the prohibition of the talking drum," according to Yale music professor and jazz musician Willie Ruff. "In terms of social engineering, in terms of . . . the complete eradication of a cultural phenomenon, nobody did a better job than the slavemasters of North America because when they made the law prohibiting the talking drum, they took away our memory of African languages and African names. We got named Willie, John, Susie, and Mary."

SAIL AWAY

Deprivation of an ancestral name was the most benign intrusion awaiting slaves-to-be. Their reculturization began before they ever boarded a ship. Many had already been confined by a warring neighbor tribe for some time before they were sold into slavery. Once they were handed over to the Europeans, though, slaves relinquished all hope of returning to anything resembling home or the relatives who could only guess at their fates. In great throngs they stood on the beaches, bound together at the neck and ankle, stripped of their former lives and uncertain of what they might become.

The scattered reminiscences left behind by slave traders suggest some felt twinges of pity for their cargo during the voyage to the New World. Slavers expressed bewilderment watching the Africans sing and dance during the Atlantic crossing, even as belowdecks their neighbors and loved ones succumbed to the lethal swill of sewage and disease where they lay fettered. "They (sang) songs of sad lamentation," in the words of one witness who made the crossing. "The words of the songs used by them were, 'Madda! Madda! Yiera! Bemini! Madda! Aufera!' that is to say, they were all sick, and by and by they should be no more; they also sung songs expressive of their fears of being beat, of their want of victuals, particularly the want of their native food, and of their never returning to their native country."

If blacks really "sang" and "danced" their way into bondage, it's certain that whites either instigated or encouraged the activity even while misreading the Africans' complicity. On one crossing, a ship's officer described his cargo as a good-natured lot who "jumped to the lash so promptly that there was not much occasion for scoring their naked flanks. We had tambourines aboard, which some of the younger darkies fought for regularly, and every evening we enjoyed the novelty of African war songs and ring dances, fore and aft, with the satisfaction of knowing that these pleasant exercises were keeping our stock in good condition and, of course, enhancing our prospects of making a profitable voyage." Some used the voyages as seagoing orgies, spending as much time drunk and sampling the merchandise as possible, secure in the knowledge that most of the Africans were too debilitated from malnutrition or disease to pose much threat of insurrection.

In her book *Jookin: The Rise of Social Dance Formation in African-American Culture*, author Katrina Hazzard-Gordon pieced together an archetypal onboard routine from various accounts: "Usually, several crew members paraded on deck with whips and cat-o'-nine-tails, forcing the men slaves to jump in their irons, often until their ankles bled. One sailor explained to Parliament that he was employed to 'dance' the men while another person 'danced' the women. On ships with no designated musician, music was provided by a slave thumping on a broken drum, an upturned kettle, or an African banjo, or by a sailor with a fiddle, bagpipe, or other instrument. As they danced, some slaves sang, incorporating their experience into their music."

Under these circumstances, music became the slaves' link to sanity, a bond between the captives and a remnant of the reality they were leaving behind. In many respects, they were dead people whose lives were inexplicably continuing without them. Far from singing and dancing in recreation or celebration as Westerners do, slaves were likely trying to retain a semblance of identity and community in the face of horror and chaos. In many African cultures, dancing and singing were considered an extension of being alive, not some momentary intermission from a daily routine as was common in Western Europe.

Requiring blacks not to sing or dance would have meant an even greater deprivation—tantamount to hobbling white slaves or cutting out their tongues. In some tribes, rhythm was taught to youngsters as a holistic method of developing coordination. Call-and-response vocal exhortations helped impart language by repetition, which was of vital importance since African cultures were based on oral traditions rather than on reading and writing. Instead of the comparatively monotonal Western speech patterns with larger vocabularies, Africans had fewer words, but a mellifluous way of expressing subtlety through pitch and percussive sound.

"Melodic improvisation was as characteristic a feature of the music as was singing 'extempore,'" Eileen Southern writes in *The Music of Black Americans*. "The first affected the second to some extent: a singer would invent a song on the spot, then naturally change the repetitions in the melody to fit the ever-changing text." For Africans, music was not a permanent artifact like a well-crafted letter to a friend, but rather a dynamic conversation in progress. Africans communed on two planes simultaneously through music. One was an elastic exchange between communicator and the intended recipient, the other an evolving process between the performer and music itself. None of this seemed intelligible to members of white society, whose music was written—most often for church services or tavern dances—such that the player's responsibility was simply to re-create these tunes as faithfully as skill would permit. For Africans, the concept of music as a rigid set of notes repeated without deviation was likely as pointless as watching an idiot who wanders the streets endlessly muttering the same phrase. And while both peoples shared a devotion to music commemorating important events in the life of their communities, Africans didn't stop there. Through music, they passed messages of all sorts, from the mundane to the most deeply cherished tenets of cultural identity from one generation to the next (just as rap music still does today), all without benefit or need of written communication. Distinctions between "illiterate" and "nonliterate" cultures were lost on slave traders. They failed to grasp that, for Africans, music was not mere recreation, but a means to convey information as revealing of time and place as any sonnet by Shakespeare might be for the English.

Arguments about whether musicality is a learned or inherited trait begin here as well. A Zulu proverb opens Samuel Floyd's book, *The Power of Black Music*, proclaiming that "The calves follow their mothers. The young plant grows up near the parent stem. The young antelope leaps where its mother has leaped." Floyd then goes on to introduce a concept he calls "cultural memory," a Jungian notion that imbues members of a society with a collective identity—including musical talent. These traits, he writes, "exist not merely in the sense that African American music has the same characteristics as its African counterparts, but also that the musical tendencies, the mythological beliefs and assumptions, and the interpretive strategies of African Americans are the same as those that underlie the music of the African homeland, that these tendencies and beliefs continue to exist as African cultural memory, and that they continue to inform the continuity and elaboration of African American music." This theory, while not inherently racist, runs perilously close to the idea of "native ability," theorizing that blacks are genetically predisposed to excel as music makers.

Even at the outset, white Americans appear similarly conflicted in their responses to African American music. Hubris and xenophobia allowed slaveholders to cling to assumptions of black inferiority while continuing to value and covet the musical talents demonstrated by their "property." The slavers' ignorance also wrought serious consequences. First, the lack of literacy among African peoples permitted traders and slaveholders to convince themselves they were more evolved than their prisoners.

The second and undoubtedly more tragic result was that once denied language and music as means of expression (since those speaking in similar tongues were frequently separated for fear of revolt), African Americans' cultural memories began to disintegrate. Rituals either lost essence or were mangled in endless retellings by slaves whose understanding of ancestral lore grew increasingly spotty. "That's a huge supposition," counters Dr. Horace Boyer, "failing to take into account the constant import of Africans into North America, which continued long after the trans-Atlantic slave trade became illegal. And every time a new African arrived, those cultural ties to home were reinvigorated. The truth is that we can only guess how much African culture was preserved because slaves were very good at presenting one image to their captors and keeping the rest to themselves. And while the nature of these totems remains a mystery, you can bet what they showed to white people was certainly just the tip of the iceberg." Even so, other experts believe that behind the veil of what writer Lerone Bennett calls the "Cotton Curtain" of secrecy, Africans' tribal memories began to fade, surviving as a vestigial link to their homeland or as traditions no longer relevant to the Africans' current situation in life. In this sense, blacks were now not only slaves, but orphaned from their societies as well—no longer African, and far from American.

Deprived of their drums and other native instruments, many newcomers did the only thing they could do: sing. Blacks used their voices to preserve the telling details of themselves—who they were, what they ate and wore, what the weather was like, and how they hunted and farmed and raised their youngsters. But as they sang among and to one another, they also sang of the present, and recollections of the past were quickly supplanted by more immediate concerns. Overseers soon recognized several important advantages to having slaves sing at their labors as well: first, they were distracted from the grueling routine of the task at hand, and, second, slaves singing in unison were effectively prevented from murmuring plots of revolt to one another. Finally, the songs themselves became a mechanism for coordinating group effort. And the results could be impressive.

In a woodcutting song, for example, hundreds of slaves would pair off in twos and time their ax blows to the rhythm:

> A cold frosty morning
> The niggers feeling good
> Take your ax upon your shoulder
> Nigger, talk to the wood[1]

Because African music was forbidden, its absence undoubtedly accelerated the slaves' isolation from their homeland. Prohibition of native music also prompted the need for something to take its place—and, more importantly, it created a conduit for the first meaningful exchange between the races in the New World. Much of the music from Western Europe rang familiar to both cultures (both derive from similar scales, many ethnomusicologists agree), and Africans quickly recognized the call-and-response aspects of Western religious music as similar to their own. The ideas of rhythmic timekeeping and different vocal parts sounded simultaneously—the building blocks of harmony—were principles of structure mutually understood by the time blacks and whites began their awkward coexistence. Thus singing in English became an acceptable pastime for slaves approved by their masters.

It's difficult with a 21st-century moral compass to grasp how slaveholders could hear work songs wafting over the fields and conclude that because slaves sang at their labors, they must be living contented lives. Yet that seems to be the case. "The system by which men are degraded to the level of brutes, or the arguments which justify such bondage, every unprejudiced mind must turn from with horror," one white observer wrote. "But when this is admitted, if it becomes a question whether the slave can be happy in his bonds—if not exposed to actual bodily suffering—the seven years I had an opportunity to be out witnessing his constitutional vivacity make me reply in the affirmative . . . . Toil, in ordinary cases, is but a dam to his animal spirits, which overflow with a greater violence at the hour of relaxation. A dance, a song, and a laugh are his sole desiderata. All this is, no doubt, merely sensual, and far inferior to the pleasures which an elevation to his just dignity would afford him; but still, nothing can be more erroneous than the impression that the Negro is not to the full extent as happy as any of the other unenlightened laborers with whom Europe abounds."

At work and leisure, African Americans used exclamations called "cries," "calls," and "field hollers" to keep each other company, beckon their deities, and remain entertained. Academics today can claim only a vague understanding of these spontaneous and free-form outbursts of music. "Most have a hard time explaining the difference between cries, calls, and field hollers without using examples," Boyer allows. "They're easier to distinguish from hearing them than by offering any kind of concrete definitions, and since the slaves who sang them didn't categorize them, the definitions we use are more for us than for them. Of course, we only know what they really sounded like from the anecdotes we have, and the recollections of ex-slaves recorded in the 1930s may or may not be what was actually heard in the fields early on."

By the broadest definition, then, "calls" tended to be more denotative, consisting of simple declarations or the most elementary (and literal) word-of-mouth advertisements. Generations of food vendors, chimney sweeps, fix-it specialists, and salvage men had calls specific to their trades intended to attract public attention. Innumerable nationalities worked in professions where the strongest and loudest call made the difference in getting a job or making a sale—and in this earliest form of advertising, blacks had plenty of competition.

Cries, however, were entirely African in origin and could be characterized as sudden emotional outbursts, often without words. Comprised of hair-raising falsettos, staccato growls, and syncopated yelps, these sounds could make the uninitiated bolt upright in bed. They were a part of the homeland lexicon for many displaced Africans, and keeping them in circulation was one more way to cling to life before slavery. "Unexpected wordless birds of flight coming out of the stillness of the fields," author Harold Courlander called them after a chance encounter. Cries existed independent of structure, theme, or other Western preconceptions. "It is often completely free music," he writes, "in which every sound, line, and phrase is exploited for itself in any fashion that appeals to the crier."

Some musicologists contend that field hollers are the true predecessors of modern blues because of their expressiveness. They could be profoundly emotional, whether evoking ecstasy or pathos, and were readily identifiable, first because they were usually sung a cappella and solo, and second because they were typically performed while the slave worked at some nonrhythmic chore, cotton picking being a fairly obvious example. *Music in the New World* author Charles Hamm recounts one such overheard holler:

> Oh, if I ever make it, baby, I be long gone.
> Wo, I'm goin' down in Lou'siana, oh, don't you wanna go.
> Wo, I'm goin' down in Lou'siana, don't you wanna go.
> Wo, you look for me in Lou'siana, oh, I be long gone.
> Wo, you look for me in Lou'siana, I be long gone.
>
> Wo, you can tell everybody that I'll be gone.
> Wo, I'll be by to see you 'fore the summer gone.
> Wo, I might be in a hurry, I can't stay very long.

Although delight at their charges' musical dexterity is well documented, so too are the suspicions of whites worried about what subtexts slave music might hold, no matter how benign or self-evident the message might appear. Henry Knight, a white man who witnessed a black funeral around this time, reported with a palpable shudder that it appeared commonplace for slaves to "sing and dance and drink the dead to his new home." Unfamiliarity with African customs launched whites into paroxysms of paranoia. In 1680, the Virginia Assembly proclaimed "the frequent meetings of considerable numbers of Negroe [*sic*] slaves under pretence of feasts and burials is judged of dangerous consequence."

White fear of black revolt was almost as motivating for slavers as white brutality was to slaves. In the American South, where farmers were spread farther apart and slave revolution was considered as much an eventuality as a drought or flood, blacks were kept on a short tether, whereas more parental attitudes prevailed further north. Yankee Cotton Mather reflected, "I would always remember that my servants are in some sence [*sic*] my children, and by taking care that they want nothing which may be good for them, I would make them as my children . . . Nor will I leave them ignorant of anything, wherein I may instruct them to be useful." This was a far cry from business-as-usual in the South, where slaves were forbidden to learn to read and write.

LIFT EVERY VOICE

When the Church of England established a Society for the Propagation of the Gospel in Foreign Parts in 1701, Northern colonists set about saving the "heathen souls" of their property. The settlers applied liberal doses of religious indoctrination and encouragement in singing the Psalms of the day—a task slaves met with dexterity and passion. As psalmody presented the first opportunity for black and white Americans to raise their voices together in song, their collaborations were more significant as history than as music, because psalmody is more accurately described as chanting than singing. In practice, lines from the Psalms were first intoned by a chosen "precentor" who, if all went well, began and concluded at a preordained pitch. The congregation then followed suit, repeating the line and often embellishing the tune as it went. That was called "lining out," which gained popularity in many Pentecostal churches—black and white—and remains a cherished tradition of many rural services today.

Christians felt obligated to convert their servants in part since they were often living under the same roof. But the teachings of Christ—among them, "Do unto others as you would do unto yourself"—made for some steep theological hurdles. Missionaries learned to tailor scripture to their needs, emphasizing the belief that man's toil on Earth would be rewarded by an afterlife paradise. Initially those colonists bent on baptizing their servants met with responses ranging from indifference to aggression. But the "Great Awakening" religious revival of the early 1700s began with a burst of evangelism and a proliferation of sects. A new generation of evangelists replaced solemn scripture reading with wild-eyed sermons that many slaves recognized as a counterpart to the trances of the African shaman. Sacred music was evolving as well, with psalmody losing popular ground to the more poetic hymns that carefully altered Biblical texts into rhyming melodies more easily sung, played, and memorized. Both were enormously appealing for blacks, who eventually relinquished their ancestral notions of the hereafter and embraced Christianity with a fervor that outstripped their masters.

Colonist Samuel Davies described his day at devotions across from the slave pews and gushed, "I cannot but observe, that the Negroes, above all the Human Species that I ever knew, have an Ear for Musick [sic], and a kind of extatic [sic] delight in Psalmody; and there are no books they learn so soon, or take so much pleasure in . . . I can hardly express the pleasure it affords me to turn to that part of the Gallery where they sit, and see so many of them with their Psalm or Hymn Books, turning to the part then sung, and assisting their fellows who are beginners, to find the place; then all breaking out in a torrent of sacred harmony, enough to bear away the whole congregation to heaven."

Still, reminders that Africans were invited to America at gunpoint constantly negated even the most harmonious exchanges between blacks and whites. The most vicious injustices of slavery were not wreaked upon the blacks who first strode onto these shores, however. They were visited remorselessly on their progeny, whose rights and identities were systematically plowed under as the slave trade became more profitable in the New World. In fact, until Africans slipped on the social scale from servitude to slavery at the onset of the 18th century, there was a glimmer of hope that they might be able to lead happy, productive, and independent lives of their own. In the Northeast particularly, blacks experienced diminished citizenship, but were not generally looked upon as subhuman.

Blacks even had their own corresponding traditions, including Election Day in New England and the North Carolina John Canoe Festival, known by various names from Africa and the Caribbean to ports up and down the Atlantic Coast. For some, the African-influenced winter solstice celebration was John Conny, while others recognized festivals called John Kunner, John Connu, or Junkanoo, the latter still observed today in the West Indies. Another celebration, Pinkster Day, sprang up in Dutch settlements as an observance of Pentecost Sunday in the mid-1600s and was subsequently embraced by English New Yorkers. Once the festivities were under way, blacks commandeered the grounds in vivid re-creation of traditional African dance and song. Revelries continued through most of the following week, with throngs of white rural and urban observers gathered to witness the spectacle. "The festivals attracted large crowds of white spectators from both city and rural sections," according to historian Eileen Southern. The celebrations were known as "'Pinkster, the Carnival of the Africans,' and novelists incorporated scenes from the 'great Saturnalia of the New York Blacks' in their fictional works."

The center of attention was a figure called "King Charles," who played the pace-setting drum, called the dances, and was considered "the leading spirit" of the revels. In addition to the assorted percussion instruments present, there were also fifes, banjos, and fiddles—all played by blacks. And while there were booths, stalls, and tents erected on the fairground, much of the empty space on the midway was reserved for a marathon of dancing, in which new couples joined as others fell by the wayside, felled by their own exhaustion. At the end of the week, black and white celebrants straggled home to begin their observance of the Sabbath.

The festivals enjoyed moderate popularity in Manhattan but vanished with the end of the American Revolution. In 1811, all such hijinks were declared illegal in Albany, where the town council prohibited stalls from being erected on "Pinkster Hill." Similar fairs with at least some time given over to black "jubilees" for song, dance, and recreation were recorded in colonial Philadelphia and other parts of New York.

Even in bondage, these Africans could sing in hopes of a better life because their prospects were without limits, much the same as for those who immigrate to America today. But by the 18th century, white hospitality was wearing thin. Maryland came first, enacting laws in the 1660s forbidding intermarriage and proclaiming blacks slaves for life. Other states followed suit—Virginia in 1691, Massachusetts in 1705, North Carolina in 1715, Delaware in 1721, and Pennsylvania in 1725. Tensions rose on both sides. In 1741, pre-urban New York City saw more than a dozen slaves burned at the stake and eighteen others hanged by residents fearful of an uprising. What makes all these moments in history important to the music of today? The answer is obvious, but ought to be directly addressed. Point of origin aside, no element informs African American music making to such a degree as slavery.

FOR THE LOVE OF MONEY

Why did fate single out Africans to become slaves? In North America, some theorize that black subjugation simply became a utilitarian solution to a mounting problem of economics. Historian Lerone Bennett boils it down in *Before the Mayflower: A History of the Negro in America*: " . . . the rulers of the colonies were not overly scrupulous about the color or national origin of the work force." Settlers experimented with Indian slavery and found that they tended to wither and die once enslaved and that their capture could bring retaliation from their relatives encamped just beyond the horizon. There were experiments in white slavery, too, but whites were under the jurisdiction of recognized governments; they could appeal to a monarch or to local public opinion. More importantly, whites were invisible to a degree; they could vanish to a new settlement and rebuild their lives in freedom. Ultimately, Africans remained slaves because they couldn't escape unnoticed. No one would come to their rescue, and no law would be enacted to protect them.

"Africans," Bennett deduced, "from the standpoint of the colonial ruling class—did not have these disadvantages. They were strong: one African, the Spanish said, was worth four Indians. They were inexpensive: the same money that would buy an Irish or English servant for seven years would buy an African for life. They were visible: they could run, but they could not blend into the white crowd. Above all else, they were unprotected. And the supply, unlike the supply of Irishmen and Englishmen, seemed to be inexhaustible."

The final determinant may well have been a simple matter of happenstance. In the 1780s, when the prices of American-grown indigo, tobacco, and rice plummeted, depression overtook the South. Had it not been for Eli Whitney's invention of the cotton gin in 1793, the slave industry might have collapsed on its own. But the cotton gin provided a second wind for Southern planters. Once the cotton's seed was separated from its fiber mechanically, planters brought the full power of slave labor to bear on cultivation alone. So successful was this practice that by 1815, a substantial number of rice and tobacco growers turned instead to cotton production, and the demand for slaves escalated exponentially.

Much is known about slavery in the United States, but real information about slave life is sketchy. It's well documented, for example, that a sizable population of free blacks lived in the antebellum South. As many as 500,000 occupied what would today be called blue-collar jobs, filling positions as domestics, skilled artisans, and factory workers. However, these men and women were the exception to the rule. Most Southern blacks were enslaved, and most of those in bondage were owned by planters and plantation owners from the East Coast well into Texas.

In the urban centers of the Northeast, slaves were slowly making social progress. The British shrewdly offered freedom to all slaves who took up arms against the rebellious colonists in 1775, and in 1778, a number of laws were passed by the revolutionary government offering the same freedoms in exchange for military service against the crown. Massachusetts lawmakers abolished slavery in 1783. But those who were already enslaved were not set free; rather, their children born after the measures were passed were freed, and the acquisition of new slaves in the Commonwealth was prohibited.

To describe the development of a uniquely American culture among the slaves as stunted would be an understatement since their native language, common rituals, and freedom of expression were all forbidden. Yet the rudiments of structure were beginning to coalesce in the waning days of the American Revolution. By 1784, black clerics Richard Allen and Absolom Jones held licenses to preach at the Old St. George's Methodist Church in Philadelphia. Three years later, Allen and Jones were joined by six other blacks to form the Free African Society, described by Lerone Bennett as "an embryonic cell" serving as both a mutual aid society and the blueprint for a black-owned and -operated insurance company.

Another crucial linchpin was the black independent church movement, whose roots harkened back to the middle of the preceding century. The political clout of this string of churches (which ran from South Carolina to Georgia and Virginia) was strong enough to stage the first demonstration against the legal sanctions of slavery, which would become known as "Jim Crow" laws. When black parishioners began to outnumber whites at Sunday service, a confrontation was inevitable, and blacks were cast out to worship among themselves.

Social and fraternal black organizations soon followed suit. In 1787, after a failure to work out a peaceful coexistence with the white Masons, a veteran of the American Revolution named Prince Hall founded the first black Masonic lodge. Integral to the formation and success of these organizations was a single galvanizing principle: the ceaseless push for equal rights. The awareness of disparity between the races and the subsequent struggle for civil rights was passed on in house-to-house ideological combat against the imposition of white rule. It was fed to African American toddlers along with mothers' milk and reinforced at every educational gathering, social occasion, or religious observance. In forcing blacks to worship apart from those who owned them, slavers hastened the end of their dominion.

When they did attend services together elsewhere, blacks and whites eyed one another with suspicion, a case in point being the "camp meetings" ushered in as part of the Second Great Awakening of 1800. As the forerunner of today's tent revivals, camp meetings found white ministers aghast at the changes wrought in sacred music by African Americans. For example, it was not unusual for blacks to continue singing in their own quarters long after the end of the day's formal devotions, and the sounds that wound through the campfires, tents, and surrounding woods could only begin to be described as disconcerting to staid white ears.

Swedish novelist Fredrika Bremer, unlike others, was intrigued. From the segregated black quarters, she recalled an after-hours revel in which "the tents were still full of religious exhaltation, each separate tent representing some new phasis . . . In one . . . a song of the spiritual Canaan was being sung excellently . . . At half-past five . . . the hymns of the Negroes, which had continued through the night, were still to be heard on all sides."

The church's bastions of authority were not nearly so indulgent. Methodist church officer John F. Watson made clear his disdain and chastised other attendees for "errors" committed during services: "Here ought to be considered, too," he wrote, "a most exceptional error, which has the tolerance at least of the rulers of our camp meetings. In the blacks' quarter, the coloured people get together, and sing for hours together, short scraps of disjointed affirmations, pledges or prayers, lengthened out with long repetition choruses. These are all sung in the merry chorus-manner of the Southern harvest field, or husking-frolic method, of the slave blacks. . ."

Watson's rant sets a pattern typical of whites who perceive black-derived culture threatening their status quo. As Watson's hackles were raised, so too would white wrath befall the eventual creators of ragtime, jazz, R&B, rock 'n' roll, and rap. Surely, they say, nothing but trouble results from the commingling of black and white music. "The example has already visibly affected the religious manners of some whites," Watson groused. "From this cause, I have known in some camp meetings, from fifty to sixty people crowd into one tent, after the public devotions had closed, and there continue the whole night, singing tune after tune (though with occasional episodes of prayer), scarce one of which were in our hymn books."

Flooding the grounds with unsanctioned entreaties to the almighty was bad enough, but adding insult to injury was the prospect that white supplicants might be tempted to join in these sing-alongs. These hymns and their singers were now undermining the authority of the church, the fretful worried, with compositions more emotive and easier to sing and remember by virtue of their recurring choruses. Worse, blacks were contaminating Western religion with melodies and tempos bearing a disquieting resemblance to the dance tunes so popular in the slave camps of the day. The heathens were no longer at the door, but at the hearth, luring the faithful off to some primitive jubilation with siren songs of perverted Biblical verse.

The status quo was also under attack from within—in the form of a class war between white citizens over whether the new nation should embrace the entertainments proffered by the European Age of Enlightenment or strike out for new territory. Having finally secured independence in the War of 1812 and being agitated by the urban population explosion—which brought scores of immigrants from different nations into close living proximity (New York City alone ballooned from its 1840 population of 410,000 to a congested 910,000 by 1860)—many Americans wanted no part of an arts scene promulgated by the very royal courts responsible for oppressing the colonies. Average Americans wanted the United States to develop its own (white-derived) grassroots approach to art, one that would reject the pomposities of the European crowns and their caste systems. The situation soon deteriorated into street scuffles between the proponents of Old World culture and those who felt that imported dramas and musical entertainments only kept the country tied to apron strings half a world away.

Dislocated and buffeted about between cultures, the new urban émigrés gravitated toward sentimental parlor ballads that glorified the familiar—an old lamp, old chair, or old hunting dog—or an old dog lying at the feet of an old chair by the light of the old lamp. Sentimentality was in demand, and purveyors had no qualms about laying it on with a trowel. The promise of a better life in America lured many from the comforts of their native countries and families, and such ballads were passed around as remedies for homesickness. Besides, music publishers found them free for the taking. Musical compositions were not incorporated into U.S. copyright laws until 1831, and America had no real agreement over music copyrights with Britain until 1891, meaning that stateside publishers could pick and choose among the popular English works of the day without the slightest financial compensation set aside for the composer.

At the time, the principle customers were housewives who purchased music for their pianos (which were manufactured regularly in America from the dawn of the 19th century). These early books, called "songsters," promised to "offend no delicate sensibility," but to keep the purchaser fashionably informed of the latest musical trends from the continent. *The Singer's Own Book: A Well-Selected Collection of the Most Popular, Sentimental, Amatory, Patriotic, Naval, and Comic Songs* begins with the admonition that "not a single line has found admission to this book, which can directly or indirectly offend the nicest modesty, or mantle the cheek of beauty with the faintest blush."

The music had its devotees and its detractors. In researching his biography of composer Stephen Foster, author Ken Emerson came across a clipping from *The National Intelligencer* in Foster's father's keepsakes. Signed only "M.," it bemoaned, "all the sounds which are produceable from a piano are not Music [*sic*]. Oh! Is it not a torture to 'sit with sad civility' and listen to that disease (excuse the bull), called a popular song? Why, the thing is more contagious than the cholera . . . . Oh! Satan, what a sad blunderer you are to kill Job's daughters! Why did you not teach them to play on the piano, and sing, 'Come rest in this Bosom!' [One parlor favorite of the day.] Your business would have been done at once, you silly fiend. Job could not have stood it—he would have cursed and died."

Lower-class literary diversions proliferated across the nation as well. Newsweeklies rushed to fill the cultural vacuum with fanciful tales of the Midwest Expansion and the indomitable American spirit, including the ever-more-unlikely exploits of pre–comic book superheroes like the flinty Yankee everyman "Brother Jonathan" (based on Natty Bumppo in *The Last of the Mohicans*), and Davy Crockett, who came to embody America's untamed land and spirit. "I can walk like an ox," began one legendary Crockett boast, "run like a fox, swim like an eel, yell like an Indian, fight like a devil, spout like an earthquake, make love like a mad bull, and swallow a nigger whole if you butter his head and pin his ears back." The real Crockett did little to discourage such hyperbole. In fact, he was a willing participant in his own mythologizing. His response to an accusation of adultery during the 1829 congressional campaign was typically resolute: "I never ran away with any man's wife—that was not willing."

JUMPING JIM CROW

Perhaps inevitably, black counterparts to these white archetypes soon appeared in the popular imagination. While the sight of African Americans was hardly unusual in the United States, the probability of whites getting close enough to know or understand black traditions remained remote. And with little real information to guide them, myth-makers filled in the blanks by using their imaginations. Blacks, they concluded, were not particularly bright, but could be taught simple tasks and were always musical and funny.

After the Second War for Independence in 1812, Americans became increasingly inured to Negro suffrage. So long as the federal government deferred authority to the individual states, the mutual laissez-faire attitude placated Southerners dependent on a slave-based economy. Surviving playbills provide some indication of popular opinion regarding "what to do with the darkies." Often they were more welcome onstage than on the street. As early as 1767, an actor who went by the stage name Tea performed "a Negro dance" while appearing with the American Company in Philadelphia. By 1837, a few novelties crept in among the well-starched parlor pieces. These new additions were romantically distorted views of slave life, often recommended to be performed "*alla niggerando*" for maximum effect. Coarse and drenched in contempt, minstrelsy—or as it quickly became known throughout the land, blackface—became the first indigenous American art form. "I am science nigger," proclaimed one early favorite. "My name is Jim Brown."

In a very real way, however, whites had been donning black guises for centuries in playing Moors and bringing Shakespeare's Othello to life. As immigrants, many Western Europeans added their peculiar traditions to the mix. During the early 1800s, celebrants covered in chimney grime, outfitted in fanciful attire or inside-out street clothing, and calling themselves "Callithumpians" traveled house to house as part of their winter solstice observance. Inside, after receiving permission from the head of the house to perform, the callithumpians enacted a short improvised program reminiscent of European mumming plays. According to *Demons of Disorder*, Dale Cockrell's history of minstrelsy, the show served as a rite of passage for the young and as an opportunity for "role inversion," in which blackened performers were granted momentary rule of the residence for their presentation. In addition, the occasion served as what Cockrell calls "communal regulation" (or "charivari") because the invading visitors briefly had the ear of those higher on the social scale and could petition for the redress of grievances. Since the suggestions often indicated the will of the people, their advice was not to be taken lightly.

On the theatrical stage, blackface served a variety of purposes before being subsumed into the entertainment phenomenon of minstrelsy. More than a half dozen plays featuring blackfaced characters were performed around the country from 1769 through 1828. Blacks were often portrayed as dimwits or wily schemers, but there were exceptions. For example, in Frederick Reynolds' *Laugh While You Can*, the black character Sambo is a freed slave whom Cockrell calls "the primary facilitator and expediter in a play of romantic intrigue."

When minstrel tunes filtered into the hummable lexicon of the average American in the early 1800s, stage performers quickly set about fleshing out the characters described in song. And since simplicity was easier to impart than nuance for these performers (who appeared often in uneducated parts of the country), most black characters were depicted as little more than caricatures. White innkeeper and musician Micah Hawkins made a black man the narrator of his tribute to U.S. victory at the Battle of Plattsburg from the second revolutionary war. "Bow wow wow, den de cannon gin't roar. . ." ran the lyrics to "Backside Albany." (As an odd footnote, Francis Scott Key's observation of the war's next great battle, the bombardment of Fort McHenry, prompted him to rhapsodize about "rockets red glare" in "The Star Spangled Banner," while both songs relied on melodies borrowed from Ireland and England, respectively.) "Backside Albany" was greeted with enough enthusiasm to convince Hawkins to attempt a sequel of sorts, "Massa Georgee Washington and General La Fayette," an account of the Battle of New Orleans composed in exaggerated slave dialect.

In *Blacking Up: The Minstrel Show in Nineteenth Century America*, Robert Toll claims the first white man to use black idioms for profit was an English collector of African American "scraps and malaprops" named Charles Matthews. Eventually, Toll writes, "while attending a performance of the African Theater Company, a resident theatrical troupe in New York City, Matthews heard the audience demand that the black actor playing Hamlet stop his soliloquy and sing 'Possum Up a Gum Tree.' Matthews' use of this song in his act, 'A Trip to America,' was the first certain example of a white man (in the United States) borrowing Negro material for a blackfaced act."

But the first homegrown commercial collision of black and white musical idioms occurred when a performer married music and dance with his mockery:

> Lubly Rosa Sambo cum
> Don't you hear de Banjo tum, tum, tum
> Oh Rose de coal black Rose
> I wish I may be cortch'd if I don't lub Rose
> Oh Rose de coal black Rose

Love in a Cloud, the first play scripted with blackface in mind, found a warm and receptive New York audience in 1829 when George Washington Dixon stopped the show with his rendition of "Coal Black Rose." But Dixon was just warming up. He next extrapolated its protagonist, Sambo, into an independent banjo-strumming, good-time-seeking courtier and was covered in huzzahs for the next several decades when he introduced one of the enduring stereotypes of minstrelsy, Zip Coon. A popinjay composite of "uppity" blacks who donned their masters' discarded fashion wear in a comically pathetic attempt to pass themselves off as sophisticated, Dixon's Zip Coon had a basis in reality. It was commonplace for slaves at harvesttime to gather in their owners' hand-me-downs to sing, promenade in "cakewalk" dances, and engage in self-tapping rhythm excursions known as "patting Juba" or "the hambone," which called for participants to slap out rhythms on their laps, thighs, and knees with their bare hands.

Zip Coon represented the original black dandy. A composite of misconceptions, stereotypes, and caricatures, he was given to flamboyant dress and equally florid speeches, which were often rife with grammatical errors and social *faux pas*. (Courtesy of Brown University Library)

The Zip Coon phenomenon continues to resonate long after Dixon's parody was lost to the mists of time because it is still not clear which group is making more sport of the other. Obviously Dixon was lampooning blacks. But the slaves could just as well have been ridiculing their oppressors' arrogance while strutting the grounds like peacocks. And, most curiously, at the center of it all are the slaveowners themselves, cast as doting parents bemused by their children's "dress up" games, the grown-ups chuckling contentedly while their gaggle of innocents trot out Mother's well-worn heels or Father's cast-off waistcoat.

▶ According to legend, Thomas "Daddy" Rice encountered the real Jim Crow somewhere in his travels and bought everything he could of the slave's persona, including his clothes. Over the years, Rice rode those tattered coattails to fame and fortune in theaters across the country. Later, the words "Jim Crow" would become synonymous with white oppression of blacks in the South. (Courtesy of Brown University Library)

Cakewalks preceded the kind of line dances that remained popular right up through the glory years of Soul Train and disco. Considered equal parts fashion show, entertainment, and dance competition, these events allowed slaves to strut proudly before their owners in their Sunday best—which usually meant clothes thrown out of the Big House because they either no longer fit or were considered out of fashion. Slavers thought it amusing to watch their charges play "dress up," but it's just as likely that plantation blacks relished the opportunity to lampoon their owners. (Courtesy of Brown University Library)

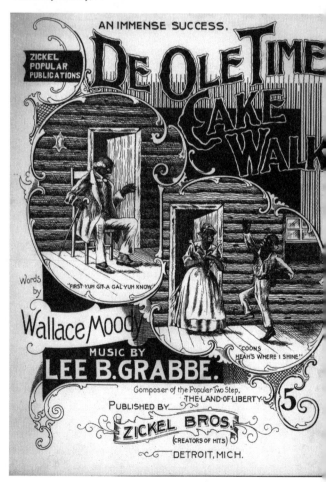

Dixon's act may have caused a sensation, but his main competitor, a New Yorker named Thomas "Daddy" Rice, set off an entertainment revolution with the creation of Zip Coon's poor Southern relative, Jim Crow. The legends surrounding his origin vary, but sometime in the early 1830s, Rice spied a hobbled black man either dancing for coins on the streets of Cincinnati or singing and shuffling in a peculiar way while at work in Louisville, Kentucky as a stablehand. This man has been described physically as everything from mangled to diseased, "his right shoulder deformed and drawn up high," ac-

JIMMY CROW.

New York: Published at ATWILL'S MUSIC SALOON, No. 201 Broadway,

cording to Toll, "his left leg gnarled with rheumatism, stiff and crooked at the knee, doing an odd-looking dance while singing: 'Weel about and turn about and do jus so/Ebry time I weel about, I jump Jim Crow.'"

Whether the stable hand was actually afflicted or simply struck Rice's Northern sensibilities as unique, the entertainer bought and paid (no amount has been recorded) for the black man's entire persona—right down to his bedraggled wardrobe. Rice inserted his Jim Crow alter ego (described as a "Kentucky corn-field Negro") into a play called *The Rifle*, and ended all speculation about whether audiences would pay to watch a white man act black. Author Ken Emerson describes the tumult: "Rice's crazy little dance, in which he executed a pixilated pirouette on the heel of one foot and landed on the toes of the other, hunching one shoulder while extending his other arm in a waggling 'hi-de-ho' salute, won him twenty encores." Both Dixon and Rice made and lost fortunes during the ensuing years, and both died impoverished and unknown. Ethnomusicologists later pilloried Rice in the court of public opinion on charges of cultural exploitation. Justifiable as these accusations appear on the surface, consider this: is Rice's co-option of Jim Crow for profit any more racist than Elvis' onstage modeling of the black-favored "cat" clothes sold at Lansky's Menswear in Memphis during the 1950s? And what about the Bessie Smith–inspired bangles and plumed feathers Janis Joplin favored in her final incarnation as an imaginary blues belter she called "Pearl," or the chains and shaved-eyebrow look Vanilla Ice took to the bank in the early 1990s? Some argue that Elvis earned the right to dress and move with black influences because he assimilated those characteristics during his childhood and was in effect "born into" the kind of music he chose to follow. Further, he and Joplin performed as they did in reverence to black idioms they admired, not in order to scorn or exploit them. But if thievery is the act of taking what is not legitimately owned and passing it off as if it were, then who among them did not steal?

Blackface is dismissed today as the antics of those with no taste attempting to please people with bad taste at the expense of those whose tastes went unconsidered. But at its core, minstrelsy sets up a paradox that has played out in American society ever since its introduction. To many a white mind, there remains something mystical and primal about the black experience. So to imitate blacks—in essence, to slough off the "white man's burden" of reserve and decorum—blackface entertainers were able to tap into a wider or at least different vocabulary of behaviors. At the time, white people would never have given themselves over to the wild physical gyrations of a Jim Crow, the Juba patting of his contemporaries, or the transcendental state blacks could reach through song. By creating the shell of a Negro with the application of burned cork, though, whites opened a portal to their own hidden creative impulses. (More than a century later, Paul McCartney explained how a similar revelation allowed him to conceive *Sgt. Pepper's Lonely Hearts Band*. Believing the Beatles had reached an artistic dead end, he decided to adopt the persona of another group entirely and see what might result.)

Melvin Patrick Ely traces the broad arc of minstrelsy midway through the 20th century in his book, *The Adventures of Amos 'n' Andy*. The characters' white creators (who played Amos 'n' Andy on radio but were replaced on TV by black actors in the 1950s) met at the Joe Bren Company, an outfit that staged minstrel shows for prominent fraternal social organizations such as the Odd Fellows and Kiwanis Clubs, among others. Ely writes that the originators of Amos 'n' Andy, Charles Correll and Freeman Gosden, understood quickly that minstrel shows went over best "when they could get the mayor, a few lawyers, maybe a college professor into the company they put together in each town. Gleeful newspaper accounts . . . show how thoroughly audiences enjoyed the once-a-year opportunity to see the local elite as blackface comics. One luminary in a North Carolina city 'out-darkied any darkey you ever heard of, whether of flesh or fable.' A doctor in West Virginia won applause 'by turning himself loose without restraint' . . . and proving that he 'possesses, in a wonderful degree, the talent to assume the exaggerated and glorified characteristics of the shuffling, singing Senegambian.'"

The crazy quilt of half-forgotten African cultures and half-learned European traditions that slaves and freedmen called their heritage was further corrupted by minstrelsy when white entertainers began substituting their (at best) revisionist accounts of what blacks did, thought, felt, said, and meant in and out of bondage. And once imitating "the Negro Way" came into vogue with the flood of performers cashing in by calling themselves "Ethiopian Delineators," blacks soon warmed to the notion that audiences might pay to see a genuine Afro-American at play. Indeed, theatergoers seemed less concerned with the race of the minstrel than with his ability to perform "authentically." In 1844, an Irishman who performed blackface jigs under the stage name "Master John Diamond" had enough hubris to challenge "Juba," a black Long Island legend, to a round of talent competitions. Their first meeting was a draw. But after two rematches, Juba (whose real name was William Henry Lane) emerged victorious with the title "King of the Dancers."

One highlight of Charles Dickens' New York visit around this time was the opportunity to witness Juba's performance at a dicey nightspot called Almack's in Five Points. In *American Notes for General Circulation*, Dickens writes with incredulity: "Single shuffle, double shuffle, cut and cross-cut; snapping his fingers, rolling his eyes, turning in his knees, presenting the backs of his legs in front, spinning about on his toes and heels . . . dancing with two left legs—all sorts of legs and no legs—what was this to him?" Juba's dexterity finally won him a dubious stamp of approval for "correct Imitation Dances of all the Ethiopian Dancers in the United States."

Negro impressions became the first American pop culture craze. Presidents Tyler, Polk, Fillmore, and Pierce all received minstrels at the White House and delighted in their frolics. A year before Juba won his crown from Master Diamond, four white men took the concept of minstrelsy a step further. Although blacks were being represented (or misrepresented) with increasing frequency in the comedies and light dramas of the stage, history credits Frank Brower, Dan Emmett, Frank Pelham, and Billy Whitlock with devising the first minstrel ensemble. Dressed in the patched and threadbare outfits of plantation slaves, the quartet opened in New York with a bill presenting "the oddities, peculiarities, eccentricities, and comicalities of that Sable Genus of Humanity."

Their union began in a completely serendipitous encounter, as Stephen Foster biographer Ken Emerson writes: "Their impromptu jam session—with Emmett on fiddle, Whitlock on banjo, Brower on 'bones' (percussion instruments made from the "sawn lengths of horse ribs like outsized castanets"), and Pelham on tambourine—created a 'horrible noise,' Emmett recalled with amusement years later, and established the instrumental lineup of the minstrel band."

Billing themselves as the Virginia Minstrels, the foursome not only established a structure that would remain a staple of blackface for the next half century, but, Emerson believes,

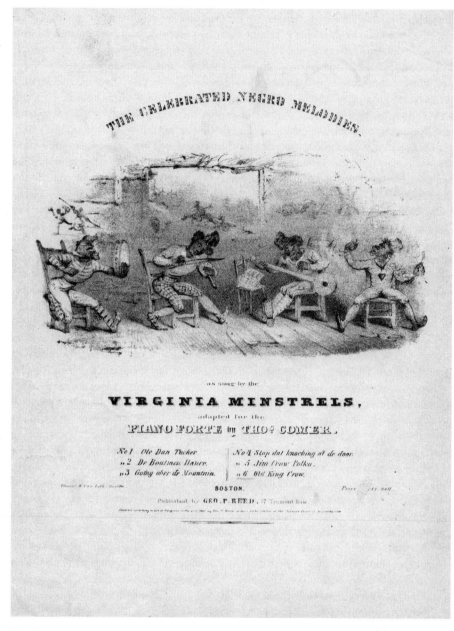

Blackface was a solo enterprise until the white Virginia Minstrels banded together to depict "the oddities, peculiarities, eccentricities, and comicalities of that Sable Genus of Humanity." Inadvertently, they also pioneered the group format—using essential instruments (fiddle and banjo) to carry the melody above a sturdy rhythmic foundation—exactly the same template used later in hillbilly, jazz, and rock 'n' roll. (Courtesy of Brown University Library)

set in place the basic group format subsequently followed in jazz, bluegrass, and rock: "The banjo shared the melody with the fiddle—like the clarinet and cornet in early jazz—while the bones chattered and the tambourine, which had a larger drumhead and fewer rattles than today's version, thumped and jingled a beat still heard 'round the world.'"

Within a matter of months, minstrel groups were either the thing to see or the thing to join nationwide. By 1855 even San Francisco, a city still in its formative years, provided enough work to support no less than five professional minstrel troupes. During the explosion that followed (the Ethiopian Serenaders, the African Minstrels, and the Congo Melodists among them), groups added refinements of their own. While the Virginia Minstrels sang only in unison, Edwin Pearce "E.P." Christy's Minstrels introduced four-part harmonies into the mix, a distinction that won them widespread acclaim, but stretched thin the already-tenuous links to actual secular black music.

For blacks and whites alike, perception was becoming reality. African Americans knew that minstrels were stitching together a patchwork of fictitious and real elements from black culture to suit their customers, but parts of that fabrication that began as counterfeit—harmony singing being one distinct example—were winning converts on both sides of the color line. Where there had once been only a handful of black Ethiopian Delineators, the box office clout of minstrelsy encouraged freedmen to seek a better future as entertainers in blackface.

Musicians of color who distinguished themselves without resorting to cork were rare, but included Francis Johnson, a military bandmaster and buglist from Philadelphia. Johnson was not only renowned as the first black musician to appear at integrated concerts alongside white players, but the first to tour the nation and the first black composer to publish sheet music. Many of his original compositions were recognized and beloved for their audacity, including his voice quadrilles, which featured the instrumentalists singing while they played, and the "Bird Waltz," which incorporated such an ornate flute obbligato that, in one critic's estimation, "the keenest perception cannot discover the difference" between the flute's solo and the chirping of an actual bird. Those present at his concerts cite the orchestra's ability to manipulate any melody into a jig, country dance, or reel—meaning, it seems, that Johnson looked at sheet music from a black perspective, as an opportunity to express the intentions of the performer as well as the composer. Johnson toured Europe with his band in 1837, and reportedly delighted Queen Victoria in a command performance.

At the other end of the Philadelphia social strata was Richard Milburn. A street performer who whistled his compositions while accompanying himself on guitar, Milburn was paid for writing "Listen to the Mocking Bird" with twenty copies of the sheet music. The song was published in 1854 by Septimus Winner under the pseudonym of Alice Hawthorne, and went on to become a favorite tune of President Lincoln. Between 1855 and 1905, it sold twenty million copies.

BEAUTIFUL DREAMER

This was the world that welcomed America's first celebrity composer. In researching his richly detailed biography of Stephen Foster, Ken Emerson found the recollections of the composer's older brother Morrison, describing Stephen's early flirtations with "show business" in Pittsburgh. Morrison writes that at the age of nine, Stephen joined his comrades and "a thespian company was formed, composed of boys of neighbor families,

Robinsons, Cuddys, Kellys, and Fosters. The theater was fitted up in a carriage house. All were stockholders except Stephen. He was regarded as a star performer, and was guaranteed a certain sum weekly. It was a very small sum, but it was sufficient to mark his superiority over the rest of the company."

Rather than deliver the ballads that moved his sister to beg their father for a pianoforte (which she knew he could not afford), young Stephen preferred the guileless emotion of minstrel fare. Most were not written in any distinguishably black dialect, but in black*face* dialect, which was an amalgam of what whites heard and could exaggerate from hearing in black speech. To hear Morrison tell it, Stephen was a peerless mimic of such sounds. "His performances of these was so inimitable and true to nature that . . . he was greeted with uproarious applause, and called back again and again every night the company gave an entertainment, which was three times a week."

In time, Stephen Foster began both sketching out tunes in the ballad fashion heard in respectable parlors and dabbling on the side with the blackface songs growing in popularity day by day. At eighteen, he published his first song, "Open Thy Lattice Love," as treacly as any standard from the songsters. Foster eventually lost his urge to perform and matured into a retiring adult who kept his own counsel as a songwriter, and he rarely performed before any audience after adolescence—possibly due to the fact that a livelihood dependent on music was considered "unmanly" at the time, or just as likely because minstrel songs were considered base until Foster's own work helped them find mass acceptance. Either way, an innate understanding of the minstrel milieu followed him into adulthood, and when he later fell in with a group of friends, he conducted them in twice-weekly singalongs. When they grew bored with the material, Foster offered to scribble out a few new melodies in the genre.

"Lou'siana Belle" was first, Morrison recalled, followed closely by "Uncle Ned." For the former, Foster borrowed the polka rhythms that had skipped across the Atlantic by 1844. The syncopation required to play these tunes properly was considered anything but genteel, and therefore easily cast in with the lot of African American styles as "disagreeable music of an uncivilized character," in the words of writer George Templeton Strong. But the lyric of "Lou'siana Belle" was even more base—suggesting an affair right under the Massa's nose. Unrefined talk about affairs already flouted every convention of polite society, but Foster demonstrates real impudence in suggesting that to own another man's beloved is immoral, no matter her color. "Uncle Ned," on the other hand, not only synthesized numerous minstrel songs; it manages to arouse sympathy for the title character. Today, the racist references in "Uncle Ned" fairly jump off the lyric sheet, but at the time, Foster's sentiments were considered bold and progressive.

> Dere was an old Nigga, dey call'd him Uncle Ned
> He's dead long ago, long ago!
> He had no wool on de top ob his head
> De place whar de wool ought to grow.
> Den lay down de shubble and de hoe
> Hang up de fiddle and de bow
> No more hard work for poor old Ned
> He's gone whar de good Niggas go.

America's original celebrity songwriter, Stephen Foster, was best known for composing the minstrel classics "Old Folks at Home," "Camptown Races," and "Oh, Susanna." Although he died impoverished and alcoholic, his songs were wildly popular on both sides of the racial divide and so popular among blacks that he was accused of stealing them. (Frank Driggs Collection)

The narrator's passive acceptance of slave life would arouse righteous indignation today (to say nothing of politically correct responses to the "N" word). But in its day, "Uncle Ned" and songs like it earned the praise of many leading abolitionists, including black freedom fighter Frederick Douglass, who publicly endorsed such songs saying that minstrel ditties "can make the heart sad as well as merry, and can call forth a tear as well as a smile. They awaken the sympathies for the slave, in which anti-slavery principles take root and flourish."

In the mid-1840s, Foster relocated from Pittsburgh to Cincinnati. There he found work as a bookkeeper and access to a wider variety of genuine black music via the bustling river traffic up and down the Ohio River. He also encountered a particularly rabid strain of racism. According to an abolitionist quoted by Emerson the biographer, "prejudice against the negro attains its rankest luxuriance not in the rice swamps of Georgia, nor the sugar fields of Louisiana, but upon the prairies of Ohio." To drive home his point, Emerson remarks that Pittsburgh's theaters may have kept blacks and whites apart with separate seating areas, but "one Cincinnati establishment reportedly advertised, 'Niggers and dogs not admitted.'"

Anyone who remembers Eisenhower's America would find a cozy familiarity in Foster's Cincinnati of the mid-19th century. Technical marvels (the telegraph, locomotive, steamboat, and daguerreotype) were changing the way people lived their lives. There was a successfully prosecuted war (with Mexico) to rekindle patriotic sentiments, and anything to do with the underclass was far from the public agenda. It's uncertain whether Foster penned his first classic in Cincinnati or Pittsburgh, but its premiere seems fixed enough. On September 11, 1847, white music spiked with black influence received its debut in a "Grand Gala Concert" at the Eagle Ice Cream Saloon in Pittsburgh. There, along with such contemporary fare as "Away Down Souf" and "Wake Up Jake," the audience heard "Susanna—A new song, never before given to the public."

It's impossible to hear Foster's tune with the ears of those who grew up more than a hundred and fifty years ago, but it's not hard to imagine the spell his words and music cast over the crowd. To begin with, "Oh, Susanna" has such an indelible melody that audiences then and now enjoy it simply as an instrumental. But Foster also used the vehicle of minstrelsy to unprecedented and astonishing effect. Cloaking himself in burned cork, he was able to comment on love, loss, race, and bewilderment at the onrush of technology. In fact, the song makes sense at so many levels its revelations remain obscure until the listener has perspicacity enough to absorb them. In contemporary performance, all that lingers in the collective consciousness is:

> Oh Susanna, don't you cry for me
> I come from Alabama, with a banjo on my knee

That's no mean feat for a song more than a century old, rarely receiving airplay (excepting costume dramas and cartoon reruns). But that snippet hardly conveys the essence of Foster's piece, which addresses migration and pioneering, but not nearly so much as other issues. Imagine understanding nothing more of Bob Dylan's intentions today than a fragment like "the answer my friend, is blowin' in the wind," or knowing only that "Smells Like Teen Spirit" refers to a brand of deodorant in its title. Here's what Foster wrote:

I come from Alabama with my banjo on my knee
I'se gwine to Lou'siana, my true lub for to see.
It rain'd all night de day I left, de wedder it was dry
The sun so hot I froze to def
Susanna, don't you cry.

Oh, Susanna, do not cry for me
I come from Alabama wid my banjo on my knee.

I jump'd aboard the telegraph, and trabbled down de ribber
De lectrick fluid magnified and kill'd five hundred Nigga.
De bugine bust and de hoss ran off, I really thought I'd die;
I shut my eyes to hold by bref
Susanna, don't you cry.

Oh, Susanna, do not cry for me. . .

I had a dream de udder night, when ebry ting was still;
I thought I saw Susanna dear, a coming down de hill,
De buckwheat cake was in her mouf, de tear was in her eye,
I says, I'se coming from de souf
Susanna, don't you cry.

Oh, Susanna, do not cry for me. . .

I soon will be in New Orleans, And den I'll look around,
And when I find Susanna, I'll fall upon the ground.
But if I do not find her, dis Darkie'll surely die,
And when I'm dead and buried,
Susanna, don't you cry.

Some disagree about the first verse's lyrical allusions to weather, one faction dismissing it as singsong nonsense, while others suggest Foster may be referring to the steady incursion of mass communications into what was once a placid agrarian life; for the first time it seems everything is happening everywhere simultaneously. (If so, the song could mark the first reference in pop culture to that compressed moment that cyberspeakers call "real time.") The "telegraph" of the second stanza hints at a pair of well-known steamboats, Telegraph 1 and Telegraph 2, and while these ships were viewed as vital forms of transportation, they were also frequently responsible for huge losses of life, being prone to sudden overheating and explosion. As Foster moves deeper into the verse, his steamboat metamorphoses into a train, for the "bulgine," Emerson explains, was a steam engine used only to power locomotives.

The remainder is fairly clear, even now. Foster augments his folksy melody with lyrics that quickly establish the fleeting travails of daily life, then dissipates to let more timeless concerns emerge. He begins with "I'se gwine to Lou'siana, my true lub for to see," the archetypal quest for treasure, adventure, or a better life. The late mythologist Joseph Campbell later called it "the hero's journey," a call to action that everyone must answer at a critical juncture in life. From the outset, Foster allows his narrator only to report on his situation: he's leaving, his reasons and destination are clearly fixed, and the circumstances (including weather conditions) will test his resolve.

Using these facts as a framework, Foster then segues into a dreamy visit from a long-absent lover, until, at the end of the odyssey, his protagonist finally arrives in the "promised land," where his fondest hopes may be made manifest. These images were in such perfect synch with the times that they resonated up and down the social ladder of the 1850s. Scores of immigrants abandoned the Old World after hearing of America's promises of freedom and prosperity, only to wake up in some grimy urban slum competing with newly arrived country folk for the same rock-bottom wages in the factories of the Northeast.

Many contemporary musicologists consider Stephen Foster the composer laureate of 19th century America. No such title was ever bestowed, of course, because none existed. But his most effective work—all written in blackface dialect—takes the pulse of Americans and returns it to them in the same cadence and tenor he received it with an unforgettable melody attached. Why Foster chose to express some ideas in formal parlor songs and others in minstrel tunes remains unclear. Certainly he was a songwriter for hire and, in that regard, really the first of his kind, so he may simply have been pairing themes with what seemed commercially viable. But blackface dialect also allowed Foster to state his emotions directly, rather than having to rein himself in to meet some arbitrary standard of discretion. "Old Folks at Home" (also known as "Way Down Upon the Swanee River"), "Camptown Races" (with its catchy chorus of "doo-dah!"), and "My Old Kentucky Home" transcend not only the times in which they were composed, but also the medium in which Foster worked. His minstrel melodies were wildly popular and sung during black gatherings as well as at those where performers corked their faces black for the amusement of whites. Many assumed Foster was credited as composer only because he bought and transcribed them from slaves in the South. Far to the contrary, he was assimilating the culture swirling around him. Foster traveled south of Kentucky only once in his lifetime, and the entire trip lasted only four weeks.

A hundred years and changes later, another singer-songwriter would hold such a clear vision of the South that his listeners assumed he, too, was a native son. Like Foster, he described his generation's migration—this time a retreat from unfriendly city dwellers and urban squalor and a return to simpler times where straightforward folks shared similar values. Ironically enough, his conveyance of choice was a fictitious paddlewheeler called the "Proud Mary." "Gosh, what a wonderful black group," Paul McCartney is said to have enthused when he first heard the Creedence Clearwater Revival classic. "When I found out they were white chappies, I was most amazed." In places, the song seems to retrace the route taken in "Oh, Susanna" back to its point of origin.

"Left a good job in the city," the song begins, "working for the man every night and day. But I never lost one minute of sleepin', worryin' 'bout the way things might have been." Like "Oh, Susanna," John Fogerty's "Proud Mary" is a traveling song—one that takes the listener down the Mississippi through Memphis (where the narrator did time as a dishwasher), all the way to New Orleans. Many have transcribed Fogerty's unique patois (where "big wheel keeps on turnin'" becomes "*toinin'*" and "Proud Mary keeps on *boinin'*") to read that the singer "pumped a lot of pain down in New Orleans." Ike and Tina Turner, in their equally famous cover version, didn't quite hear it like that. "Pumped a lot of 'tang down in New Orleans," is how Tina delivers the line—an interesting choice since "pain" now becomes shorthand for "poontang," a street slang reference to vaginal intercourse. (Fogerty himself believes Tina was singing "'tane," as in octane gas, so the mystery abides.)

In the third verse, Fogerty invites everyone down for the fun. "If you come down to the river, bet'cha gonna find some people who live; You don't have to worry," he sings, "if you got no money . . . People on the river are happy to give." Although he and Ike and Tina may have quibbled over the nature of New Orleanians' generosity, both records made it clear the narrator prefers Southern hospitality to impersonal city life.

"I actually had not been to the South before 'Proud Mary' was written," Fogerty says now, "unless my parents brought me through on some quick vacation that I don't remember. But for some reason, I gravitated emotionally, mentally, even spiritually to the South as a way of life. Back in the Creedence days, even before 'Proud Mary,' I spent some time in the South, but it was always kind of a hurried deal. It wasn't like I got to sit out for months and go cane pole fishing, which is something I would have loved to do. In the years since, I've gotten to spend much more time in little adventures in Mississippi, especially."

Like Foster, Fogerty was reared a world away from the one he envisioned so clearly. Fogerty grew up in the Berkeley, California suburb of El Cerrito. He never "ran through the backwoods bare" in Louisiana, although "Born on the Bayou" suggests otherwise; he wasn't Creole or Cajun and had little familiarity with the "flatcar riders and cross-tie walkers" his tunes memorialized. Both men created indelible images of time and place without firsthand experience. But in their imaginative synthesizing (some prefer cannibalizing) of these styles and stereotypes, they filled songbooks with melodies that became anthems to the generations they represented. For Fogerty, as for Foster, America was a tableau in motion, a mosaic of humanity waiting to be captured in song. A century separates them, but they are kindred in their ability to see black and white music as one concept, not two. In the interim, innumerable others came to different conclusions.

NOTES

1 Eileen Southern. *The Music of Black Americans: A History, Third Edition.* New York: W.W. Norton & Company, 1997, p. 162.

2 Lerone Bennett. *Before the Mayflower: A History of the Negro in America, 1619–1964.* New York: Penguin Books, 1966, 1975.

CHAPTER TWO

Rags to Ragtime

n South Carolina, slaves were whipped for singing to celebrate Abraham Lincoln's election in 1860, but when hostilities broke out at Fort Sumter shortly thereafter and the new president called the nation to arms, Lincoln's mind was on preserving the Union, not the eradication of slavery. Abolition met with shallow support north of the Mason-Dixon Line, particularly among the working-class poor, who feared being underbid by free blacks even for the most thankless of jobs. Lincoln's emancipation proclamation refocused the war into a contest of ideologies. Today, such a move would bring a storm of protest through negative ads saturating the media. In 1863, the way to appeal to the passions of the masses was through song. While speeches and the newspapers reporting them appealed to reason, songs had a way of sneaking into the heart, and both sides used music hoping that their tuneful claims to the moral high ground would win public sentiment.

Composers helped redraw the battle lines as the conflict mushroomed from skirmishes over states' rights into a five-year bloodletting, with the stakes rising to encompass the fate of the entire nation. African Americans were splintered into three groups during the war: those already free, those still in bondage, and the remainder, who were kept in limbo as captured rebel property held in the "contraband" camps of the North. Free blacks were prohibited from joining the Union Army until the fall of 1862. Soon after their induction, though, black enlistees found themselves at war on two fronts: one a battle to end slavery, the other an ongoing debate with Northern whites who discounted the value of black troops and relegated them to menial tasks. A number of white commanders considered the requisition of band instruments for their black regiments a top priority. Thereafter, time and effort was spent in extensive drills—not for combat, but for dress parades.

Music provided succor and a renewed sense of collective purpose to troops and civilians alike. On a larger scale, the Civil War also forced blacks and whites to reexamine their coexistence, and freeing the slaves challenged white Americans to either embrace real democracy or retreat into the delusion of blacks as biologically inferior. Fantastical sounds suddenly rushed in to fill the void between the races, as if two estranged families had finally started to talk again and needed to find a vocabulary that was new, yet familiar, and neutral enough to allow input from both sides. Spirituals. Blues. Ragtime. Jazz. The music forms that coalesced in the postwar years could never have come together as they did without two essential ingredients: first, the Union victory, which promised to put blacks in charge of their own destinies, and, second, the close-quarters interaction between the races necessitated by the war. Cross-cultural exposure had already resulted generations before in the synthesis of African-influenced hymns out of Western European psalms and the creation of America's first pop culture craze in minstrelsy. Now their collaborations would migrate upstream on the Mississippi waterways, picking up momentum and regional inflections from barn dances, saloons, and brothels along the way to filter out into juke joints and dance halls of the Northern Midwest and along the Atlantic coastline. Everywhere in America, it seemed, there was now a music that owed some essential component to African derivation. It was not always welcome, but it was almost always there.

Slaves predicted a "year of jubilation" at the war's end, but the Confederate defeat brought no guarantee of full citizenship for African Americans. Instead, the surrender posed innumerable questions. Whether or not blacks and whites *could* live together as equals, they most assuredly *would* live among one another as free, and no one knew what that would look like in a "Re"-United States. Every implication of the term "American" would soon change as a pair of disparate and mutually suspicious cultures were shoved together against their will. Picture social upheaval on a grand scale, and it's possible to imagine the tumblers of a cosmic time clock locking into place, releasing the floodgates of every emotion—including hostility, resentment, sympathy, atonement, and a rapacious desire to communicate those sentiments musically. In the torrent that followed, the blues would congeal into three distinct forms, spirituals would be codified and sent on evangelical missions around the world, and a surfeit of brass instruments left over after the war would help pave the way for jazz.

HOORAY AND HALLELUJAH

As Confederates gathered to battle Lincoln's armies of the North, original songs were quickly crafted to generate support, but, just as often, well-known tunes were outfitted with new lyrics to sway newcomers to one side or another. Historian Eileen Southern recounts that on the eve of the battle at Manassas, secessionists sang "Maryland, My Maryland" to the tune of "O Tannenbaum" until most of the crowd was in tears. For their part, Northerners took the melody of a camp meeting standard called "Oh Brothers, Will You Meet Us on Canaan's Happy Shore?" and recast it as an abolitionist diatribe called "John Brown's Body." (Before being hung as a traitor, Brown raided a government armory as part of a scheme to establish a freed slave camp in the Maryland mountains.) Julia Ward Howe overheard the tune sung by troops in Virginia and composed yet another set of lyrics, published in *The Atlantic Monthly* in 1862 under the title "Battle Hymn of the Republic."

Howe's reworking—guaranteed to leave a lump in the throat—accomplishes numerous feats of genius. First, it replaces the militant abolitionism of "John Brown's Body" with loftier ideals and makes certain no one mistakes the Union cause for some transitory political squabble. Then she conjures images of unflinching resolve and reasons (as Lincoln will) that when the stakes are great enough, mankind can be pressed to sacrifice. The real masterstroke, however, was her decision to retain the "Glory, glory . . ." chorus, which welds her lyric onto the song's genesis in the spiritual tradition and keeps black emancipation in mind rather than on the tongue; it's poetic without being preachy.

Across the battle lines, rebels were making use of black labor as servants at the front or back home, where they helped to maintain those enterprises considered essential to the war effort. A lucky few served in drum-and-fife positions, for which they were paid on a par with any other member of the company. The song that stirred Southern hearts was of course "Dixie," a minstrel show closer written by a white songwriter from Ohio named Dan Emmett and introduced on the New York stage by Bryant's Minstrels in 1859. The contrasts between Emmett's tune and "Battle Hymn" are striking. The latter aligns singers in a heavenly crusade. But for all its wistful imagery, "Dixie" always directs its supporters back to the here and now, where Southern ideals are under siege.

"In Dixie's Land," as it was first known, was conceived not as a call to arms, but as the reverie of a contented slave written in blackface dialect. "I wish I was in de land ob cotton," Emmett's lyric laments, "Old times dar am not forgotten, Look away! Look away! Look away! Dixie Land." It's also worth mentioning that the contented slave narrator says he's not *in* Dixie Land; he *wishes* he *were*, as if to admit with a wink and a nod that Dixie might be more a state of mind than a plot of real estate. The verses recall scenes of antebellum bliss ("in Dixie's land where I was born in, early on one frosty mornin' . . ."), but below the surface, its insurrectionist intent is clear because the utopia depicted so romantically is at odds with the country's direction—away from slavery, away from an agrarian economy, and away from isolationism.

On those terms, "Dixie" issues a challenge no Southern patriot can resist. The lyric sugarcoats its subversion by tenderly enumerating all the charms and traditions that secessionists would shed blood to preserve. "Hooray, Hooray," the song proclaims as it reaches full gallop: "In Dixie's land I'll make my stand, to live and die in Dixie." The covert incitements of "Dixie" become apparent only when the listener questions what might happen if Southerners felt their cherished institutions were under attack. Long after the war's end, "Dixie" remained the theme song of the South in homes and in public performances. In fact, the day following Lee's surrender at Appomattox, Abraham Lincoln stood before a crowd of celebrants and asked one of the bands present to play "Dixie" as an act of reconciliation. "I have always thought 'Dixie' one of the best tunes I have ever heard," the President said wryly, "Our adversaries over the way attempted to appropriate it, but I insisted yesterday that we fairly captured it. I presented the question to the Attorney General, and he gave it as his legal opinion that it is our lawful prize. I now request the band to favor me with its performance."

Almost immediately, "Dixie" was embraced as a valentine to the Southern way of life and as such became the Confederate signature in music. By depicting the Old South with the same greeting card sensibility that Norman Rockwell would later bring to his scenes of Americana, "Dixie" also sold Southerners a flattering self-portrait steeped in nostalgia. Just as previous generations professed their love for the old chair, old dog, and old lamp in parlor songs, Yankees and Rebels shared a fondness for their own bygone days—even though those idyllic times may have existed only in memory. From Protestant pleas to "Give Me that Old Time Religion" through "Happy Days Are Here Again" and baby boomer TV jingles reminding viewers that "simple pleasures are the best," familiar touchstones offer the illusion of security in uncertain times. In the first years after emancipation, black minstrels (including blues pioneer W.C. Handy) understood this and ended their shows with a medley of Stephen Foster tunes followed by an encore of "Dixie," the song linked most closely to their oppression. Exactly how Handy and his compatriots performed "Dixie"—with sarcasm, irony, or tongues planted firmly in cheek—no one can be sure.

Aside from the freedmen and slaves, a third group of blacks was neither free to roam the country nor pressed into service to prop up the Confederacy. Dubbed "contrabands," these were slaves seized as spoils of war and kept in camps under Federal protection. Without skills, homes, or prospects, they were regarded by some Northerners as little more than refugees siphoning away the Union food and medicine badly needed at the front. Federal leaders were confronted with a riddle: how could they prosecute a war when its main victims ached for the same supplies Union soldiers needed to fight effectively? Ultimately, much of the relief effort on behalf of the contraband blacks was provided by a range of charitable organizations, many of whom were also stretched thin and lacking in organization. The resultant camps were overcrowded breeding grounds for disease and confusion, but rife with music.

Memoirs from both contraband and Union soldiers describe black music making while at labor or leisure. In addition to reintroducing white listeners to shouts, cries, and hollers, witnesses in the camps recall hearing such tunes as "Go Down Moses," reworked by the slaves to commemorate their deliverance after Lincoln signed the Emancipation Proclamation. "Go down, Abraham," went the new refrain, "way down in Dixie's land/ Tell Jeff Davis to let my people go!" While the new lyric didn't stick, "Go Down Moses (The Song of the Contrabands)" remains a favorite among gospel choirs and became the first black spiritual composition published in the United States, although those who created the "transcription" had little exposure to the song as it was sung in the camps. By the time the tune was issued as sheet music in 1872, said one witness, it more closely resembled the hymns familiar to white ears, a "parlor ballad in 6/8 time."[1]

Black freedom quickly proved to be a mixed blessing. In New Orleans, for example, African Americans were sent tumbling down the social scale as a result of emancipation. New Orleans' "Creoles of Color" comprised an entire subset of free blacks born from generations of liaisons with French, Spanish, and Indian settlers. These partially black New Orleanians (sometimes referred to as "quadroons" and "octoroons," depending on the percentage of African American blood in the family's heritage) were people who had either received manumission from their masters or had been born free to former slaves. Being only a few steps from white allowed Creoles of Color a certain prestige and in some cases arrogance toward blacks still in bondage. Prior to 1861, many owned land and slaves of their own and could afford to have their children study art, literature, and music in France.

The war abruptly ended their affluence, and to many Creole minds their degradation was made complete in 1890, when Louisiana Legislative Code No. 111 stipulated that anyone of African ancestry should simply be classified Negro. Countless fortunes were lost, and degreed Creole musicians jockeyed for work alongside self-taught street players who bought their instruments in secondhand shops as war surplus. Creole violinist Paul

Dominguez bemoaned the situation years later in an interview with music archivist Alan Lomax: "They made a fiddler out of a violinist—me, I'm talking about. A fiddler is *not* a violinist, but a violinist *can* be a fiddler. If I wanted to make a living, I had to be rowdy like the other group."[2]

With the war over and Lincoln martyred, many white Americans turned inward, caught up with the politics of reconstruction, the industrial revolution, and a zeal for temperance that wormed its way into popular song. Little more than harangues set to music, these morality plays were the rage in parlor rooms across the country. The best known, "Come Home, Father" (1864), tells of a daughter's three visits to the local tavern, begging for her Papa's return. In her final plea, she laments how her sickly little brother has died—his wish to see his father one last time unrequited.

While Northern diversions included temperance ditties and debating the practicalities of Lincoln's pledge to "bind up the nation's wounds," Southerners straggled home to reconsider life without the economic crutch of slavery. African Americans had even tougher choices to make. Some kept picking cotton as sharecroppers. Others moved to the industrialized cities in search of factory jobs. Black musicians joined the exodus of former slaves who were satisfied to make a bundle of their belongings and take any road out of subjugation. For them, completion of the transcontinental railroad in 1869 and the proliferation of all-black minstrel touring companies made a tantalizing combination. In the same way rappers and sports stars are romanticized today, a black performer's career in minstrelsy dangled the promise of self-determination—even if it meant working for white producers to reinforce black stereotypes.

BACK IN BLACKFACE

Plantation life may have provided the backdrop for minstrelsy, but until the war's end in 1865, only a few African Americans were actually "blacking up" for a living. Blacks infiltrated the field en masse in the years following emancipation, billing themselves as "authentic" or "genuine" purveyors of Negro idiosyncrasies. By this time, however, minstrel archetypes had been pared down to a few pat roles, the clever trickster/wily Negro seldom seen among them. Now the variety of black characters resembled a family of circus clowns. All appeared different and interrelated, but with an Aunt Jemima, a shuffling elder, the would-be rake Zip Coon, and assorted banjo-plucking "darkies," the unmistakable intent was to portray Africans as foolish children with a knack for music making bordering on the savant. That is, blacks were born innately musical, but so slow-witted that they couldn't grasp the magnitude of their own gifts. Black artists hopped aboard and reinvigorated minstrelsy nonetheless. They corked up their faces, painted their lips, shucked and jivved, and sang and told jokes at one another's expense. In signing onto the conceit, they also invested minstrelsy with the only integrity it could ever claim.

Evidence suggests that black participation in minstrelsy was strictly fee-for-service and part of a quest for opportunity beyond blackface. Black people made a success of blackface and their purgatory in it by sheer force of will. Their perseverance helped to hew vaudeville from minstrelsy and mount the first all-black theatricals at the turn of the century. And, because freedmen and former slaves shouldered their minstrel careers as an apprenticeship rather than a yoke, their work on the circuit provided them with the experience to step onto the stages of vaudeville and Broadway as entertainers with ready-made marquee value. They sang "Dixie" and slapped their knees in hambone rhythms, but always seemed to be pushing forward. How many black parents have passed on this message of working with whatever you can get your hands on as a survival skill from the days of slavery—or even before? So many African American success stories followed the same pattern, and still do: Take what is given to you, the lesson seems to say—even if it's another person's scraps. By investing it with personal commitment, you can transform that refuse into something special, something worthwhile—something someone will pay you for. And once you've cornered the market on a product uniquely your own, you'll have *real* bargaining power.

Journalist Donnell Alexander says that this message is central to understanding American black culture in his 1997 essay for *Might* magazine, "Are Black People Cooler than White People?" Alexander maintains the very concept of "cool" derives from taking this lesson to heart. "Cool," he writes, "is all about trying to make a dollar out of 15 cents":

"Cool was born when the first plantation nigga figured out how to make an animal's innards—massa's garbage—taste good enough to eat. Hog maws and chitlins became good enough to cherish and long for wistfully. That inclination to make something out of nothing—to devise from being dumped on—and then to make that something special, articulated itself first in the work hymns that slaves sang in the fields and in the songs at the center of their secondhand worship."

Such possibilities help explain why a generation of black performers were willing participants in their own humiliation. Still, the image of African Americans "blacking up" is only one strand in the complex web of minstrelsy. The tougher question asks us to consider the relevance of blackface now. Do remnants still exist in today's media? In a 2001 biography called *Where Dead Voices Gather*, author Nick Tosches (who is white) attempts to uncover the true story of a white minstrel named Emmett Miller. Early in the book, Tosches defends blackface as no more demeaning than any ethnic smear promulgated by the entertainment industry. Tosches next upbraids *The New York Times* for its politically correct headline of a book review dealing with minstrelsy. He doesn't take the easiest shot against revisionism, the inherent unfairness of judging behavior of a hundred and fifty years ago by today's standards. He chooses instead to defend minstrelsy as merely rowdy good fun. Tosches quotes the offending headline ("Minstrel Tradition: Not Just a Racist Relic") and then counters, "as if to imply that the blackface caricatures of minstrelsy were somehow more racist than the insidious stereotype of today's popular entertainment; as if to imply the playing of blacks by whites to be more demeaning or more momentous in absurdity than the playing of Italians by Jews and WASPS, from *Little Caesar* to *The Godfather*, and every other manner of ethnic fraud upon which our popular culture has to this day been based."[3]

Heaping insult onto injury, Tosches goes on to paint America as a land of dreams and dreamers in which minstrel shows were never mistaken for reality. "If the halcyon lark of antebellum plantation life invented by minstrelsy was a sham," he argues, "it was at least a sham that few took for reality." This seems patently absurd, since it's still commonplace to switch on a TV talk show and hear an actor describe being hailed in public by his or her character name because a fan wanted to offer advice in handling some random plot twist. Americans of the 19th century had no mass media and were less traveled and less educated than audiencees today. Therefore, it's at least logical to conclude that most observers had no idea how much (or little) truth might be behind blackface. "The same," Tosches says, "cannot be said of modern cultural shams such as the fantasy of African American roots perceived in, say, Kwanzaa, a fake holiday invented in 1966, and no closer than minstrelsy to the reality of any true African culture." Tosches overlooks the fact that every holiday can be traced to a point of origin, and that what Kwanzaa has in its favor (leaving aside its design to ennoble rather than denigrate) is that it was invented by the same people who practice its observance. It was not something foisted upon a minority by a xenophobic majority.

Tosches gets one thing right: every group has members who enjoy seeing the misconceptions and stereotypes of their culture trotted out for public amusement. Just as some Southerners are tickled by comedian Jeff Foxworthy's "You Might Be a Redneck" routine, there are pockets of Italian Americans who'd never miss *The Sopranos* and gay bars where patrons flock to watch *Queer Eye for the Straight Guy* on television. To the bewilderment of many social critics, black devotees of minstrelsy stretch back long before *Amos 'n' Andy* brought blackface to radio in the early 20th century. Our ability to laugh at ourselves and at one another is not unique among world cultures, but perhaps because we readily accept and celebrate our mongrel origins, self-deprecation has always been a central feature of American mass entertainment.

While black entertainers did ultimately turn minstrelsy to their own advantage, there's scant evidence that they ever donned blackface to dispel the stereotype of the dim but happy plantation slave. Instead, black minstrels worked hard to satirize their lot more believably than their white rivals. Handbills boasted casts of "real coons" and reviewers noted large and supportive black crowds "attracted by the novelty of a corps of 'real nigger' performers." Simultaneously, minstrelsy was undergoing other changes, evolving from small, self-contained units of song-and-dance men who told jokes and staged skits.

Touring troupes now boasted huge casts, with each company promising "spectacular and diverse" entertainments. In some cases, they pared back Negro parodies, while in others they excised white minstrels entirely rather than suffer by comparison with black performers. Increased competition meant the addition of evermore bizarre sideshow attractions, including animal acts, circus freaks, and Greek and Roman "statuary" tableaus—that is, girls posing in tights, a presentation considered titillating at the time. These entertainments took several turns. Some emphasizing the scantily clad ladies took the low road into burlesque. Singer/producer Tony Pastor took the opposite approach in 1880, downplaying minstrel escapades and replacing tawdry diversions with more wholesome acts. Families descended in droves to see his shows at New York's Fourteenth Street Theatre, and the result was vaudeville—the forerunner of the variety shows that lasted well into the 1970s.

As early as 1861, Duprez and Green's minstrels began two show business practices that survive to the present: the adoption of signature uniforms and nonstop touring. Duprez and Green also displayed a knack for generating publicity; they promoted themselves by hosting free events and serenading newspaper offices the way modern performers visit a radio station to spark interest in a show or record release.

Minstrelsy also held prospects of excitement and adventure. There was travel, instant approval from the audience, widespread notoriety, and disposable income. However, despite the fact that minstrels enjoyed freedom on a longer tether than sharecroppers or other unskilled ex-slaves, there were drawbacks aplenty. For example, unless the company was flush enough to travel by rail with onboard accommodations for the company, lodgings were unpredictable—especially since signs reading "Don't Let the Sun Set on You, Nigger" still stood on the outskirts of towns around the country. Some towns had hotels catering to a black clientele, and on other occasions, private citizens would open their homes to a visiting troupe. If not, they camped together outside town, hoping that "keeping to their own kind" would keep them safe.

Outside their tiny traveling bubble of influence, existence could be precarious for black minstrels, particularly by comparison with the ex-slaves who remained in familiar surroundings. Author Edward Berlin recounts two instances of black performers who ran afoul of the law. Berlin first reports that in 1902, Billy McClain was arrested in Kansas City for wearing excessive jewelry when the authorities surmised he could not have come by such wealth honestly. That same year, according to Berlin, came the death of Louis Wright, a 22-year-old member of Richard and Pringle's Famous Georgia Minstrels.

After a parade to herald his company's arrival in New Madrid, Missouri, Wright and a friend were walking to the opera house when they were pelted with snowballs by white youngsters passing by. Wright yelled obscenities at them, which convinced the assailants that such a "vile insult" demanded retribution. In an attempt to capture and whip Wright, they ambushed the cast at the theater after the performance. Shots were fired and several members of the troupe wounded. All were arrested.

"The next day," according to Berlin, "each one was taken to the court and asked who among them had fired the gun. They all denied that any of their members owned a firearm. They were returned to jail for another night. At 11 on Sunday night, Wright was taken from the jail. Two young boys testified they had seen the handle of a revolver sticking out of his pocket.

"The following morning," Berlin concludes, "the minstrels were released and found Wright hanging from a tree near the train depot. He was later cut down, put in a box and shipped C.O.D. to his mother."[4]

So, with Jim Crow laws replacing the promises of Reconstruction, mocking one's race for the amusement of others provided both the best and the worst America could offer newly freed blacks. Individually they enjoyed the obvious benefits of steady employment with a touring group. Talented artists—those with real vocal, comic, or dancing abilities—could live in hopes of stardom. Few minstrels were getting rich, but many were getting noticed. James Bland, the composer of "Carry Me Back to Old Virginny," was one of many drawn to the light of the minstrel stage and left scorched by his encounter. At the height of his fame, he was known as the "Idol of the Music Halls" and the "World's Greatest Minstrel Man."[5] Although university educated, Bland took the plunge into minstrelsy in 1875 after teaching himself to play banjo and by entertaining friends, often with songs he'd written himself.

Bland worked the burned cork circuit with a number of troupes until an 1881 tour of Europe with Haverly's Colored Minstrels convinced him to strike out on his own. When the company returned to America, he resigned himself to solo work, remained overseas, and struck gold. Estimates suggest he earned as much as $10,000 a year on tours of England and Germany, but when he returned stateside in the 1890s, his fortunes imploded. Audiences winced at his dated material, and such lyrics as "all dem happy times we used to hab will ne'er return again" from "Virginny" trapped him like a mosquito in amber. Although credited with some 700 songs, including the classic spiritual, "Oh, Dem Golden Slippers," Bland was unable to make the transition into the emerging era of Negro musicals. He died impoverished in Philadelphia in 1911, and nearly half a century later his ode to antebellum Virginia became the official state song.

Another marquee favorite, Billy Kersands, had an act sure to thrill audiences, irrespective of color or refinement. Music historians credit him with popularizing (if not the outright invention of) a dance called "the Essence of Old Virginia," which soon came to fame as the soft-shoe. His execution of another step, the "buck and wing," also became the standard for other hoofers to follow. As a black comic, Kersands was best known for his dimwitted characters and the "talent," because of his large mouth, of being able to place an entire cup and saucer inside. While performing before Queen Victoria, he is said to have assured the monarch that had his mouth been any larger, "they would have to move his ears."[6] His crowd-pleasing repertoire included a song of intrablack racism, "Mary's Gone with a Coon," in which a father bemoans his daughter's choice of husband as too dark. "My heart is tore," says the score, "when I think de matter o'er . . . De chile dat I bore should tink ob me no more den to run away wid a big black coon."[7]

And so it went. More entertainers in the field led to greater diversity among them, and once blacks became their own promoters, selecting their own material, they chipped away at conventions, and new producers began to finance more realistic theatricals. A pair of black performers, Emma and Anna Hyer, became producers of light opera and dramatic musicals, including *Urlina; or The African Princess, Colored Aristocracy,* and *Plum Pudding.* The Hyer sisters financed road shows ranging from serious to comic opera and tested the limits of minstrelsy's burned cork frolics. The business-savvy sisters helped a number of black artists up the ladder to stardom, particularly Sam Lucas, the most popular black minstrel of his time.

Lucas made his debut as a minstrel in 1869, jabbing still-raw nerves with selections that dared to celebrate the end of slavery.[8] By the time he left show business in 1915, he not only appeared in the Hyers' musical dramas *Out of Bondage* (1876) and *The Underground Railroad* (1879), he also took the title role in the first serious production of Harriet Beecher Stowe's *Uncle Tom's Cabin,* and starred in *The Creole Show*—the first black musical revue, which ran in New York during 1890. Lucas was also center stage for the first black musical, *A Trip to Coontown* (1898), before reprising his Uncle Tom role in 1912 when the play moved onto the silent screen.

Minstrelsy was slow to die, but its dominance of the American stage ended with the turn of the century. Nonetheless, radio and television versions of *Amos 'n' Andy* and community minstrel shows across the country kept its traditions alive well into the Eisenhower Administration. Uncle Ben, Aunt Jemima, and Sambo remained among the nation's most recognizable black "celebrities" alongside Louis Armstrong, Lena Horne, and Joe Louis. Revisionist observers from both sides of the color line (many with a vested interest in how history is interpreted) continue to weigh what blackface says about the collective American psyche.

There's little dissent from the notion that minstrelsy became a metaphor to help whites assuage their guilt for subjugating African Americans. After all (the logic goes), if blacks were savage, didn't white Christians owe it to them to look after them and give them meaningful duties in life? Seen through this prism, minstrelsy is merely a theatrical extension of Manifest Destiny doctrine: being born white is to be superior, because that is what God wants. And, if the most meaningful work a black person can do is amuse a white audience, shouldn't that be enough?

Ultimately, blackface minstrelsy may be too protean to allow easy understandings. On the surface, it was farcical pastiche. Below the burned cork, though, minstrelsy reveals itself as one of humanity's intermittent attempts to put a face on the primordial bogeyman. Minstrel shows tutored white America for nearly a century with parables of how blacks were *other*—different and scary, yet enchanted and enthralling. As the inheritors of that society, we have yet to come to terms, not with our revulsion at minstrelsy, which is readily granted in this era of political correctness, but with the fascination that tears at us with claws that penetrate far deeper. It's plain that blackface didn't attempt to depict African Americans so much as to outline the fears and suppositions surrounding them. Most minstrel songs and routines were white inventions, so it's reasonable to conclude that blackface says at least as much about white concepts of blackness as about blackness itself.

Set aside for a moment the damage minstrelsy did to African Americans. What did the white *attraction* to blackface antics say about America? Why were white audiences captivated? What continues to draw white artists to incorporate black influences? In part, it's all a matter of economics. Box office receipts and record company profits demonstrate that the formula remains as potent today as it was when Jim Crow first jumped, Jolson first crooned, and Elvis first shook pelvis. But other than preferring rappers' hip-hop fashions to the burned cork of a minstrel, what separates today's performers from the minstrel images that make us cringe with shame? Doubtless there were Caucasian blackface performers who did not like black people, but who can say that there are more or fewer of them today, all willing to shuck and jive their way to success?

The less cynical view holds that white performers working in today's rap, rhythm and blues, and hip-hop idioms do so out of devotion. But many are artistically at an impasse, too timid (or too intimidated by their labels and fans) to venture beyond the provided blueprints that led to their multiplatinum sales. There are numerous examples: Kid Rock, Limp Bizkit, and Linkin Park harken back to the 1980s black metal band Living Colour with their hybrid of riffs and raps. The Red Hot Chili Peppers have taken those same concepts and expanded their dynamic range to include quiet ballads and pop-friendly melodies. Conversely, Justin Timberlake's 2002 solo album, *Justified*, is both ambitious and derivative in attempting to update Michael Jackson's *Thriller*. In each case, the music bears an unmistakable stamp of personality, but falls short of breaking new creative ground.

It's hard to fault these artists for their inspiration, though. Blacks have historically been the urban adventurers, the ones who popularized cool by living large under duress. Unlike white icons Donald Trump and Ben Affleck, black celebrities often begin as street heros who can take whatever they have and make it look desirable irrespective of start-up capital or good bone structure. But what happens when a generation of followers catches up to the standard-bearers, only to find them milling around at the end of a blind alley?

"As valid a form of art as it might be, rap is not about making music," says singer-songwriter Lyle Lovett. "You've got music on the one hand and words on another, but they're not the same, and that's why I like bands like the Blackeyed Peas, the Roots, and Outkast—you have musicians actually up there playing live instruments. I don't know why that's so important to me, but it is. Maybe it's because I think about what's going to happen years from now—I mean, where will rap be able to take music in the future?"

Black hip-hoppers—those artists whose forebearers always illuminated paths to the *future*—have used their recent time in the limelight not to innovate, but to erect a new racial stereotype built on bottles of Kristal, pimped rides, bling-bling, and two-hundred-dollar-a-pair Air Jordans. In many ways, this modern minstrelsy is the new cool, reinforced through movies, Web sites, and weekly episodes of MTV's *Cribs*.

Minstrelsy today is supposedly deader than Latin, a subject fit for dissertations on how one entertainment genre begat another. Certainly there's cultural value in seeing how the organization of minstrel troupes (with their designated positions for instrumentalists, rhythmatists, and an interlocutor) began a paring-down process that reduced ensembles to their most essential elements, an evolution that would pave the way for jazz trios and rock groups.

But blackface lives; it's seeped into the bedrock of our collective being. Minstrelsy as historical era may be dissected and catalogued, but it's anything but over, especially when those who trade in black caricature continue to bank huge paychecks and influence visual and musical trends on a global basis. The evidence is everywhere—from showboating diva concerts and interviews in *Vibe* to hip-hop videos where smut is somehow both ultrahip and inherently funny.

When Missy Elliot raps in her 2003 hit "Work It" about shaving her "cha-cha" and groping her date "to see how hard I gotta work ya," it's hard to know how to react. Charges that she's objectifying black women are somewhat blunted since she's calling the shots and getting rich in the bargain. Besides, rock and rap have a long tradition of scoffing at prudes. Some sociologists believe such music is an expected outgrowth of the need for teenagers to establish identities separate from their parents'. But when lyrics are stripped of all romance, all that's left is unchecked abandon—the same indictment leveled against black-inspired music for hundreds of years. A segment of society remains appalled while others defend Missy E as merely "representin'" what happens in everyday life. But if the equation for minstrelsy is "race + exploitation = profit," how do we account for Missy Elliot, 2 Live Crew before her, or even the guitar-humping theatrics of Jimi Hendrix?

Check the magazine stands or flip through the current cable TV lineup and the stereotypes still pop up like ducks at a shooting gallery. No art form influences American entertainment to the degree that minstrelsy still does, but because its evidence is scattered around us in familiar and comfortable places, it slips past us unnoticed. We'd recoil if today's artists rubbed their faces with burned cork and slurped watermelon onstage while crooning plantation ditties. But when Vanilla Ice imitates MC Hammer or MTV's Carson Daly nods along while the singer from an all-white boy band explains his group likes "chillin' with the homies and keepin' it real, yo," Americans race to download their latest hits instead.

Cool, we are now told, is as close by as the nearest specialty store and as easy to obtain as one's credit limit will allow. But there was a time when portraying blacks as obsessed with sex and status was considered an insult rather than clever marketing. Before America was sorted by demographics and every aspect of life became packaged (including outsider status and all its essential accessories), black talent was regarded as something sacrosanct, even magical, by both races.

SPIRIT OF '76

In 1876, the same year the Hyer Sisters organized their first permanent colored musical-comedy troupe, Marie Selika Williams made her debut as a concert soprano in San Francisco. Dubbed "Queen of the Staccato" by the press and her fans, Williams was one of at least five black prima donnas earning international acclaim through her dexterous handling of sacred and classical compositions.

All of this represented progress for African American performers, considering what they had come to expect. Less than a generation earlier, a black soprano from Natchez, Mississippi named Elizabeth Taylor Greenfield became the darling of the Eastern cognoscenti and was sent to Europe in 1853, where she was presented not so much as a singer as a wondrous fluke of nature. Greenfield received some vocal training in Philadelphia as a youngster, then relocated to Buffalo, New York, where she quickly earned a reputation as "The Black Swan." In 1853, she took England by storm, according to author Harriet Beecher Stowe. Greenfield's recitals typically included "Old Folks at Home," with the Swan delivering "one verse in the soprano, and another in the tenor voice," according to the novelist. Greenfield's accompanist then offered up a demonstration of the singer's range by striking notes at random on the piano, which she would then duplicate vocally. "She followed with unerring precision," Stowe reports, "striking the sound at nearly the same instant his fingers touched the key. This brought out a burst of applause."[9]

Black performers could astonish audiences with their mastery of Western styles, but so long as they were compelled to perform someone else's music, they risked being regarded as human mynah birds. For them, emancipation meant more than slipping out of slavery's shackles; it meant replacing preconceptions about black creativity.

Half a continent away at Fisk College in Nashville, a missionary named George White made the next move: he would take his all-black school's chorus on a fundraising mission (following the route of the Underground Railroad) and in the process present a sheaf of previously unknown slave spirituals to largely white audiences. The resulting tours not only provided financial resuscitation for Fisk; they offered compelling evidence of slaves who used songs of faith to steel themselves against oppression. Ultimately, White and the Fisk Jubilee Singers would make their case before royal courts and concert halls across the globe and set a standard followed by every gospel choir since.

Fisk College was established in 1866 on the grounds of what had been a field hospital for Lincoln's army of the North—a facility, rumor had it, where patients received treatment more often for venereal disease than for wounds inflicted by the enemy. As the fledgling school angled for respect in a city crowded with carpetbaggers and secessionists, the idea of presenting a cultured black chorus performing Western sacred music made for good public relations. Privately, Fisk administrators also hoped the pastime would prevent their student body of former slaves from reverting to paganism, or—heaven forbid—embracing "the Papal Church with its pictures and dresses and music and gaudy trappings and showy ceremonies."[10]

One of the founding faculty members was George White (actually, he *was* white), a Union soldier-turned-instructor who agreed to provide music lessons in his spare time to students who showed promise. Unbeknownst to White, his students were also gathering by themselves to revisit the music they had sung in bondage. When the director found out, he asked them to share their songs with him for collection and transcription. Doubt-

White audiences didn't know what to make of the Fisk Jubilee Singers, pictured here with their founding members around 1880. Initially the former slaves were taken for a novelty act because they dressed in suits and gowns. Their repertoire of originals included "Swing Low, Sweet Chariot" and "This Little Light," which one critic dismissed as "cornfield ditties." (Frank Driggs Collection)

less the singers were conflicted about whether White could be trusted with such a bounty, since these compositions were created secretly and not intended to be heard by anyone other than the slaves who created them. Eventually, pianist Ella Shepherd contributed "Swing Low, Sweet Chariot," and "Before I'd Be a Slave" (songs her mother later claimed to have written). Submissions piled up quickly, and White began to rehearse his choristers in the material. Because so many of the songs were fluid inventions of endless variety, White's arrangements tended to force the material into a structure that could be repeated from one performance to the next. Those familiar with the spirituals before White wrestled them onto paper found the transcribed versions less malleable and spontaneous and preserved with a formality typical of Victorian sacred music.

Western notation techniques may have hampered White's attempts to capture the subtext of each tune, but when his singers took them over, much of the missing passion returned. Choir member Georgia Gordon recalled that White "would keep us singing them all day until he was satisfied that we had every soft or loud passage to suit his fastidious taste." Ironically, in a genre accepting of hollers and shouts, White honed his singers' approach to pianissimi until they could sing with one voice in a hushed whisper. According to those present, the conductor rehearsed them to sing as forcefully and quietly as they could. "If a tiger should step behind you," White coached, "you would not hear the fall of his foot, yet all the strength of the tiger would be in that tread."[11]

Beguiled as he was by the possibilities, White vacillated in his concern about how the music would be received. What would Nashville's white community make of such songs? These pieces were worlds removed from the leering tone of blackface and yet their African-derived elements also removed them from what locals recognized as devotional song. Musically, they were brimming with emotion; lyrically, they were frankly personal and casual in addressing the Almighty.

The first spirituals were forged in the fire of what slaves called "ring dances," postworship sessions where the pews were set aside and a kind of trance-dance ensued. Ring dances (long a tradition in West Africa) provided a context by which shouts, cries, and hollers could intermingle freely, with the participants clapping, dancing, and singing their pleas to heaven. Author Andrew Ward separates these spirituals into two basic groups. One includes the so-called "sorrow songs" suggested by "Swing Low, Sweet Chariot" and the like, and the other incorporates "jubilees," typified by such up-tempo numbers as "This Little Light of Mine" and "Gospel Train." And, much like the songs of their African ancestry, these sacred songs "not only declared faith but carried news, raised protests, expressed grief, asked questions, made jokes, lubricated a slave's never-ending toil."[12]

Fisk administrators considered White an ambitious and reckless man, and were convinced that his touring scheme was rooted in ego rather than interest in promoting the choir or its college. But with funds dwindling and the singers leaving favorable impressions at every appearance, the dissenters relented and White was allowed to tour with his group. His detractors reasoned that if he succeeded, Fisk would benefit. If not, they could dismiss him without appearing petty.

On October 6, 1871, White and accompanist Shepherd headed north from Nashville on borrowed funds with a complement of eleven singers and a teacher who served double duty as chaperon. Things did not go well. Ward notes that even though White had secured first-class train passage for his troupe, they were forced to ride in the caboose, little more than a rattling "chicken box." At one venue after another, audiences arrived half expecting a comedy revue, and even the singers' stage attire of simple gowns and suits seemed to suggest a joke in progress with its punchline just around the corner.

At the outset, White's objective was not to present spirituals, but to put his vocalists on display singing difficult popular standards to show how much progress had been made in the short years since emancipation. Just the same, there were such numbers as "Go Down Moses," "Broken-Hearted, Weep No More," and "Washed in the Blood of the Lamb." At every juncture, White's desire to impress the crowd favorably succeeded, but not always as he'd hoped. Some mistook the Jubilees for a novelty act. Once, when Ella Shepherd sat down to play informally, a group of whites gathered around her to marvel. One who could not contain his awe exclaimed, "Only see! She's a nigger!" Other places on the route would accept only minstrel fare, forcing the Jubilees to enlist the help of an eight year old who would sing, "I'm a roving little darky/ all the way from Alabam'/ and they call me Little Sam."[13]

Reviewers' "insights" included assertions that the vocalists had likely sung since infancy "because they could not help it," and they winced at the zeal of the Jubilees' delivery. Naked emotion offered without restraint, one writer suggested, bespoke a degree of amateurism. Still, he concluded, "the unaffected, simple fervor, breathing forth the soul, were remarkable and touching qualities of the performance."[14]

Slights in the press and from the audience were nothing compared with the less-than-warm welcomes that greeted the Fisk singers as they made their way north. When money became scarce, the choir resorted to singing in one city to pay for lodging and transport to the next. Ohio proved impervious to their charms at first, as they were turned away by a succession of hotels and prohibited from eating with other guests when they did find refuge. In Columbus, White hit upon the idea of naming his troupe the Fisk Jubilee Singers, after "the year of jubilee," a slave reference to emancipation. Finally in Delaware, Ohio, the group began to see daylight. Earnings finally began to outstrip expenses and the local press described the Fisk singers as "no Negro minstrel affair, but an elevating, a refining, and remarkably delightful entertainment."[15]

Two events vaulted the Fisk singers out of obscurity. First, they created a firestorm at Oberlin College that November, rising, according to an account by *The Lorain County News*, to sing several religious songs "in the characteristic style and weird cadence of their nation, and with remarkable effect." Legend has it that the Fisk Jubilee Singers sent a shiver through the crowd with their ghostly pianissimo entrance to "Steal Away."

> Steal away . . . steal away . . .
> Steal away to Jesus
> Steal away . . . steal away home . . .
> I ain't got long to stay here

It was a moment of exquisite triumph. The song carried the congregants back to the world of plantation field hands who used melody the way a spy uses code, where slaves would quietly answer by repeating the tune, then fan out through the fields for meetings in secret. As performed by the Jubilees, the song required every voice to begin at the same instant in a barely audible hush, which was then embellished more rapturously with each pass through the chorus. Witnesses to the concert included members of the famous Beecher clan (all related to Harriet Beecher Stowe), most especially the Reverend Thomas K. Beecher of Elmira, New York and his brother, America's preeminent preacher, Brooklyn's Henry Ward Beecher. In addition, another valuable ally joined them after the concert: a seminarian at Oberlin named George Stanley Pope, who agreed to travel ahead of the troupe and act as advance man.

The adulation was far from unanimous. Some quibbled with the technique, others the subject matter, marginalizing the Fisk canon as "cornfield ditties." Critics were similarly divided. In New York, *The Musical Gazette* called their performance "a burlesque on music, and almost on religion. We do not consider it consistent with actual piety to sit and be amused at an imitation of the religious worship formerly engaged in by ignorant but Christian people; and as for calling their effort a concert, it is ridiculously absurd."[16]

Not all sympathies were so hard won; some listeners were smitten instantly. America's best-known author embraced them from the start. "I think these gentlemen and ladies make excellent music," wrote Samuel Clemens, a.k.a. Mark Twain, "and what is as much to the point, they reproduce the true melody of the plantations, and are the only persons I ever heard accomplish this on the public platform. The so-called 'Negro minstrels' simply misrepresent the thing; I do not think they ever saw a plantation or ever heard a slave sing. I was reared in the South, and my father owned slaves, and I do not know when anything has so moved me as did the plaintive melodies of the Jubilee singers."[17]

Once Henry Ward Beecher took a shine to them, the Fisk Jubilee Singers' fortunes improved considerably—although Northern periodicals now sometimes labeled them "Beecher's Negro Minstrels." A year later, at the World Peace Jubilee in Boston in 1872, the Fisk Singers became heroes when a concert attempting to unite a bevy of choirs proved too unwieldy to direct. During "Hymn of the Republic," a local black chorus was to begin, with the remaining multitude chiming in at the refrain. The orchestra began at too high a pitch, and only the Fisk singers could reach the notes.

J.B.T. Marsh picks up the tale in his book, *The Story of the Jubilee Singers*: "The great audience was carried away on a whirlwind of delight . . . Men threw their hats in the air and the Coliseum rang with cheers and shouts of, 'The Jubilees! The Jubilees forever!'" White and his troupe used the publicity to launch subsequent tours that poured $150,000 into the Fisk coffers. Eventually, the Fisk Singers themselves were earning good money—as much as $500 per tour—while entertaining the crowned heads of Europe and presenting what had been black folk music created in secret to appreciative audiences from Germany and Switzerland to Great Britain. The enterprise was so successful that it fostered a cottage industry of its own, as colleges from Virginia and South Carolina soon formed touring choruses in order raise money.

Until slave hymns found an outlet through the Fisk chorus, whites were largely oblivious to any such music. Missionaries who heard spirituals before White tidied them up derided their emotionality as either uncouth or blasphemous, and couldn't fathom how such a ruckus could pass for communal prayer. One white Presbyterian minister committed his misgivings to paper: "Superstition permeates their whole society," he wrote, "and manifests itself as an atmosphere about the world of piety they inhabit. Visions, revelations, and rhapsodies sweep through their confused ideas of worship until their religion becomes an inebriation."[18]

While praising the singers' vocal abilities, author Samuel Floyd suggests that their overtraining kept the public from ever hearing spirituals sound as they had originally. "In the Jubilee Singers' renditions, the Negro spiritual had been transformed into a fine imitation of itself," he grumbles, "But the transformation was not complete; it was to continue, generation after generation, until audiences would no longer hear spirituals even as the Jubilee Singers themselves had first sung them, let alone as they had been sung by the slaves."[19] Like the songs of Stephen Foster, the spirituals most commonly available today are versions delivered with crisp diction in a steady meter, either in cookie-cutter arrangements ideally suited to department store background music or in earnest dulcimer-meets-granola "New Age" recordings.

George White remains a pivotal figure in gospel lore as yet another white man responsible for turning black music into a financial windfall by making it palatable to the (white) masses. For some, he is the man who reworked spirituals into a higher-class minstrel show in which the clowns were sad-sack rubes rather than grinning idiots. But it's impossible to dismiss the flip side of the argument: without White's contribution, much of the slave repertoire might have been lost altogether. Without his determination, the tours might have been abandoned before they proved profitable; without his reining them in, it's possible that white audiences might have found spirituals as incomprehensible as the missionaries who first heard them.

ELITE SYNCOPATIONS AND COON TUNES

In the secular world, freedmen acclimated quickly to the fringe benefits of capitalism, and one of those was access to the piano. Their fascination was twofold: in the first place, they had long mastered and explored the breadth of stringed instruments, so the piano represented unconquered territory; in the second, owning any kind of keyboard carried with it a certain cachet, since pianos were also a talisman of success in the white man's world. It was the era's state-of-the-art entertainment center, as much a source of recreation as radio in the 1930s, jukeboxes in the 1950s, or the latest Xbox or iPod. George Washington Carver's autobiography recalls his dining with a family in Alabama and learning that while they only had one fork between them on the table, off in a corner stood an organ they were buying through installments of $60 per month.

African American musicians wasted no time testing the limits of the new contraption, and, as expected, they brought their previous musical experience to bear in making the instrument their own. They tore apart the music they played, separating it into the polar components of rhythm and melody, leaving it effectively in "rags." Eileen Southern writes, "The style of piano-rag music, called 'jig piano' by some—was a natural outgrowth of dance-music practices among black folk. As we have seen, the slaves danced in antebellum times to the music of fiddles and banjos, the percussive element being provided by the foot stomping of the musicians and the 'juba patting' (knee slapping) of the bystanders. In piano-rag music, the left hand took over the task of stomping and patting while the right hand performed syncopated melodies, using motives reminiscent of fiddle and banjo tunes."[20]

The exact source of ragtime remains as much a mystery as that of spirituals or the blues. Clues to ragtime's origin have been found in Southern brothels, where the proprietors found piano players cheaper than ensembles, in the Midwestern homes of middle-class blacks, and in the theater and tenderloin districts of the East Coast. There's little debate that ragtime rhythms converged from a variety of dance music forms, most likely the cakewalks and two-steps that came to prominence in Industrial Age America, while the sprightly ragtime sound derived in some measure from the jigs and walkabouts of minstrel fame. If that's so, it makes for a poetic reclamation of music that had supposedly been "stolen" from blacks during slavery. Unlike minstrelsy, however, ragtime was not an imitation or a joke, but a real product of black minds and hands—an idea revolutionary enough to trip alarms throughout the conservative establishment.

Reviewers schooled in the classics shuddered at ragtime syncopations, calling them vulgar, even demonic. They were aghast to find young white couples drawn to the staccato rhythms and hummable melodies of such songs as "Hello, Ma Baby" ("Hello, my ragtime gal") and "Bill Bailey, Won't You Please Come Home," from 1899 and 1902, respectively. Most music pundits regarded ragtime as either unworthy of their consideration or further evidence of modern social decay. In the words of New England music writer Daniel Gregory Mason, such music was simply a "comic strip" depicting America's "vices," which "poisons the taste of the young." His assessment of a musical style that rested its melodies between beats rather than soundly upon them was that it was full of "bangs and explosions, like a criminal novel."[21] Others fretted the public would lose its appetite for "quality."

"Ragtime has dulled their taste for pure music just as intoxicants dull a drunkard's taste for pure water," Herbert Sachs-Hirsch decreed in 1912 in a periodical called *Musical America.* Well ahead of the 1960s theory that the Beatles were invented by a Soviet think tank in order to disorient young minds in the West, Francis Toye had similar qualms about ragtime: "These 'crotchety' accents, these deliberate interferences with the natural logic and rhythm, this lengthening of something here and shortening something there, must all have *some* influence on the brain."[22]

Much worse than losing taste for "good music" or scrambling synapses was the prospect of America being negrified as a result of emancipation. Surely devolution would follow as whites succumbing to ragtime were pulled down the ladder of civilization. Ragtime-inspired music, fumed a 1913 issue of *The Musical Courier,* "is symbolic of the primitive morality and perceptible moral limitations of the Negro type. With the latter sexual restraint is almost unknown, and the widest latitude of moral uncertainty is conceded . . . America is falling prey to the collective soul of the Negro."

Concurrent attempts were made to discredit the originality of ragtime (to blunt claims of black creativity) by pointing out syncopations in works by Beethoven, Mozart, and other respected composers. A 1906 submission to *Musical America* calls any discussion of ragtime as an American art form ludicrous—and for the most obvious of reasons: "The so-called Negro melodies, even if they be original with the colored race, cannot be considered as American, for the Negro is a product of Africa, and not of America."

Educated African Americans distanced themselves, too. Their preachers sermonized about ragtime as a road map to vice, and those blacks intent on assimilating quickly denounced rags and the lifestyle they evoked. When they saw whites seize upon rags as a race-baiting tool, a chorus of black intellectuals joined in opposing them. "White men also perpetuate so-called music under the name 'ragtime,'" a writer opined in *The Negro Music Journal,* "representing it to be characteristic of Negro music. This is also a libelous insult. The typical Negro would blush to own acquaintance with the vicious trash put forth under Ethiopian titles. If *The Negro Music Journal* can only do a little missionary work among us, and help us to banish this epidemic, it will go down in history as one of the great benefactors of the age."[23]

Composer Antonin Dvorak was one of the few to defend publicly black music in general and ragtime in particular. As a musician who understood how folk melodies had inspired and been lifted verbatim by the composers of Western Europe (including Rimsky-Korsakov and Mussorgsky), he saw in Negro melodies an untapped wellspring of possibility. "Here," he wrote in a February 1895 contribution to *Harper's New Monthly Magazine,* "for those who have ears to hear are the seeds from which a national art may ultimately spring."

True to other forms of black-derived music, ragtime appeared in performance long before reaching the printed page. Pianists were heard "ragging" their music in Chicago at the 1893 World's Columbian Exposition—among them a young black composer from

Texas named Scott Joplin. The son of a former slave whose father played the violin, Joplin began his career playing at "social clubs" in the Mississippi Valley and learning music theory from a German immigrant named Julius Weiss.

By all reports, Joplin was a soft-spoken gentleman, friendly but not effusive. His refinement made him a much-needed poster boy for ragtime, especially since the music gave offense almost as often as it won converts. Joplin's mild manner and challenging works transformed him overnight into the one ragtimer who one day might redeem himself as a "real" composer, according to the pundits. Unassuming as he may have been as a personality, Joplin was nonetheless an iconoclast who succeeded on a grand scale and took the popularity of ragtime with him when he died from syphilis complications in 1917.

While other pianists honed their stage skills (and considered Joplin a middling player at best), Joplin focused on composition, turning out one elegant tune after another, from his initial success with "Maple Leaf Rag" on through "Elite Syncopations" and "The Entertainer" (a soundtrack hit decades later as the theme song from *The Sting*) and on to such ambitious projects as the ragtime operas *Guest of Honor* and *Treemonisha*.

Throughout the most productive years of his career, Joplin was promoted by his white publisher, John Stark. The story of their first meeting has been repeated so often and with so many embellishments that no one really knows for certain how they met. In the most fanciful version, Joplin visited the publishing house Stark owned and played "Maple Leaf Rag" in hopes that Stark would buy the rights to print the sheet music. Stark supposedly demurred, believing the piece too difficult for a novice player to master. Joplin countered with a bet: if he could find someone on the street to play it, Stark would publish it. Joplin left and returned moments later with a teenager who sat and played it verbatim the first time through. Legend has it that the boy couldn't read music at all and that Joplin had taught him the rag for just such a purpose.

Joplin and Stark struck up a symbiotic business relationship. Their August 1900 contract for "Maple Leaf Rag" stipulates Joplin's one-cent per copy royalty at a time when most tunes (particularly those by black composers) were purchased outright. For his part, Stark owned exclusive rights to publish the most beloved rag of the day. By 1903, he was able to gloat on a back cover advertisement that "one million copies have been sold and no abatement of demand. There will be a temporary stop to its sale when every family in the civilized world has a copy."

With an instinct that would rival any modern public relations firm, Stark touted his client's genius in a 1905 letter to *The New York Sun*—neglecting to mention his bias as Joplin's publisher. "His pieces bud out from his own consciousness and are real creations," Stark enthused. "They are not light and trashy. They are profound and difficult . . . There are a number of them, not all rags—and mark this prediction: They will find their way to all countries, be played by the cultured musicians everywhere and welcomed into the drawing rooms and boudoirs of good taste."

While ragtime was gaining ground with music lovers, a craze of so-called "coon songs" kept bigotry alive and well with a hit parade that included "All Coons Look Alike to Me," written by black composer Ernest Hogan. The original Hogan lyric was "All Pimps Look Alike to Me," but when black vaudevillians Bob Cole and Rosemond Johnson put the tune in their act, they changed the lyric. The song finally became so well known that it

At a time when black songwriters typically sold all rights to their songs outright, ragtime composer Scott Joplin negotiated royalty payments with his white publisher, John Stark. Joplin rags enjoyed resurgence in the 1970s, when they served as the musical centerpiece of Paul Newman and Robert Redford's buddy caper, *The Sting*. (Frank Driggs Collection)

was used in ragtime competitions for years, with each performer having to "rag" the tune for two minutes' time.

In New York, coon songs and rags became cornerstones of the black musical. After *The Creole Show* proved that white patrons were willing to support Negro-themed shows that did not include blackface, black entertainers became a common sight on stages around the city. John Isham, the booking agent behind *The Creole Show*, opened a black variety revue in 1895 called *The Octoroons*. The night's big number: "No Coon Too

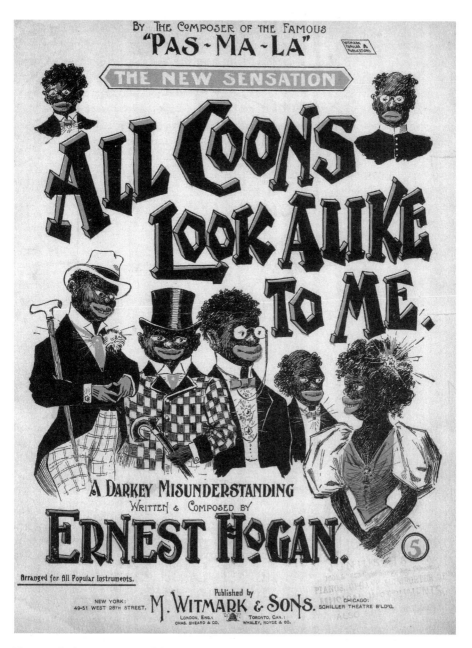

The so-called "coon songs" of the early 1900s revisited the demeaning exaggerations and misconceptions promoted during the minstrel age. The most popular of these was "All Coons Look Alike to Me," a song familiar enough to become a set piece of many ragging competitions. (Courtesy of the Hogan Jazz Archive, Tulane University)

Black for Me." Emboldened by its success, Isham reached even further with a show called *Oriental America*, in which classically trained vocalists presented a medley of opera scores. For a short time in 1896, the show played on Broadway, the bastion of white conservative culture. Bob Cole and Rosemond Johnson (along with Billy Johnson) returned with *A Trip to Coontown* in 1898, and by the early years of the new century were working on a straightforward dramatic piece with music entitled *The Shoo-fly Regiment*. The narrative presented Cole as an Alabama college graduate who turns his back on a teaching career in order to fight in the Spanish-American War. Favorable notices and full houses earned the participants a satisfying payday, but the national tour was cut short when Cole suffered a nervous breakdown on the road. In 1911, he committed suicide.

Many of these pioneers had come an astonishing distance in the quarter century since emancipation and wore their achievements with a pride that bordered on hubris. Will Marion Cook was the volatile composer behind *Clorindy, or The Origin of the Cakewalk* (1898). As a young man, he had studied at Oberlin Conservatory and briefly under Dvorak. When he joined forces with vaudeville minstrels Bert Williams and George Walker for *In Dahomey*, *In Abyssinia*, and *Bandana Land* (all before 1908), he hit commercial pay dirt, but soon the balm of appearing on "the Great White Way" was not enough to quell his anger at having to compose coon songs and other novelties that denigrated his heritage. Years later, Duke Ellington recalled (in *Music Is My Mistress*) how a newspaper critic received Cook after lauding him in a review as "the world's greatest Negro violinist." An enraged Cook smashed his violin on the man's desk, shouting, "I am not the world's greatest Negro violinist. I am the greatest violinist in the world!!" Cook rarely played again in public. Black theater tumbled into disarray, reeling from the deaths of Cole, George Walker, and Ernest ("All Coons Look Alike") Hogan, as well as the loss of comedian Bert Williams, who was snapped up by *The Ziegfeld Follies*.

Neither the sparkle of these shows nor the growing market for ragtime sheet music was lost on New York's community of white musicians. Most Americans had not been to the red-light districts of a major city, and had no firsthand knowledge of how truly complex rags could be. As every publisher knew (long before John Stark's deal with Scott Joplin), the people buying sheet music were hobbyists, not entertainers, and they would never master the intricacies of ragtime without playing them as frequently as the composers themselves. So when it came time to mimic ragtime styles, white composers cut corners—shaving off a beat here or a flourish there—knowing that the melody was what the customer really wanted anyway. This diluted ragtime clattered into one home after another, enticing Americans to break free from Victorian values and dance into a new century.

And, just as consumers were deluged with disco recordings in the late 1970s from artists who had no real grasp of what it was, New York songwriters jumped at the chance to cash in on the public fervor for ragtime. One of the first to do so was Israel Baline, a sheet music salesman-turned-composer who renamed himself Irving Berlin and helped make ragtime respectable with "Alexander's Ragtime Band." Berlin's song was the musical event of 1910: easy to sing, simple to play, impossible to forget, and not one measure actually composed in ragtime.

Ethnic novelties, sentimental ballads, and songs in the same vein as "Alexander's Ragtime Band" ushered Tin Pan Alley onto the national stage. Supposedly named for the jangle of

As minstrelsy gave way to vaudeville at the close of the 1800s, entertainers like Bert Williams (pictured) found that show business afforded blacks both mobility and some measure of financial independence, if not dignity. Until the onset of World War I, black performers were expected to wear burned cork onstage. (Frank Driggs Collection)

pianos up and down New York's 28th Street, where music publishers sifted through material, Tin Pan Alley was a centralized hive of publishers and songwriters who survived a war of attrition over rivals from Philadelphia, Boston, Chicago, and other eastern commerce centers. By 1900, songwriters who peddled their tunes in the district were reaping results with such hits as "My Wild Irish Rose," "In the Good Old Summertime," and "Sweet Adeline."

On Tin Pan Alley, music made by African Americans was just one more ingredient in a stew brimming with ethnic influences. Irish, Jewish, and German newcomers mixed with Negroes, Slavs, and other minorities, each seeking to embrace the culture of their adopted homeland. With Broadway only a few blocks from the chaos of Tin Pan Alley, music of every description ricocheted from building to boulevard until even the songwriters were hard-pressed to say how or where they'd gotten an idea. A few, like George M. Cohan, managed to straddle both worlds—on Broadway, he was known as a charismatic entertainer, while Tin Pan Alley steadily cranked out his patriotic tunes, including "Yankee Doodle Boy" and "You're a Grand Old Flag," alongside such sentimental showstoppers as "Give My Regards to Broadway."

Ragtime finally yielded to more elastic approaches. In the coming decades, musicians would explore the possibilities of a tune by jazzing it up or giving it a bluesy reading. But the requirements of ragtime were fairly rigid, and once its rules and procedures were applied, the results were not far from expectations. Ragtime was more a style of playing than a kind of music, and for that very reason, it was gradually accepted to be a creative dead end. Its greatest historical contribution was to provide a bridge between minstrelsy, vaudeville, blues, and jazz.

At the same time, advances in recording technology liberated consumers from having to play transcriptions for enjoyment. Now they could play a performer's version on a prerecorded disc, cylinder, or piano roll. In 1909, a copyright law was passed to ensure composers received payment and attribution when their work was used, and in 1914 musicians assembled to form the American Society of Composers, Authors, and Publishers, or ASCAP, in order to further protect the artists' ownership of live and recorded performances.

ALL THAT JAZZ

Down in New Orleans, the end of the Civil War started a chain of coincidences that no one could have foreseen or planned. In less than a dozen years, they would blossom into what television documentarian Ken Burns calls "America's only truly indigenous art form," jazz.

From Congo Square (where slaves from neighboring homes were permitted to dance together on their "free day") to the well-heeled Creole community, African American music had been a part of the city's musical character for generations, regularly intermingling with the sounds of French, Spanish, and Caribbean émigrés. Emancipation and disbanding military bands after the Civil War translated into a surplus of cast-off band instruments quickly snatched up by amateurs seeking to entertain tourists on the street or looking to play in pickup bands for festivals and funerals.

Add to that a constant influx of freedmen fleeing the Jim Crow laws that were quickly restoring white supremacy throughout the South. Sharecroppers and itinerant farmworkers migrated to New Orleans to work on the docks and in the city's comparatively open marketplaces, and with them they brought the rudiments of the blues.

Labeled often—and simplistically—as the earthy sibling of the spiritual, the blues began in slave camps as a catchall for many of the same African music traditions that transformed hymns into spirituals: call and response, work songs, shouts, cries, and an intention to cope with life's burdens by setting them to music. No matter how many antecedents they held in common, spirituals and the blues would never share the same point of view. Spirituals promise that those who repent will live an eternity in bliss; for them, life is a process of becoming, where the glass is half full and on the way to overflowing. Conversely, the blues consider life to be a hardship in which every man, woman, and child is an orphan and anyone (including the narrator) is potential victim and culprit. With cautions that range from world-weary to enraged, the blues hold a profound understanding of the same glass as half empty. While Christians sing that all sins will be forgiven and all wrongs redressed come Judgment Day, a blues singer simply states what is: they're beaten down by bosses, betrayed by lovers, swindled by friends, at the mercy of the bottle, or dodging the law. Other differences crop up as well: to "have the blues" diagnoses the victim as depressed and downhearted, but singing them out offers release, rejecting sorrow (as an act of will rather than faith) in hopes of a brighter future. And while spiritual singing began and generally remains a group exercise, the blues were often delivered by a soloist with minimal accompaniment.

By the war's end, at least three distinct approaches to the blues were already codifying in different areas of the country. East Texas players favored a percussive attack that lent a gritty realism to depictions of a harsh life in prison, on the railroad, or sharecropping. Less jazzy and lighter were the blues rising out of the Piedmont, which included Virginia from Richmond south to Durham, North Carolina and Atlanta, Georgia, then led west to the Appalachian Mountains. But the first strain to fall on receptive ears in New Orleans was the sound that drifted down the waterway that was the city's lifeblood: The Mississippi Delta blues.

The blues were built on a simple but elastic song form consisting of three chords most often arranged in twelve-bar sequences. Guitars and harmonicas, once again being easy to master and portable, were ideally suited to blues making, meaning desire was practically all anyone needed to reshape any experience into a personal musical statement. In New Orleans, where everything is done with flash and flair, the blues found its way into the hands of classically trained Creoles, ragtimers, and brass players alike. All these musics cascaded into one in the mind of New Orleans cornet player Buddy Bolden, whose horn blew from one century into the next with what the world would one day call jazz.

Bolden's ability to reimagine the blues as a music conceived for brass remains one of the earliest markers pointing the way to jazz. He ruled the nightspots of New Orleans in the 1890s and earned the ire of Creole professionals who thought his sets too bluesy, too slow, and too damned loud. By 1906, he was known throughout the city as "King" Bolden, a larger-than-life character whose volume behind the horn was matched only by his unquenchable thirst for liquor. Increasingly erratic behavior led to a mental breakdown, and after agreeing to play in a parade, Bolden wandered away from his bandmates somewhere along the route. In 1907, his mother committed him to the state asylum. He was 29 and would live another quarter of a century in the hospital, hearing voices, seeing visions, and, as a physician described him later, tearing at his clothes and picking things off the wall.

Bolden's disappearance took a toll, but he was not jazz incarnate. Just as he synthesized blues, marches, dance music, and ragtime, others were doing the same and making names for themselves playing in this "hot" style rather than playing the "sweet" dance music considered de rigueur in respectable entertainment venues. In Bolden's wake, the city proclaimed a former mandolin and accordion player named Freddie Keppard New Orleans' new "King of the Horn."

The creation of jazz involved not only Bolden and Keppard cutting across the grain of what was expected of brass instruments, but a nurturing environment unwittingly provided by New Orleans as well. If jazz could be called "the pearl of American music," then surely the Storyville district was a perfect shell to ensure its survival. This incubator was put in place by New Orleans Alderman Sidney Story, who only wanted to stifle complaints about prostitution in the city's red-light district. In October 1897 it became "unlawful for any prostitute or woman notoriously abandoned to lewdness, to occupy, inhabit, live, or sleep in any house, room, or closet" outside a thirty-eight block area. To hear Jack Buerkle and Danny Barker tell it in their book, *Bourbon Street Black*, Storyville, as it became known, was a place unlike any other on the planet: "While some legitimate enterprises were conducted in the area, Storyville was primarily a collage of cabarets, whorehouses, cafes, cribs, honky-tonks, houses of assignation, 'dance-schools,' gambling joints, and clip-joints, all devoted to fleecing the adventurous sensualist of his money."[24]

This hedonist hothouse was precisely the kind of situation needed to graft together experienced Creole musicians and the talented amateurs who played by ear without knowing (or caring) which influences they had assimilated. Work was plentiful in Storyville, even if prestige was not. Early jazz players worked in the district, often without the knowledge of their relatives. For Creole sax and clarinet player Sidney Bechet, playing in Storyville was an embarrassment. Jelly Roll Morton, who later claimed to have invented jazz, was kicked out of his grandmother's house at 15 when she discovered he was plying his piano trade in the dives of Storyville.

While ragtime had toes tapping elsewhere around the country, New Orleans spun its syncopations in several directions at once. Percussion parts, whether played on drums or as the bass parts of a piano, were polyrhythmic. Brass players sharpened their skills in cutting contests—those spontaneous competitions that determined who could "blow the hottest"—which could erupt as easily in a parade as in a brothel. Calling this new amalgam "jazz" did the music and its players a disservice, Bechet would later argue. Jazz was too confining a term to wrap itself around music so immense. It was a kind of music that could only have been borne on the first gusts of freedom blowing through the world of Black Americans. "It was like they were trying to find out in this music what they were supposed to do with this freedom: playing the music and listening to it—waiting for it to express what they needed to learn, once they learned it wasn't just white people the music had to reach to, nor even to their own people, but straight out to life and to what a man does with his life when it finally is his."[25]

Storyville lasted just long enough to see jazz through its infancy. In the early days of World War I, four soldiers were killed inside the district within weeks of each other, and both the Army and Navy demanded Storyville's pleasure palaces be shut down entirely.

Despite the mayor's attempts to thwart the edict, the district was voted out of existence on October 2, 1917, and a little more than a month later a mass exodus ensued. In effect, New Orleans had gestated jazz and now unceremoniously shoved it from the nest.

For a time, Storyville's musicians vied for jobs at parties and riverboats on Lake Ponchartrain, fanning out on occasion to Southern Louisiana and Mississippi, then on to Georgia, Alabama, and Florida. By 1911, Jelly Roll Morton was gone, Bechet had moved on, and the Original Creole Band had lured Freddie Keppard to join them on the road. Others joined the circuses passing through, and while the Storyville years endowed them with an ability to play in a variety of styles, it also irreversibly altered them. They would never hear or want to play music within the same rigid confines again.

Less than a year before Storyville was turned inside out, 18-year-old Louis Armstrong waved goodbye while his mentor Joe "King" Oliver boarded an Illinois Central train bound for Chicago. Armstrong's talent sparkled among the thinning ranks of New Orleans musicians and his career accelerated when, on Oliver's parting advice, Armstrong was hired by bandleader Kid Ory. It was stable and rewarding work, but not enough to satisfy Armstrong, who, having spent time in the Colored Waif's Home, was driven to escape poverty. Armstrong jumped at a gig aboard the steamboat *Sydney*, a job which gave him a glimpse of life outside New Orleans—and gave listeners a preview of his rapidly accelerating genius. "Little Louis" received on-the-job training when bandleader Fate Marable threw the young cornet player into a throng of professional musicians who could read music as well as improvise. In his autobiography, *Satchmo*, Armstrong describes the experience:

"I could pick up a tune fast," he recalls, "for my ears were trained, and I could read a little, too, but not enough for Fate Marable's band . . . Fate knew all of this when he hired me, but he liked my tone and the way I could catch on. That was enough for him. Being a grand and experienced musician he knew that just by being around musicians who read music I would automatically learn myself. Within no time at all I was reading everything he put before me."[26]

Another group of Crescent City musicians was soaking up everything that drifted out from the bordellos of Storyville and out into the night air—a group of five white players who became the first to make a jazz recording. They were led by Nick LaRocca, a man who, like Jelly Roll Morton, would claim to have "invented" jazz. New Orleans jazz scene veteran Preston Jackson remembers seeing LaRocca and his bandmates at Billy Phillips 101 Club, hanging on every note played by Joe Oliver. "One of the best numbers I ever heard Joe play was 'Eccentric.' He took all the breaks, imitating a rooster and a baby. He was a riot in those days, his band from 1915 to '16 to 1918 being the best in New Orleans. The LaRocca boys of the Dixieland Jazz Band used to hang around and got a lot of ideas from his gang."[27]

Al Jolson, who was already a star of the vaudeville stage, spotted LaRocca's ensemble during a Chicago café engagement. Jolson was in town touring with *Robinson Crusoe, Jr.* (source of the unlikely hit, "Where Did Robinson Crusoe Go with Friday on Saturday Night?"). According to reports, LaRocca and his band drove Jolson to tears. He secured the Original Dixieland Jazz Band (ODJB) an enviable New York residency at Reisenweber's restaurant, where they turned the town on its ear with an up-tempo free-for-all jazz style incorporating animal sounds and other novelty effects. Within weeks, they recorded

"Livery Stable Blues," barnyard impressions intact. A well-circulated rumor held that the Victor Recording Company had offered a recording contract to Freddie Keppard and his Original Creole Band, but Keppard declined, supposedly in fear that other players could copy his style from records and put him out of work.

Of all the musicians in America playing jazz at the time, it's ironic that the first ones to issue a record were white—and not only white, but apparently racist as well. Toward the end of his life, LaRocca became increasingly embittered that white jazz musicians had been eclipsed by the likes of Jelly Roll Morton, Sidney Bechet, King Oliver, and Louis Armstrong. "Nigger" was a word that percolated throughout his correspondence. Historians continue to argue whether the band, whose most memorable hit came later with "Tiger Rag" ("Hold that tiger!"), was playing its jazz from genuine inspiration or offering up a minstrelized version of what they heard and playing jazz for laughs and cash. In reading his correspondence and listening to his music, it's plain that LaRocca worked as hard as any man ever has to claim something he didn't own.

Thirty-one days after the release of the ODJB's first record, President Woodrow Wilson led the United States into The Great War. Even so, "Livery Stable Blues" and "Dixieland Jass Band One-Step" (LaRocca changed the "Jass" spelling after discovering that local hooligans made a sport of scratching out the "J" on his band's posters) sold more than a million copies at 75 cents per copy—outselling recordings from every popular performer of the day, including patriotic tunes from John Phillip Sousa and traditional pieces by Enrico Caruso. The Victor company demanded more ODJB product, and soon the band was before the microphones again, cutting "Fidgety Feat," "Clarinet Marmalade Blues," and "Tiger Rag."

With jazz now captured on disc, the hyperactive frolics of LaRocca and his bandmates could reach anyone who had access to a phonograph. For a short time, they were the face of jazz in America, a circumstance that likely chafed Jelly Roll Morton, Freddie Keppard, and Joe "King" Oliver, some of whom had been familiar with "hot music" for decades. Even in New York, musicians had been playing ragtime at an accelerated pace for years. One of them was James Reese Europe, the African American who would become the living bridge between black and white musical influences, the missing link between ragtime and big band jazz, a real-life war hero, and perhaps the most underrated figure in the annals of American music.

Europe grew up in Washington, D.C., carefully tended and tutored by a pair of musician parents. At 14, he entered a songwriting contest and had to settle for second prize when his sister Mary walked away with top honors. Europe moved to New York in his early 20s, playing piano in cabarets to supplement his ongoing music education. By 1905, he was writing for a group called the Memphis Students and holding down a gig at Baron Wilkin's Nightclub in Harlem—where seven-year-old George Gershwin would loiter outside for hours listening to Europe play.

Bob Cole and Rosemond Johnson hired Europe to conduct the orchestra for *The Shoo-Fly Regiment*, and when black musicals fell from favor in 1910, Europe formulated a plan to keep African Americans influential and employed: the Clef Club. Equal parts fraternal order, clearing house, and union, the Clef Club promoted local musicians in its orchestra showcases—eventually leading to a series of annual performances at Carnegie Hall and high society bookings as far away as London and Paris.

Bandleader James Reese Europe ushered in a new era for black musicians in America. Not only was he at the forefront of helping black musicians unionize, he inspired the fox trot, brought jazz to the European continent, and returned home a war hero. He was also the first African American bandleader signed to a recording contract. A few short years later, the first public funeral procession ever accorded a black man in New York City was held for Europe. (Frank Driggs Collection)

While the venerable pianist Eubie Blake was still rising through the ranks of New York musicians, he was one of many who looked up to Europe, not only as a creative mentor, but as a man possessed of uncanny business sense. For example, Blake noted, even though Europe's bands were "reading sharks" whose acuity was such that "if a fly lit on that paper, he got played," Europe had his ensemble set aside their sheet music as soon as they'd learned it, because in polite society it was believed that Negro musicians played everything by ear.

Europe was a man of his time, and espoused some popularly held opinions without batting an eye. "The Negro has an inimitable ear for time in dancing," he told a reporter for the New York *Evening Post* in 1914. "As a matter of fact, this instinct for dancing time is an awkward virtue when it comes to training a symphonic orchestra. You would laugh at some of our rehearsals when, in a moment of inadvertence, the players begin to transpose their parts into ragtime. We get some undesignedly funny effects that way."

Confident in his belief that the music of his race should be allowed to develop independently of (white) western confines, Europe used this rationale to explain why his orchestra played only music by Negro composers. "I know of no white man who has written Negro music that rings true," he said. "Indeed, how could such a thing be possible? How could a white man feel in his heart the music that a black man feels? There is a great deal of alleged Negro music by white composers, but it is not real. Even the Negro ragtime music of white composers falls far short of the genuine dance compositions of Negro musicians."

Such pronouncements were all a part of Europe's multifaceted makeup. Since the Clef Club was also a social organization, not all of the 150-strong membership could actually play. Fakers often filled out the orchestra, some with enough skill to scrape by in performance, others simply sitting with instruments clutched as props. Europe always seemed to have a larger purpose at work. Before the organization was founded, musicians were expected to do double duty as waitstaff and bartenders; under the aegis of the Clef Club, they were hired exclusively as talent and were also afforded room and board plus travel expenses.

Despite the collapse of the black musical and years ahead of "Livery Stable Blues," Europe became in 1913 the first African American bandleader to land a major recording deal. During one of his engagements abroad, he met and fell into a fast friendship with an English actor/dancer named Vernon Castle and his American wife, Irene. By the time Europe met them, the Castles had a revue sanitizing the latest dances, most of which revolved around ragtime, into something even European bluebloods could embrace. Indeed, the Castles' air of nobility demonstrating "The Texas Tommy" or "Turkey Trot" (both African American in origin) did much to soothe Victorian sensibilities. In America, they invented a dance step of their own, the "Castle Walk," and returned to find the entire continent of Europe in the midst of a dance mania. When the Castles met Jim Europe on the society circuit, the attraction and the opportunity for mutual benefit was apparent to all three. Irene Castle wrote later that Europe "was one of the first to take jazz out of the saloons and make it respectable." For Europe, providing musical support for the world's premiere dancers was a smart career move, since it put him in the best halls and connected him with wealthy patrons.

Their performances provided a shot of adrenaline for the crème de la crème on both sides of the Atlantic. Once during a lull in the proceedings, the Castles overheard

Europe noodling at a tune called "Memphis Blues," the first blues published by the self-proclaimed "Father of the Blues," W.C. Handy. Europe considered the tune more a dance than a song, according to biographer Reid Badger, and asked the Castles if they didn't think it might make an interesting departure from their faster numbers. What the Castles worked out to "Memphis Blues" became the dance sensation of the age—the Fox Trot.

With the advent of World War I, Vernon Castle joined the Royal Air Force, Irene continued performing, and Europe enlisted in New York's 15th Regiment, later renamed the 369th Infantry. Once again, Europe saw the big picture: "I have been in New York sixteen years," he told fellow volunteer Noble Sissle, "and there has never been such an organization of Negro men that will bring together all classes of men for a common good. And our race will never amount to anything, politically or economically, in New York or anywhere else unless there are strong organizations of men who stand for something in the community."[28] With the imprimatur of the Armed Forces behind him, Europe organized what has been called the finest military band in history, "The Hellfighters," a nickname given them by the French troops who witnessed their valor in combat.

American high command still refused to allow blacks to fight alongside U.S. troops, so Lieutenant Europe's regiment was assigned to assist the French. There at the helm of his machine gun outfit in April 1918, Europe became the first black U.S. Army officer to lead troops into battle, and his band was received with frenzied delight by the French and American forces stationed abroad. Less than two months later, Europe was hospitalized when a German gas attack severely damaged his lungs. During his convalescence, the bandleader composed "On Patrol in No Man's Land," which he later presented with all the bravura of Tchaikovsy's "1812" overture: the piece required performers to mimic machine guns, explosions, sirens, and artillery blasts. For their 191 consecutive days of combat, the 369th Infantry took home 171 decorations for bravery—more than any other American unit in the war. Off the battlefield, they conquered French villages and their doughboy countrymen with a potent mix of plantation melodies, French and American marching tunes, and Europe's rousing American hit, "Memphis Blues."

Europe returned a hero and on February 17, 1919, he and the band took part in a welcome home parade where an estimated one million New Yorkers greeted them along a route stretching from Madison Square Park to 110th Street, then proceeding onto Lenox Avenue north to 145th street. Excepting the officers, the entirety of the old 15th was comprised of black troops recruited from Manhattan, Brooklyn, and Harlem. *The New York Age* reported that when the Hellfighters Band crossed 110th Street onto Lenox, the response "bordered on a riot."[29] Europe hastily arranged a national tour of the Hellfighters to capitalize on their newfound fame, and the band actually worked in a few recording sessions during a Philadelphia stopover. A few days later, the ensemble returned to Boston. After playing its first set on May 9th, 1919, the bandleader called his drummers to his dressing room, and after a short argument, one of them stabbed Europe in the neck with a penknife. He gave instructions to finish the concert and was taken to a local hospital, where he bled to death.

Days later, James Reese Europe received the first public funeral ever bestowed upon an African American by the city of New York. Thousands turned out. Jim Europe may have foreseen the Jazz Age, but he would not witness its arrival.

NOTES

1 Crawford, Richard. *America's Musical Life: A History.* New York: Norton, 2001, p. 415.

2 Barker, Danny and Jack V. Buerkle. *Bourbon Street Black: The New Orleans Black Jazzman.* New York: Oxford University Press, 1973, p. 10.

3 Tosches, Nick. *Where Dead Voices Gather.* New York: Little, Brown and Company, 2001, p. 13.

4 Berlin, Edward A. *King of Ragtime: Scott Joplin and His Era.* New York: Oxford University Press, 1994, p. 124.

5 Southern, Eileen. *The Music of Black Americans: A History, Third Edition.* New York: W.W. Norton & Company, Inc., 1997, p. 238.

6 Toll, Robert C. *Blacking Up: The Minstrel Show in Nineteenth-Century America.* New York: Oxford University Press, 1974, p. 254.

7 Ibid., p. 256.

8 Morgan, Thomas L. and William Barlow. *From Cakewalks to Concert Halls: An Illustrated History of African American Music from 1895 to 1930.* Washington, D.C.: Elliott & Clark Publishing, 1992, p. 19.

9 Crawford, Richard. *America's Musical Life: A History.* New York: Norton, 2001, pp. 427–428.

10 Ward, Andrew. *Dark Midnight When I Rise: The Story of the Jubilee Singers Who Introduced the World to the Music of Black America.* New York: Farrar, Straus, and Giroux, 2000, p. 100.

11 Ibid., p. 115.

12 Ibid., p. 113.

13 Ibid., p. 133.

14 Ibid., p. 129.

15 Ibid., p. 133.

16 Ibid., p. 157.

17 Ibid., pp. 164–165.

18 Ibid., p. 104.

19 Floyd, Jr., Samuel A. *The Power of Black Music: Interpreting Its History from Africa to the United States.* New York: Oxford University Press, 1995, p. 61.

20 Southern, Eileen. *The Music of Black Americans: A History, Third Edition.* New York: W.W. Norton & Company, Inc., 1997, p. 315.

21 Whitcomb, Ian. *After the Ball: Pop Music from Rag to Rock.* Pompton Plains, New Jersey: Limelight Editions, 1994, p. 19.

22 Berlin, Edward A. *King of Ragtime: Scott Joplin and His Era.* New York: Oxford University Press, 1994, p. 88.

23 Ibid., p. 89.

24 Barker, Danny and Jack V. Buerkle. *Bourbon Street Black: The New Orleans Black Jazzman.* New York: Oxford University Press, 1973, p. 19.

25 Crawford, Richard. *America's Musical Life: A History.* New York: Norton, 2001, p. 565.

26 Barker, Danny and Jack V. Buerkle. *Bourbon Street Black: The New Orleans Black Jazzman.* New York: Oxford University Press, 1973, p. 25.

27 Ibid., p. 104.

28 Badger, Reid. *A Life in Ragtime: A Biography of James Reese Europe.* New York: Oxford University Press, 1995, p. 142.

29 Ibid., p. 8.

CHAPTER THREE

Big Band Theory

T
he *New York Times* measured the loss of James Reese Europe in a single word: "Incalculable." As one of those who kept watch over Europe's interests at home while the conductor was abroad, Eubie Blake said simply, "He was our benefactor and inspiration. Even more, he was the Martin Luther King of music."[1] Absent many of the guiding lights who shepherded black music into the new century—Joplin, Europe, and the pioneers of black theater—ragtime ran its course and blacks quietly disappeared from the Broadway stage. It was an inauspicious beginning for an era that would usher in the blues, gospel, and country and witness the rise and fall of swing.

From Prohibition's dank cellars to its brightly lit speakeasies, hot jazz blossomed from a rickety cornball diversion into a critically accepted art form capable of expressing the full range of human emotion. Everyone, it seemed, had a strategy for the next turn jazz should take. Its most readily identifiable components (blues, improvisation, brass, and rhythm) broke apart, mutated, and recombined so often that a single label was meaningless. "Jazz" became the one-size-fits-all designation for such disparate musical outpourings as Gershwin's "Rhapsody in Blue," Fats Waller's piano-based boogie, the pop-swing of Glenn Miller, and the trailblazing bop pioneered by Charlie Parker and Dizzy Gillespie.

While politicians attempted to explain how the country would "return to normalcy" after Germany's defeat in the War to End All Wars, the pastoral security that Americans knew before 1917 vanished forever. In its place were the promise and apprehension of a nation's unknowable future, and jazz was the screaming infant keeping America awake at night.

THE GREAT WHITE WAY

As the Jazz Age of the 1920s began, smoldering racial antipathies ignored for the war's duration roared back to life, with lynchings on the rise and the reputedly liberal President Woodrow Wilson introducing segregated washrooms in the nation's capital. Returning black veterans were slapped in the face with reminders that just because they had helped secure liberty overseas didn't mean they could expect the same freedoms back home. Of the seventy black Americans lynched in the last months of 1919, ten were members of the U.S. military still serving in uniform.

The Great Migration from the South entered a second wave as scores of blacks moved north seeking work in the job-rich cities of Philadelphia, Detroit, and Kansas City. In New York alone, the black population more than tripled in the years between 1910 and 1930, surging from 100,000 to 328,000. Metropolitan whites now had to confront their own biases as they vied for work in the rail yards, steel mills, and stockyards alongside black laborers.

In New York, many of Tin Pan Alley's most talented songwriters were becoming bankable Broadway attractions. Just as George M. Cohan made his name with patriotic fare (including "Over There," the tune that sent Americans marching to war) and Irving Berlin distilled vaudeville and ragtime into complete musical revues, a 17-year-old George Gershwin crossed over from song plugging into composition. Minstrel man Al Jolson overheard Gershwin playing "Swanee" at a party and, instantly recognizing its crowd-pleasing potential, slipped the tune into his musical vehicle of the moment, *Sinbad*. Within a year, a Jolson recording of the song sold a million copies; sheet music sales doubled that. The success of "Swanee" helped Gershwin launch an original piece, *La, La, Lucille*, and earned him a slot scoring one of the town's hot attractions, George White's *Scandals*, which competed with the Ziegfeld *Follies*. Churning out tunes for the *Scandals* kept Gershwin busy for the next three seasons until he left to focus on plot-driven musicals.

Gershwin and Jolson had independent but intertwined destinies. Both were born to Russian/Jewish immigrant families much the same as Irving Berlin and the then-unknown Benny Goodman. Gershwin was born in Brooklyn, New York as Jacob Gershowitz in 1898; Jolson's given name was Asa Yoelson (his exact birth date is uncertain, but was in the vicinity of 1886). Yoelson's father Moses left Lithuania to work as a cantor in a Washington, D.C. synagogue, where he earned enough to book passage for his family to the New World. By the time Asa turned 10, he and his older brother and sisters had arrived in Washington, where the boys fell quickly under the spell of the boisterous streets. They joined a gang of local toughs and often came home singing popular tunes—much to the dismay of their father, who felt that all musical efforts should be directed with reverence to God.

The boys grew wild and unrepentant, and even anglecized their names (older brother Hirsch changed his to Harry and Asa became Al) before seeking their fortunes in show business. Harry then abandoned Al, telling him that he was headed for Broadway. Young Jolson soon hopped a freight train to New York, but his brother was nowhere to be found. Al wound up literally singing for his supper at a cheap dive in the Bowery. He then worked in the circus and sang in burlesque shows and bars up through the ranks until he was without question the most famous vocalist of his time. Along the way, he developed a repertoire of hits, including "April Showers," "California, Here I Come," and "Mammy," the latter often delivered in blackface. Comedian George Burns considered Jolson remarkable: "Jolson used to walk on the stage in blackface and sing, 'I gotta a Mammy in Alabammy,' and people believed him."

Jolson also made a lasting impression on Samson Raphaelson, a University of Illinois undergraduate who met the singer after a performance of *Robinson Crusoe, Jr.*, probably around 1916. Convinced that Jolson was really a cantor in secular clothing, Raphaelson wrote "The Day of Atonement," a short story revolving around a Jewish boy who runs away from his ghetto home to become a singing sensation. The denouement finds him returning home on the Day of Atonement to perform at a synagogue service in tribute to his dying father. Eventually, Raphaelson decided to turn his story into a stage play he retitled *The Jazz Singer*.

In his preface to the early version of the melodrama, the playwright opined that "Jazz is Irving Berlin, Al Jolson, George Gershwin, [and Broadway entertainer] Sophie Tucker . . . . Jews are determining the nature and scope of jazz more than any other race—more than the negroes [*sic*], from whom they have stolen jazz and given it new color and meaning." The "new meaning" to which Raphaelson refers is the grafting of Tin Pan Alley harmonies and other melodic elements onto African rhythms.

Once musical numbers were added, *The Jazz Singer* opened in Stamford, Connecticut on July 1925 starring George Jessel. At the time, Jolson told the author: "Son, if there's anything I can do to make this show a success, just say the word. If it flops, I'll put my own money into it to keep it alive." The notoriously insecure Jolson (who ran water in his dressing room to avoid hearing how much applause his fellow performers were getting onstage) must have turned green when Jessel and the show practically sprinted to Broadway. Raphaelson's tale clearly touched something profound in the patrons who flocked to see it. Like the parlor ballads of the nineteenth century with their soothing musical reminders of the faithful dog, familiar lamp, or cozy rocking chair, *The Jazz Singer* lamented the erosion of Old World values. Cannily, it did so while promoting the very art form responsible for luring young people away from tradition. Raphaelson had it both ways, as audiences on either side of the debate felt *The Jazz Singer* spoke to them.

Warner Brothers picked up the movie rights, and an enterprising young executive named Darryl F. Zanuck suggested that *The Jazz Singer* could help launch the company's new Vitaphone sound system. Jessel, concerned about how appearing in "talkies" might affect his career, asked for $10,000 to reprise his role on-screen. Zanuck's response? "For that kind of money, we could get Jolson." In fact, Jolson did visit Hollywood long enough to sign up for the part—staying in the same hotel as his pal, George Jessel.

The film did for Jolson what the *Thriller* videos did for Michael Jackson. Already the King of Broadway, Jolson was now at the vanguard of a new era in motion pictures as well. Looking at *The Jazz Singer* today, these achievements are difficult to appreciate, as Jolson plays on camera to the nonexistent "cheap seats" in the house and his hystrionics appear incomprehensibly larger than life.

The conclusion of the film finds Jolson down on one knee, calling out "Mammy" in blackface. "I always have a picture in my mind," Jolson later reflected, "of a black boy and his life story when I sing that song. A southern Negro boy who has found life a bitter and terrible tragedy . . . just about ready to give up the battle of life in despair, brokenhearted over cruel fate when he thinks of his 'Mammy' . . . . There was the one who loved him, whose arms are open to him, one who is ready to comfort him, and the thought gives him renewed faith in life and the future."[2]

While pretending to be black remained a profitable enterprise in the emerging mediums of radio and film (the *Amos 'n' Andy* characters were household names by the end of the decade), actually *being* black and talented offered no guarantees of work at any level of show business. Changing public tastes had effectively blocked black theater folk from the Great White Way for the better part of the 1920s. In the vacuum left by Jim Europe's murder, Noble Sissle took on Eubie Blake as a partner in a song-and-dance act billed as the "Dixie Duo." They dressed to the nines, refused to cover their faces with burned cork, and took vaudeville stages by storm. Sissle remembered that Pat Casey, Jim Europe's former agent, agreed to represent them and informed other promoters that Sissle and Blake had "played in the houses of millionaires and the social elite (as part of Europe's Society Orchestra) and they dressed in tuxedos and he'd be damned if he'd let us go on-stage in old overalls and act like a couple of ignoramuses."[3] They performed an endless variety of duets, but always closed with "On Patrol in No Man's Land," in remembrance of Europe.

As they made their way up and down the showrooms of the Atlantic seaboard, Sissle and Blake worked to get themselves and black theater back on the boards of New York. Like-minded artists were hard to find, but in 1920 they came across a pair of comics named Flournoy E. Miller and Aubrey Lyles. The four struck up a fast partnership, with Miller and Lyles providing the key Sissle and Blake had been seeking: a premise sturdy enough to support a full-length musical. Intrigued by a Miller–Lyles routine that cast them as rivals in a small-town race for mayor, the composers developed the sketch into a full evening's entertainment by adding their own songs and dance numbers into the mix.

Their musical arrived in New York in May of 1921 under the title *Shuffle Along*, with Blake behind the piano while Sissle, Lyles, and Miller led the cast. Despite worries that the night's central romantic song, "Love Will Find a Way," would draw boos from white audiences for depicting a black romance without burlesque or blackface, the show was favorably received, and *Shuffle Along* was pronounced one of the great delights of the theatrical season. Entertainment writer Heywood Broun gushed in *The Evening World*, "We don't suppose the members of the cast and chorus actually pay for the privilege of appearing in the performance, but there is every indication that there is nothing in the world which they would rather do. They are all terribly glad to be up on the stage singing and dancing. Their training is professional, but the spirit is amateur. The combination is irresistible."[4]

Before it finally closed, *Shuffle Along* spawned a series of sheet music and recorded hits, including "Love Will Find a Way" and "I'm Just Wild About Harry." African Americans had been so long in exile from the stage that by the time these "new" talents came to the public's attention, many cast members were already seasoned veterans. The production helped launch the careers of several major black talents, including comedienne Florence Mills, singer Paul Robeson, and the chorus girl who became a star, future banana-skirt dancer and Parisian chanteuse Josephine Baker.

Sissle's autobiography states that Baker auditioned for the show at its inception, but they were reluctant to cast her. "We had turned her down when she tried out for us in Philadelphia because she was not yet sixteen," he says. "We had wanted to hire her, but by law we couldn't. She was heartbroken." Baker, who was more likely fourteen or fifteen when she tried out, would not take no for an answer. She slipped into the second company performing *Shuffle Along* on the road in the Northeast, then joined the New York cast in 1922. With classic showbiz panache, Baker proved that there are no small parts, only small players. It took her only a few weeks to become one of the evening's standouts, mugging and dancing up a storm. Sissle remembered, "Every place we went, people buying tickets asked: 'Is the little chorus girl here who crosses her eyes?'"[5]

Shuffle Along, with its brisk pace, emphasis on rhythm, and perfect grasp of the moment, marked not only a return of blacks to Broadway; it helped reinvigorate theatricals altogether. Patrons on both sides of the color line were drawn to the catchy score, contemporary dances, and innocuous humor. Overnight, the Sissle and Blake imprimatur became a stamp of quality. Sissle landed a recording contract for Emerson Records (accompanied by Blake, who also moonlighted backing the legendary black vocalist Alberta Hunter), and the pair dashed off a dozen tunes for *Elsie*, a 1923 show with no overt connection to black theater. Somewhere in the rush they found time to re-create part of their vaudeville act for an experimental marriage of sound and visuals called *Snappy Songs*. The pioneering Phonofilm music video did little to advance talkies, but nonetheless captures Sissle and Blake mugging through performances of "Affectionate Dan" and "All God's Chillun Got Shoes." Soon they launched a second musical, *The Chocolate Dandies* (1924), and when that show closed in September 1925 they boarded the R.M.S. Titanic's sister ship, the Olympic, to spend eight months touring England. By the tour's end, Blake was ready to return to America. Sissle, still seduced by continental attitudes and sophistication, chose to remain, and they parted as a team.

BLUES WAR

If black performers entered the Jazz Age frustrated by their inability to woo Broadway, they could at least claim progress in recording. On Valentine's Day 1920, in the New York studio of the General Phonograph Corporation (which issued the Okeh label), a pair of black artists laid down the first documented recording by an African-American female. Vaudeville singer Mamie Smith cut a pair of songs written by her manager, Perry Bradford, "You Can't Keep a Good Man Down" and "This Thing Called Love." These earned enough attention to warrant Smith's return to the studio, where on August 10 she recorded the first black hits in the blues idiom, "It's Right Here for You" and "Crazy Blues."

Sales of "Crazy Blues" suggested the presence of a large untapped source of revenue—a base of black music fans ravenous for "race records" in a style of music that had so far gone unrepresented. The label debuted Okeh "Original Race Records" in 1921. Over time, Louis Armstrong and King Oliver would record for the label, as would blues artists Lonnie Johnson and Sippie Wallace. Columbia Records soon followed suit with releases from Ethel Waters and Bessie Smith, followed in short order by Paramount, which dispatched talent scouts and portable recording gear to rural America with one directive: to find, record, and return with the next blues hit.

Even blues progenitor W.C. Handy momentarily had a finger in the pie as part owner of a music publishing company that moved from Memphis to New York in 1918. By 1921, though, Handy and partner Harry Pace had separated, leaving Pace to rechristen his enterprise Pace Phonograph Company and issue records under the "Black Swan" imprint—now recognized as the country's first black-owned label. Although his stewardship of Black Swan was short-lived, Pace did hire a young black musician named Fletcher Henderson to act as recording manager, and while still at the helm, Pace also oversaw Ethel Waters' rise from Harlem favorite to nationally known recording star via "Down Home Blues" and "Oh, Daddy" in 1921.

Black Swan sent Henderson to accompany Waters as one of her Black Swan Troubadours, and during the tour she provided him with a hands-on introduction to the blues—

literally. "Fletcher wouldn't give me what I call 'the damn-it-to-hell bass,'" she sputtered in her autobiography, *His Eye on the Sparrow*. To help Henderson find "that 'chomp-chomp' stuff of real jazz records," she brought him piano rolls and he practiced with them until his fingers matched every keystroke. Henderson then grafted those blues ideas onto the concepts of big band orchestration he'd learned from James Reese Europe's Clef Club. In his spare time away from Black Swan in 1923, Henderson booked a ten-piece orchestra into the all-white Club Alabam in New York, where he began to hone a formula. By directing the ensemble to state its opening chorus followed by solo passages for his instrumentalists before returning to the stated theme, Henderson and his sax-playing partner Don Redman fashioned a structure so simple and flexible that swing bands, jazz combos, country acts, and pop groups have kept it alive ever since. And, in the early 1930s, it was Benny Goodman's orchestra playing Fletcher Henderson's charts that actually began the swing craze.

Paramount Records bought Pace out of bankruptcy in 1924, but his place in history was already assured. *The Chicago Defender* touted Pace's company as having "forced white record companies to recognize the large market for recordings by black performers" as well as compelling them to publish race-music catalogs and requiring that they advertise in black newspapers.

The sudden clamor for blues records caught the executives at Columbia Records flat-footed. But in February 1923, their fortunes improved abruptly when a girl who grew up singing for pennies on the street corners of Chattanooga, Tennessee walked into their studios. Bessie Smith's reputation at the time couldn't have been more impressive; she was a featured vocalist in a Philadelphia theatrical called *How Come?* and the toast of the town there. Her greeting at New York's Columbia offices that day was decidedly more subdued. According to one witness, Smith "looked like anything but a singer, she looked about seventeen, tall and fat and scared to death—just awful."[6] Her first session was a disaster, but the next few days of studio time muscled the dark thunder of her voice onto a pair of records. "Down Hearted Blues" (written by Alberta Hunter and Lovie Austin) was a hit by summer, and by year's end it sold 780,000 copies, allowing Smith to charge $1,500 per week as a headliner. Smith would prove to be America's first diva in the modern sense, as her fame owed as much to her tantrums as to her Wrath-of-God voice. She'd take lovers of both sexes, pursue her husband firing a pistol, foil a Ku Klux Klan attempt to stop her show by chasing them from the premises, and rip the stage curtains down around her if things didn't go the way she liked.

Smith's recording career lasted less than a decade, but the image she created of the hard-suffering, booze-fueled blues shouter survives to this day. Janis Joplin modeled her alter ego, "Pearl," in part on the Smith legend. In life, Bessie Smith owed her fathoms-deep voice in equal parts to her size and an apprenticeship on the vaudeville circuit as part of a troupe featuring fellow blues belter Gertrude "Ma" Rainey. The enduring sides Smith laid down in the mid-1920s—when she and Louis Armstrong created a new vocabulary for the blues duet—are her real artistic legacy. Before they joined forces, Smith seldom strayed from the formula that made her a celebrity, keeping to spare accompaniment, usually with a bare-bones ensemble—a single violin or piano simultaneously driving the melodic line. But in "St. Louis Blues" and the ragtime classic "You've Been a Good Old Wagon," Armstrong and Smith stand toe-to-toe as musical foils, Satchmo

The hard-loving and harder living Bessie Smith could not only sing the blues, she could make her cabaret audiences feel them, too. Decades later, her outrageous offstage behavior and gutbucket singing style would serve as inspiration for Janis Joplin's free-spirited alter-ego, "Pearl." (Frank Driggs Collection)

augmenting Smith's pleas with his own. It's a rare instance of Armstrong riding shotgun as an accompanist for someone else and in this case losing to Smith, who demands her share of the limelight. Oddly enough, the Louis who taught the world to swing provides virtuosic moments on the track, but his riffs spring from the melody and beat, rather than from Smith or the lyrics. Armstrong's flashy interjections would have swamped a lesser singer, but no one ever stole the show from Bessie Smith.

DOWN TO THE CROSSROADS

Northerners may have preferred their blues from gussied-up ensembles at urban nightspots, but down South where the music began, the sounds of hard living were only a few paces away from the squalid realities of everyday life. In the Mississippi Delta and Southeastern Texas, low wages, hard labor, and humidity went hand in hand, and when the day's work was done, many counted themselves lucky to have energy left to raise their voices. Here, the blues was not just a style of music but a way of being, and its practitioners passed the hat for food and shelter alongside the folks who gathered at honky tonks, cheap eateries, and street corners to listen for a while. The success of race records and the invention of portable recording equipment scattered talent scouts on a cross-country search for more of the same, but what they found was something much more harrowing.

These "down-home," "country blues," or "folk" performers knew little of record making; some were barely literate. They were experts on life at the bottom of the social scale, however—well versed in such topics as suffering, survival, and what could be wrought from a battered guitar or banjo. Their music was typically sung solo (predominantly by men) to the accompaniment of a single instrument, often used in unison or call-and-response tandem with the singer carrying the melody—devices that would later resurface in the hands of electric guitar-slingers ranging from B.B. King and Jimi Hendrix to Stevie Ray Vaughan and Lenny Kravitz.

The foundation of modern blues rests on the shoulders of only a few recorded artists, all of them black. Among them was Dallasite Blind Lemon Jefferson, an inventive composer who parlayed his distinctive vocals and fretwork into two parallel careers, one as a popular headliner who had his own chauffeur, and another under the pseudonym "Deacon L.J. Bates," recording religious material. Jefferson's songs ("Matchbox Blues" and "Black Snake Moan" among them) outlined the subject matter that still defines the blues, including the cycle of endless toil and empty pockets leading to unfaithful women, getting drunk, and landing either in jail or in a pine box. His work in turn inspired Texan Huddie Ledbetter, who was serving time in a Louisiana prison when he was discovered in 1933 by white traveling music archivists John Lomax and his son, Alan. Leadbelly, as he became known internationally, would continue to have scrapes with the law, but he also introduced a wealth of songs—including "Goodnight Irene," "The Midnight Special," and "Rock Island Line"—that transcended the blues to become permanent staples of popular music.

Texans like Jefferson and Leadbelly helped codify the blues, but the enduring image of a bluesman as a latter-day Faust could arise only from the Mississippi Delta. There, Charley Patton and a trio of interconnected black musicians—Son House and his stylistic protégés, Robert Johnson, and Muddy Waters—would take lyrics that had once been mundane recitations of misery and weave them into captivating ghost stories infused with supernatural dread and a dark sexual undertow. Son House's "Death Letter Blues" hits like a bucket of icewater down the spine, as his terror turns to grief: "I got a letter this morning," he intones, "how do you reckon it read? It says hurry, hurry down . . . Your love is dead . . . ."

Decades later, hearing Son House would begin a lifelong romance with the blues for Bonnie Raitt. "It's just one man and guitar," she says, "or one person with a guitar. In terms of making the connection from Son House to Robert Johnson and Muddy Waters, there's nothing more powerful than the Mississippi Delta Blues, that kind of stark, lonely blues that came out of that one area of Mississippi . . . . For me, John Lee (Hooker), Son House, and Muddy Waters really capture that. There's a purity to their style that derives from the way they sound being an extension of who they really are."

Eventually Son House disciple Robert Johnson (who died in 1938 at age 27) came to personify the very crossroads he described in song, as his life story became an intersection where fact and fiction trafficked freely. According to a yarn attributed to Son House, Johnson sold his soul to the devil in exchange for supernatural skill as a guitarist. The rumors swirling around Johnson's death were no less sinister. According to most sources, Johnson was poisoned when his fancy for the wife of a jealous honky-tonk owner came to light. Johnson wrote "Sweet Home Chicago," "Love In Vain," and, of course, "Cross Road Blues," songs that launched dozens of careers and sustained countless others. The twenty-nine sides he recorded in Texas in 1936 and 1937 remain among the few certainties about him, and his songs only grew in stature during the quarter century they were out of print. When they were finally unearthed for a 1961 LP called *Robert Johnson: King of the Delta Blues Players*, they became the holy grail of blues records for British devotees like Eric Burdon, Keith Richards, John Mayall, and Eric Clapton. The tracks have since been remastered for compact disc, and for an album to live up to such gargantuan hype may seem impossible. But Johnson delivers one staggering performance after another, creating a firestorm of sound and emotion that ranges from the rhythmic chug of "Preachin' Blues" to the delicate fingerings of "Ramblin' on My Mind" and the riveting imagery of "Hell Hound on My Trail."

Johnson's renditions of his material have gone largely unnoticed by radio listeners and programmers, but they live on through a legion of superstar acolytes. Black blues legend Elmore James scored one of his biggest hits by electrifying Johnson's "Dust My Broom" in the late 1940s. In his wake, Muddy Waters and John Lee Hooker recorded Johnson tunes and played them onstage throughout their careers. In the rock era, the Rolling Stones paid tribute to Johnson early on by tackling "Love In Vain," and Led Zeppelin joined the fray with their barely recognizable take on "Traveling Riverside Blues." But Johnson's biggest devotee remains Eric Clapton, who recorded "Four Until Late" and radically re-imagined "Crossroads" with Cream in the mid-1960s, then over time recorded "Steady Rollin' Man" and "Ramblin' on My Mind." Finally, in 2003, Clapton spent an entire album examining Johnson's songs and the hard-to-navigate rhythmic style in which he played them with *Me and Mr. Johnson*.

Today's blues titans may regard Johnson as an immortal, but it's hard to picture him contemplating posterity—food and shelter were probably much more on his mind. Like everyone around him, Johnson was trying to get by and to do so he had to play more than the blues; any dreams of real stardom would have meant expanding beyond a largely

Son House served as mentor and inspiration to generations of blues singers, including Robert Johnson and Muddy Waters. Unlike the brassy women who filled Chicago nightclubs with their piano-based combos, Son House and his contemporaries often worked alone. For Bonnie Raitt, there was no turning back after listening to him. All that feeling, she says in wonder, and "it's just one man and a guitar." (Star File)

black audience. Blues singers understood that they appeared at the behest of a paying clientele, and as such their repertoires included jigs, two-steps, rags, and reels—anything that might convince a customer to order that all-important next drink.

A half century after his passing, generations of blues artists from Johnny Winter to Jonny Lang have been weaned on Johnson's otherworldly moans, but there are those who find the music impenetrable. Some fans who've spent a lifetime getting their blues through an amplifier admit that they're challenged to embrace the quiet rusticism of Johnson and his contemporaries. Just as the fast edits in music videos have shortened viewers' attention spans and the digital advances of *The Matrix* make the special effects of Fritz Lang's *Metropolis* appear quaint by comparison, appreciating the unadorned voice and guitar of a man more than fifty years dead requires a willingness to meet the music more than halfway.

While a malleable structure has kept the blues timeless, its confessional tradition has made it arguably the most personal of American musics. Artists who work in the medium are expected to bring their listeners into a circle of confidants—in effect acting contrary to human nature by exposing rather than hiding ugly truths. "The blues are classic and universal," says Bonnie Raitt, "and its appeal goes far beyond the boundaries of the black community that created it. I could relate to the blues at 14 because at the time I was a miserable little girl. Songs of heartbreak can touch people at every age and across every ethnic line or any other line you can think of. A great song with a lyrical or melodic hook that grabs you will touch you right to the core, whether it's jazz, blues, country, or anything else."

THE PICKUP ARTIST

In 1925, the year that Blind Lemon Jefferson cut his first tracks, electricity was being introduced to music—not through amplifiers, but in recording equipment. The resulting improvements in fidelity meant that music fans at home were hearing more detail and dynamics than ever, and a new industry boom was under way. Riley B. King was born that same year in Indianola, Mississippi, where he was raised as his forbearers were, to pick plantation cotton. His attraction to the blues began long before he rose to local fame as a Memphis disc jockey, adopted the nickname B.B. ("Blues Boy") King, or landed his first date with a guitar named "Lucille." In fact, B.B. King's love affair with the blues predates the electric guitar entirely.

"Blues was around before jazz, and it has sort of been the great grandfather of a lot of the music we hear today," King explained from the road the week of his 75th birthday in 2000. "But where I was playing and on the plantation where I lived, we couldn't have 'gone electric.' We didn't have electricity. My pastor in church played an electric guitar that was amplified by an electrifiying pickup that they'd put on it, and so that was the first time I heard an electric guitar."

In all its sizes and guises, the electric guitar has become an icon of modern culture on a par with the airplane or automobile. Guitar bodies are often shaped to curvaceously feminine specifications, but if slung low enough on the body and grasped by the neck, they transform into a universally recognized phallic symbol. Guitars can be crafted by hand to appear rustic and voluptuous or as tiny and high tech as a spy gadget. Like pets, they tend to take on the personalities of their owners. The Fender Stratocaster Buddy Holly strummed to fame in the mid-1950s came off as a gangly contraption with its kidney-shaped body and a whammy bar that made it look like an oversized kiddie toy. Ten years later, Jimi Hendrix had the same model spitting artillery fire on "Machine Gun" and used it to turn "The Star Spangled Banner" into a display of musical pyrotechnics at Woodstock.

Electric guitars are taken for granted in the computer age, but coaxing the genie of electricity into the guitar was a clumsy process full of false starts. In 1924, an engineer for the Gibson company developed an electric "pickup" for the viola and string bass with a mechanism that could pass sound through the guitar bridge to a magnet and coil system that first recognized vibrations, then transmitted them via an electric signal to an amplifier. Unfortunately, the original signals were weak, and although the guitar was louder, it was still too quiet to compete with a surrounding group. Only when electromagnets were brought into the equation did electric guitars become a real possibility. The first working model was a Hawaiian lap guitar from Rickenbacker Electro Instruments that looked like a frying pan with an oversized handle. But because the U.S. Patent Office couldn't decide whether the product was an instrument or an appliance, the technology was never secured from copycats.

Gibson guitar engineer Lloyd Loar developed the first "Spanish" (as opposed to lap-played) model called the Vivi-Tone, but the hollow-body electric didn't catch on until Gibson worked out the bugs and shipped the first ES-150 from Kalamazoo, Michigan on May 20, 1936. In less than a year's time, Charlie Christian had one and from that moment on, he was rarely seen without it.

"Coming up, we all had our favorites," says B.B. King. "I listened to Lonnie Johnson—not Robert Johnson, but (Louis Armstrong and Duke Ellington sideman) Lonnie Johnson—and Blind Lemon Jefferson. Those were two of my early influences, and after that came the electric guitar with Charlie Christian and then Django Reinhardt and later T-Bone Walker. I could never play like any of the great artists that I idolized, so I had to settle for sounding like myself."

Southern blues continued to resurface periodically through the remainder of the century ("It never went completely mainstream, but never really disappeared, either," Raitt says); crooners, folkies, and country stars all took turns with Leadbelly's "Goodnight Irene" and "Rock Island Line," while "The Midnight Special" became the eponymous title and theme song of a late night 1970s TV show featuring live rock acts. In addition, artists across the spectrum—from Django Reinhardt and Dinah Shore to Taj Mahal and Leon Redbone, the Squirrel Nut Zippers, and the performers behind the wildly successful *O Brother, Where Art Thou?* soundtrack—have more than adopted the songs of the South. Some pay their respects with letter-perfect cover versions, while others try to extend the musical bloodline by composing new tunes in the mold of the originals.

"As a society we have evolved very fast," says newcomer Susan Tedeschi, a torchy white blues singer who burst onto the scene in the late 1990s. "Music has come a long way technologically, along with a lot of other things, including the way people think. I think the real thread between then and now is that there are certain things common to the human condition, things like pain and losing people and hard work. If you can understand that, then you know exactly what the singer is singing about, whether it's Charley Patton and Robert Johnson, or Irma Thomas and Koko Taylor, or Eric Clapton and Stevie Ray Vaughan."

But for many of the pioneers of down-home blues, the roar of the 1920s was little more than the sound of time rushing by. Just as they approached the brink of national exposure, the stock market collapsed and dragged the world into the Great Depression. Phonograph sales slumped in 1932 to less than six percent of what they had been only five years earlier. By the time the industry finally stabilized at the end of World War II, guitars were being electrified and many in the first generation of blues performers found themselves back in the same weather-beaten dives where they were discovered.

Theirs was not only a misfortune of time, but also of place. While memberships in the Ku Klux Klan soared to record heights during the decade, black migration to the job-rich industrial north helped to create greater tolerance in the cities—meaning that for all the lynching and discrimination in the hinterlands, urban blacks were experiencing greater economic and civil freedom than ever. That progressive wave reached full flower during the Harlem Renaissance, a kind of black Brigadoon that flourished and disappeared within a dozen years.

THE JOINT IS JUMPIN'

Hailed as the epicenter of cultural and intellectual freedom, the Harlem Renaissance rose up out of uptown New York City in the early 1920s, where a black entrepreneur named Philip A. Payton bought up the area's overdeveloped real estate and sold it piecemeal to black homesteaders through his Afro-American Realty Company. Black poets, musicians, artists, and thinkers responded as if the promise of American self-determination was materializing before their eyes. Bolstered by the support of surrounding neighbors, Harlem's "New Negroes," as they preferred to be called, believed prosperity could be won through the efforts of a self-reliant and interdependent black community. James Weldon Johnson, in his Harlem history called *Black Manhattan*, remembers the movement beginning in a giddy rush of optimism. "Harlem has provided New York Negroes with better, cleaner, more modern, more airy, more sunny houses than they ever lived in before," he writes. "And this is due to the efforts made first by Mr. Payton."

The Harlem Renaissance conjured prospects for a society where "separate but equal" might actually come to mean "live and let live," and few on either side of the color line objected. Blacks were still banned from employment at any New York utility company and even denied jobs at city department stores during the 1920s. But postwar prosperity and exposure to European customs during the Great War persuaded many Americans of the social alternatives to Victorian morality. Meanwhile, radio broadcasts and evermore sophisticated recordings raised the profile of music throughout the country. Then on January 20, 1920, teetotalers won their battle with alcohol through passage of the Volstead Act, but they lost the war when Prohibition went into effect nationwide. Instead of putting rumrunners and gin joints out of business, it put a "speakeasy" on nearly every block of metropolitan America, where for the first time, black and white women joined men at their leisure.

At least part of the speakeasy appeal was that it provided thrillseekers a chance to thumb their noses at convention. The soundtrack of their disaffection was jazz, with its insouciant lyrics, herky-jerky rhythms, and underground cachet. Speakeasy entertainment, like the establishments themselves, ran the gamut from slick to sleazy. Consider this lyric attributed to cabaret singer Lucille Bogan:

> Your nuts hang down like a damn bell clapper
> And your dick stands up like a steeple
> Your asshole stands open like a church door
> And crab walks in like people

Such amusements sprang up wherever people could gather to drink openly in secret, often under the noses of well-bribed police and government officials. The entire town of Kansas City was run by the corrupt Pendergast organization during the "Roaring '20s," leaving the town "wide open," in the words of newsman Walter Cronkite, whose journalism career took off there. "The music moved up the Mississippi River, branched off into the Missouri River, and got to Kansas City," Cronkite recalls, "and as a result we had a really lively nightlife scene full of top-notch jazz bands. They were nearly all black; in fact, I can hardly remember any white musicians.

"The main clubs were on 12th Street, which is where 'The 12th Street Rag' comes from. Smaller clubs featured individual black artists who were exceptionally good, all with followings of their own. So we'd all go around town at night seeing these acts of principally acoustic entertainment. One gal played piano and sang risqué songs, and her favorite bit of business was a connecting phrase which went, 'two old maids in a folding bed, one turned over and the other'n said . . .' and then she'd launch into something like (he sings) 'Yes, We Have No Bananas . . . .'"

Kansas City was the most libertine city in the heartland, and the jazz the locals called "Chicago-style music" kept patrons and the laissez-faire-minded authorities drinking, gambling, and frequenting whorehouses side by side. Most of the musical action of the city revolved around 12th Street, "a black street in the black community," Cronkite says, "but it was a main street, so it didn't deter anybody. I don't know that there was much of a question about integration in Kansas City; we didn't have a very large black population, but black musicians were there all the time. Let me put it this way: among the whites, there was no consciousness about segregation there. I'm sure among black people there was, but the black population was very small in the city."

With the help of radio, jazz overran the banks of the Mississippi to saturate the American Midwest. Artie Shaw, arguably the greatest clarinetist of the age, started out as a teenager playing small venues around Cleveland. "When I was there, we played dance music," Shaw recalled, "just the current popular tunes. Some was good and some was pretty terrible, but it wasn't jazz or what some people called 'hot music.' I always thought those were corny names for it, anyway. We sure didn't have black audiences at that time in Cleveland, although we did have after-hours jam sessions occasionally and those were almost always mixed."

Shaw migrated to California, playing Hollywood parties and club dates, where "some of the tunes were so terrible, you couldn't even describe them. We would take the chord structure, something like Gershwin's 'I Got Rhythm,' or a tune like 'More than You Know,' and improvise on it. But it was more or less stock material, and there wasn't much of a scene musically happening."

Omnivorous in his hunger for what he called "American music," Shaw toured the country while jazz was entering its awkward adolescence, "and the music kept becoming more sophisticated because it kept on being played," he said. "But I didn't really notice things changing until 1928, when I spent the summer in Chicago before moving to New York. That's where I heard Louis Armstrong live for the first time, so I was finally hearing some good players. I would get together with the guys around there after work—we'd work until 4 o'clock in the morning and then I'd go sit in with (black) bands like Earl Hines'."

Those endless nights in the Windy City also put Shaw in touch with jazzmen Frankie "Tram" Trumbauer and Leon "Bix" Beiderbecke, Midwestern white men who would leave their own indelible marks on jazz, together and apart. "To be a white musician, and hearing Beiderbecke and Trumbauer was something else," remembered Shaw, who was also in search of a musical identity at the time. "You knew they had definite goals in mind for their music rather than just aping what they heard around them." When Shaw caught them as part of the Jean Goldkette Orchestra in the late 1920s, he told *JAZZ* author Geoffrey Ward he considered them "the first really great white big band . . . unbelievable. They swung like mad." Though neither was a gifted rhythmatist, Trumbauer and Beiderbecke excelled in tone and finished each other's phrases with a skill that approached clairvoyance. Trumbauer, the music-reading sophisticate, became the perfect bookend for Beiderbecke, the untrained oracle from whom music flowed like water from a tap. For many aspiring white players, including Shaw, Beiderbecke and Trumbauer provided a glimpse beyond the hit parade into the realm of creative possibilities.

Their tag-team symbiosis is the centerpiece of "Singin' the Blues" (1927), in which Trumbauer hands off from his C-melody saxophone to the clear, confident Beiderbecke, who sounds well ahead of his contemporaries in jazz thinking. His solo unfolds with a controlled grandeur, swaying inside the tempo rather than pushing or tugging it along, which were typical approaches of the day. There's a bit of strutting machismo here, too, and a kind of joy in music making that white folks were supposedly too self-conscious to create.

Unable to meet payroll, the Goldkette orchestra collapsed under its own weight in September 1927, leaving Tram and Bix scrambling for steady work. Neither could believe their luck when, just a few weeks later, they dropped in on a Minneapolis appearance by the Paul Whiteman Orchestra. The pair met the bandleader at intermission, accepted his invitation to play during the second set, and were offered permanent jobs later over dinner. "Whiteman also hired people you've never heard of," Artie Shaw recalled, "and he hired them because he liked their sound. He liked Bix's playing and he liked Trumbauer. He liked Jimmy and Tommy Dorsey, too."

The portly and amiable conductor could afford to be magnanimous. Whiteman was a convert from classical music who embarked on a very public crusade to "make a lady of jazz" by removing its "stigma of barbaric strains and jungle cacophony," which he did by pulling rhythmic punches and having solos written down and played from the sheet music. To many minds, Whiteman (yes, he was white) represented the antithesis of real jazz; to staid white sensibilities, his approach was just the whip and chair needed to tame this unruly noise. Whiteman cemented his place in history by introducing the world to "symphonic jazz" through a 1924 New York concert that leapfrogged from "Livery Stable Blues," in recognition of the Original Dixieland Jazz Band, to a new work composed especially for the occasion, "Rhapsody in Blue" by George Gershwin.

Paul Whiteman, the conductor who liked to claim that he'd "make a lady" of jazz, is pictured conferring with composer George Gershwin (left) and Dana Suesse (right) just before a Carnegie Hall concert scheduled for November of 1932. Eight years earlier, Whiteman introduced the public to Gershwin's amalgam of black jazz and white symphonic music, "Rhapsody in Blue." (Frank Driggs Collection)

According to a 1997 appreciation in *The New York Times*, Gershwin's rhapsody remains the 20th century's single highest-grossing piece of music. On the surface, its abiding popularity is due in part to catchy melodies that attempt to meld jazz and classical forms into a seamless whole. But, as Gershwin himself was soon to lament, the entire work was actually cobbled together in three weeks. Gershwin had originally turned down the offer to compose a piece for the concert, but then read a newspaper column announcing that he was at work on a symphony for the program.

This was heady stuff for a popular tunesmith. Feeling the tug of prestige at his sleeve (and likely with the same excitement and trepidation that later attracted Billy Joel and Paul McCartney to explore symphonic composition), Gershwin changed his mind and plunged forward. The rhapsody was a manifesto intended to challenge highbrow notions that jazz was shallow music meant for dancing. "Jazz, they said, had to be in strict time," he later wrote. "It had to cling to jazz rhythms. I resolved, if possible, to kill that misconception with one sturdy blow. Inspired by this aim, I set to work composing with unwonted rapidity. No set plan was in my mind—no structure to which my music would conform. The rhapsody, as you see, began as a purpose, not a plan."[7]

"Rhapsody in Blue" premiered at Aeolian Hall in Manhattan in 1924 to great fanfare, attracting the glitterati and critics of note from all the cosmopolitan news outlets. Reviewers generally overlooked the contributions of Ferdie Grofe, the arranger on Whiteman's staff responsible for scoring the piece. Instead they huddled over the rhapsody like overstuffed guests picking at the carcass of a Thanksgiving turkey, arguing whether Gershwin had really turned a corner in American composition.

"Exciting," "bold," and "daring" were common appraisals, and while some observers rightly chastened Gershwin for the episodic structure and meandering connective passages of his work, all agreed that the composition had merit. Deems Taylor's evaluation in the *World* was fairly representative: "It was crude, but it hinted at something new, something that has not hitherto been said in music. Mr. Gershwin will bear watching; he may yet bring jazz out of the kitchen."[8]

Spectacular as it is, Gershwin's rhapsody is more a flirtation with jazz than the real thing, and most recorded versions have either buried or stripped away the few intended nods to African American influence—most notably the "laughing" clarinet glissando up to high B-flat at the beginning and the banjo that adds so much depth and poignance to the legato section near the end.

Subsequent productions piled on instruments until the piece became a lumbering behemoth gutted of nuance. Grofe himself rescored the rhapsody for a full symphony shortly after Gershwin's death in 1937. Woody Allen used a garden-variety performance as the musical backdrop for his 1979 black-and-white romance, *Manhattan*. The Disney studios set Gershwin's score to animation for *Fantasia 2000*, and by the end of the century the epic conclusion had been reduced to an airline's TV jingle.

A decade after the rhapsody cemented his reputation, Gershwin spent considerable time in developing themes and songs for his greatest work, *Porgy and Bess* (1935). The folk opera, as Gershwin liked to call it, began as a 1926 novel by DuBose Heyward. Generally recognized as the first major American novel written by a white man that does not condescend toward blacks, *Porgy and Bess* took America by storm, and Gershwin along with it. Not long after the book came to his attention, Gershwin took up a correspondence with the author, continually expressing an interest in creating an opera around Heyward's characters but always too busy elsewhere to perform the necessary research. Gershwin believed that in order to write believably in the voices of Porgy and Bess, he needed to immerse himself in the black experience—to whatever extent possible for a well-to-do white sophisticate.

By the time Gershwin began collaborating with the author, *Porgy and Bess* had already been fashioned into a stage play (in 1927) and slipped through the fingers of Al Jolson as a movie musical. In 1933, Heyward sent Gershwin news that Jolson wanted to put *Porgy and Bess* on the big screen with songs by Jerome Kern and Oscar Hammerstein II. Gershwin did not oppose this; rather, he waited patiently until the deal fell apart. By November 1933, notice of the Gershwin/Heyward opera was in the papers, and the pair had already begun sketching out individual scenes.

The music Gershwin composed for *Porgy and Bess* (which includes "Summertime" and "I Got Plenty of Nothin'") does not masquerade as black music, but is presented as a respectful nod from a peer. Frequently when explaining the project to the press, Gershwin explained that while *Porgy and Bess* adheres to most conventions of classic opera, its text abandons Western European pageantry to follow Heyward's luckless characters in their struggle for survival. Gershwin spent time in South Carolina among the Gullahs, an insular black community renowned for their embrace of African traditions long since abandoned by most American blacks. Early on, Gershwin decided not to appropriate Negro melodies for the score, but to compose from the inspiration provided by the Gullahs and other black folk musicians. On several occasions, Heyward saw Gershwin demonstrate a near-mystical ability to channel and reinterpret what he heard.

"The Gullah Negro prides himself on what he calls 'shouting,'" Heyward commented later. "This is a complicated rhythmic pattern beaten out by feet and hands as an accompaniment to the spirituals, and is indubitably an African survival. I shall never forget the night when, at a Negro meeting on a remote sea-island, George started 'shouting' with them. And eventually to their huge delight stole the show from their champion 'shouter.' I think he is probably the only white man in America who could have done it."[9]

Porgy and Bess was not an immediate hit. Subsequent productions staged after Gershwin's death in 1937 have proved more profitable. Nearly everything he touched turned to gold, and not only did Gershwin die as one of the most beloved figures in the music world—he helped to make many of the names around him famous as well.

As a result of the concert at Manhattan's Aeolian Hall, Whiteman was knighted by critics as "The King of Jazz." (In 1930, a film biography of Whiteman features Gershwin performing "Rhapsody in Blue" alongside the orchestra.) For his part, Whiteman accepted the kudos—along with the money and endless string of engagements—but never mistook his work for the jazz firmly rooted in New Orleans and its tradition of improvisation. He did do everything in a big way though, and the size of his orchestra swelled to nearly three dozen by the time Tram and Bix hopped aboard. The pair remained a part of Whiteman's ensemble until alcohol-related mishaps forced Beiderbecke off the road, where he died of pneumonia after several unsuccessful attempts to get sober. Louis Armstrong later said that when he heard the news, he wept all night long. In an era renowned for its cutting contests, he and Bix never blew a note in competition.

In Nat Shapiro and Nat Hentoff's book, *Hear Me Talkin to Ya*, Satchmo remembered Beiderbecke as a gentleman and a colleague. "When Bix would finish up at the Chicago

Theater at night," Armstrong reminisced, "he would haul it out to the Sunset where I was playing and stay right there until the show was over and the customers would go home.

"Then we would lock the doors. Now, you talkin' about jam sessions . . . ," Satchmo recalled haltingly, "those were the things, with everyone feeling each other's notes or chord, et cetera, and blend with each other instead of trying to cut each other. Nay, nay, nay . . . . We did not even think of such a mess. We tried to see how good we could make music sound, which was an inspiration within itself."

Death ennobled Bix in a way that his life never could. In 1950, Hollywood slathered another coat of varnish onto his legend via *Young Man With a Horn*, a biopic featuring Kirk Douglas as the muse-driven cornet player. With so little actually known about Bix, fans filled the void with half-imagined tidbits. Sadly, those who actually spent time with Beiderbecke scarcely knew him better than those who pored over records and articles looking for any clues about the inner man. "I did share rooms with Bix for a very short time," Artie Shaw recalled later, "and I didn't really get to know him. He was hard to know, because he was drinking an awful lot at the time."

Bing Crosby, who launched his singing career as part of Whiteman's trio of Rhythm Boys, also roomed with Bix on the road. He says it was music, not drink, that proved Beiderbecke's undoing. "It wasn't booze that killed Bix," Crosby told Nat Hentoff. "He wasn't an alcoholic. He was a jolly absent-minded sort of fellow, but he was so totally immersed in music that he never ate or slept properly. His health broke from exhaustion. Of course, it seemed none of us went to bed in those days. It's amazing that some of us survived."[10]

Whatever passions Beiderbecke harbored aside from booze and music he kept to himself. As the mysteries compounded over time, they only added luster to his appeal, transforming him into a Jazz Age martyr who gave all for his art, particularly for those who sought to follow in his footsteps.

COTTON TALE

High-rolling establishments needed bigger bands like the Whiteman Orchestra; their sound helped fill the cavernous halls of the large venues and their drawing power helped ensure full dance floors and hefty bar receipts. Expansive orchestras and evermore ornate show palaces popped up like the morning toast. Black customers were turned away from many nightspots, while inside, black bands were working the white crowds into a frenzy. Harlem's Cotton Club stands as the apotheosis of New York nightlife during the Roaring '20s. Located at Lenox Avenue and 142nd Street, the club conjured images of the antebellum South, with a stage draped in Plantation-era kitsch and souvenir programs depicting a world of sex and savagery where light-skinned women were ravished by dark-skinned satyrs.

Of course, black access to the Cotton Club was confined to the bandstand—an irony apparently lost on all but the performers who worked there. The shows were always expertly crafted, but frequently reached back into minstrel tradition for inspiration, according to club regulars. One contemporaneous review smacks of lechery, with an observer from *Variety* endorsing the chorus of "almost Caucasian-hued high yaller gals . . . possessed of the native jazz heritage." The writer was visibly impressed by their "hotsy-totsy performance," leaving the impression that the show was as much a burlesque as a

Duke Ellington holding court at the legendary Cotton Club, which one reviewer called "a seething cauldron of Nubian mirth and hilarity." With Ellington at the bandstand, the venue attracted the Hollywood elite, gangsters, and politicos, all anxious to be seen among the Harlem hoi polloi. (Frank Driggs Collection)

musical revue. "The brownskins' shivaree," he wrote breathlessly, "is worth the $2 couvert alone."[11]

Being named the house band for a venue like the Cotton Club was as close to job security as any musician of the era could imagine. When King Oliver declined an offer to become the club's featured attraction at the end of 1927, Duke Ellington's group won the coveted slot, where they remained until the hit "It Don't Mean a Thing (If It Ain't Got That Swing)" lofted them to stardom in 1932. When the Duke departed, the club's mob musclemen expeditiously "liberated" Cab Calloway from his contractual obligations to the nightclub owner a few blocks away. Ellington's subtle innuendoes were replaced by jitterbugging pep rallies with Calloway at the megaphone barking, "Are You *All REET?*" before launching into "Minnie the Moocher." The Cotton Club clientele answered each "Hi-De-Ho" with one of their own and loved every minute. Calloway stage shows were a blur of whipcrack arrangements, jived-up lyrics, sweat, and flailing hair. In short, he was the perfect complement to the club's party atmosphere, where whites could carouse in style and intermittently ogle the black sensuality traipsing by for just that purpose. "You have your own party and keep to yourself," opined a Manhattan visitors' guide. "But it's worth seeing how they step."[12]

"Slumming," as the uptown pilgrimage became known, became a major attraction in part because it offered the chance to get "up-close and personal" with negroes without actually having to touch any. It's as if whites were expecting something akin to a guided tour through *Jurassic Park*. These voyeurs were not only intrigued by the mysteries of black sexuality, but by the possibility that some stick-up artist among them might be concealing a switchblade or pistol. In combination, the chance to dip a toe into the salacious Negro world coupled with the abstract threat of near-death (like a horror movie scare) was as irresistible as it was exhilarating. As the neighborhood's reputation spread, the lines quickly blurred between what was hip and what was hype. Gossip columnists spotted Cole Porter, Marlene Dietrich, and Orson Welles among the Cotton Club's revelers; even the nation's head G-Man J. Edgar Hoover (surely aware of the club's mob ties) had to see for himself. The *Variety* critic was beside himself with excitement: "Harlem's night life now surpasses that of Broadway itself," the reporter gushed. "From midnight until well after dawn it is a seething cauldron of Nubian mirth and hilarity."[13]

One of Harlem's "New Negroes" was writer Langston Hughes, who recounted the unfolding scene in *The Big Sea: An Autobiography*. Whites, he lamented, were "flooding the little cabarets where formerly only colored people laughed and sang, and where now, strangers were given the best ringside seats to sit and stare at the Negroes—like amusing animals in a zoo." Ellington pronounced the Cotton Club atmosphere particularly "degrading and humiliating to both Negroes and whites," but he also thought it mad fun, and a good deal more upscale than what he'd been exposed to elsewhere on the club circuit.

Just a few blocks away at the Savoy Ballroom, interracial dancing was permitted, and swing dancing escalated into aerial displays of muscle and nerve. The latest craze was the Lindy Hop (after aviator Charles Lindbergh), and according to author Hughes, dancers there enjoyed flaunting their skill before the eyes of disbelieving tourists. "The Lindy-Hoppers at the Savoy even began to practice acrobatic routines," Hughes notes in *The Big Sea*, "and do absurd things for the entertainment of the whites, that probably never would have entered their heads to attempt merely for their own effortless amusement."[14]

The locals were mortified. "For nearly 20 years, musicians and dancers of all backgrounds frequented the ballroom," writes Katrina Hazzard-Gordon, the author of *Jookin: The Rise of Social Dance Formation in African-American Culture*. "But its truly integrated atmosphere generated much attention, particularly among the police who expressed concern about interracial dancing." Numerous campaigns were mounted to write the mayor regarding the menace of "white whores" and miscegenation at the club.

Second-tier venues sprang up in the fertile soil sown by the Savoy, the Cotton Club, Connie's Inn, and Roseland Ballroom (where Fletcher Henderson's band had been the resident attraction since 1924), and all needed entertainment to attract curious passersby.

A cheaper cover charge meant less glitz and smaller combos—which also meant more money for each performer working that night. Soon enough, piano players became the most sought after of all musicians, because they could be heard over the din of clinking glasses and conversation, and when called upon they could also lay down a wall-to-wall groove that could be heard half a block away. Ragtime piano virtuosos (called "professors" by their admirers) injected their sets with dance-friendly rhythms and the "walking bass," a left-handed attack that propels the bassline from one octave to the next over a few short measures. Soon, these party-hardy pianists had fashioned something entirely new from the remnants of ragtime, a thunderous derivative called "stride" (named for those swinging left-handed leaps across the keyboard), and that fad soon triggered its own spinoff in boogie-woogie, a more propulsive version of the same.

The black stride masters of Harlem, James P. Johnson (the composer of "The Charleston") and Willie "The Lion" Smith, among them, saw their reputations rise through the late-night cutting contests that kept Harlem hopping into the wee hours. Johnson's wife, according to local lore, often had to go "from street to street, until she heard the piano . . . recognize his style and then go up to the apartment to get him out of there and take him home."[15]

Artie Shaw arrived in the city hoping to make a name for himself as a session man. One night while he was walking down the street, a sound he'd never heard before blared out through an open window. "That's how I found Willie ('The Lion' Smith)," Shaw recalled. "And we got to know each other. Things then weren't like they are now; there was no black anger detectable. They were glad to have you, as long as you could play. Certainly being Jewish had nothing to do with it; nobody ever asked what religion I was. I wasn't practicing any kind of religion then, so if somebody had asked me, I would have answered that I didn't have one. It was a miserable period of my life, but musically interesting."

Since soloists were usually cheaper and adapted quickly to the needs of the occasion or venue, stride and boogie-woogie stompers were among the most well-traveled players of the time. When the buzz surrounding King Oliver and Louis Armstrong reached Los Angeles, Jelly Roll Morton abruptly quit the city in 1923 and headed for Chicago himself. Once there, he made terrific records as a soloist (Morton's deft touch on a 1926 instrumental called "The Pearls" is an oft-cited example) and with his Red Hot Peppers straight through the decade, but spent his free time lecturing anyone within earshot on the finer points of his "real" New Orleans style. A publicity still of the Peppers finds Morton comfortably seated among his men with a professorial finger raised while the standing bandmates supposedly await his next "pearls" of wisdom. Jelly Roll was a raconteur nonpareil who loved telling his hostage pupils how he invented jazz "one summer's day in 1902," although if that were true, he'd have been juggling his "inventing" with puberty, since he was twelve years old at the time.

So long as they had gigs to sustain them, New York and Chicago musicians logged thousands of miles trekking back and forth, often with the New Orleanians among them hosting informal jazz tutorials after business hours. "For example," as Artie Shaw recalled, "in New York City, we had a pool of musicians who were among the greatest in the world. There were Tommy Dorsey, Benny Goodman, me, Mannie Klein . . . there was Jimmy Dorsey, who was in the doldrums at that point, but the rest of them, Arnold Brilhart and Alfie Evans, they were terrific players (also all white). Who wound up with the gig just depended on who got the contract. You were being hired by musicians; you had that advantage, but the music you were playing was unbelievably bad. It really was beneath playing, but you had to play it because that was your living."

At the center of it all was Louis Armstrong, who cared less about a musician's color than his ability to play. "I'm a spade, you're an ofay," he once remarked to white trombonist Jack Teagarden. "We both got soul. Let's blow."

One night at the Hoofer's Club in Harlem in 1923, Armstrong encountered Fats Waller, the rotund stride apprentice to professor James Johnson. Waller was quite nearly cartoonish in appearance: nearly three hundred pounds of black dandy from the neck down, Waller was set off above by a gap-toothed grin and rubbery eyebrows, then topped maraschino-cherrylike with a derby two sizes too small. But when he sat down to play he was all business, with a rhythmic wrecking ball for a left hand and a sugary tickle to his right. They crossed paths again on live radio, at record dates (as "Perry Bradford's Jazz Phools"), and at Chicago's Vendome in 1927. Two years later, Fats would provide Satchmo with his first mainstream hit, "Ain't Misbehavin'," a frothy number lifted from Waller's score for *The Hot Chocolates.*

When Armstrong's professional home at the Chicago Savoy grew financially unstable, he set about relocating himself and the entire band to New York in 1929—despite receiving an invitation meant only for him. The entire company found work quickly, though, and were soon thrilling white clubgoers at Connie's Inn in Harlem, where *Hot Chocolates* was born. The combination of Waller's music and Armstrong's showmanship proved such a potent brew that the revue was moved downtown to Broadway, where it ran 219 performances. Armstrong originally delivered the tune from the orchestra pit, but before long the producers moved him to the stage, where his spot became a centerpiece of the show.

For Waller, *Hot Chocolates* marked the beginning of an ascendance that would continue right up until the winter of 1943, when he died of pneumonia on an overnight train trip at the age of 39. Fats, according to all concerned, spent his short life in nonstop pursuit of song, women, money, food, and liquor. He was also a warmly funny fellow who used humor to spice up his songs, lest they "get boresome." Along with Cab Calloway, Waller improvised an entire lexicon of jive phrases ("Let's get sweet and hot," to start a tune, "Turn it loose," "Mow me down," and "Send me, son" at the breaks, and "Cease, gentlemen, cease," at the close) that, in complement to his interminable mugging, made him the focal point of every gig. Waller returned by proxy to Broadway in 1978 when the musical *Ain't Misbehavin'* played 1,600 performances and launched the career of actress/singer Nell Carter. More than most, Waller seems to stand apart from time, and his song canon—which includes "The Joint Is Jumpin'" "Honeysuckle Rose," "A Handful of Keys," and "Smashing Thirds"—has never gone out of style. Someone, somewhere, is either covering a Fats Waller song or pinching a riff from one of his signature piano runs.

Nonetheless, many middle-class blacks believed the Calloway, Armstrong, and Waller stage shows undermined "New Negroes," first by making them look silly, and second by suggesting the entire black race endorsed insipid behavior as a means of attaining white approval. Those trying to convey an image of respectability winced whenever Satchmo rolled his eyes or Calloway shook his slick black locks from the bandstand. They cringed at the Waller party parodies where floozies got smacked around and Fats had to dash to their rescue. "Don't hit that chick! That's my broad!" Waller bellows in "The Joint Is Jumpin'"(1937), "Boy, I'll knock you to your knees!"

Calloway was dismissed out of hand as a novelty act, even though his arrangements were top flight and his players included, over time, Dizzy Gillespie, Cozy Cole, and Jonah Jones—all estimable talents even in their formative years. Critics confronted with such tunes as "Are You Hep to the Jive?," "Come On with the 'Come On'," and the "Hep Cat's Love Song," caught the kitsch, but missed the music. Waller's prowess as a songwriter and stride player made him less vulnerable. "A lot of what we did wasn't easy," says Al Casey, the guitarist in Waller's traveling group, the Rhythm, "but he made it look easy, like he did with everything else. We were all used to Fats' style of singing and playing so it was never a problem. There was mutual admiration between all the bands, but it was competitive, too, depending on the kind of work you did. Of course, when you're playing with someone with his reputation, there wasn't much problem getting respect from other players. I mean, it's Fats Waller."

It didn't help matters that Fats' zest for the good life kept him broke. He wrote and sold songs practically on the spot, sold them cheap, and often sold the same one more than once—a little passive/aggressive leverage to ensure he'd eventually collect what his work was worth. Even when his notoriety as a performer eclipsed the fame of his songs, he continued to record prodigiously. As early as 1929, Waller sat in on sessions with a white band that included Jack Teagarden, Gene Krupa, and Eddie Condon. It was an audacious move for the time, but less risky since it was studio work and not a live appearance. Musicians loved working with Fats, who gave as much as he took—and that was considerable.

"Yes, he drank," Casey admits, "but that man was a very professional man and a very intelligent man. He drank, but he never messed up a job. Fats let you be the person and the player you wanted to be, as long as you carried yourself right. If you didn't carry yourself well, you didn't have a gig. To me, I appreciated that."

Armstrong didn't get off so easily. When Satchmo recorded "Ain't Misbehavin'," he inadvertently crossed a line in the sand into mass popularity, and diehard jazz fans perceived his move the same way Elvis fans would come to regard the King's Army hitch. Subsequent Armstrong records emphasized singing over trumpet virtuosity and signaled the end of a golden era. When Satchmo took to bugging his eyes and mugging for the crowds who flocked to see him, early supporters turned away in disgust. Armstrong was selling out, they said, and the great architect of jazz was now chipping away at his own iconic image. Armstrong's final act of betrayal may have been in selecting the rough-hewn Joe Glaser as his manager for life. In a 1935 handshake deal that was never formalized, the most famous black musician in America cast his lot with Glaser, a white man who allegedly learned his strong-arm negotiating tactics from pals in the mob. Through his association with Armstrong and the other acts who flocked to him, Glaser became a millionaire. In return, Glaser repositioned Satchmo in the public mind as a national treasure—exactly as he is regarded today.

Tastemakers continue to heap huzzahs on Armstrong's work from the 1920s, particularly his sides with the Hot Fives and Hot Sevens. But as his stature grew beyond the jazz community, those records became a bittersweet reminder of the creative path Armstrong abandoned in order to become America's first black superstar. "I feel there's a certain amount of Uncle Tom that he did," Wynton Marsalis explained in an interview published in *Best of New Orleans* magazine in 2000 on the occasion of Satchmo's centennial anniversary. "It just came with the territory in one way, but it was also part of the whole descendancy of the minstrel show tradition."

Billie Holiday—no stranger to criticism herself—once offered an explanation of her own. "Louis may Tom," she conceded, "but he Toms from the heart."

BLACK AND TAN

As the ire aroused by Louis Armstrong's supposed defection from jazz to the pop world continued to ricochet through the music community, Edward Kennedy "Duke" Ellington stood blithely apart from the fray, content to make music on his own terms while paying little attention to commercial trends. He treated his songs as if they were jewels, each containing just one facet of his personality (and that of his orchestra), and didn't seem to care whether the public favored one cut over another. Fans could partake of what they liked now and return for more whenever their tastes caught up with his.

Just as Beethoven preferred to work for art's sake alone rather than compose for wealthy patrons, Ellington had no patience for the confines of popular opinion. "Categories are sometimes used by a person who feels that the one he's talking to doesn't know enough about the language in which he speaks," Ellington offered in his 1973 autobiography, *Music Is My Mistress.* "So he uses lines, boxes, circles, and pigeonholes to help the less literate one to a better understanding . . . , On the other hand, categories are sometimes used as a crutch for a weak artistic ability to lean on. The category gives the artistic cripple's work an attractive gloss." He concluded, "An agreeable smell is in the nose of the one who smells it."

A generation earlier, no environment in America could have produced Duke Ellington or his colorblind grasp of music, and, even today, the musical utopia he envisioned remains elusive. Alongside Louis Armstrong, Ellington elevated what people called jazz from a comic novelty into an art form. Both men were born at the turn of the century, affable, and gregarious, but in many ways they were worlds apart. Armstrong wore his hardscrabble roots as a badge of honor. A man of robust tastes and fast and enduring friendships, Satchmo was the same man onstage as off, a performer who never condescended or attempted to hide the hot music roiling up inside him. By contrast, Ellington was the epitome of cool. With his Mona Lisa smile and continental bearing, Ellington the man was every bit as fascinating as the music he wrote.

Both men galvanized a country well prepared to classify them as the latest incarnations of the classic Jim Crow/Zip Coon stereotypes—a broad-brushed simplification later conveniently used to describe such opposites as Joe Frazier and Muhammad Ali, Otis Redding and Marvin Gaye, and today's bejeweled hip-hoppers and their postgangsta counterparts. But Armstrong and Ellington refused to be straitjacketed by the roles society had waiting for them—they broke their bonds and refashioned those caricatures into something closer to the truth. Armstrong's brawn behind the horn and approachability offstage became one model of black masculinity, while to others, Ellington's cerebral reserve provided an attractive cloak for the sensualist within. "The Duke" may have promoted his image as a fey dandy, but with translucent nocturnes like "Warm Valley" (and later, "Satin Doll") in his repertoire, Ellington left little doubt that you'd want to keep a close watch on your female companion if his gaze ever fell upon her.

Armstrong was born an impoverished son of the New Orleans slums; he learned to live by his wits as a child and turn every moment to his advantage by finding the places where he best fit. Ellington was a product of the nation's capital, a light-skinned mama's boy pampered into manhood who became the master of his world by creating it around him as he went. One set of life circumstances taught the merits of improvisation and showcasing individuality without a showboating ego. The other seemed tailor-made to encourage a creativity fed through contemplation, ideal for a composer's inner-world explorations. At the zenith of their powers, they were two sides of the same coin—Armstrong with his unique approach to rhythmic time, and Ellington a man who pushed his music past the conventions of popularity, race, and complexity into timelessness. Both men *thought* jazz—mankind's most artful feat of improvisation—but they thought it very differently, and that thinking manifested in the way each dealt with race.

Ellington typically ignored bigotry as beneath his consideration. In a 1944 New Yorker profile, writer Richard Boyer wrote of a St. Louis cop meeting Ellington and gushing, "If you'd been a white man, Duke, you'd have been a great musician." The unperturbed Ellington replied, "I guess things would have been different if I'd been a white man." For decades, music writer Nat Hentoff followed the Duke around, watching as his worldview evolved. The recorded Ellington legacy contains brilliant sacred music and ambitious elongated pieces alongside the dance classics "It Don't Mean a Thing (If It Ain't Got that Swing)," "Ko-Ko," and "Cotton Tail," which fueled his success on both sides of the color line.

Even though his music was meant for anyone who had ears to hear it, Ellington took deep pride in his ethnicity, and composed numerous pieces in tribute to his racial heritage. Ellington was intent upon not only broadening his musical horizons, but in widening the scope of black themes in popular song. Where there had once been a void, Ellington helped to establish a black context for life in America through music. This life was not the subsistence-level despair of the bluesman, but an exquisite, sophisticated, expansive life—the same dream harbored by millions of white Americans during the Great Depression. Decades later, his work still sounds fresh and innovative, from 1931's "Dreamy Blues" (later retitled "Mood Indigo," where the high notes are scored for trombone and the low ones assigned to the clarinet), up through "Sophisticated Lady" in 1933, the band's still-catchy 1940s theme song, "Take the 'A' Train," and "Black Beauty," his 1960s tribute to Florence Mills, a black star who first rose to fame with Sissle and Blake.

Music as diverse and complex as Ellington's demands serious consideration. Is it black? Is it all blues based? What does the organic blend of his instrumentalists (hand-picked by Ellington based on flexibility and distinct individual sound) say about his concepts of orchestration? And, since his compositions depended upon dense harmonic structures—some of which seemed far removed from the blues—is it even jazz? According to Nat Hentoff, Ellington toyed with the idea of abandoning the word "jazz" entirely during a visit with Fletcher Henderson. "Why don't we drop the word jazz?" he mused to Henderson. "We ought to call what we're doing Negro music."[16]

Musicians and critics continue to tug at the fabric of Ellington's life's work, trying to separate black threads from white, but Armstrong's talent inspires a rare unanimity among them: Satchmo's playing comes from the soul—a decidedly African American one. And such an improvisatory gift, whether it flows from a Bach, a B.B. King, or a

Beatle, posits that intuition is a legitimate source of expression—one which allows the artist freedom to respond to what he or she hears instantly rather than having to weigh every element of music theory before striking a note. In a very real way, improvisation reintroduced a concept once at the core of African music making, the notion of the performer engaged in a spontaneous exchange with other musicians or even in a dialogue with the music itself.

Aspiring jazz players could take stock of Ellington—his music, manner, and education—and believe the same success might be theirs one day, black or white, if they applied themselves diligently. But Armstrong? No, a Louis Armstrong, like a da Vinci, Jules Verne, or Einstein, comes along once every few centuries—rooted in the present, but able to anticipate the future. "Louis Armstrong I am unequivocal about," says Ken Burns, the television documentarian whose PBS series, *JAZZ*, reacquainted America with its musical heritage in 2001. "This is a man who is maybe not even a man, but someone who was sent to Earth to bring the healing power of the blues to us," says Burns, "and we need it now more than ever."

Armstrong alone inspires such superlatives among aesthetes, and deservedly so. Before him, players were lashed to the meter, singers vocalized often ignorant of dynamics, and all were detached from the emotions in the pieces they played. For Armstrong, music was a baseball diamond where he played every position better than his teammates. He could lay back and support others, as records throughout his career aptly demonstrate. He could play off, on, and around a melody in a seemingly infinite variety of tonal shadings. As a singer, he'd ditch the lyrics altogether if he could better set the mood by singing gibberish, which caught on as the "scat" vocalizing fad brought to greater fame by Cab Calloway and, later, Ella Fitzgerald. Satchmo's performances onstage and on record exuded so much joy that he actually sounded like he was at play, rather than playing—one more reason opinion makers accused him of Uncle Tom-ism. By the time his wife (musician Lil Harden Armstrong) convinced him to leave King Oliver for a solo career in 1924, Armstrong was a local luminary. But his short stay in Fletcher Henderson's band became New York's crash course in swing, and when it was all over, Armstrong had shown the Big Apple how to loosen up. He returned to Chicago triumphant and made the Hot Five and Hot Seven recordings that preserved his legacy in wax.

Ellington's intricately conceived charts swing from the head down. Armstrong's best work swings from the hips up. Juxtapose the seductive sweep of Ellington's orchestra in 1927's "East St. Louis Toodle-oo" with the swagger of Satchmo's introduction (in three different tempos) to "West End Blues," recorded with his Hot Fives ensemble just after Armstrong switched from cornet to trumpet in 1928. Black and white musicians alike scratched their heads trying to re-create and build upon the sounds of both men, and with radio beaming their music across the nation, Americans found themselves faced with a short list of options: they could resist, they could listen, or they could dance.

RITES OF SWING

Radios and broadcast outlets grew exponentially throughout the 1920s, and became not only a boon to jazz, but to the music business in general. And when the stock market took a nosedive in 1929, the new medium became a source of calm for a nation in economic freefall. The Ellington orchestra had been on the air from its early Cotton Club days, and that in turn propelled the Duke and his band to Hollywood in 1930, where they appeared in a forgettable Amos 'n' Andy comedy (this one, unlike the TV series, starred the white minstrels who created the roles) called *Check and Double Check*. If Ellington and company were disgruntled by having to appear alongside blackfaced comedians, they never let on; it was exposure, and the band exploited every opportunity possible.

For those without gigs in Hollywood or the handful of show palaces across the country, making a living was tough—especially if the profession could be deemed expendable. With one of every four wage earners in the country jobless, even menial jobs were hard to come by—including the lousy ones musicians generally took when gigs were scarce. In Atlanta, one citizens group made its priorities perfectly clear: "No Jobs for Niggers Until Every White Man Has a Job." According to *JAZZ* author Geoffrey C. Ward, "The music business came close to collapsing. Membership in the American Federation of Musicians fell by one third—even after their dues were cut in half, many musicians could no longer pay them. More than one hundred New York dance halls closed their doors and nearly half the theaters on Broadway were shut down or turned into movie houses. In Chicago, shivering jobless men burned old phonograph records to keep warm. American record companies, which had sold more than 100 million discs a year in the mid-'20s, were soon selling just six million. Okeh, Gennett, and Paramount Records all went out of business. Warner Brothers teetered on bankruptcy and the RCA-Victor Talking Machine Company stopped making record players altogether for a time. Even Paul Whiteman had to lay off ten members of his thirty-man orchestra and ask the rest to take a fifteen percent cut in pay."[17]

Then, in 1933, the music world hit bottom when Prohibition was suddenly repealed. As soon as a neighborhood liquor store would open, a half dozen nightclubs would reel from the impact. Booze by the bottle kept many patrons at home, and without a sizable paying audience, proprietors felt no need for a small combo, let alone an orchestra. Even the few bands whose fame innoculated them against having to disband entirely scrambled for bookings on occasion.

It was against this backdrop that Benny Goodman found himself in New York struggling to keep his orchestra financially afloat. A reprieve came in the form of a steady job playing for NBC on a three-hour Saturday night radio program called *Let's Dance*. The show was broadcast live across the nation at 1 a.m. Eastern Standard Time. By sheer chance, it also launched Benny Goodman's career and a frenzy for swing music that would last until the end of World War II. Goodman, who included arrangements he'd bought or commissioned from Fletcher Henderson (and others, ultimately), was the first white swing outfit to play what was essentially black music for white audiences.

The show was largely overlooked on the East Coast, where its starting time was too late to become the centerpiece of an evening's entertainment. But in the West, where the show aired at 10 p.m., adolescents were riveted in the same way that some 40 years later their children would throw parties to watch *Saturday Night Live* on television. Once *Let's Dance* caught on in Los Angeles, entire evenings were organized around the broadcast, and anyone who was anyone didn't want to miss an episode. Goodman was oblivious to the show's appeal three time zones away; he considered himself lucky to have a forum and paychecks for his orchestra.

Then came the hot months of 1935. George Gershwin was making headlines with *Porgy and Bess* ("Old hat," and hardly "Negro music," said Duke Ellington), and the black Chick Webb Orchestra, long a fixture of the Harlem nightclub circuit, began recording with a young scat singer named Ella Fitzgerald. A few blocks away, a shoplifting arrest set off a race riot when a crowd of black onlookers first attacked the arresting officers and then turned on their reinforcements. The mob ransacked and burned white-owned stores, triggering the end of the Harlem Renaissance and the beginning of ghettoization. Big band music moved downtown to 52nd Street, nuzzled comfortably in and among the theaters that already attracted a huge tourist trade. There, the Flamingo Club, the Onyx, Jimmy Ryan's, the Famous Door, the Three Deuces, and a reconstituted Cotton Club became the nucleus of New York's "Swing Street." Economics forced the same consolidations on the other side of the country, with such Los Angeles nightspots as the Cocoanut Grove and Billy Berg's luring celebrities and in turn the tourists who wanted to rub elbows with them.

When a company strike forced the sponsors of *Let's Dance* to cancel the show abruptly midway through 1935, Goodman agreed to tour in hopes of building on his name recognition. Benny, whose business acumen was surpassed only by his desire to make the best music possible, was well received in the urban Midwest by offering up a conservative mix of "sweet" dance music and the saucier Henderson charts. But enthusiasm waned across the Rockies. The band was playing joints that stank (literally—one was a fish barn) and on at least one occasion had its stage security provided by chickenwire. The crowds had grown unpredictable and by the time the band hit California, Goodman's mood vacillated between despair and resignation. As Goodman's orchestra filed onto the stage August 21 at the newly remodeled Palomar in Los Angeles, Benny was already weighing his options once the troupe disbanded. From the stage that night, the Palomar must have looked like a musicians' Little Big Horn—intimidating in its cavernous sprawl, with a horde of inscrutable onlookers strewn across the floor. For an hour, the band waded through its catalog of sweet arrangements to a throng of restless spectators.

As the legend now goes, trumpet player Bunny Berigan was the first to declare he'd had enough. "Let's cut the shit, Benny," he yelled from the brass section. Goodman later confessed that he too was ready to go out with the proverbial bang rather than with a whimper. "I decided the whole thing had gotten to a point where it was make or break," the bandleader recalled. "If we had to flop, at least I'd do it in my own way, playing the kind of music I wanted to. For I knew, this might be our last night together, and we might as well have a good time . . . . I called out some of our big Fletcher arrangements."[18]

The audience, finally hearing what they'd hoped for, rushed the stage en masse. They were the leading wave in a torrent of Americans anxious to ignore the Depression for a few hours and kick up their heels. Again and again across the country, such bands as New York's Casa Loma and Jimmie Lunceford Orchestras, the Chicago-based Glenn Miller and the Dorsey Brothers, and Kansas City's Count Basie faced the same roar of approval. Even parents who once condemned jazz as "the path to degradation" (in the words of *The Ladies Home Journal*) wanted to learn a few of the latest steps.

NIGHT AND (LADY) DAY

On July 2, 1936, Goodman stepped back into the studio to back up a twenty-year-old black singer who had barely an octave's range to her voice. She and Goodman shared a brief fling two years earlier after being introduced by John Hammond, the wealthy impresario who would later sign recording deals with Bob Dylan and Aretha Franklin. The vocalist was the former Elanora Fagan, born illegitimate in Philadelphia and shunted from one home to another throughout childhood, raped at eleven, and a full-time prostitute by twelve. In Alice Dean's whorehouse on the waterfront she sang along with the house Victrola for extra money. By the time she met Hammond in New York, she'd found her way out of the brothels and into the small cabarets that dotted the city. She sang for tips without a microphone and mulled over stage names for herself before settling on Billie Holiday.

Artie Shaw remembered her well: "I had known Billie ever since she was seventeen and I was nineteen," he said. "We met in Harlem, which was where you would meet anyone black and in music in those days. I was waiting for my union card, and you had to wait six months before you could play legitimately anywhere. During that six-month period, I found my way up into Harlem and I was playing with Willie the Lion and anyone else who'd let me sit in. So I'd run into Billie up there, and I really liked the way she sang, and she had what I'd call a really keen musical intelligence. Writers have said she didn't have much range, but how much range do you need? How much did Fred Astaire have? An octave and a tone. Eight notes."

Holiday hit her stride after a series of flings fronting big bands, which tended to overwhelm the subtle mischief of her voice. In 1937, she signed on with Count Basie, whose Kansas City boogie woogie ignited a second stage of the swing explosion. She called him "Daddy" Basie (as she would many significant men in her life); he referred to her with mock formality as "William." Like Bessie Smith before her, Billie was a force of nature. She checked her femininity at the stage door, and on the road she gambled, drank, and cursed like the most hardened veteran. In time, Holiday's phrasing would influence nearly every serious singer to follow. Frank Sinatra claimed her as an influence, as have Willie Nelson and Joni Mitchell. When Diana Ross depicted her troubled life and drug-related demise in the 1972 film *Lady Sings the Blues,* she earned herself an Academy Award nomination (the movie received five altogether)—and the everlasting ire of Holiday fans who considered her pop-friendly re-creations tantamount to sacrilege.

Billie's life and legacy are rich in anecdotal opportunities. She was a proud and resilient woman who bowed to no one, yet was brought low by an insatiable desire for the drugs that led to her premature death at the age of 44. Basie let her go in 1938, citing financial disagreements. That she would next ally herself with an iconoclast bandleader like Artie Shaw is typical of Holiday; that the white bandleader would flout Jim Crow conventions by undertaking a tour of the South with a black vocalist was pushing the envelope for all concerned.

In the first place, promoters disapproved of blacks and whites in the same bands because the combination turned every contract negotiation into a peace treaty. But when the practice began with Goodman, Shaw, and a few others, agents and managers began trying to work around the problem. "Well, Billie could sing, and the audience liked her," Shaw maintained, "but in the hotels, she couldn't take the front elevator. I didn't care about the audience, and I didn't care whether the promoters liked it or not, but the problem was, we'd go to a hotel and have to work at night, and she couldn't take the elevator like anyone else because the hotel got a lot of complaints: 'You take *blacks* in here?' In those days, you didn't. We had this peculiar superstition about anyone with darker skin."

Even with a half century of hindsight, it's anyone's guess where Shaw and Holiday's bravery ended and irascibility began. It's safe to say that neither evinced much tolerance for fools or bigots. In Canada, she was treated as every bit the star her talent warranted. When it came time to head down below the Mason-Dixon line, she expressed reservations but Shaw convinced her to come along.

"And then we had an incident one night along the way," he said, "where someone piped up and said, 'Have the nigger wench sing another song.' And Billie must have blushed under her tan, because she had a short temper. So she started mouthing the word 'motherfucker' at him. This is *way* down South, with my '36–'37 band. We hustled her

Billie Holiday working the white crowd at Manhattan's downtown hotspot, Café Society, in 1939. Famed wordsmith S.J. Perelman (in glasses) sits at the front table. (Frank Driggs Collection)

out of there quick before anything could get started, but I think she realized what was going on, and she was scared."

Upon her return to New York, Holiday swore off dance bands and settled into steady work at an avant-garde Greenwich Village club called Café Society, where races mixed freely and patrons were encouraged to sit and listen. There, in April of 1939, she was approached by a Jewish high school teacher who put music to his grisly depiction of a Southern lynching. The incendiary lyrics persuaded composer Abel Meeropol to take refuge behind the pen name Lewis Allen—a psuedonym that remains on the sheet music to this day. Billie's label recommended against recording it, which only reinforced her belief in the song. She obtained permission to record it elsewhere, and it soon became a staple of her live act. She'd sing it framed in a tiny pin spotlight that barely illuminated her face; she stood immobile, arms limp at her side. Tears would flow but not stop the ghastly blues, which proceeded dirgelike until the final chords reverberated inside the walls, floors, rafters, and fixtures, along with the hearts and minds of everyone present. Holiday would then vanish without returning for a curtain call or encore. None who saw it were likely ever to forget the event, and not all were pleased to find their night of gaiety shattered on such a somber note.

While "Strange Fruit" sent a collective shiver through each new patron in attendance, singing the tune nightly took its toll on Holiday. The upbeat numbers that had made her sound both carefree and insubstantial gave way to such langorous torch songs as "Lover Man (Oh, Where Can You Be)," "Good Morning Heartache," and her own masterpiece, "God Bless the Child." Holiday's song, more than the many she made her own, provided a template for songwriters of the 1960s. It's too worldly to be considered religious, and too hopeful to qualify as a simple blues. "Them that's got shall get; them that's not shall lose," she wrote after her mother once refused to loan her money, "so the Bible says, and it still is news . . . ." Her triumph, like those of the southern blues masters, is in refitting her personal setback onto a universal framework: "Mama may have, and Papa may have," she affirms, but "God bless the child that's got his own."

The traumas Holiday endured and pursued ate away at her voice, but throughout the 1940s and 1950s she etched her star-crossed dignity into dozens of records. While she clearly raised the bar for performers in terms of committing heart and soul to a body of work, fans had to wonder: did her onstage excursions into misery ("You've Changed," "I Cried for You," and "Lady Sings the Blues") deepen her depression, or were they, as many believed, merely reflections of her everyday torments? Holiday was hospitalized in the spring of 1959, suffering from cirrhosis and malnutrition. As she lay there wasting away, authorities served her an arrest warrant on narcotics charges. Five days later, she died.

By way of contrast, Holiday's onetime boyfriend Benny Goodman lived to be seventy-seven. Childhood deprivation aside, Goodman endured few of the disadvantages Billie encountered through life—he was imbued with a near-fanatical devotion to the American work ethic, drove himself and his bandmates with a humorless discipline, and, of course, was born white. No sooner did he become famous (the "King of Swing," claimed the press, ignoring Count Basie just as Paul Whiteman gave the white media an excuse to pass over Armstrong and Ellington) than he put together a small combo featuring black and white performers playing together live. And this was not a loose aggregate of interchangeable players. Black pianist Teddy Wilson and vibraphone virtuoso Lionel Hampton (who joined a short time later) were the perfect foils for Goodman and Gene Krupa, the flashy drummer from Goodman's orchestra. Each man held an indispensable role in hearing and responding musically to the other three. It was jazz of the highest order, though not always ideal for dancing. Here, for the first time, was a group made up of black and white musicians who were doing the unthinkable—making music and money as full creative partners. Some critics suggest the project worked because Goodman could afford to squander some of his popularity on the risky enterprise of an integrated band, while others attest that Goodman didn't give a damn what antiblack sentiments he stirred up, so long as the music was worth playing.

SWING AND A STRIKE

Records and radio gave jazz a national platform, but by the mid-1930s, disparate factions of the music industry moved to claim larger shares of the new technology's market. First, the American Society of Composers, Authors, and Publishers (ASCAP) demanded a royalty increase for songs played over the air. Then in 1939, CBS, ABC, and NBC countered by establishing Broadcast Music Incorporated (BMI) in order to collect royalties on music composed specifically for the airwaves. A legal morass ensued in which each party charged the other with infringement. Often the battle was characterized in racial terms, since ASCAP principally regulated popular standards and show tunes, while BMI represented more recent jazz and swing pieces.

At the same time, record companies were fending off attempts by the American Federation of Musicians (AFM) to gain compensation for union players who lost live gigs to recorded music in venues around the country. And if that wasn't enough, the U.S. government issued a series of directives during the war that called for rationing shellac and vinyl (the prime ingredients of both records and a variety of war necessities) and instituted a twenty percent surtax on any entertainment that included dancers or vocalists. For some reason, instrumental music remained exempt. The War Department did issue a few recordings of service bands under its own imprint as "V-discs," but these were intended only for airplay, and were never available as commercially viable releases.

Following the attack on Pearl Harbor, President Franklin Roosevelt led America into its second world war—one far less romantic than the first. This time, blacks were granted essential roles in domestic defense and the military. But integration was out of the question, and each branch of the Armed Forces remained segregated to the point that even blood supplies were kept separate. Correspondent Walter Cronkite recalls that from his vantage point, there was very little interaction between black and white troops, over music or anything else. "I must say that I didn't really see music bringing people together during the war in London while the blitz was going on," Cronkite remembers, "but that's because there really wasn't a lot of music around at the time. And with the liberation of France, there wasn't much either. People were too preoccupied. There wasn't a lot of entertainment anywhere. I can't even think of any jazz joints in London."

The record industry joined Hollywood in promoting the war effort. For every Clark Gable and Betty Grable, the music community offered up a Glenn Miller Army Air Force Band and appearances by the Andrews Sisters—all squeaky clean, patriotic to a fault, and, not coincidentally, white. When jazz star-to-be Gil Evans reported to his outfit clutching a collection of government-issue V-disks, his bunkmates wanted to beat him up for embracing "colored music."

Musicians were allowed to be at the war, but not always in it. Artie Shaw's band never attended boot camp, and when the sailors stationed in Sydney, Australia found out, the players faced unrelenting ridicule. "We also went unrecorded during the war because I refused a commission," said Shaw. "Glenn Miller's band got recorded because he was *Major* Glenn Miller. They wanted me to play officers' dances, and I wanted to play for the enlisted men. So where are you gonna record that close to the front lines, in the jungle? It was a very low point in my life, I was a wreck psychologically, emotionally, and physically. We were as close to the action as you can get without being shot, and by the end of the war, I was half nuts."

At home, the war of public relations was being waged largely in terms of race. Government-sanctioned propaganda set about convincing Americans that Germany was overrun with jackbooted sadists, that Italians were swarthy thugs, and that every Asian was a Jap saboteur in waiting. Anti-Semitism was also on the rise at military bases and anywhere servicemen gathered to drink. In April of 1943, several enlistees in Harlem reported they had contracted venereal disease from women who frequented the Savoy Ballroom. That gave local authorities all the justification they needed to permanently close the club, sparking riots uptown. Across the country a few weeks later, rowdy servicemen declared a month of open warfare on black and Latino jitterbugs from Los Angeles' rough-and-tumble east side, with fights erupting regularly in nightclubs and into gang warfare in the streets. In 1998, a whitewashed account of their rampage gave the Cherry Poppin' Daddies a retro-swing hit called "Zoot Suit Riot."

Civilian dissent during the war years all but vanished after Pearl Harbor, allowing the U.S. government to act with impunity toward minorities. They were able to ship law-abiding Japanese-American families into internment camps, maintain segregation in the armed forces, and offer towheaded German prisoners of war the kind of restaurant seating that many African Americans never lived to see.

Legal battles and the war abroad kept many swing era favorites off the air for nearly two years while listeners made due with big band interpretations of the classics and various folk songs from the public domain. Many labels also anticipated the fracas and hoarded studio material to ration at their leisure. During that twenty-four-month lull, far from the ears of jitterbugs who were overseas battling the Axis powers, a group of jazz renegades staged a palace coup against the tyranny of swing.

BIRTH OF THE COOL

Mass appeal lofted swing to recognition as "America's Music," but it also discouraged its stars from tweaking a proven formula for success. Lindy-Hoppers, after all, were waiting for that next four-on-the-floor stompfest, not the arrival of anything new. Just as profiteers reduced ragtime to its most recognizable identifiers in order to attract the widest range of customers, swing became musical wallpaper for dilettantes more interested in high times than good music. In the monotony, free thinkers grew bored and annoyed with audience demands to stay the course. "Let's face it," Artie Shaw said in disgust, "no matter how carefully and deeply you bury shit, people will sniff their way to it, dig it up, and buy it in vast quantities."

As the 1930s drew to a close, a new generation of black musicians entered the field itching to push past the dance hits that held the country in Lindy-Hopnosis. And very quickly, these young talents—Dizzy Gillespie and Thelonious Monk, soon to be joined by Charlie Parker, Kenny Clarke, and Miles Davis among a host of (mostly black) players—forged an alternative to the uniformity of swing.

For Charlie Parker, the instant of his epiphany was unforgettable. He remembered running through a tune called "Cherokee" at an uptown chili parlor in December, 1939. "And, as I did I found that by using the higher intervals of a chord as a melody and backing them up with appropriately related changes, I could play the thing that I'd been hearing. I came alive."[19]

The visionaries of bebop believed, as French philosopher Jean-Paul Sartre stated in a 1947 article for the *Saturday Review of Literature*, that "Jazz is like bananas—it must be consumed on the spot." Stylistically, their music was cobbled from at least two identifiable sources. Jam sessions in Harlem helped players move toward a rough schematic of bebop, but the fierce cutting competitions in Kansas City taught them to think on their feet or be left behind. There, two of the city's favorite sons, Charlie Parker and Lester Young, began to chafe under the yoke of big bandleaders and went truant from their written parts whenever possible. After work, they'd take a tune (Gershwin's "I Got Rhythm" was a favorite) and explore its every permutation inside and out. The notes tumbled out in flurries, not soft as snowflakes, but in sparks and embers. Bebop was "no love child of jazz," Parker later insisted, but merely a matter of "playing clean and looking for the pretty notes." Many boppers saw swing as escapist tripe, while their music's discordant harmonies and shifting rhythms accurately reflected the uncertainties of modern life.

By developing a signature instrumental approach, beboppers plotted to wrest jazz back from the hitmakers and return it to a platform of individual expression. Gillespie later explained, "Some of us began to jam at Minton's (nightclub) in Harlem in the early 1940s. But there were always some cats who couldn't blow but who would take six or seven choruses to prove it. So on afternoons before a session, Thelonious Monk and I began to work out some complex variations on chords and the like, and we used them at night to scare away the no-talent guys. After a while, we got more and more interested in what we were doing as music, and, as we began to explore more and more, our music evolved."[20]

Many white players assumed these insults were intended for them. Renowned black drummer Art Blakey shared many a stage with white musicians, and found them to be generally punctual, easygoing, and adept at delivering dependable (albeit predictable) sets. But he scoffed at their creativity. "The only way the Caucasian musician can swing," he snapped, "is from a rope."

By the 1950s, such attitudes were pervasive enough to earn the nickname "Crow Jim," since they exemplified reverse discrimination. In his book, *Jazz in Black and White*, Charlie Gerard describes a scene where white bopper Art Pepper was informed that two of his black accompanists were actually making faces behind his back during a show. "Over the course of the next few nights, Pepper indeed found them to be sneering at him," Gerard writes. "He confronted (drummer) Lawrence Marable, who told him, 'None of you white punks can play.'"[21]

Still, when the movement began, the beboppers received more criticism—from both sides of the color line—than they were able to mete out. "Mezz" Mezzrow, a white jazzman who'd been on the scene for decades, decried the music as "frantic, savage, frenzied, and berserk." Cab Calloway—who once fired Gillespie when an argument of theirs resulted in Calloway's being nicked with a carpet knife—pronounced bebop "Chinese music." Louis Armstrong called it "crazy, mixed-up chords that don't mean nothing at all." At the end of the century, Wynton Marsalis would lead others to similar condemnations of free jazz and fusion.

The jazz world split into three reactionary camps: one in relentless pursuit of the biggest hits, crowds, and purses; a second faction (dubbed "moldy figs" by jazz writers) who proclaimed that the only true jazz was the New Orleans "Dixieland" variety; and a third front representing the growing throng of insurgent boppers.

While Dizzy Gillespie and a few others deserted commercial jazz for bebop, others were content to have it both ways. Benny Goodman first heard the protobop guitarist Charlie Christian when John Hammond intervened once again. The well-meaning but meddlesome Hammond arranged to have Christian show up unannounced, plugged in and ready to play, at a Goodman gig. What Goodman reluctantly heard sent his mind spinning. Christian had reinvisioned the guitar as an electric instrument, alternately chording and picking single-note counterpoints inspired in part by Lester Young's sax solos. After hearing the possibilities in Christian's playing, Goodman hired him on the spot. Their association was tragically brief, however; soon after he burst onto the scene, Christian became ill with tuberculosis and died in 1942, only 25 years old.

As had happened before and would recur many times during the remainder of the century, popular music continued to splinter and jazz drew dwindling crowds of elitist devotees. "Hard bop" became a militant variant of bebop and "modern jazz" took the coldly logical approach of mathematicians at work. A white West Coast trumpet player named Chet Baker (a favorite of Charlie Parker's) used his mute and matinee idol looks to help create a soothing suburban romantic strain called "cool jazz." By the end of the 1940s, swing had vanished, big bands were dying, and the jitterbugs who loved them both returned home to attend college and start families of their own.

FUNNY VALENTINES

Like all art, jazz is essentially a conduit of communication. It's ironic that in dealing with the origins and significance of jazz, ideologues from both sides have been talking *at* one another rather than *to* each other since its inception. Back and forth it goes: black players grousing that white players can't swing, whites countering that black musicians shun or mock their Caucasian counterparts. Blacks accuse white performers of attempting either to steal the entirety of jazz for commercial gain (and there's nothing new there, since that accusation is leveed against whites whenever a new black-derived music emerges), or to hijack its direction as happened during the big band era with swing. Whites point out how black jazz stars perform as though they're doing the world a favor. Miles Davis was a prime offender in the eyes of some, turning his back on audiences and wandering offstage whenever he wasn't the center of attention. Most remarkable of all, though, is the notion that black people are better jazz players by dint of race alone.

Wynton Marsalis makes his opinion clear during a possibly apocryphal "interview" with an unnamed journalist in his 1994 book, *Sweet Swing Blues on the Road*. When asked what made blacks better jazz players, Marsalis let jazz writer Stanley Crouch take the heat: "Crouch says 'They invented it,' People who invent something are always the best at doing it." Using this logic, modern art cannot compare to the work of cave dwellers, Greek tragedy surpasses Shakespeare, and white guys make the best basketball players.

As if to ignore the assertions of slavers and minstrels who surmised that black talent was no more than a savantlike manifestation of random genes, African Americans began to proclaim that nature had indeed blessed them with a gift for music making that whites could only hope to approximate. Even Malcolm X agreed. "The white musician can jam if he's got some sheet music in front of him," Malcolm told organizers of the Organization of Afro-American Unity in 1964. "He can jam on something that he's heard jammed before. But that black musician, he picks up his horn and he starts blowing some sounds that he never thought of before. He improvises, he creates, it comes from within. It's his soul; it's that soul music."[22]

The apparent chasm between the races here could be nothing more than a semantics disagreement. Even if scientists can one day isolate cultural identifiers that separate black from white players, the idea that Benny Goodman, Gene Krupa, Woody Herman, and Gil Evans couldn't swing remains a stretch of the imagination. Perhaps they didn't swing the same way, with an identical sense of phrasing, dynamics, and rhythm, but they could and did move audiences of every color.

But many black musicians insist that if jazz is their intellectual property, they should be entitled to set its parameters. "Black people toiled and suffered, playing and nurturing this music when it wasn't popular and no one was paying to hear it," according to Denton, Texas–based jazz guitarist Don Bell. "And if you have people who weren't there, didn't do the work, and now want to tell the creative inheritors of jazz that their opinions don't matter . . . well, I think it's fair to say something's wrong."

"I don't know how anybody can even think about that," Artie Shaw said. "It's a black myth today. 'It's *our* music,' they keep saying, and that kind of attitude is gradually attenuating their audiences to the point where they don't have much of an audience anymore. If they'd stop thinking about whose music it is and start playing for audiences, they'd have a chance. But what they're doing is playing for themselves mostly. Listen to a big band like McCoy Tyner; they have a hell of a band there, but I mean, who knows what they're doing?"

As for whites reaping the greatest economic benefits from the music, documentarian Ken Burns says that through most of the century, the populace of the United States was more white than anything else—and therefore, they supported the musicians who looked and sounded most like them.

"A lot of that has to do with demographics, right?" Burns explains. "You essentially have a white society, with ten to twelve percent of them African American. Duke Ellington, Fletcher Henderson, Chick Webb, and, of course, Louis Armstrong basically invent and promote big band swing, but it is going to be the Benny Goodmans and the Glenn Millers—particularly a Glenn Miller who has his feet so much out of the art and into the pop world—who are going to have the general widespread response. Still, they would all be the first to acknowledge their debt to the African American community. Now that may not compensate for the fact that Benny is going to sell ten times more than Duke Ellington, but that's the case."

All but the most strident racists will grant that black and white artists collaborated to create jazz and many of its offshoots, with blacks providing most of the inspiration and guidance. But if jazz could have been patented, and blacks were majority stockholders on its patent, then they have precious little to show for it on the ledger books. Why? Most obviously and conveniently, such ideas cannot be traced to their original owners. More troublesome is the realization that when jazz broke through to mainstream success, it somehow *ceased to be black.*

Swing, epecially such big band smashes as Benny Goodman's "Sing, Sing, Sing," Artie Shaw's "Begin the Beguine," and Glenn Miller's "A String of Pearls," helped to persuade listeners that this was not an ethnic music, but a style anyone could adapt. And since jazz never went through an era that didn't have its share of white stars, who can blame the casual listener for not understanding how much music filtered down from black inspiration?

There should be no ducking the reality that white-owned record companies, radio networks, club owners, and musicians made more money than their black counterparts from music that clearly owes more to black influences than white. But the case is not so cut-and-dried, because jazz was never entirely derived from or even played exclusively by blacks—even at its inception.

In his book, *Jazz in Black and White*, white author Charlie Gerard describes how black music ideologues are galled that "each style of jazz—and each variety of blues, rhythm-and-blues, and rap for that matter—has been appropriated from the African American community almost from the day after it was first heard there." If that is so, how can jazz ever be considered a pure expression of African American culture? Since white artists were present at birth to rob jazz from its ethnic cradle, their playing also influenced what was being created, and music—which knows no color—would have commingled white and black characteristics indiscriminately from the outset.

BODY AND SOUL

"The reason the story of this music is so interesting," says Ken Burns, "is because it's like Cinderella. It's the person you keep down and leave back at home to sweep the hearth who is going to be the Belle of the Ball. Everybody knows that in their guts. The most pernicious racist knows that the person whose head is underneath his boot is somehow going to come back. And out of that resiliency, we know we've seen anger manifest in our society in crime and other things. But in music, and jazz in particular, you have a tremendous art form that's affirmation in the face of adversity."

During the decades between 1920 and 1950, the music forms created by African Americans proved resilient enough to withstand threats of every stripe, including adaptation and exploitation, internal purist revolts, and a global economic depression. The reasons are simple enough. All were soundly rooted in the structure of the blues, allowing them to be endlessly reconfigured to suit changing times. At the same time, advances in broadcast and recording technology (including talking pictures) during the 1920s delivered the sounds of city jazz, country blues, and singing cowboys to a new generation of converts.

Escalating sales of radios and phonographs at every level of society also meant a wider audience and an increasing demand for product, but what's missing from that capitalist equation is *how* Americans were evolving as listeners. Patrons no longer had to wait for a touring musician to share their appreciation as part of an audience. Music became a solitary affair as well as a public occasion, and one person in a room with a radio or a handful of records could absorb dozens of artists and styles in one sitting.

The modern fan was born when listeners began to have private relationships with the disembodied sounds they welcomed into their homes (just as the Walkman and Internet file sharing would revolutionize music in the 1980s and 1990s). Faraway performances held the now-undivided attention of listeners who huddled in the dim light around a radio or Victrola, each straining to hear the next blue note or rhythmic turn. Those who liked the music but preferred not to race-mix or visit a club in some unfamiliar part of town could now be entertained by Negroes without actually having to interact personally with them.

Records and radio not only kept listeners entranced separately; they trapped music in time so that aspiring players could memorize a song, an arrangement, or even a performer's specific style, regardless of race. In the final analysis, these performances served as common language between artists and their fans, particularly those who aspired to music careers. Without the music makers in the room and with black and white influences constantly recombining, identifying a performer by race became exponentially more difficult, and, finally for some, irrelevant.

NOTES

1 Kimball, Robert and William Bolcom. *Reminiscing with Noble Sissle and Eubie Blake.* Lanham, Maryland: Cooper Square Press, 1973, p. 72.

2 From "You Ain't Heard Nothin' Yet" available online at dinesp.fsnet.co.u/youaint.html

3 Kimball, Robert and William Bolcom. *Reminiscing with Noble Sissle and Eubie Blake.* New York: Cooper Square Press, 1973, p. 80.

4 Ibid., p. 95.

5 Ibid., p. 128.

6 Jasen, David A. and Gene Jones. *Spreadin' Rhythm Around: Black Popular Songwriters, 1880–1930.* New York: Schirmer Books, 1998, p. 290.

7 Goldberg, Isaac. *George Gershwin: A Study in American Music.* New York: Frederick Ungar Publishing Co., 1958, p. 139.

8 Ibid., p. 151.

9 Ibid, p. 322.

10 Hentoff, Nat. *Listen to the Stories: Nat Hentoff on Jazz and Country Music.* New York: HarperCollins Publishers, 1995, p. 58.

11 Ward, Geoffrey C. and Ken Burns. *Jazz: A History of America's Music.* New York: Alfred A. Knopf, 2000, p. 147.

12 Ibid., p. 147.

13 Ibid., p. 145.

14 Hazzard-Gordon, Katrina. *Jookin: The Rise of Social Dance Formation in African-American Culture.* Philadelphia: Temple University Press, 1990, p. 134.

15 Ward, Geoffrey C. and Ken Burns. *Jazz: A History of America's Music.* New York: Alfred A. Knopf, 2000, p. 95.

16 Hentoff, Nat. *Listen to the Stories: Nat Hentoff on Jazz and Country Music.* New York: HarperCollins Publishers, 1995, p. 6.

17 Ward, Geoffrey C. and Ken Burns. *Jazz: A History of America's Music.* New York: Alfred A. Knopf, 2000, p. 174.

18 Ibid, p. 223.

19 Nisenson, Eric. *Blue: The Murder of Jazz.* Cambridge, Massachusetts: Da Capo Press, 1997, p. 112.

20 Ibid, p. 111.

21 Gerard, Charley. *Jazz in Black and White: Race, Culture, and Identity in the Jazz Community.* Westport, Connecticut: Praeger, 1998, p. 9.

22 Ibid., p. 28.

CHAPTER FOUR

When Worlds Collide

Long Tall Sally, she's built for speed
Got everything that Uncle John need . . .
"Long Tall Sally" by Little Richard

Long Tall Sally has a lot on the ball
Nobody cares if she's long and tall . . .
"Long Tall Sally" as recorded by Pat Boone

B y the end of World War II, the pied pipers of bebop were leading jazz down a commercial blind alley. For the first time in the music's fifty-year history, the medium's most creative minds—including Charlie Parker, Dizzy Gillespie, and Thelonious Monk—were more interested in innovation than in enrolling converts. A dwindling audience of enthusiasts was delighted, but America was not amused. Jitterbugs had no idea what this new sound meant or what they were supposed to do with it. Was it tribal or cerebral, or both? Was its discordant jumble of notes a product of the avant-garde or merely the latest incarnation of some ancient African tradition? How do you move to it? Satirist Mort Sahl spoke for the perplexed nation when he quipped that nowadays "a waiter drops a tray, and three couples get up to dance."

Since it was practically impossible to hum a Parker obligato or match steps to an intricate Thelonious Monk riff, bebop launched jazz into a commercial tailspin. Worse, it distanced mainstream audiences from jazz altogether, a hefty ransom for reclaiming what the music boppers considered their cultural birthright. Listeners cast about for music that better represented the world they knew, and they found it. Many middle class (predominantly white) fans embraced the soothing warble of Frank Sinatra, Rosemary Clooney, and Nat "King" Cole. Largely black audiences flocked to the movies, where they could watch early music shorts featuring Louis Jordan's hot dance combo, the Tympany Five.

(These shorts were brief performance clips without plot points that could be snipped from a film before white audiences could be offended by them.) As the record industry began to recover from wartime rationing, the only topic the major labels (Columbia, RCA, and the rest) seemed to agree upon was that swing was dead and that their audience was now sampling everything from mambos and polkas to hillbilly and gospel.

APPALACHIAN STOMP

Sometime during the 1990s, the term "roots music" emerged for any American musical idiom considered rural in origin or believed to embody the values and yearnings of the heartland. Whether it was folk, gospel, country, blues, Cajun, or Tejano, the reputation of each rested on a kind of Shakeresque quality in which form always fit function. Stripped bare or gussied up with ornate arrangements, the compositions remained at their core simple declamations on life and how to deal with its hardships—in other words, topics so universal they transcended skin color. By sticking to the basics, gospel and hillbilly in particular flourished, and when their first practitioners abandoned the clapboard shacks and one-room churches of the country for city life, they brought their music with them.

None of these musics or their subsets can claim a racially pure pedigree. Just as jazz had its white contributors present at creation, and Fisk Jubilee choirmaster George White brought his Western European sensibilities to bear in transcribing "Steal Away" and "Swing Low, Sweet Chariot," other white musicians had an effect on the black-derived music they encountered, including hillbilly.

For generations, slaves in the field and white farmworkers were playing many of the same melodies on the fiddle and banjo. By the time archivist John Lomax first published "Home on the Range" in a 1910 anthology called *Cowboy Songs and Other Frontier Ballads*, rural white America had long been incorporating elements of the blues into their renditions of Scottish reels and Irish folk songs.

In 1922, Texas fiddler Alexander "Eck" Robertson opened the door for country when he and Virginian Henry Gilliland visited New York. At Victor Records studio, one sporting a Confederate uniform and the other decked out in cowboy gear, they recorded "Arkansas Traveler" and "Turkey in the Straw" before anyone knew what to call their music. A year later in Atlanta, a visiting Victor Records representative named Ralph Peer recorded Fiddlin' John Carson's renditions of "The Little Old Cabin in the Lane" and "The Old Hen Cackled and the Rooster's Going to Crow"—then watched the record outsell his most optimistic projections.

In May of 1927, an aggregate of black and white string players calling themselves Taylor's Kentucky Boys recorded a few folk standards, including "Soldier's Joy," "Forked Deer," and "Gray Eagle," marking (according to *The Devil's Box*, a book by music historian Charles Wolfe) the first interracial recording in American history. Two months later, Peer descended on the small Tennessee town of Bristol. He unloaded a trunk crammed with recording equipment into what was once a hat factory and set about capturing the sound of (white) rural America on disc. In order to promote his visit, Peer invited a local reporter to watch singers Ernest Stoneman and Eck Dunford cut their version of "Skip to Ma Lou" in a single afternoon. The story made front-page news in Bristol; prominently featured in the account was Stoneman's $100 paycheck for the session. Overnight,

Peer was deluged with hopeful amateurs, among them two cornerstones of the genre: the Carter Family; and Jimmie Rodgers, who became famous as "the Singing Brakeman."

Rodgers' audition almost didn't happen. In fact, he was lucky to be alive.

Serious bouts with tuberculosis forced him to quit the railroad work that had taken him cross-country and exposed him to a variety of American music styles. When he heard about Peer's talent search, Rodgers and his string band set out from Asheville, North Carolina for Bristol, but when the group decided their odds were better without him, they ditched Rodgers the night before the audition. Rodgers performed solo the next day and, true to his bandmates' prediction, Peer left unimpressed.

A few months later, Rodgers approached the label again at the company's Camden, New Jersey studios, and made an altogether different impression. The song he brought with him, "Blue Yodel," became an instant hit, a country classic, and a convincing demonstration of how thoroughly mongrelized America's music had become by the 20th century. Better known by its lyric, "T for Texas, T for Tennessee," the song features not only an indisputably blues-based performance by a white artist, but the high lonesome yodel that became Rodgers' musical calling card. In 1928, at a time when the nation's economy was faltering, Jimmie Rodgers became the best-selling artist in the genre. Although he died in 1933, remnants of his style have filtered through much of the music recorded in his lifetime and ever since in artists ranging from Leadbelly to Hollywood's "Singing Cowboys" Gene Autry and Tex Ritter. In 1961, Rodgers was named the first inductee of country music's Hall of Fame.

Conservative urban whites were quick to embrace the values espoused by "old-time" hillbilly music. Neither its lyrics nor dance steps betrayed overt references to African American influence, while more subtle nods—the bent blue notes, solo singing, and tales of woe—were well hidden in its ancestry. Auto tycoon Henry Ford latched onto hillbilly music as the common-sense alternative to jazz, which he condemned as "waves upon waves of musical slush that invaded decent parlors and set the young people of this generation imitating the drivel of morons." Jazz, he believed, was infested with blacks, Jews, and Communists, while his square dances and fiddle contests were wholesome events the whole family could enjoy.

Southern radio programmers soon discovered that their hillbilly acts dispensed not only entertainment, but a boost in morale to those hit hardest by the Depression—and that made them a marketer's dream. Although some performers had been performing on the air since the early 1920s on radio stations from Fort Worth to Atlanta, it was the *Barn Dance* on WSM in Nashville that set the standard in 1925 with a slate of local musicians vying for applause every Saturday night. Two years later and under a new name, the Grand Ole Opry unified hillbilly music under one banner. Among its first stars was a black harmonica player named Deford Bailey, who remained with the show (and attracted an incalculable number of black listeners) until his refusal to quit playing copyrighted music during the American Society of Composers, Authors, and Publishers (ASCAP) strike forced him out in 1941. Race is said to have played a part in his dismissal, but had his bosses been looking for a reason to fire him, surely they would have found one in less than fifteen years.

The Opry laid bare what hillbilly practitioners and devotees had known for some time: that this music was already a mosaic of wondrously tangled influences, despite its reputation for simplicity. Not only were Western European folk songs and African American traditions thrown into the mix, but song structures and ideas from the minstrel era and jazz as well. Blackfaced minstrel man Emmett Miller apparently wandered back and forth across the boundaries at will and took a cast of moonlighting luminaries with him. His 1928 recording of "Lovesick Blues" eerily foreshadows the Hank Williams hit version that followed twenty years later, and backing Miller are "His Georgia Crackers," an aggregate of jazz players led by Tommy and Jimmy Dorsey. Later editions of the Crackers included trombonist Jack Teagarden and the pounding drummer behind "Sing, Sing, Sing," Gene Krupa.

From the hills to the bayous and Texas Panhandle, these music forms resembled the Dust Bowl era that spawned them—untold billions of particles tumbling over and into one another until they were reshaped by technology and the swing craze into something else entirely. Suddenly southern bands were augmenting their fiddle sections with horns and blending them with the vocal harmonies that crossed the border from Mexico. Fort Worth bandleader Milton Brown pioneered the style that came to national attention as Western Swing, but in 1936, he sustained serious injuries in an auto accident that resulted in his death a few days later. In due time, the world crowned Brown's former bandmate Bob Wills as "The King of Western Swing" instead. Wills began his career in the 1920s as a blackface fiddler in Fort Worth medicine shows. According to Ray Benson, whose band Asleep at the Wheel updates western swing for audiences in the new millennium, "Bob was such a fan of the blues he once rode fifty miles on horseback to see Bessie Smith perform. The blues is right at the core of what Bob Wills took and then turned into western swing." One of Wills' earliest recordings featured an adaptation of Smith's "Guitar Rag," which became the band's theme for several years as "Steel Guitar Rag." Wills' accessible mix of dance, jazz, swing, fiddle, and honky-tonk attracted fans of every stripe, and a string of hits ensued, including "San Antonio Rose," "Take Me Back to Tulsa," and "Deep in the Heart of Texas."

In radio interviews, performers often exaggerated the southern twang of their voices in an attempt to show that they rose from the same stock as their fans. But black influences sprang to life as soon as they began to sing. Bluegrass pioneer Bill Monroe (from whom Elvis learned "Blue Moon of Kentucky") acknowledged that he grew up listening to both black and white blues singers. Ralph Stanley is an elder statesman of bluegrass who appears on the soundtrack to the Coen brothers' film *O Brother, Where Art Thou*. On his solo, "O Death," he demonstrates the same melisma (embellishing a vocal line with a series of improvised notes where only one may be called for) practiced by southern black gospel groups. While the voice is all Stanley, his approach is audibly more Afro-American than hillbilly.

Demands for factory workers during World War II attracted farmers to the cities of Nashville and Memphis, which in turn provided a market for country music on radio and in dances around town. By the time Hank Williams arrived on the postwar music scene, the parameters of country music were well delineated. But while the singers and songwriters delivered their songs as if they were reading a stranger's mail aloud, Williams hit paydirt by singing from the heart—what artists today would have no trouble classifying as "soul." Was this ability a God-given instinct, or a skill developed over time? No one seems certain, but Williams repeatedly cited a black street musician named Rufus "Tee-tot"

Payne as a major influence. "All the music training I ever had was from him," Williams divulged in remarks to *The Montgomery Advertiser* in 1951. The following year, he went into greater detail, discussing his roots with country chronicler Ralph J. Gleason: "I learned to play the git-tar from an old colored man .... He ... played in a colored street band .... I was shinin' shoes, sellin' newspapers and followin' this old Nigrah around to get him to teach me to play the guitar. I'd give him fifteen cents, or whatever I could get a hold of, for the lesson."[1]

Perhaps Williams needed help with technique, but his experience with life's miseries was all his own. Hank's wife Audrey spent years bucking for a singing career, but her ambition eclipsed her talent, and largely out of jealousy she shunned him while spending every spare dime she could grab. Williams, troubled by a bad back and rocky marriage, used pills to get him from the next gig to the next bottle and the next one-night stand. He had pain to spare. Once, when Hank's friends called Audrey to say they were bringing him home after he'd fallen from the stage (drunk) and reinjured his back, she shot back, "I don't care what you do with the son of a bitch, just don't bring him out here." A short time later, Audrey called them and asked what had happened to her money—the proceeds Williams had just earned singing. "Lady," the friend replied, "as far as I know, you ain't got no damned money. I gave *Hank's* money to Jim (Denny, Hank's business associate)."[2]

Williams' own songs, which took off after "Lovesick Blues," joined sturdily crafted melodies to lyrics that ached from longing. The woman he yearned for in song and in reality would always remain just out of reach in varying degrees. Sometimes, she'd have a "Cold, Cold Heart," at others he'd admit "I Can't Help It If I'm Still in Love With You" and wonder in his sadsack voice, "Why Don't You Love Me Like You Used to Do?" In the studio, Hank guaranteed his songs' longevity by insisting they be kept free from faddish musical adornments. He used two words for instruction: "Vanilla, boys."

The memorable tunes and basic arrangements had the desired effect. Cajun and zydeco fans still revere "Jambalaya" as though it was composed in New Orleans' French Quarter, "Cold, Cold Heart" became a crossover pop hit for a newcomer named Tony Bennett in 1951, and in 1962, Ray Charles resurrected "Your Cheating Heart" and changed the face of country music forever.

WASHED IN THE BLOOD

Grassroots music was slow to catch radio programmers' attentions. It fell to the honky-tonks and a loosely interconnected string of churches to nurture and disseminate the sounds of rural America before they slipped quietly into the city.

Songs of worship received far less radio exposure than hillbilly, and for years a majority of black churchgoers looked askance at gospel music's embrace of modern instruments and syncopation. Gospel coursed north through many of the same furrows bloodied by Sherman's March through the Confederacy, and by the turn of the century, the Fisk Jubilee Singers (who continued to tour with replacements as original members dropped out) and the myriad troupes that sprang up in their wake had created a vast market for spirituals, not only as a concert attraction, but as product in the form of sheet music.

In 1901, a Philadelphia-based black Methodist minister named Charles A. Tindley began to compose and self-publish original hymns. A well-known proponent of racial equality, Tindley publicly denounced blackface theatrics and was injured in a demon-

Hank Williams and band posing at a 1949 Nashville recording session. Williams, who learned to play guitar "from an old colored man," worked at a different kind of soul—singing country tunes from the aching void of a troubled marriage, a bad back, and frequent bouts with alcohol. (Frank Driggs Collection)

stration while railing against D.W. Griffith's defamatory portrayal of blacks on-screen in *The Birth of a Nation*. Tindley's works included "The Lord Will Make a Way," "What Are They Doing in Heaven Today?," and a piece he first titled "I'll Overcome Someday," which evolved over time into the civil rights anthem, "We Shall Overcome."

In 1910, a white choirmaster named Homer A. Rodeheaver began to publish the black-derived religious music he heard while touring alongside evangelist Billy Sunday. The first of these were considered no more than the latest iterations of "sorrow" and "jubilee" spirituals that had been accumulating since the Civil War. Over time, Rodeheaver's collection grew to include the enduring standards "His Eye Is on the Sparrow" and "The Old Rugged Cross." Taken together, the assortment displays a stark contrast between spirituals and this newer music, dubbed "sanctified" because of its origins in the Pentecostal church. In retrospect, spirituals can be seen as black-derived music from the fields being made palatable to the masses via white reinterpretation, while the nascent gospel sound suggests that blacks were returning to vocal traditions from the slave centuries and before.

Numerous black congregations prohibited music of any kind, believing it opened the door to sensuality. Conversely, the sect of Primitive Baptists only forbade instruments. Much of their music was sung a cappella (another characteristic of spirituals), but these churches welcomed any kind of accompaniment the human body could provide, including clapping, patting, and stomping. Their services were worlds apart from the conservative praise-singing heard in white churches. Primitive Baptists were among the so-called "holy roller" sects reinvestigating their cultural heritage. They sang much as their ancestors had—throats wide open, punctuating phrases with call-and-response, falsetto, and embellishments from the blues scale—all while following a leader who provided the starting pitch. As a chorus, they were at once completely united and disparate individuals, with the ensemble anchoring the melodic line while various soloists tagged in and out to urge the song to climax.

By the early part of the 20th century, the shouts, calls, and hollers once used in the fields were welcomed indoors as an integral part of black Pentecostal worship. These services bore at least a passing resemblance to camp meetings of a hundred years before, where penitents were derided for their pursuit of religious ecstasy through music. The controversy now reignited in the teens and early 1920s, with church members debating whether this strain of sacred music was "too worldly" and its celebrants too intoxicated by its persuasive tug.

A variety of sanctified services were released in their entirety during the 1920s, with music and sermons featured side by side. At the time, a popular religious recording ("The Downfall of Nebuchadnezzar," by Reverend J.C. Burnett, for example) could outsell a blues record by someone of Bessie Smith's stature nearly four to one. Okeh Records, already an established entity with a roster of secular artists, recorded some 30 tunes by a blind Dallas gospel singer named Arizona Dranes between 1926 and 1928. Although the spread of gospel was undoubtedly stunted by the Great Depression, recorded gospel began to soar commercially in the 1930s when quartet singing came into vogue. Ensembles included the Dixie Jubilee Singers (who recorded "Swing Low, Sweet Chariot" on film for a 1929 musical called *Hallelujah*), Reverend Tindley's group—the Tindley Quaker City Gospel Singers—and the Famous Blue Jay Singers.

The man most responsible for forging a gospel sound by combining hymns and spirituals with elements of black secular music was Thomas Dorsey (who was black and no relation of the swinging Dorsey brothers). Dorsey began his music career as a pianist known as Georgia Tom, Texas Tommy, Smokehouse Charley, or Barrelhouse Tom, depending on the occasion and locale. He served as aide-de-camp to Ma Rainey during the peak of her career in the early 1920s, and for a while, it seemed he might juggle careers between sacred and secular music. Dorsey relished personal freedom and loved music, but as a minister's son, he was well acquainted with the serenity claimed by those who renounced temptations of the flesh. Like many who would follow the same path (including Little Richard, Elvis Presley, Donna Summer, and Prince), Dorsey equivocated through the 1920s, trying to see which was the better fit for him. In 1921, he composed a religious tune called "If I Don't Get There" before returning to work with Rainey.

In 1928, Dorsey had a mainstream hit (with the innuendo-drenched "It's Tight Like That") before permanently settling on a life in religious music. He joined Chicago's Pilgrim Baptist Church and composed his most famous works, including "Take My Hand, Precious Lord" in 1932 and the enduring classic, "Peace In the Valley" (written for his protégé, Mahalia Jackson), in 1939. At first, congregants were uneasy with the confessional and bluesy elements of Dorsey's work, but as throngs soon discovered, his tunes were spectacularly successful in transporting worshippers from the here-and-now into a state of devotional rapture.

Entertainers on the church circuit came to regard religious hysteria as a barometer of their appeal. Groups calling themselves the Pilgrim Travelers, Golden Gate Quartet, and Soul Stirrers (which included Sam Cooke through most of the 1950s) took it upon themselves as a sacred quest to make sure the congregation was "swept up in the spirit." Traveling from town to town, they quickly took the congregation's pulse, then worked the crowd into a state of uncontrolled jubilation. It became a mission superseded only by hitting the notes and staying in time.

In *You Send Me*, Sam Cooke biographer Daniel Wolff says the phenomenon earned a nickname. "It all turned on Sister Flute," he writes. "That's what the Stirrers called her, a name they'd first heard around New York City. There was a Sister Flute in every congregation: the archetypal church mother, the one who started the shouting. When she fell out—when she danced the holy dance and locked rigid with the Spirit, so caught in the throes of possession that the deacons had to come and wrestle her back into the pew so that she wouldn't hurt herself, her eyes rolled up, her heels pounding the hard wood floor, her best Sunday hat crushed and forgotten beside her—once Sister Flute got to moaning and amening, the rest would follow."[3]

Some churches embraced Sister Flute, while others took pains to ensure she would never be summoned. Future gospel star Mahalia Jackson was more eager to hear Ma Rainey and Bessie Smith records than what was being provided by New Orleans' traditional Baptist services. She'd slip across town to the Holiness church, where waves of sanctified passion crashed in around her and carried her away. No choir. No organ. It seems the only instruments were percussion—triangles, cymbals, tambourines, and drums. But, as Jackson says in *You Send Me*, "Everybody in there sang, and they clapped and stomped their feet and sang with their whole bodies. They had a beat, a rhythm we held onto from slavery days, and their music was strong and expressive. It used to bring tears to my eyes."

Progressives in the church claimed that "falling out" had a basis in scripture (one frequently cited passage had to do with "making a joyful noise unto the Lord"), while traditionalists disapproved of such histrionics and challenged the faith of gospel singers who performed secular music in nightclubs and concert halls. Prime offenders—aside from Dorsey himself—included "Sister" Rosetta Tharpe, who recorded Dorsey's "Hide Me in Thy Bosom" under an alternate title, "Rock Me." She also signed a mainstream contract with Decca Records and had a string of well-known hits, ranging from the gospel-tinged "Down By the Riverside" to "My Man and I." At least one surviving film captures a gospel choir clustered around Sister Tharpe while she shouts a bluesy paean to heaven and negotiates a series of flashy riffs on her guitar.

Mahalia Jackson and Clara Ward (another Dorsey discovery and one of the greatest influences on Aretha Franklin) seldom strayed from religious material, although Jackson was

After gospel music gave birth to doo-wop and the rhythm and blues music of the 1950s, it returned to the churches and auditoriums from which it sprang. Singers like Cissy Houston continued to work the same magic on congregants and secular crowds, though, and provided not only a musical foundation but inspiration to artists ranging from Aretha Franklin to her stylistic descendants, including Mariah Carey and neo-soul singers Jill Scott, Angie Stone, and Alicia Keys. (Jim Cummins/Star File)

signed for a time to Columbia Records. She relocated from New Orleans to Chicago in 1927, and became Dorsey's frequent musical partner for the next fifteen years. After working as a nurse and a domestic, Jackson finally became a professional singer after a record executive heard her sing at a funeral. By 1947, she was gospel music's most recognized voice and scored the genre's first million seller, "I Will Move on Up a Little Higher."

What began in the fields and became legitimized by the church soon gained renown elsewhere. In the late 1930s, John Hammond produced a pair of concerts at Carnegie Hall to showcase the breadth and sophistication of American black music. The first was staged on December 23, 1938 as a tribute to the recently deceased Bessie Smith. Segments of the program offered up spirituals and Holy Roller hymns, blues, harmonica playing, boogie-woogie piano, swing, and New Orleans jazz. The following year, the presentation was even more audacious: *From Spirituals to Swing* featured Count Basie and his band (Charlie Christian sat in to trade licks with his inspiration, Lester Young) and Benny Goodman's mixed-race sextet, with vibe virtuoso Lionel Hampton and Christian on guitar. The bill also included blues singer Ida Cox and spirituals by the Golden Gate Quartet.

In Washington a year later, black concert singer Marian Anderson's bid to sing at Constitution Hall was thwarted by the Daughters of the American Revolution. She resorted instead to an outdoor performance at the Lincoln Memorial, where she sang "My Country, 'Tis of Thee" before a large audience that included first lady Eleanor Roosevelt. (Anderson would have an encore, too: she returned to the site in August 1963 for the March on Washington, where she performed "He's Got the Whole World in His Hands" on the same program that included Martin Luther King's "I Have a Dream" speech.)

Throughout the 1930s and 1940s, vocal groups sliced through the blare of big band music, with a few black ensembles managing to dent the pop market. In 1940, the all-black Ink Spots cut "When the Swallows Come Back to Capistrano," a record that made such an impact that even cartoon characters were heard singing it. Like their contemporaries the Mills Brothers, the Ink Spots were seasoned performers (the Mills Brothers had been around since 1922; the Ink Spots formed in 1934) famed for their close harmonies and clean-cut style. During much of the swing era, the Mills Brothers provided velvety vocal beds for tracks led by Louis Armstrong, Bing Crosby, and Ella Fitzgerald, while the Ink Spots quietly racked up hits, including "If I Didn't Care" and "Glow Worm."

More than a century before, black singers found common ground with whites in praise singing. Now many white listeners recognized similarities to barbershop harmony in the vocal blend of gospel quartets. These sounds became increasingly familiar to listeners during the ASCAP/ Broadcast Music Incorporated (BMI) licensing battle that lasted through most of World War II. Numerous performers slipped through the quarantine by recording a cappella, leading to hits by Frank Sinatra (backed by the Bobby Tucker Singers), Bing Crosby (fronting Trudey Erwin and the Sportsmen Glee Club), and the Mills Brothers, who scored the biggest record of the decade with "Paper Doll" in 1942.

Billboard magazine dropped its references to "race records" that same year, opting to call its chart of top sellers "The Harlem Hit Parade." (Two years later, editors introduced the first country survey, "Most Played Juke Box Folk Records.") *Billboard* reporter Jerry Wexler tweaked the title yet again in the summer of 1949. Wexler renamed the Harlem listings "Rhythm and Blues," although as it has often been pointed out, the records represented were not required to be either rhythmic or bluesy. Rather, the term was universally understood to connote black music without ever actually mentioning race. Today, that phrase has been replaced with the equally ambiguous and more politically correct term, "urban."

In the calm between World War II and the threat of communism rising in the East, popular music took a backseat to other concerns. Records by bandleaders Desi Arnaz and David Rose ("Babalu" and "Holiday for Strings," respectively) continued to sell, and by 1947 the industry finally broke its pre-Depression sales record set a quarter of a century earlier. Music was sound business again—pun intended—but hardly a galvanizing cultural force. Postwar consumers had more interest in cars, appliances, and basking in the soothing cathode glow of television than in what was topping the current Hit Parade.

TOO MARVELOUS FOR WORDS

Returning GIs stormed the business world with the same vigor they'd shown on the beaches of Normandy, resulting in a proliferation of independent record labels and newly licensed radio stations popping up everywhere—all of them looking for That Thing that would make them stand out from everyone else.

Depending on one's personal politics, the 1950s was either the decade when the country started to grasp its preeminence on the world stage or a time when Americans began to believe their own hype. After the tribulations of the Great Depression and World War II, white Americans returned home to family incomes that had doubled during the war. Those of black households tripled. What could possibly be beyond the country's reach? The United States split the atom, stopped polio in its tracks, and invented the freeway and fast food. President Truman integrated the armed forces in 1950. America was now the home of Marilyn Monroe and Joe DiMaggio, a place where white-gloved policemen in double-breasted tunics stood on street corners ready to assist a senior citizen or help a lost child find his or her mommy. For some it was the societal ideal. For the rest, it was a velvet coffin—ornate, constricting, and emblematic of a premature surrender to conformity.

Either way, Utopia didn't last long. Norman Rockwell scarcely got it all down on canvas when the juvenile delinquents of rock 'n' roll began to mock the nation's self-congratulatory grandeur. America entered the decade as one people—with blacks as second-class citizens, but complacently so to white eyes—and ended it a nation straining at the seams. The same white working-class couples who helped win World War II suddenly saw their suburban preserve under siege. On one front, they were beset by blacks who wanted into the world of white prosperity. On the other, they were being betrayed by their own children, privileged kids trapped inside someone else's dream of success and stifled by the ennui of their own affluence.

As a result of changing child labor laws and the postwar economic boom, America had a new citizen and a new subculture: the teenager. Prior to the Depression and World War II, adolescents were either children (under twelve) or "young men and women," subject to spontaneous tirades on the gravity of impending adulthood. (Contrast that to the era's black youth, who remained all but invisible.) In 1937, the *Andy Hardy* film comedies introduced Mickey Rooney as a teenager improvising his way into maturity. His missteps invited homilies not only from his father the judge, but from anyone else in the adult world who cared to offer a reprimand. While Rooney's antics and romance with Judy Garland did respectable business at the box office, other moviegoers were more taken with a group of miscreants from the far end of the social spectrum. In a Humphrey Bogart whodunit released that same year, *The Dead End Kids* burst onto the screen with a Bugs Bunnyesque sarcasm that earned the young actors instant acclaim, and soon they were the stars of their own low-budget capers. The Kids glamorized petty crime and contempt for their elders, rebelled through the clothes they wore, and spoke in a nearly impenetrable convolution of jive and Brooklynese. Over time, the core group—which included Leo Gorcey and Huntz Hall—morphed into the East Side Kids and the Bowery Boys, but by the release of their last film in the late 1950s, the damage was done. Adolescents had learned to defy authority.

BLUE EYES

As before, Americans felt the need to establish an identity wholly separate from one's parents. But the swing-obsessed jitterbugs of a generation earlier raised more amusement than concern, and were considered no more dangerous than the flappers of the 1920s for whom rebellion was a brief stopover on the road to adulthood. All of that changed in 1942 with the arrival of a blue-eyed stack of bones from Hoboken, New Jersey calling himself Frank Sinatra. Within three short years, Sinatra had gone from singing as a restaurant waiter to fronting the Harry James Orchestra and on to become the voice of Tommy Dorsey's world famous big band.

What separated Sinatra from the competition was not just the stick-figure physique that made bobby-soxers (girls still too young for nylons) want to drag him home for a hot meal and a night of passion. Sinatra contrived to distinguish himself in any way possible from his contemporaries. He was the first modern white vocalist to invest emotion in the lyrics he sang, a trait he later attributed in part to Billie Holiday. A longtime smoker, Sinatra swam in order to expand his lung capacity, which allowed him to sculpt phrases for dramatic effect and hold notes long after most singers had blown themselves out. The singer also used his wistful songs to mold a romantic public persona, and, in him, crush-prone girls found the ideal receptacle for their budding sexual fantasies. Sinatra became the modern archetype of youthful yearning nicely done up in a suit and bow tie.

While black singers had been displaying real emotion in song for some time (and few country singers had delved so deeply), the early Sinatra style was considered overwrought in many white circles. To those looking in on Sinatra-mania from the outside, he was less a singer than a flimsy excuse for pubescent girls to swoon. More staid settings revealed him to be a vocalist of marked restraint, and one who constantly impressed even the most jaded musical collaborators. In 1943, an East Coast society gig at the Waldorf-Astoria put New York's elite in his back pocket—a feat he'd already managed before an audience of skeptical Californians a few months earlier. When symphonies around the country were strapped for cash, Sinatra bolstered his own stock by appearing at the Hollywood Bowl alongside the Los Angeles Philharmonic (although one attending soldier-turned-critic remarked to his companion, "I hope they won't forget to flush the Bowl"). But Frank could also be his own worst enemy. From the outset of his career, he engaged in a series of love/hate relationships—with the press, with his fans, and with his own image. He enjoyed the ingenues (privately sampling their favors on innumerable occasions), but longed to be taken seriously as an artist; he worked hard for approval, but lashed out at those who dared disagree with him; and his tenderness at the microphone evaporated when he heard the stage door catch behind him. He was a tough SOB who relished and nurtured his mob associations, even when they later cost him his friendship with playboy president John F. Kennedy.

For those born after his first two careers—first as a teen heartthrob and second as a movie star and nightclub überswinger—the pop landscape without a Frank Sinatra is unimaginable. Certainly before him there had been media idols—Valentino providing an oft-cited example. But until Sinatra, none of them were artists who could greet everyday people on their own turf, then transport them to another plane of existence. Sinatra used his songbook to craft an idyllic dreamscape, and his strength of conviction as a singer allowed legions of lovestruck fans to buy into it as well. Bing Crosby, Sinatra's early hero and immediate predecessor as a singing icon, was detached and aloof. Sinatra was anything but. Sometime later, writer Gene Lees described Frank's gift succinctly: "After Sinatra, if you sounded like him you were imitating, but if you didn't, you sounded like you were doing it wrong."

At least some of Sinatra's impact can be chalked up to serendipity. Commercially and artistically, he was as much the right man at the right place at the right time that Elvis Presley would prove to be in 1956. But he also sought every opportunity to press an advantage. When Sinatra began entertaining during the big band era, vocalists were but one component at a bandleader's disposal. They were featured soloists, but hardly stars in their own right and no more highly valued than a talented clarinet or trombone player. Vocalists were to be heard but seldom seen, and were usually kept seated beside the orchestra until the time came to offer up a chorus. Then, on cue, the singer would stroll to the microphone and enter a phrase with all the pizzazz of a spelling bee contestant before returning to be seated once more. Sinatra helped change all that. When public tastes shifted from swing to the more soothing alternatives, pop vocalists appeared to fill the void, and suddenly Sinatra and his contemporaries became front men for their bands and rarely left the limelight.

During his formative years, popular songs were also in transition, evolving from statements without subtext (think "Happy Days Are Here Again") into more varied expressions. By the time Sinatra left the Dorsey band for a solo career in the mid-1940s, he was picking new material to address a more sophisticated listening audience; the result would be an entire genre known by century's end as "standards." Sure, the era's composers could be a bit Goody Two-shoes—"Zing! Went the Strings of My Heart" and "Ac-cent-tchu-ate the Positive" leap to mind—but with Cole Porter, the Gershwins, and Irving Berlin providing a template, many tunesmiths pushed past clichés to create statements of profound beauty and subtlety. "Night and Day," "Someone to Watch Over Me," and "All of Me" were early choices that demonstrated Sinatra's intuition not only for what clicked with his voice and image, but what would appeal to the public.

All of these developments combined to make contemporary tunes more reflective of real people with real emotions, which included naked lust and loves that somehow didn't last forever. Pop fare could still be ridiculously childlike, and would remain so with such novelty hits as "I'm Looking Over a Four-Leaf Clover" and "How Much Is That Doggy in the Window?" yet to come. Sinatra suggested an alternative. When he resurfaced in 1952 on Capitol Records after a dry spell, his voice boomed with a newfound authority and crept through torch songs with an ache fleshed out by experience. Unlike Crosby, who kept his own counsel and whose skeletons remained closeted until after his death, Sinatra wore his public wounds (many self-inflicted) with pride, and they added luster to his performances on record. These were the sides that inspired vocalists on both sides of the color line, from Nat "King" Cole and Billy Eckstine to Peggy Lee and Bobby Darin.

Debates about whether Sinatra was a jazz or pop singer miss the point, because Sinatra rewrote the template in his own image. His material may have been middle of the road, but jazz phrasing and rhythm were integral to Sinatra's swing. By comparison, most of his white male contemporaries sound like pitchmen crooning jingles. Because his rhythmic judgment was sound and his belief in portraying the emotions of a lyric so right (who would argue the logic in presenting a song the way an actor would flesh out a character role?), they became the new gold standard and transformed the way white artists in particular approached a song. His palate of vocal colors became so widely copied that Frank eventually risked self-parody in using them. Such second-tier talents as Vic Damone, Perry Como, and Steve Lawrence forged entire careers as Sinatra copycats; others—Tony Bennett, Mel Torme, and Harry Connick, Jr. included—have acquitted themselves intermittently by trying to extrapolate from what Sinatra began.

African Americans developed a taste for Sinatra as well; to some he represented what could happen when whites finally internalized the siren call of black-inflected music and put it to use in their own work. Frank showed what it was to loosen up and start to swing. All of this was made more palatable for blacks by the fact that Sinatra was nearly reckless in his support of civil rights. In 1945, he sponsored an Oscar-winning documentary short called "The House I Live In," which depicted him preaching racial harmony to schoolchildren and performing the title song written by the same Lewis Allen who composed "Strange Fruit." The gesture earned him cachet in the black community, but aroused suspicion wherever discrimination remained in vogue.

SEPIA SINATRAS

Another catchphrase of the era arose during the controversy of the Supreme Court's 1954 antisegregation ruling in *Brown vs. the Topeka Board of Education*. The notion of "separate but equal" was not a new one, and was often applied in disciplines far from the political arena. Since Sinatra had come to embody America's notion of the modern metropolitan Casanova, it made good sense to groom and market a black counterpart.

Fortunately, the best song interpreters cast from the Sinatra mold proved better suited to portray themselves. Nat "King" Cole was a Chicago transplant who moved to Los Angeles at the crest of big band swing. Cole honed his deft keyboard touch in a constellation of race-mixing nightspots, working with small bands and a group of jamming buddies that included a pair of electric guitar pioneers, black bandmate Oscar Moore and white guitar legend Les Paul. Since a Los Angeles statute prohibited clubs with a white clientele from admitting blacks and the Negro Musicians' Union (Local 767) forbade its members from playing impromptu, Cole and his pals learned to keep one eye on the bandstand and the other scanning the entrances and exits. As added insurance, they all had numerous stage aliases—Les Paul was Paul Leslie, and Nat was alternately Shorty Nadine, Sam Schmaltz, and—after the title of one of his songs—"Nature Boy."

Cole earned his reputation as an inventive jazz pianist, but what endeared him to mainstream America was his strangely arresting vocal approach. Where Sinatra ad-libs in-

Nat "King" Cole, one of many to wear the "sepia Sinatra" mantle, posing alongside Francis Albert Sinatra, the man who revolutionized popular singing in the 1940s. Their emotive styles influenced generations of vocalists to come, from Tony Bennett to Harry Connick, Jr. and Norah Jones. (Frank Driggs Collection)

cluded the occasional "koo koo" or "ring-a-ding-ding," Cole articulated every syllable as though he'd been coached by *My Fair Lady*'s Henry Higgins. This was black music that white America could embrace without self-reflection, because Cole sounded—thanks to Sinatra—whiter than the white guy next door. It should have sounded stilted, but it didn't, and it shouldn't have worked, but it did. Like Sinatra, Cole was blessed with an internal jazz metronome that kept his music swinging even when the arrangements were syrupy and the lyrics pretentious. Moreover, Cole proved before James Brown, Otis Redding, or Mick Jagger that clever wordplay runs a poor second to emotion when trying to convey the essence of a song. Ella Fitzgerald and Louis Armstrong knew this, and toyed with colloquialisms and scat singing. Cole did the opposite. While the lyrics of his story songs ("Mona Lisa," "Too Young," and "Unforgettable" were among the biggest) were understood with crystalline clarity the first time through, Cole infused them with a winking nuance that intrigued and delighted his fans.

Because his piano technique appealed to hardcore boppers (their sole complaint was that he didn't play jazz often enough) and his pop vocals endeared him to middle America, Cole became one of the first modern artists to "cross over" from black to white popularity. By 1956, his track record stretched back more than a decade to include such gems as "(Get Your Kicks) on Route 66," the Yuletide classic "Christmas Song" (". . . Chestnuts roasting on an open fire . . ."), and a Charlie Chaplin evergreen called "Smile." But the year was to be the singer's rockiest yet. On a promotional swing through the South, Cole and the other acts on the bill played to segregated houses in Texas, and then moved on to a two-show appearance scheduled for April 10 in Birmingham, Alabama, where Nat's sister had been born.

The first concert was intended for an all-white crowd, while the second would allow Cole's black fans to see him perform. Midway through the second number of the first show, five white men jumped onstage and scuffled with the artist, one of them knocking him onto his piano bench with force enough to make it split. While the stunned police clambered onstage to subdue Cole's assailants, one of them grabbed the singer's leg and began twisting it. Visibly shaken, Cole hobbled offstage, but returned to take a bow and apologize for not continuing. He explained, "I just came here to entertain you. That's what I thought you wanted." Nat did perform the second, all-black show as scheduled, but not before confessing his disillusionment. "Man, I love show business," he confided backstage. "But I don't want to die for it."

Vindication of sorts arrived six months later when NBC announced they would be giving Cole his very own variety series on television. The program first aired in November—without sponsors, since most advertisers were afraid to put money behind "a colored entertainer." The network was so strongly committed to the idea that they considered the program a loss leader, and reviews suggested that if the company could hold out long enough, advertisers would see the wisdom in reaching millions of black and white music fans devoted to the show. After less than a year on the air, NBC expanded the series from 15 minutes to a full half hour, and many of Cole's celebrity pals dropped by to endorse him. Just as a few daring advertisers offered some financial daylight, the network inexplicably began shuffling the show's airtime in the NBC lineup, making it difficult for viewers to find. Shaky support from within and without convinced Cole to decline a renewal, and it wasn't until NBC introduced the Diahann Carroll sitcom *Julia* in 1968 that a black performer would headline a network series again.

Other entrants in the Sinatra derby included the Bay Area's Johnny Mathis, whose supper club aplomb scored points on both sides of the color line. Madison Avenue couldn't have created a better product to promote assimilation than Mathis, with his quavering vibrato, gently processed hair, and preppy *savoire faire*. He didn't have Cole's reputation as a virtuoso, but "It's Not for Me to Say," "Misty," and "Chances Are" (his hits between 1957 and 1959) showcase a voice that's as slick as Cole's but more nuanced and loose. Blacks who believed Cole was clipping his diction to appeal to whites had less trouble with Mathis' saccharine, emotive delivery.

Guiding Mathis' career was Columbia Records chorus master Mitch Miller, who handpicked much of the material and personally crafted the arrangements. Miller's treatments coated Mathis' voice in a candy shell, nearly overwhelming the singer's mollified ethnicity. Mathis' place in the pop music firmament remains unclear as a result. For years, he has been criticized for downplaying his heritage in order to boost sales, while those who can separate Mathis' talent from his image hold him in higher regard. While Mathis was not often seen at the leading edge of civil rights marches, he supported causes with generous donations and charity work. Not everyone is meant to storm the battlements with banner in hand, and if Mathis' only crime is to have made memorable pop records (admittedly, some sound cheesy by today's standards), then that work should be allowed to speak for itself.

Any number of black vocalists have tried on the Sinatra persona since. Sam Cooke and Marvin Gaye both held aspirations in that direction (Sam more concerned with cracking the casinos of Las Vegas; Marvin more interested in suave bachelor swing). In the early 1970s, even the pubescent Michael Jackson posed underneath a single streetlamp, overcoat slung over his tuxedoed shoulder and a Sinatra-esque fedora perched atop his enormous afro. But none blur the line between Sinatra's black and white influences more dramatically than Sinatra's showbiz pal, Sammy Davis, Jr.

Davis was born in Harlem in 1925 to a pair of vaudevillians; his mother was a chorus girl and his father one of the featured dancers with a group led by headliner Will Mastin. As a three year old, young Sammy was awarded ten dollars and a trophy for his own hoofing in a Philadelphia amateur contest, and his father immediately reinvested the winnings in a pair of tap shoes for his son. The boy's precocity landed him a role opposite Ethel Waters in a 1933 film short called *Rufus Jones for President*. In it, the diminutive Davis nods off in his mother's arms to dream he's been elected to the highest office in the land, and in the process delivers a startlingly assured rendition of Louis Armstrong's "I'll Be Glad When You're Dead, You Rascal You." Davis Sr. and his son worked in pared-down versions of the Will Mastin Trio throughout the Depression until Sammy the younger was drafted during World War II.

Military service became one long stream of racially motivated attacks, Davis recounts in his autobiography, *Yes I Can*. At 5'3" and 115 pounds, Sammy was easy pickings for anyone who wanted to bully a black recruit. All of this came as a huge surprise to Davis because, like the black minstrels of yesteryear, he had been sheltered by life on the Chitlin Circuit, where the people he met knew him as a talent, if not a star. Davis went through the Army's basic training four times. He heard himself regularly referred to as "nigger," and had his nose broken in a fight after he refused to dance for his tormentors and swig from their beer bottle filled with urine. On another occasion, when a group of GIs caught

No matter how many stars surrounded him, Sammy Davis, Jr. did his best to shine the brightest of the bunch. More than most of his peers, Davis was caught between the pre–civil rights notions of blacks in entertainment and the Black Power movement of the soul era. Here in 1950, Davis is flanked by singer Patti Page and swing sensation Benny Goodman. (Frank Driggs Collection)

him chatting up a white woman, they ambushed Davis in the latrine and whitewashed his body in obscene graffiti.

After the war, Davis rejoined Mastin and his father and renewed an old acquaintance with Frank Sinatra, whom he'd met before the war while Sinatra was fronting the Dorsey band. By the 1950s, Davis had become Frank's favorite vanity project. Sinatra insisted the Mastin Trio open for him in New York and threw his considerable weight behind making sure Sammy was treated no less deferentially than Frank himself in social situations.

Davis repaid Sinatra with an unwavering loyalty and emulated his ring-a-ding style so closely that Frank had to warn him off. Davis outlasted vaudeville, but it left its stamp on him, even after the Mastin Trio finally dissolved in the mid-1950s. Sammy could dance, but not innovate. He was a nondescript singer who sold his tunes through dint of personality rather than vocal technique, and as a film actor, he worked too hard to create believable characters. He was far better suited to stage work, where his workaholic ethic paid off with the 1956 success of *Mr. Wonderful* and a Tony nomination a decade later for *Golden Boy* (he lost to *Fiddler on the Roof* star Zero Mostel). The original *Golden Boy* score contains "Yes, I Can," a song Davis identified with enough to give his autobiography the same title.

Audiences and critics agreed that Davis poured heart and soul into every performance, and that the results were often showstopping. But they had a harder time forgiving his off-stage excesses—the pursuit of white women and white affluence, and an unflagging enthusiasm to act as Sinatra's personal prop. Of course Sinatra loved it. He used Sammy onstage to set up object lessons on racial tolerance that created a scene more often than a statement. When they performed as part of the Rat Pack (alongside Dean Martin, Kennedy-in-law Peter Lawford, and comedian Joey Bishop), their schtick veered wildly from slick to smarmy and back again. Much of their onstage patter survives on recordings as a reminder that all present enjoyed their concoction of arrogance, brotherly love, and misogyny punctuated by song snippets and movie star impressions. A live album called *The Summit* was recorded on the outskirts of Chicago in 1962, and it fixes each in his role. (Joey Bishop, the group's usual color commentator, is replaced on this occasion by a bewildered Johnny Carson, while Peter Lawford is AWOL as well.) Here, Sinatra is the emcee, Martin the drunk, and Davis the earnest kid whom the others tease with racial (but not rac*ist*) jokes and occasional comments about his stature and conversion to Judaism. "How did that little ol' colored Jewish boy get out on the stage?" typifies the Sinatra one-liner. Dean and Frank are playful and relaxed, but Sammy is in full-court press at every turn, and is caught once again straining from exertion. In the end, he remains third of three and finds himself in the most ironic of duets opposite Sinatra: "Me and My Shadow."

Sammy Davis, Jr. matters now because he so visibly and uncomfortably straddled the fence between what had been demanded of blacks in America during his youth and what they would soon demand for themselves in his maturity. He was active in the civil rights movement and supported liberal democrats Robert Kennedy and Hubert Humphrey, but is best remembered for snuggling up to Richard Nixon. At his worst, he actually chastised Louis Armstrong for taking a stand against racism in 1957 when Satchmo refused to represent America as a goodwill ambassador abroad while black children were being denied entry to Arkansas schools at home. Davis joined a chorus of black and white detractors (including the well-known black leader Adam Clayton Powell, Jr.) to rebuke Armstrong, who Davis felt "did not speak for the Negro people." On October 12, a reporter from *The Pittsburgh Courier* quoted Sammy denouncing Armstrong for condemning separate-but-equal practices in education while continuing to play segregated venues, "which Satchmo has done for many years."

Understandably, those who follow in Sammy's wake remain divided on his legacy. Actor and dancer Gregory Hines stooped to kiss his shoes during a television tribute taped just before Davis died in 1990. Producer Quincy Jones is quoted in a Sammy Davis CD anthology saying, "A lot of young black entertainers don't understand all that Sammy did for them, but the truth is there's a lot of his blood on their road to success."

On the other hand, singer-songwriter Bill Withers contends that "the only thing Sammy Davis integrated was Las Vegas. He didn't integrate America. Sammy Davis being able to sleep in a hotel in Las Vegas didn't have a damned thing to do with whether somebody was going to take me seriously in my profession or not. When I was trying to convince people that I could work on their airplanes and fix them, and they won't crash (Withers' day job before his music career took off), that has not a damned thing to do with Sammy Davis, Jr. hanging out in Las Vegas with Dean Martin and sleeping with some showgirl with blonde hair. The two don't relate. It's nice and it's idealistic, but one has nothing to do with the other."

Davis got a few lucky breaks, but most came at a price. The public could have embraced his performance as Sportin' Life in MGM's 1959 remake of *Porgy and Bess*, but they were more interested in his scandalous affair with a white Hollywood bombshell named Kim Novak. They could have sided with Sammy when he and another blonde bride-to-be, actress May Britt, were disinvited from John F. Kennedy's inaugural gala at Kennedy's insistence. Instead, the press castigated Davis for trying to live a white life in black skin, and the status quo agreed. They could have praised him for breaking the Vegas color barrier by being admitted to hotels and casinos where blacks before him were only allowed to serve or entertain. But instead, they saw him as grasping at the white acceptance that would never be his, flanked onscreen by Sinatra, Martin, and the other white Rat Packers, or spotted around town with a Swedish bride in tow. He sang, "I've Gotta Be Me," but who was he? "The Candy Man"? "Mr. Bojangles" in a jumpsuit and bowler? Penultimate hipster or pathetic square?

Sammy's dilemma was black America's struggle writ large. He longed for respect, but always seemed to be chasing approval. As a running gag on the 1960s comedy series *Laugh In*, Davis played a gavel-wielding soul brother who popped into sketches rapping, "Here Come Da Judge." But he could never really decide whether he belonged with the freedom fighters or with the cocktail set who shook their heads at such rabble.

MANNISH BOYS

Most of Sammy's contemporaries never got within spitting distance of the Sands, the Desert Inn, or the Frontier Hotel. Many began as sharecroppers' children in the South, where any hope of prosperity led inevitably to the job-rich cities. And while Davis was polishing a new extravaganza called "The Birth of the Blues" for his nightclub act in the 1950s, a slow parade of black Southerners drifted north to see the blues born again.

Americans collectively tightened their belts during the Great Depression, but this wave of black migrants knew the true meaning of deprivation. For them, mind-numbing factory jobs were a Godsend compared with manual labor or unemployment. Nearly three million of them trekked north in the decades between 1940 and 1960. In the sense that they were unskilled workers moving to the city for lower-echelon jobs, they resembled the former slaves who fled the South after emancipation. But in their favor, they did have both information and an infrastructure waiting. An already established network of friends and relatives provided valuable insights into how urban life worked, with its own pace and peculiar customs—including racism.

"I've seen more problems up North than I ever did in the South," claims blues guitarist Buddy Guy, who relocated from Baton Rouge, Louisiana to Chicago in the 1950s.

Urban bigotry, he says, differs from the rural variety. "I look at it like rattlesnakes," he explains. "There's poisonous snakes everywhere, but a rattlesnake will make a noise to let you know to get the hell out the way. Other poisonous snakes show up in other places where you don't expect to find them, and they don't warn you. They *show* you. They got neighborhoods in the North where they (whites) didn't want you living; in the South they wanted you around because you were working for them."

A good-sized metropolis like Philadelphia, Detroit, or Chicago could absorb thousands of these newcomers and render them invisible, but it could not smother their culture. When the job boom lured black Southerners to the cities in the late 1930s and early 1940s, Mississippi Delta music was among their undeclared baggage.

Radio became their common denominator and provided a conduit between the world they knew and the one they faced. In November of 1941, a harmonica player named Sonny Boy Williamson (born Willie Miller) joined Robert Johnson's stepson Robert "Junior" Lockwood to host a country blues–based program on KFFA in Helena, Arkansas. *King Biscuit Time*, named for the show's sponsor, proved so popular that the duo quickly expanded into a full-fledged group and later added a simulcast on WROX in Clarksdale, Mississippi.

These broadcasts brought the blues to its widest audience yet at the moment of its greatest change. Traditional views of the music as male dominated, acoustic, and mournful dissipated overnight. They were replaced by a new breed of blues artist steeped in the Mississippi Delta tradition, but also influenced by the abundance of jazz, folk, and pop music on the radio.

Encouraged by the success of *King Biscuit Time*, other stations tried their luck with blues programming. By the late 1940s, both Howlin' Wolf (Chester Burnett) and B.B. King hosted blues shows in Memphis, and, in 1951, Ike Turner began his own stint as a deejay in Clarksdale. By then, Lockwood and Williamson had become household names throughout the listening area, and they used *King Biscuit Time* as a bully pulpit for their favorite unknowns. A glance at their guest roster reads like a blues Who's Who. Studio visitors included Elmore James, "Little Walter" Jacobs, and a fiery young shouter named McKinley Morganfield, the man who would popularize the electric blues as Muddy Waters.

The son of a farmer, Waters spread the delta blues of his mentor Son House throughout the club circuit up and down the Mississippi. He traveled to St. Louis in 1940 and joined the Silas Green traveling tent show, and shortly thereafter, Library of Congress archivist Alan Lomax learned about Waters from a black scholar from Fisk University named John Work III. Lomax made the trek to Waters' home and recorded him there in the summer of 1941. Those recordings came and went without notice (in fact, Lomax never paid Waters the twenty bucks he promised for them), and Muddy returned to plantation work. But in 1943, Waters quit. Despite the fact that his field hand work kept him out of the war (he provided a "vital service" by harvesting cotton), and that he was already twice married and had children, Waters packed his bags and headed to Chicago. He settled in with a half sister and her husband, took a factory job, and set about establishing himself on the club circuit.

First and foremost, Muddy Waters was a realist and a utilitarian. He left the South because he knew he'd never escape poverty otherwise. He began playing electric guitar because no one could hear him over the din of a Chicago juke joint without amplification.

At the end of World War II, a former field hand named McKinley Morganfield electrified the blues as Chicago bluesman Muddy Waters. After an abortive attempt to find fame through archivist Alan Lomax in Mississippi, Waters moved north, where his earthy blend of blues and braggadocio quickly caught on with transplanted Southerners. (Frank Driggs Collection)

As he later recalled to biographer Jim Rooney, "When I went into the clubs, the first thing I wanted was an amplifier. Couldn't nobody hear you with an acoustic . . . you get a more pure thing out of an acoustic, but you get more noise out of an amplifier."

Muddy was also a proud man, and because amplification made his mistakes more apparent, he worked hard to develop a clean, direct style. He wisely surrounded himself with experienced specialists (pianist Sunnyland Slim, guitarist Jimmy Rodgers, and blues harp great Little Walter), then began boiling his sound down into a thick, pungent roux. The fearsome breadth of Waters' vision became apparent at Chess Records in the late 1940s, when each new release arrived like a battle cruiser sailing into a yacht club. Fat, seditious beats were bolstered by jabbing guitars and swirling harmonica fills. "Rolling Stone" was first, followed by "I Can't Be Satisfied" and "I Feel Like Going Home." Although he never had anything but the best sidemen (over the years, they included Otis Spann, James Cotton, and Buddy Guy), Waters' booming voice remained the focus of every track. His best records, "I Just Want to Make Love to You," "Mannish Boy," and "Got My Mojo Working" (all recorded between 1954 and 1956) packed enough sexual heat to be sold shrink-wrapped and marked for adults only.

Muddy Waters was the alpha male of the blues—the majestic, supremely self-confident sultan who could entice any woman into his harem. John Lee Hooker worked his charms from another angle entirely. He didn't seem to give a damn what men thought of themselves; he was all about the women. Where Muddy sauntered, John Lee seduced. For years, they jousted on the nation's jukeboxes, and if a randy customer with a handful of coins knew what he was doing, one of them would break the most strident lady's resolve. If Waters' bluster couldn't close the sale, Hooker could be summoned to whisper his stream-of-consciousness come-ons and visions of carnal delight. They made perfect foils.

On the occasion of Hooker's passing, sometime collaborator Bonnie Raitt looked back on their twenty-year friendship in *Rolling Stone* magazine. She reminisced about their duet on Hooker's "I'm in the Mood," clearly taken with this man several generations her senior and intrigued at the prospect of "playing his sexual foil for real." Raitt wrote that "we surprised each other, because after all the flirtation, it turned into something that made me shake in my boots a little bit. I was losing it. There's actually a point on the tape where I say, 'Man, I need a towel.'"

Hooker was raised in Clarksdale, Mississippi as one of eleven children. His early interest in music (he played an inner tube stretched across the family's barn door) was rewarded with guitar lessons from his stepfather, Will Moore. Today, Hooker is principally known as a singer-songwriter, but he never harbored any particular affinity for words, chords, or even melodies. For him, music began and ended with two elements: atmosphere and beat. Hooker's most representative work, "Boogie Chillen" (1948), "Boom Boom" (1962), and "One Bourbon, One Scotch, One Beer" (1966) seem dredged from the primordial ooze—someplace older than the blues, ancient and entrancing. In the liner notes to *The Very Best of John Lee Hooker*, Van Morrison allows that the Hooker style may be "repetitive, but it's never boring. He's like a shaman, a witch doctor."

The so-called "cock rock" bands of the early 1970s reinvigorated Waters' classics with a transfusion of hippie testosterone. Led Zeppelin covered "You Shook Me," "Good Morning Little Schoolgirl" became a Johnny Winter concert evergreen, and "I Just Want to Make Love to You" made Foghat a staple on FM radio. But Hooker remained the sole master of his own sound, despite a marketing scheme to pair him in his later years with such younger talents as Keith Richards, Carlos Santana, and Jimmie Vaughan. In the 1960s, British Invasion bands such as the Animals and Them cranked up their amps to cover Hooker's "Boom Boom," but they couldn't approach the mulekick of the original.

In 1951, Hooker's first recording of "I'm in the Mood" (on Modern Records) sold a million copies. Since he had the market on his own sound cornered, Hooker discs suddenly popped up on a half dozen labels under as many pseudonyms. From one tune to the next, he might be John Lee Booker, John Lee Cooker, Johnny Lee, Texas Slim, Delta John, Boogie Man, Birmingham Sam, or Johnny Williams. Fans weren't fooled for an instant. Clearly Hooker was a touchstone for those Southern newcomers who missed the sights and sounds of the world they'd surrendered. A new Hooker record, under any name, was as welcome as a home-cooked meal at Mama's house.

JUMP, JIVE, AND WAIL

Just as the joys and anxieties of city life reshaped the blacks who moved North, their music metamorphosed to keep pace. Nothing made that more evident than the ascent of the guitar through electricity. Overnight, amplification transformed the acoustic guitar from a time-keeping device into what players had been seeking for decades: a genuine solo instrument.

Charlie Christian was an early convert to electricity who sharpened his guitar skills in Oklahoma City—publicly on the road with the local Cotton Club Orchestra and privately under the tutelage of Chuck Richardson. Another of Richardson's pupils was a childhood friend of Christian's, a Dallas native named Aaron Thibeault (T-Bone) Walker. As a youth, Walker apprenticed himself to Blind Lemon Jefferson and later spent time as a sideman for Ma Rainey, Cab Calloway, and dancer Bill "Bojangles" Robinson. Blues guitar was merely Walker's means to an end; his real ambition was to be a star. Always as thrilled to watch a great show as to perform one, Walker was hugely impressed by the theatrics of Cab Calloway and his contemporaries. In his early solo days, T-Bone played banjo (louder than an acoustic and therefore harder to ignore, he reasoned) and while working as a dancer, his finale included hoisting and twirling a table—with his teeth.

The electric guitar gave the extroverted Walker his ticket to notoriety. In return, he gave succeeding generations their first lessons in stagecraft and established the guitar as an extension of the player's personality. Eschewing Christian's light touch, Walker developed a technique grafting bluesy melodies onto a swinging beat, thereby creating a hybrid that dancers soon dubbed "jump blues." As a composer, he held the copyright on the drowsy blues classic, "Stormy Monday"; as a performer, he was a city-slicker dandy who could play behind his back *while* doing the splits. As a picker, he remains in a class by himself. Echoes of his fretwork can be heard in B.B. King's single-note runs, the chord shadings that made Chuck Berry and Keith Richards famous, and the freewheeeling solos of Albert King, Eric Clapton, and Stevie Ray Vaughan.

The ingredients of jump blues came together as if some scavengers' party was assigned to collect anything that might aggravate a responsible parent. The squealing saxes and stripped-down beat were leftovers from swing, song lyrics were spiked with bawdy jokes and double-entendres, the accompanying dances called for vigorous body contact, and—most frightening of all—every element could be traced to black origins.

At the center of this roughhousing was Louis Jordan, a talented black sax player who rose from roadwork with the Rabbit Foot Minstrels (which at varying points also included Ma Rainey and Bessie Smith) to a spotlight role at the Savoy Ballroom with the Chick Webb Orchestra in 1936. Webb soon grew disenchanted with his discovery, perhaps because Jordan was one of the few who could pull focus from the band. A skillful player, Jordan was an incurable show-off who gave the audience more than their due and a capable vocalist who occasionally sang opposite Webb's star attraction, Ella Fitzgerald. Although Jordan was married and Ella barely out of her teens, the two took up an indiscreet romance, and within months, Jordan was fired.

During his tenure, however, Louis made a name for himself and vowed to form his own group. His swing experiments yielded little until he beefed up his sound while paring down the instruments. After carefully surveying the crowd during his gigs, Jordan began to construct records to magnify his party boy stage image (his first recording, in 1934, was "I Can't Dance, I Got Ants in My Pants"). Black and white, the public ate it up. His decision to approach everything he recorded with a sense of humor (including the ballads) resulted in a string of novelty hits, and, to complement his records, Jordan devised another gimmick. He'd get the drummer to play timpani. One day, when the instruments wouldn't fit onstage at one of his gigs, Jordan summarily dropped them from the act. Typically thereafter, the Tympany Five included six to eight members and no timpani whatsoever.

In 1938, a sanitized version of "Barnacle Bill the Sailor" set his course for the next quarter century. Jordan was a sponge for material, and paid for it wherever he found it, regardless of the composer's color. "I'm Gonna Move to the Outskirts of Town" hit as the nation was gearing up for World War II, and Jordan was seldom absent from the charts for the next ten years. "What's the Use of Gettin' Sober (When You're Gonna Get Drunk Again)" and "Five Guys Named Moe" were both Top Five hits on the Harlem Hit Parade in 1942 and 1943, respectively. In *Honkers and Shouters*, Jordan tells author Arnold Shaw that "Is You Is, or Is You Ain't (My Baby)?" (1944) and "Choo Choo Ch' Boogie"(1946) were both written by whites.

Jordan explained that "Is You Is, or Is You Ain't (My Baby)?" was written with a white man whom he met during an engagement at Lakota's Lounge in Milwaukee. "He was a little humpback fellow about the size of Chick Webb," he told Shaw. Every night, the fellow would drop in to work on the affections of a girl as if she were a math problem to be solved. "He just loved me," Jordan said to Shaw, "and he'd hang around so long as I was there. She'd be talkin' to someone else, and he'd say to her, 'Is you is or is you ain't ma baby?' And he was strictly Caucasian—no black blood in him at all. Soon I started sayin' it. And he said, 'Let's write a song.' You can't say because of color or race that a person would not say a thing or do a thing."

"Caldonia (What Makes Your Big Head So Hard?)" was written by Jordan, although credited to his wife of the time for financial reasons. "Saturday Night Fish Fry" paired Jordan with composer Ellis Walsh. "That's how we did it in the early '40s," he explained to Shaw, "so that we drew everybody. I was trying to do what they told me: straddle the fence. I made just as much money off white people as I did colored. I could play a white joint this week and a colored next."

To overlook a talent of Jordan's luminescence would have been difficult. He made certain it was impossible. Most of his songs feature him as lead vocalist, and he rarely allowed anyone else to solo during the instrumental breaks. Live, no one else worked the crowd as hard, and unlike many of his contemporaries, Jordan had no qualms about bugging out his eyes or cutting up if he thought it would win audience approval. He developed a character, "Deacon Jones," who sported a top hat, oversized white-frame glasses, a loud tie, and gloves—were he alive today, he could play Grandpa to Public Enemy's Flava Flav. Plans were made to feature Jordan and his band in an all-black film while the group was visiting Los Angeles in 1943. That deal fell apart, but led to three days of work filming *Follow the Boys* for Universal, in which Louis and His Tympany Five shot a film version of "Is You Is, or Is You Ain't (My Baby)?" In effect, Jordan used the movie to launch and promote his record. By the mid-1940s, he and the band also had a presence wherever "soundies" were offered, those being band performances played through a film-configured jukebox for ten cents a throw.

By marketing his sense of the absurd and completely saturating the existing media of the time, Louis Jordan made himself one of black America's most familiar faces. A native Arkansan, he toured the South throughout his career unfazed by Jim Crow laws or segregation. When "Caldonia" was made into a film short, *Billboard* magazine claimed the featurette was "one of the very few all-Negro productions to get bookings in Southern white theaters." In fact, the tune itself has something of an interracial history: In 1945, white bandleader Woody Herman caught a show with Louis and His Tympany Five and rushed to record the song, which was such a smash for Columbia that another version (by Erskine Hawkins) was rushed out by RCA Victor. Only then did Decca Records release Jordan's original, which proved a solid hit on its own.

"Mr. Personality," as he was now billed, began mounting small vignettes onstage to create lasting impressions of his songs. In "Beware" (1946), Louis slips into another comic role, acting this time as a hellfire-and-brimstone preacher lecturing his flock on the wiles of the fairer sex. It became an integral part of his stage show, just as Michael Jackson's live re-creations of the "Beat It" and "Thriller" videos evolved into set pieces that barely changed after 1984.

Aaron Izenhall, a longtime member of the Tympany Five, saw a rock 'n' roll sensibility creep into Jordan's act years before anyone understood what it was. "What Louis was trying to do was present his audiences with a Technicolor picture of a live band," he tells Jordan biographer John Chilton in *Let the Good Times Roll*, "getting the musicians to imitate a movie onstage. Eye-catching costumes and nonstop action lent the show a Hollywood flair, he says, "and that's what Louis wanted. We were the first one to wear those bright colors and that became an automatic part of rock, and even now you can go back to our version of 'Beware' and realize that it's the earliest sort of rap."

B.B. King had been watching the band's soundies for years by the time he first saw Jordan and company on stage. "He was a Louis Armstrong in his own way," says King, who released a Jordan tribute album during the swing revival of 1999. "And he made his own contribution, even if he hasn't gotten anywhere near the same amount of attention. He just had fun with lyrics, but he was bluesy with them when he wanted to be. He played jazz as well as most people I know; so he could do it all; he was way ahead of his time."

Jordan set the table for rock 'n' roll, and the swing revival of the late 1990s owes much of its sensibility to records by the Tympany Five and Cab Calloway. Their visuals may recall the Cotton Club in its heyday, but the attack is decidedly punk—since many of the players (including members of the Brian Setzer Orchestra, Big Bad Voodoo Daddy, Royal Crown Revue, and the ribald Cherry Poppin' Daddies) migrated to jump blues after early careers playing Ramones-derived rock. Their take on swing is less nuanced than the era that provided their inspiration, but as hits like "Jump, Jive, and Wail" and the Squirrel Nut Zippers' "Put a Lid on It" illustrate, the sense of mirth survives intact.

Those groups reconnected black music half a century old to the multiculti pop radio of the approaching millennium, an easy task considering that at its core, rock music has never strayed too long or far from the music of Jordan and his acolytes. In fact, it's arguable that Louis Jordan is responsible for much of what rock music has become since he first took the stage. Rock's propulsive rush of energy and carefree mischief were Jordan's stock-in-trade, and his interracial appeal certainly provided reassurance to artists like Chuck Berry and Berry Gordy that white audiences would spend money on black entertainers—if the product could be packaged attractively enough.

SOUL PROPRIETORS

Women were major contributors to the blues' metropolitan makeover at the end of the second World War. Like Muddy Waters, LaVern Baker got her start in Chicago. A few subway stops from Thomas Dorsey and Mahalia Jackson, Baker—billed as "Little Miss Sharecropper"—was singing the blues in small clubs. Her first recordings for an independent label (King) were trifles, but her luck changed after making the switch to the then-fledgling Atlantic Records. Together with contemporaries Ruth Brown and Etta James, Baker gave the 1950s "blues mama" image a modern makeover.

At first glance, Brown's "Mama, He Treats Your Daughter Mean" and Baker's "Jim Dandy" (1953 and 1956, respectively) appear cut from the same cloth as the cabaret woes of Bessie Smith and Billie Holiday, but they couldn't be more different in approach. Brown and Baker were women asserting themselves, not victims. Brown appears hellbent on ditching "the meanest man" she's ever seen, while Jim Dandy's rescue has to do with an aching libido, not a damsel in distress. After decades of companies trying to cash in on fads or looking for songs that could be sung as well by anyone, Atlantic's brass abruptly changed strategy. They followed the artist's muse by allowing these women—and their other acts—to be themselves.

Atlantic was guided by Ahmet and Nesuhi Ertegun, a pair of brothers born to a Turkish diplomat. Ahmet describes his mother as a music enthusiast who introduced the boys to jazz and records by Josephine Baker, the Mills Brothers, and Mae West. When their father announced they were being reassigned to Washington, D.C., Ahmet was delighted: "Oh, thank God," he remembers in his autobiography, *What'd I Say: The Atlantic Story.* "I'm going to the land of cowboys, Indians, Chicago gangsters, beautiful brown-skinned women, and jazz."

At 14, Ahmet's mother bought him a record-cutting machine. Ertegun describes it as "more than a toy; it was an amateur recording machine which cut acetate discs," similar to the machinery used by real professionals. Meanwhile, the brothers witnessed firsthand growing up in the nation's capital how blacks and whites interacted during the war. Not surprisingly, as Turkish Muslims living in the embassy of a foreign country, the boys identified with the outsiders. "Black and white musicians did play together," Ertegun recalls, "but it was not easy. It was more possible in New York, particularly in Harlem, but in Washington at that time, it was virtually impossible. I went to college in Annapolis, Maryland, and one night three of my school friends and I went to hear a band at a black nightclub, and we were arrested coming out of the place. I asked the judge, 'Where is the law written which states that we cannot go into this club?' And he replied, 'It's not written, but it's understood.'"[4]

Waves of disgust coursed through the family whenever such comments were made. According to Ahmet, the ambassador occasionally received letters from congressmen grousing that "a person of colour [sic] was seen entering your house by the front door." The elder Ertegun invariably shot back, "In my home, friends enter by the front door—however, we can arrange for you to enter from the back."[5]

The Ertegun brothers couldn't collect records or friends fast enough. As young adults, they produced shows of their own and rubbed elbows after hours with John Hammond, Duke Ellington, Lena Horne, Jelly Roll Morton, and Charlie Parker. After their father died in 1944, the Erteguns weighed their prospects, decided to remain in America, and gravitated toward the record industry. In November of 1947, the first Atlantic session featured a group called the Harlemaires in a recording of "The Rose of the Rio Grande."

Nesuhi moved west and left record making to Ahmet and a business partner, Herb Abramson. But with the swing market imploding, Ahmet had to wonder: would it be better to cast the company's lot with a onetime winner (jazz) now in the doldrums, or to ante up for what might be the sound of tomorrow (rhythm and blues), even though it had no established mass appeal and might prove to be a fad?

Atlantic temporarily hedged its bets with small successes on both fronts, actually piggybacking Ruth Brown's first studio date onto the end of an Eddie Condon session in 1949. White Condon's jazz group backed up Brown on "Rain Is a Bring Down," and through such choices Atlantic became known as a company blind to color and open to new ideas. Nesuhi rejoined the fold in 1955 and ushered in a cadre of fresh jazz talents that ranged from the Modern Jazz Quartet to the Afro-funky bassist, pianist, composer, and *enfant terrible* Charles Mingus. In the 1960s, Atlantic became home to John Coltrane, the most original sax player to surface since Charlie Parker.

The label's greatest coups came in 1952, with the signing of Ray Charles, and in 1953, when a white Jewish *Billboard* reporter named Jerry Wexler (the man who coined the term "rhythm and blues," or R&B) came aboard as a business partner. Wexler soon demonstrated a flair for transmuting raw talent into commercially viable art. When his performers reached a creative roadblock during a session, Wexler would offer advice by assuming the role of Man on the Street. He became the quintessential fan—the music nut who drums on the steering wheel when his favorite song appears on the radio (listen for Wexler wailing behind Big Joe Turner on the chorus of 1954's "Shake, Rattle, and Roll"), the white guy mysteriously up on all the latest dances (he demonstrated "the Jerk" for Wilson Pickett and guitarist Steve Cropper to help them find new rhythmic accents for "In the Midnight Hour"), and the guy who knew, *just knew*, he'd get great music from Aretha Franklin—if only she'd agree to leave Detroit and record in Alabama with an integrated band. In contributing random moments of brilliance and inspiration, Wexler was worth his weight in gold records.

"The R&B I liked best," the producer recalls decades later, "had strong links to jazz and blues. But the progression of blues and jump blues to R&B happened in almost imperceptible increments. As our roster expanded, we developed a reputation based on our tastes and our sensibilities, and there are only two major companies where the owners produced the records: Atlantic and Motown."

Finding Ray Charles, of course, was like unearthing the lost treasure of Tutankhamen: the embodiment of a culture, all in pristine condition, and all in one place. He was the living essence of black music in America. But the surprise that awaits anyone who digs deeper than "What'd I Say," "Georgia on My Mind," and "America the Beautiful" is that Charles was a one-man repository of *every* music considered distinctly American. Fed through his sensibilities as an individual as well as a black man, his music took on the characteristics of its keeper.

"As far back as I can recall, I was extremely impressed by music, period," Charles confessed in 2000. "I never thought about picking it apart. All music had impact on me—it wasn't just gospel and the blues. Country and western had an impact on me, jazz had an impact on me . . . I didn't know all these different 'types' that the media use to put labels on things. All I knew was, I liked it or I didn't like it. That was it."

As a child, Charles (who lost his sight over a period of months and was blind by the age of seven) was drawn to the personalities who projected themselves through music, regardless of color. In the liner notes to the box set *Ray Charles: Genius & Soul*, he told biographer David Ritz that his first musical hero was Artie Shaw. "Didn't even know he was white," he confided. "Didn't even care. Even more than Benny Goodman, Artie Shaw had the clarinet technique I loved. That perfect tone, that sweet sound. Plus he swung his ass off. Artie Shaw is the reason I took up the instrument myself."

Educated at a Florida school for the blind (which was segregated even though the students couldn't see one another), Charles dropped out of school at 15 and turned pro. He made the rounds from Jacksonville to Orlando and Tampa, picking up gigs as a peerless impersonator of Nat "King" Cole or blues shouter Charles Brown. He even performed in a band called the Florida Playboys that featured fiddles and a steel guitar. Three years of scuffling later, Ray decided he could make it anywhere. He chose the city farthest away: Seattle.

Once there, he gathered a small following in the nightclub community as a musical mimic. "That's when I decided to quit doing Charles Brown and Nat Cole," Charles recalled. "I remember people coming up to me saying, 'Hey Kid, you sound just like Nat Cole,' or 'Hey Kid, you sound just like' . . . whatever else it was. And I woke up one morning thinking about it. You know how things just come in your mind? I thought, nobody knows what my name is. I'm just a kid. *Hey Kid.* I started telling myself that if you're ever going to be anything, you gotta go back to that thing your Mom always taught you: you gotta go back and try to be yourself. I could make money sounding like Nat Cole, because I could get hired sounding like him and Charles Brown. You're going to have to start being yourself and find out if you're good or not."

Charles began to transmute the gospel, blues, jazz, and hillbilly sounds of his childhood into something altogether new. Song by song, Charles clambered out of the shadow of his mentors; "Confessin' Blues" (1949), recorded for the independent label Swingtime just before Ray moved to Los Angeles, evinces a heavy debt to Cole. But by the time of "Baby, Let Me Hold Your Hand" in 1951, Ray had replaced his heroes with a husky baritone of his own.

Ray Charles may not have been able to see, but through his unique musical vision, he was able to unite blues, gospel, and country under one banner. At the time of his passing in 2004, Charles was the subject of a major motion picture, *Ray*, and had a string of hits stretching back four decades on the pop, R&B, and country charts. (Frank Driggs Collection)

When Charles' contract came up for sale, Ahmet Ertegun jumped at the opportunity. "My success really took off (at Atlantic) when I finally started being myself," Charles stated flatly. "And that was with 'I Got a Woman,' (#2 R&B hit, 1955) that was the opening thing." The melody is all gospel, the arrangement is a heady brew of jazz and blues concepts, and the voice features the same groans and growls that inspired vocalists from Marvin Gaye to Joe Cocker, Tina Turner, and Lyle Lovett.

"In any medium as a consumer," Lovett says, "you want to see a great artist's mind working. You want to witness a talent like that at work, and that's what you got to see in Ray Charles. In his country phase, those records really sounded more like Ray than like country. But the popularity of genres is a faddish and a fickle thing. So seeing someone make his mark independent of that, to where it really becomes more revealing of the person and less about a specific song, I think that's what makes real art and memorable music.

"Talking about race is tricky," Lovett concedes, "because there are differences between people. How do you articulate that? When you say that someone like Louis Armstrong had a natural talent, are you talking about him specifically, or are you referring even in part to some kind of genetic makeup?" For Lovett, Ray Charles presents the same kind of quandary. Clearly, Charles was black and talented. But how much of his talent had to do with his being black?

"To make a broad generalization," Lovett says after some deliberation, "I believe black music is from the soul and white music is a more cerebral thing; you could call it 'music from the head.' And emotion is always a quicker way to people's humanity. The thing about the best music is that it doesn't try to convince you intellectually—it gets right to the heart of the matter. And that's what Ray Charles' records did. My parents had a lot of Ray and Nat 'King' Cole records in their collection and I remember watching Red Skelton, The Hollywood Palace, and The Ed Sullivan Show and seeing him regularly on programs like that. And I was always drawn to that kind of music, and I can recall taking guitar lessons and learning all about how rock and jazz came from the blues."

Ray Charles was a repository of all those sounds. "Making a Ray Charles record was like working on a textbook that would serve you forever," Wexler attests. "He was a contracted artist signed to us, but we were also there to serve him. He is the consummate singer/accompanist, because he perfectly understands how to stay out of his own way and still create a wonderful background."

Each of his Atlantic albums was a tautly drawn passion play. From "Drown in My Own Tears" (#1 R&B hit, 1955) to "Hallelujah I Love Her So" (#5 R&B hit, 1956), Charles confidently mapped out new terrain for blues and pop-gospel, and then in 1958, he wheeled about to release a hard bop collaboration with Milt Jackson of the Modern Jazz Quartet. Wexler struggled for new superlatives to herald the duo.

"We called it 'Soul Brothers,'" Wexler says of the first time the word "soul" was used in print to imply a profound depth of feeling. "It was my title, and at the time, it just seemed like something natural, something that wasn't a cliché. The thing about Atlantic was that we were making black music to sell to black adults. To me, it was part of us knowing who we were. Like the other up-and-coming labels of the time, including Specialty (Little Richard's label) and Chess (home to Muddy Waters and Chuck Berry), we knew our strengths and tried to develop our own particular skills."

Charles departed Atlantic at the end of the 1950s, leaving behind two landmark tracks. One was "What'd I Say?," the rousing encore number bowdlerized into a TV commercial pitching shower massage in the late 1990s and revived for Robert Altman's film, *Dr. T and the Women*, in a reverential cover by Lyle Lovett. With its Latin rhythms, blues inflections, and call-and-response denouement ("Make me feel so good," Ray would yelp, quickly echoed by the Raelettes), "What'd I Say?" slithered off the bandstand and up the nation's spine as a hypnotic invitation to dance.

The other track was "I'm Movin' On," (#11 R&B and #40 pop hits, 1959). In his autobiography, *Brother Ray*, Charles recalled his disappointment in the tune's anemic chart performance: "That's a Hank Snow song (Snow being a white country artist), and it became the first country and western number I ever recorded. I wanted Chet Atkins to play his country guitar on the date, but he was already booked up that afternoon. I would have liked 'I'm Movin' On' to have become a hit, but it was put on the flip side of 'I Believe to My Soul,' and, as best I remember, that was the one more people asked for and listened to."

When Ray surfaced at ABC Records the following year, he made a few more refinements that would reverberate throughout the music industry in the years to come. For starters, he quit composing. He'd had as much success with his own tunes as any he recorded (and his own "What'd I Say" remains his biggest hit), but the urge slowly disappeared. "I really prefer to do good songs written by other people," he said without regret. "When I was writing, it'd take me two or three days to write one song. I write lyrics and tear them up because I don't like them. It's not my love, like playing the piano. That's my love, that's my art. Once I got over to ABC and I had a lot of writers exposed to me, I just preferred to use other people who can write, because a good song is all I care about. I don't have to write them as long as I can get them."

If Charles had been completely unrestricted in his artistic choices at Atlantic, why then did he jump labels? First, he says ABC laid a hefty advance on the table. "Then," he explained, "when I was signing the contract, they wanted me to produce my music in addition to being a recording artist, paying me seven and a half cents out of a dime. So when I was talking with Sam Clark, the company president, I said, 'If I'm going to produce, I want to own my own masters.' I just asked for it and they gave it to me."

The possibility of a label surrendering ownership of its finished product to a contract employee has become, since then, the Holy Grail of most artists' wish lists. Ray Charles was among the first to realize the value in such a concession. And, he said, everything he needed to know about leverage and negotiation he learned from his mother, who died when Ray was 15: "My Mom taught me, 'You can get two answers from people, yes and no, and you respect both of them. So if you want something, just ask. If they say no, it's no, and if they say yes, it's yes.'"

SH-BOOM

With Ray Charles leading the way, pop began cannibalizing the sounds of gospel, hillbilly, and various strains of the blues. Just as New Orleans bordellos nurtured jazz in its infancy and the dismantling of Storyville forced that music out and up the Mississippi at the turn of the century, new combinations of familiar sounds were appearing everywhere through cross-pollinating bands and the media. This time, thanks to technology, the revolution would take place simultaneously via hundreds of broadcasts across the country.

Because so much happened in such a short time, conceptual and geographic imprints quickly became a tangle of clues leading back into a labyrinth of gospel, blues, jazz, and hillbilly influences. A Chicago gospel quartet might emphasize one set of vocal traits, while street singers harmonizing on a Brooklyn stoop might highlight others. But as church groups toured and maturing neighborhood kids began to sing alongside adults at Sunday service, they developed styles that each would recognize and neither would own. The sorting of one urban culture from the next, gospel harmony from doo-wop, and jump blues from R&B became for the average listener a pointless exercise in hairsplitting.

By 1950, the gospel circuit was a grassroots machine, with churches regularly sponsoring tours and occasional "battle-of-the-band" competitions for quartets to spar in a singing variation on the jazzmen's cutting contests. That same year in New York, a gospel tutor named Billy Ward formed the Dominoes, a group he fronted expressly for the purpose of recording secular tunes. And although Ward's vocalists were steeped in the gospel tradition, a generation removed from the Ink Spots or Mills Brothers, their material concerned more lusty pursuits. Indeed, "Sixty Minute Man," generally acknowledged as the first record to "cross over" from the R&B charts to pop charts in 1951, left little to the imagination. "There'll be fifteen minutes of kissin'," the chorus calls, "then you'll holler 'please don't stop,'" (to which Domino Clyde McPhatter replies in falsetto drag, "*Don't Stop!!*"), followed by "fifteen minutes of teasin', fifteen minutes of squeezin', and fifteen minutes of blowin' my top."

In 1953, when McPhatter left the Dominoes, Ahmet Ertegun tracked him down in Harlem and signed the singer instantly. Atlantic allowed him to handpick a group of his own (the first incarnation of The Drifters), but within two years, McPhatter was so well established he left them permanently for a solo career.

The run of luck that began for McPhatter with "Sixty Minute Man" reverberated through every stratum of the music industry, but was felt differently by blacks than by whites. African American performers, especially those with experience singing in church, were intrigued by the prospect of secular fame and fortune. White artists and the major labels took another view. Most of these black performers and their tunes would go unnoticed by mainstream record buyers—unless someone came along to polish them up for mass consumption.

In the summer of 1954, Atlantic released "Sh-Boom," by the black vocal group the Chords, which many consider (along with the Delta Cats' "Rocket 88" featuring Ike Turner) to be the first rock 'n' roll record. Others make a case for Bill Haley's "Rock Around the Clock" or Elvis Presley's "That's All Right, Mama" as more likely. (*Suggestion: Start this conversation at any party that's gone on too long and watch the room clear.) The Chords' record rose to #2 on the R&B charts, only to be eclipsed on the pop survey by a tepid remake by an all-white Toronto group called the Crew-Cuts. In all likelihood, the practice of whites recording covers of R&B hits before a black indie (independent) record could cross over to pop owed less to an artist's color than the color of cash. R&B acts had long covered the white-composed songs of Tin Pan Alley and Hollywood, and by the time rock 'n' roll arrived, most entrepreneurs knew that black records would be played on R&B stations while white groups were more likely to win out on the Top 40. So the roots of this very real segregation were in format first and race second. The major labels and their artists simply capitalized on a system they knew worked in their favor.

Undoubtedly the Crew-Cuts' single was rushed to market to siphon sales away from the Chords, but it wasn't a note-for-note copy. The arrangers jettisoned the Chords' nods to jazz and the a cappella introduction for a bloated brass treatment and a bouncing timpani to answer the chorus ("Sh-Boom, Sh-Boom") like some burlesque drummer's rimshot punctuation of a bad joke. The Chords' guileless harmonies were replaced with a barbershop schmaltz that rendered the song cloying and tinny. Just the same, the Crew-Cuts sold a million copies and scored a #1 pop hit.

The Chords' "Sh-Boom" also helped to launch the short-lived reign of black doo-wop, a strain of vocal music using nonsense syllables to establish a rhythm or weave a melodic counterpoint. The best of these, including "Earth Angel" by the Penguins and the Five Satins' "In the Still of the Night," depended less on gimmickry than upon a solid tune and the rough-hewn sincerity of the artists, many of whom were entering a recording studio for the first time. By the time the Platters arrived on the scene with "Only You" (#1 R&B and #5 pop hits, 1955), "The Great Pretender," "The Magic Touch," and "Twilight Time," supper club élan began to overtake the naiveté of early doo-wop. And, when that amateurism vanished, so did the daydream that any kid, black or white, could walk out the door and record tomorrow's #1 single.

Anything climbing the charts was considered fair game for a hit-hungry record company, and competing against an indie label lacking legal and business expertise simply increased the odds of a cover outselling the original. The relationship was oddly symbiotic. Without black vocal groups, there would have been no need for the Crew-Cuts (who also had a #3 pop hit with "Earth Angel" in 1955), and without New Orleanian rockers Fats Domino and Little Richard, Pat Boone might have ended up becoming a school teacher as he'd expected.

Growing up in Tennessee, Boone regarded making records as little more than a hobby. But once he established himself in 1955 by remaking "Two Hearts, Two Kisses" by Otis Williams and the Charms and Fats Domino's "Ain't That a Shame," he and his handlers knew they'd found a niche. Boone was unassailably virtuous, a gleaming icon of Eisenhower-era virtue. His producers handed him one of the raunchiest rock 'n' roll songs ever conceived and watched as he turned a song about cornholing into confetti. In Little Richard's stage show, the tune began as "Tutti Frutti, good booty . . ." and featured the line, "If it don't fit, don't force it / You can grease it, make it easy . . ." The song was well sanitized by the time Little Richard committed it to vinyl, but it took Pat Boone to bleach it white.

Half a century later, the question remains: should Boone and other R&B raiders be thanked for exposing this music to white audiences who might never have heard "Tutti Frutti," or "Ain't That a Shame" otherwise? Should Little Richard and Fats Domino be thankful that these impersonations were so vacuum-packed that teens dashed to find the originals instead? Or were Boone and his cronies merely thieves with a legal loophole?

Boone makes his case in Fred Bronson's *Billboard Book of Number One Hits*. "Ninety percent of radio stations in America wouldn't play R&B hits no matter how big they were," he says simply. "To get them on radio, other artists had to do them. I talked to Fats and Little Richard. There was a definite ceiling on how far they could go. When a white artist came along and sang their songs, they were introduced to audiences they couldn't get to themselves."

Robert "Bumps" Blackwell, the man who discovered and guided Little Richard's early years, concurs—to a point. "The white radio stations wouldn't play Richard's version of 'Tutti Frutti' and made Boone's cover #1," he tells author Charles White in *The Life and Times of Little Richard*. "So we decided to up the tempo on the follow-up and get the lyrics going so fast that Boone wouldn't be able to get his mouth together to do it. The follow-up was 'Long Tall Sally.'" Implausible as it seems that Blackwell and Richard could have foreseen a second Boone incursion, they did what they could to fend off any cover version. "We kept re-recording because I wanted it faster," Blackwell says. "I drilled Richard with (the line) 'Duck back in the alley' faster and faster until it burned, it was so fast. When it was finished I turned to Richard and said, 'Let's see Pat Boone get his mouth together to do this song.'" The final tally: Little Richard's "Long Tall Sally" reached #6 on the pop charts in early March 1956; at month's end, Boone's cover peaked at #8. While Boone might well be convicted in courts of public opinion for being excessively white, it's hard to detect any animosity on his part. When ABC offered him a TV series (*The Pat Boone–Chevy Showroom*) in the late 1950s, Boone enthusiastically presented Little Richard as a guest, and has often credited him since. Still, it's not entirely clear Pat Boone would have had a variety show had it not been for the black artists he covered.

"The pop charts wouldn't play my records when I started out," Richard says in hindsight, "even though long before I ever became famous, whites loved my music. I always played the kind of music that brought a joyful sound that everyone could like. All I know is that when Pat Boone and the others covered my music, they opened the door for me and made my songs acceptable on the pop charts, where they hadn't been before."

From R&B to pop, the raids continued unchecked, with the smaller independent labels often outmaneuvering the sluggish majors. The indies may have lacked the facilities and industry contacts, but they weren't hamstrung by overhead costs or corporate responsibilities, either. They simply dumped product onto the market and waited to see what caught the public's fancy before committing money to its promotion. And they weren't going to make it easy for poachers. In 1954, Hank Ballard gave his group the Royals (later rechristened the Midnighters) an R&B smash with a slice of double-entendre called "Work With Me, Annie." If Annie was "working" at all, she was likely plying the oldest trade known to man. "Annie, please don't cheat," Ballard begged. "Gimme *all* my meat." Even though the original was regarded by white programmers as smut set to music, it was redone several times, once by a promising black vocalist named Etta James (as "Roll With Me, Henry"), and again by Georgia Gibbs (watered down to "Dance With Me, Henry").

The gouging and name-calling turned uglier once the American Society of Composers, Authors, and Publishers (ASCAP) and Broadcast Music Incorporated (BMI) joined the fray. The ASCAP board was still smarting from a series of legal setbacks, including a federal antitrust finding in 1941 that identified the organization as a monopoly and reprimanded them for price fixing.

In 1958, ASCAP executive Billy Rose told a *Variety* magazine reporter, "Not only are most of the BMI songs junk, but in many cases they are obscene junk, pretty much on a level with dirty comic magazines." Frank Sinatra, never one to bury a grudge, blamed his commercial stumble in the early 1950s on BMI. When ASCAP forced the issue, congressional hearings were held in 1958 by the Senate Interstate and Foreign Commerce

Subcommittee on Communications. ASCAP representatives presented a letter claiming that BMI was monopolizing the airwaves, and was therefore responsible for the "deteriorating quality of music on radio and TV." A constellation of Hollywood stars, including Bing Crosby, signed the complaint.

PRINCE OF DARKNESS

By the mid-1950s, scores of artists, label representatives, and disc jockeys were fumbling with America's repressed sexual urges like impatient teens at a drive-in. But everything changed when a struggling Memphis record producer named Sam Phillips discovered Elvis Presley. With Phillips' guidance, Presley put his finger on the unholy union of opposites that everyone had been searching for: black and white, hillbilly and blues, and sleaze and salvation. Once he found it, Elvis pinched that G-spot until the nation let out a collective squeal.

Historically, there's much to be said about Elvis Presley the man, and many of his friends, colleagues, and ex-lovers are still around to offer their insights or spin. It's still possible to wander through Graceland, talk to his teachers, chronicle what he ate and wore, and list the songs he liked to sing as a kid when he got up enough nerve to perform. But no one has words for the synaptic meltdown that dissolved his distinctions between hillbilly, gospel, and R&B. Somewhere in that acid bath, those music forms merged into a thing of fearsome beauty with its own zeal to survive—through him, and anyone who heard him.

Overnight, as if to prove that losing one's virginity really could clear up a complexion, Presley's appearance changed, too. He still favored the "cat clothes" he'd seen in the windows at Lansky's department store in Memphis (a shop known more for catering to black tastes than to whites), but the confidence, the smoldering eyes, and the slicked-back hair gave him a feral look that couldn't be mistaken for anything but sex.

Presumably Elvis was less shocking for blacks who were accustomed to the raw sounds of R&B and understood that sexuality had a place in music along with other aspects of the human experience. For the white establishment, though, Presley was a sucker punch to the gut. Red-blooded American boys weren't supposed to dress, dance, or sing like *that*. Like the Crew-Cuts and Pat Boone, Presley recorded tunes by black artists—including such chart toppers as "Don't Be Cruel" and "All Shook Up" by Otis Blackwell, and Arthur Crudup's "That's All Right, Mama." Unlike his white rivals, however, Presley didn't downplay the records' blackness. He amplified it.

In 1956, Elvis graduated from Phillips' Sun Records and shows at the Louisiana Hayride to a major label contract with RCA, a management deal with Colonel Tom Parker (a former carny huckster whose rank was self-conferred), and TV appearances on variety shows hosted by the Dorsey Brothers and Milton Berle. When Presley appeared on Berle's program the second time in June 1956, his grinding performance of "Hound Dog" set off titters in a studio filled with people who'd never seen a white man so blatantly open the throttle on his libido. Elvis preened, sneered, gyrated, and laughed in the face of America's inability to let go. In return, the arbiters of taste crucified him.

Presley, according to *Daily News* critic Ben Gross, was "appalling musically," and "gave an exhibition that was suggestive and vulgar, tinged with the kind of animalism that

Originally billed as "the Hillbilly Cat," Elvis Presley shook the music world to its
core in 1956. Pictured here on *The Ed Sullivan Show*, Presley not only cobbled
together a style that reflected his R&B, gospel, and country roots—he introduced
a raw sexuality that many black audiences recognized immediately, and
conservative whites found repulsive. (Frank Driggs Collection)

should be confined to dives and bordellos." While most of the diatribes lambasted Presley's singing (or "caterwauling," as many reviewers heard it) and hypersexed stage act, others made the inevitable connection between sensuality, savagery, and race. "He can't sing a lick," wrote TV critic Jack O'Brien, and "makes up for vocal shortcomings with the weirdest and (most) plainly suggestive animation short of an aborigine's mating dance."

They demanded to know why the nineteen year old refused to behave himself on stage. Considering Tom Parker's show business background, many assumed his moves were a hoochie-coochie gimmick devised to set Elvis apart and cover up what they considered to be his meager singing abilities. They understood Presley's defiance as an act of will, and once they felt satisfied he had heard them, his noncompliance sent them into a sputtering fury. They couldn't grasp that Elvis disagreed and, without intending offense, meant to stand his ground—and occasionally wriggle on it, too. In interviews, he politely declined to court their approval, and that incensed them even more. Regardless, Presley continued to perform as he felt, his fans loved it, and it remained part of his stage persona until he entered the Army in 1958.

The sex Elvis put onstage had no precedent in white culture. It's a matter of record that white girls went wild for it and that his first string of hits presaged the sexual revolution of the 1960s. Black girls also found him attractive, which became a cause of some dismay in many African American households. In Memphis, a prominent black disc jockey named Nat Williams publicly groused about the melee Elvis created while visiting the local fairgrounds on "colored night." Williams asked why "colored girls would take on so over a Memphis white boy . . . when they hardly let out a squeak over B.B. King, a Memphis colored boy . . . Beale Streeters are wondering if these teenage girls' demonstration over Presley doesn't reflect a basic integration in attitude and inspiration which has been festering in the minds of your womenfolk all along."

Presley's sex appeal was such that even heterosexual males marveled at its potency. Jim Dickinson, a Memphis musician and producer, describes the phenomenon in *Sun Records: An Oral History.* "Anyone who saw Elvis and said they were inspired to have a career in music is lying, because seeing him was like seeing something that wasn't human," Dickinson says. "Nobody in their right mind could look at Elvis Presley and say that they could do what he was doing, because it was *that strange.* . . . He didn't even have to sing. And you lose sight of it in contemporary society, but what he was doing was completely revolutionary and liberating. Just shaking his leg—just the simple act of shaking his fucking leg—began the whole sexual revolution and changed the way every man on earth walked, talked, and combed his hair."

Elvis may have found that swaggering self-confidence on his own, but many of the outward manifestations (including his vocal style) bore an unmistakably black imprint. When the lacerating reviews exhausted his patience, Presley uncharacteristically explained himself to a writer in Charlotte, North Carolina: "The colored folks been singing it and playing it just like I'm doin' now, man, for more years than I know," he defended. "They played it like that in the shanties and in their juke joints, and nobody paid it no mind 'til I goosed it up. I got it from them."

Had Elvis played his role for laughs, it might have been different. But because he performed in deadly earnest rather than as a jester in blackface, he instantly became Public Enemy #1 insofar as the sentries of morality were concerned. To his credit, Elvis never denied his assault on convention. Rather, he suggested with a wink and a curl of the lip that surrender only hurts for a moment. Equal parts Paul Revere and Rhett Butler, Presley reassured chaste America that the spoils of submission were far sweeter than resistance. Virginity was not something for men to take from ladies; it had to be ditched by women before the real fun could begin. "Have you heard the news," he'd ask, borrowing from black shouter Wynonie Harris, "there's good rockin' tonight!!"

ROCKIN' AND REELIN'

Too little and too late, the antirock movement lurched into motion. A 1955 film called *Blackboard Jungle*, in which Glen Ford played a schoolteacher grappling with a class full of juvenile delinquents, defined the rift. Kids loved its anti-establishment tone and embraced its soundtrack—led off by Bill Haley and the Comets' "Rock Around the Clock." Parents thought the movie endorsed anarchy, and began to fear that there was more to rock 'n' roll than primitive beats and salacious lyrics; now it stood for insurrection. Elvis, Bill Haley, and Buddy Holly—their polite manners notwithstanding—quickly became examples of good boys who had stumbled into degeneracy, and something had to be done before the entire nation was swept away on a wave of miscegenation. A pamphlet distributed in the mid-1950s to Southern shopkeepers read: DON'T BUY NEGRO RECORDS. "If you don't want to serve Negroes [*sic*] in your place of business, then do not have Negro records in your jukebox or listen to Negro records on the radio. The screaming idiotic words and savage music of these records are undermining the morals of our white youth in America. Call the advertisers of radio stations that play this type of music and complain to them."

Asa Carter, the executive secretary of the North Alabama White Citizens' Council, dumped fuel on the fire in 1956 when he became obsessed with removing rock 'n' roll from jukeboxes in Birmingham and Anniston. Not only was the music "immoral" and "sexualistic," in his view, but the music represented "the basic, heavy-beat music of Negroes. It appeals to the base in man, brings out animalism and vulgarity." Carter believed the National Association for the Advancement of Colored People (NAACP) was to blame for this *coup d'état* effort to drag whites "down to the level of the Negro" and set the course for the "moral degradation of children" while serving "the cause of integration."

But the virus had already taken hold. "Hound Dog," in fact, was written by Jerry Leiber and Mike Stoller—a pair of white students at Los Angeles City College—and had already been a hit on the black charts for "Big Mama" Thornton in 1953. "Actually, I think we wanted to be black," Leiber later told *Flowers in the Dustbin* author James Miller. "Black people had a better time. As far as we were concerned, the worlds we came from were drab by comparison."

Buddy Holly, a native of Lubbock, Texas—where kids were raised to know better—blurted out an opinion guaranteed to make white parents shudder. He and the Crickets had just returned from an otherwise all-black tour in 1957, where they picked up invaluable lessons in stagecraft. Of course, they had to leave the caravan once it headed South, because they were barred from playing integrated shows, even to segregated houses. In *Time Passages: Collective Memory and American Popular Culture*, writer George Lipsitz finds Holly responding to his mother's inquiry about living and working among blacks. "Oh, we're Negroes, too," he told her. "We get to feeling like that's what we are."

The problem was, with Elvis sounding so black and this Chicago guitar player Chuck Berry sounding so white, even Asa Carter was challenged to pick the real "Ni-grahs" out of a Top 40 lineup. Ironically, Presley, Berry, Little Richard, and piano-pounder Jerry Lee Lewis—rock 'n' roll's Four Horsemen of the Apocalypse—undid themselves in ways their enemies never could and left pop music a cultural wasteland in the process.

By 1959, Elvis was in the Army and his rebel image was being cured like a hide in the sun by Tom Parker. The singles Presley recorded before his induction kept coming, but each one retreated further from the sound that made him famous. Every rocker ("One Night," for example) led to a Dean Martin knockoff ("It's Now or Never" took the melody of the Italian standard "O Sole Mio," written in 1899), or such doe-eyed treacle as "Are You Lonesome Tonight?" Many still feel that Hollywood and the Army emascu-lated Elvis. But if anyone was responsible aside from Presley, it was Tom Parker, a man with no love for rock 'n' roll and a platinum meal ticket to protect.

A short time earlier, Little Richard renounced pop music after a midflight engine fail-ure convinced him to preach the gospel instead. Besides, for Richard, whose outrageous-ness made even Elvis more acceptable, there were few heights to scale. "Oh, yes," Richard confides in his decorous Southern drawl, "I just wanted to be different, flamboyant, pretty, and striking. You know, I think the women were more shocked than anyone else. I was wearing the same things they were, wearing eyelashes and looking more glamorous than some of the women in the audience." Rural one-nighters were wearing him down, too. "It was hard playing them raggedy old places," he said. "You couldn't find a nice place to stay or a decent meal. You would find yourself eating by the side of the road and going behind a tree to take a leak."

Chuck Berry's case was different. Once Muddy Waters introduced Berry to the own-ers of Chess Records in 1955, his ascension rivaled that of test pilot Chuck Yeager. Berry set up an office appointment, and drove businesslike to Chicago from St. Louis. There he played a short reel of demos for label chief Leonard Chess, who thought one particu-lar "hillbilly" tune stood out. A few days later, they recorded "Ida May," and changed its title to "Maybelline" (#1 R&B and #5 pop hits, 1955). A burst of pop hits followed, in-cluding "Roll Over Beethoven," "Rock & Roll Music," "Sweet Little Sixteen," and "Johnny B. Goode."

But by 1959, Berry was under two separate indictments for violations of the Mann Act, which prohibits the interstate transportation of minors for immoral purposes (Berry summarized the charge in his autobiography as "white slavery"). Although acquitted in one court and convicted by another, both trials smacked of bigotry. Were the charges true? According to one jury, yes. Would Berry have been so zealously pursued if he hadn't been a rich black man driving an unchaperoned teenage girl cross-country in a peach Cadillac? The answer seemed self-evident, especially to Berry. He was sentenced to a $5,000 fine and five years in federal prison, of which he served two.

Jerry Lee Lewis, like Chuck Berry, couldn't understand what all the fuss was about. His fire-and-brimstone piano playing had earned him a nickname, "The Killer," and a monstrous pair of 1957 hits in "Whole Lotta Shakin' Goin' On" (which not only scored #1 R&B and # 3 pop, but #3 on the country charts as well) and "Great Balls of Fire" (#2 pop and #1 country). But that December, Lewis admitted his new bride was also his thirteen-year-old third cousin, Myra Gayle Brown. Fans recoiled in horror and Lewis plummeted from view, only to be reconstituted a decade later as a country artist.

So it went. Buddy Holly—the Big Bopper—and Ritchie Valens died together in a 1959 plane crash, and Eddie Cochran, the man who started power pop and punk with "Summertime Blues," was killed in a London car wreck a year later. With rock 'n' roll's varsity team thus dispatched and the herd of redshirts thinned by attrition, teen-oriented music was in greater demand than ever and desperate for anyone who could make it.

PHILLY CHEESE

In Philadelphia on Monday, August 5, 1957, a crisply dressed young man stood waiting for his studio camera to light up. When it did, he smiled. "Hi," he said, "I'm Dick Clark. Welcome to *American Bandstand.*" Swamped by well-pressed local teens recruited for his live dance show, Clark launched two revolutions in the same breath. One was a crusade to bring the latest tunes, styles, and dances to a nation hungry for something fresh. The other was a plan to get rich while avoiding the slightest suggestion of impropriety, even if it meant promoting the most bathetic performers in the milieu.

The first host of the show was forced out after a scandal, and ABC's first choice to replace him was a disc jockey named Alan Jarvis, according to *Rock 'n' Roll Is Here to Pay* author Steve Chappel. Jarvis declined the offer, Chappel discovered, because "the networks wanted no black artists appearing. Clark willingly conformed to the racist network policy."

While Clark did eventually integrate the show, he made sure to do it in carefully measured steps that took years to realize. Sex and danger may have been at the core of rock 'n' roll, but both were in short supply on *Bandstand*. Elvis Presley appeared on the program only once—unseen and by telephone. And when Clark learned of the trouble Jerry Lee Lewis was having in explaining his teen bride to the press, he hastily canceled the Killer's upcoming appearance. Instead, the show tended to favor such third-string pop stars as Fabian, Connie Francis, and the three Bobbys—Vee, Vinton, and Rydell.

Within months of its debut, *Bandstand* became the highest rated series on daytime television, and Dick Clark became not only the face of teenage America, but the vanguard of a new medium altogether. In fact, he was so far ahead of his time as a "veejay" (a disc jockey, or deejay, on video) that the term wouldn't be coined for another quarter century with the dawn of MTV. In Clark's hands, the show evolved into a virtual teen club where wholesome youngsters gathered—and could become minor celebrities through weekly TV exposure—to rub shoulders with pop stars who dropped by to lip-synch (or mime) their latest recordings. At its crest of popularity, *American Bandstand* claimed some 20 million viewers and aired on more than 100 stations around the country.

At the center of the program were the kids, 150 strong, mostly white and working-class, and always on their best behavior. Black youth was represented too, one *Bandstand* alumnus explained to the *New York Post* in 1958. "It is station practice to let eight or nine colored kids in at a time," said the insider, "and not to focus the camera on them." Regulars on the program say they discovered the steps that became the Stroll, the Bop, and the Twist at Philadelphia's integrated high schools. They'd learn the dances from black kids and bring them to the show, where Clark had them toned down before airtime. Although his career began in radio, Clark instinctively understood the power of television and that his telegenic image would fit the cool medium easily. Not all deejays were so lucky or so shrewd.

Most simply wanted to hang onto their jobs and had little inkling that they were a vital linchpin in the American postwar economy. But deejays were among the few adults who could understand kids' desires and articulate them to the business world. As such, programmers and advertisers relied on radio jocks for advice about an endless variety of adolescent purchases, from hose and hair tonic to cars and restaurants. By 1957, according to *Scholastic* magazine's Institute of Student Opinion, teen incomes were estimated at $7 billion annually, which equated to $10.55 per week—an amount comparable to the disposable income of an entire family a dozen years earlier. Just three years later, *Seventeen* magazine editor Sigana Earle reported that teenage girls alone commanded some $4.5 billion per year. Because their livelihoods depended on it, deejays listened attentively to their callers, then began to reiterate the concerns that came over the request lines. Inadvertently perhaps, they evolved into the voice of restless American youth, and not only did they discover what teens wanted—they learned what kids could be *led* to want.

A few years earlier, a white radio deejay named Alan Freed was playing the classics in Cleveland when he discovered through a record store acquaintance that kids were spending a good deal of cash on "Negro music." Freed convinced his boss to allow him to program something similar and he introduced *The Moon Dog Rock 'n' Roll House Party* in 1951, showcasing current R&B singles and the inimitable Freed as the jabbermouthed jock who chatted kids up in the vernacular to which they had become accustomed. The show was such a sensation that the following spring, Freed assembled a program of black R&B acts that drew nearly 25,000 black and white teenagers (twice the venue's capacity) and provided the catalyst for the first modern music riot. Freed threw himself into the music, which he was the first to call "rock 'n' roll," and became its most ardent supporter. He also kept a little piece of the pie for himself and was listed for years as one of the composers of "Sincerely" by the Moonglows and Chuck Berry's "Maybelline," although he had nothing to do with either aside from airing them.

Freed suffered serious injury in an auto accident a few months later, but recovered sufficiently to stage another "Moon Dog Ball" the following year. The concert proved lucrative enough to tour, and Freed was soon exporting his shows from Ohio to New Jersey. Eventually *The Moon Dog Show* landed a syndication deal and was relaunched as *Alan Freed's Rock 'n' Roll Party* and broadcast from WINS in New York City. But where Dick Clark tried to maintain a tame and pale image for *Bandstand,* Freed lauded black originals over white cover versions and otherwise let the tastes of his listeners guide him. So many black artists got airplay on his New York show that the station manager had to quell complaints from Harlem businessmen unhappy that Freed was taking work (and money) out of black households.

Freed forged ahead. He began staging shows in New York and briefly hosted a TV series intended to rival *Bandstand.* CBS aired the short-lived *Rock 'n' Roll Dance Party,* which was canceled either because (a) of complaints having to do with the show's sponsor, Camel cigarettes, or (b) during one episode, black Frankie Lymon ("Why Do Fools Fall in Love") of the Teenagers was caught on camera dancing with a white girl. Freed's final tumble began with a riot at one of his "big beat" concerts in Boston on May 3, 1958. Jerrry Lee Lewis was but one of seventeen draws for the event, which lured 5,000 young fans and guaranteed all the security 20 uniformed police officers could muster. When the house lights were turned up to full because kids were dancing in the aisles rather than remaining seated, Freed sealed his own fate. Over the house public address system he groused, "I guess the police here in Boston don't want you kids to have a good time." Outside after the show, more than a dozen people were assaulted or robbed by unknown assailants.

Freed's station in New York declined to voice any support, triggering his departure to WABC, but he didn't last long there, either. The more Freed played the martyr for rock 'n' roll—which he defended vigorously at every turn—the more conservatives held him responsible for their teens' corruption. His role in the Boston fracas earned him two separate indictments for inciting to riot. One had to be dropped because there was no evidence he'd tried to topple the federal government, and the other was filed into oblivion after Freed changed his plea from not guilty to no contest.

By the time he and Dick Clark figuratively faced off in the congressional payola hearings of 1959, Freed had become rock's straw man with the stuffing beaten out of him. *American Bandstand*, by contrast, was raking in $12 million a year. At WABC, Freed was told to sign an oath that he'd never taken payola (money in exchange for playing a record), while Clark, an employee of the same company, was never asked to issue such a pledge.

It's fair to say that at the time, the laws were murky and both men had their share of temptations. But Freed was ruined and vilified as a "nigger lover" (as he was often called behind his back), while Clark emerged fresh as a laundered hankie. Just before the hearings began in November 1959, the *Bandstand* host announced he had just divested himself of holdings in thirty-three different companies. By his own admission, those investments had already made him a millionaire, according to Linda Martin and Kerry Segrave's *Anti-Rock: The Opposition to Rock 'n' Roll*. "Between 1958 and 1959," the authors reported, "*Bandstand* played eleven records by Duane Eddy a total of 240 times, which was more than Clark programmed Presley. At the time, Clark managed the guitarist, owned stock in his company, and held all the publishing rights to the songs."

Even the music trade journal *Billboard* voiced suspicion. "According to the gossip," one report ran, "Clark owns a piece of every record he plays, whether it be the artist, the copyright, the label, or even the distributor who hands him the record." Oddly enough, this man who helped launch rock 'n' roll, with its subsequent *New Year's Rockin' Eve* celebrations, *Bandstand* grills, and *Rock, Roll, and Remember* series, claimed no real affinity for the music. When he was asked to appear on Edward R. Morrow's *Person to Person* TV interview program, Clark had contacts send him a pile of empty album sleeves to display onscreen in his office because he had no records of his own.

Materially speaking, not much was achieved by the payola investigation. A number of music historians say the hearings were a last-ditch attempt by ASCAP to undermine BMI by asserting that the only way "cheap music" (to many, a euphemism for black influence) could survive was if the jocks and their bosses had been paid to play it. But no proof ever surfaced that BMI had circumvented the law. The ASCAP board won their battle against Freed, but they lost the war against rock 'n' roll.

Congressmen and industry execs pronounced Dick Clark an acceptable spokesman for the new pop ("a fine young man," in the words of committee chairman Oren Harris), and Clark did everything he could to ensure the success of his personal cash cow. He proclaimed it "the basic form of American popular music" in the press and compared adult discontent with its rhythms and lyrics to their parents' concerns over swing and the Lindy-Hop. Rock 'n' roll, as the saying goes, was here to stay.

A SUMMER PLACE

The Rolling Stone Encyclopedia of Rock & Roll offers in-depth discussions of the origins of reggae, disco, grunge, and other genres of contemporary popular music. The entry under rock 'n' roll says only, "the term is a blues euphemism for sexual intercourse."

But rock—rock 'n' roll, rockabilly, folk rock, jazz rock, pop rock, rap rock—still thrives today because it is all things to all people. Listeners can pick from a pantheon of stars and styles to find the ones who speak most personally to their needs. The last fifty years show that the music has survived through its own system of checks and balances. A raucous trend (whether it's Elvis Presley or Marilyn Manson) always creates a market for a cuddly counterpart (think Fabian in the 1950s and the boy bands and Jessica and Ashley Simpson today). And, much like the generation that first embraced rock 'n' roll—and every one since—this music wants to defy the conventions of its elders, but be loved for its fierce independence. This music uses every conceivable charm to have it both ways. Parents in the 1950s who found "Jailhouse Rock" crass and insipid could be soothed when Elvis wooed them a little with "Love Me Tender" or "Are You Lonesome Tonight?" Hate Bobby Darin's "Splish Splash" or Etta James' "Roll With Me, Henry"? Don't worry; these same kids would soon be vying for casino dates in Vegas with "Mack the Knife," "Beyond the Sea," and "At Last."

Rock 'n' roll really is, as Little Richard described it, not much more than black-inspired R&B played up-tempo, although to be fair, white musicians did as much as anyone to jettison the democratic interplay of piano, guitar, and sax in favor of making the electric guitar rock's preeminent voice. White contributors ditched the overt innuendos and subtle rhythmic nuances, then played up any element that could broaden the possibility for rock 'n' roll to communicate and pay off while doing so. Some would call that the lowest common denominator; others, like Hank Williams, might call it beauty in simplicity. Both are right.

With the 1950s nearly a half century gone, the era's threats to conformity—Elvis, Brando, Little Richard, Marilyn Monroe, and Jerry Lee Lewis—seem no more anarchic now than an episode of *Happy Days*. Marlon Brando's leather-jacketed antihero in *The Wild One* calls to mind a Village People prototype; Marilyn Monroe, fixed in time on the subway grate with her skirt billowing around her, appears more ceramic than sensual. Mention Elvis, and a volley of associations flicker by—not of the white-hot dervish too salacious for Ed Sullivan—but of postage stamps, the *True Hollywood Story* of his crumbling marriage, and late-night TV offers for the 2002 compilation *ELVIS: 30 #1 Hits*. At one time, these iconic figures were regarded as subversive; they were labeled antisocial and antithetical to the American way of life. Now they survive as emblems of our innocence.

The era lingers sweetly in memory for a number of reasons, perhaps because the nation was at peace and times were prosperous or because rock 'n' roll was new and in its own infancy. But war at home and abroad would change all that. Once nonviolent protesters were set upon with attack dogs and flesh-ripping fire hoses, race pride turned from determination to defiance. Doo-wop and teen ballads seemed absurd in a world where the Federal Bureau of Investigation dragged Southern swamps for the bodies of civil rights activists and examined how innocent children could be blown up at Sunday school. And that was only the beginning. America was on a bloody march, and ready for a brand new beat.

NOTES

1 Escott, Colin. *Hank Williams: The Biography.* Boston: Little Brown and Company, 1994, p. 11.

2 Ibid., p. 160.

3 Wolff, Daniel. *You Send Me: The Life and Times of Sam Cooke.* New York: William Morrow and Company, 1995, p. 83.

4 Ertegun, Ahmet. *What'd I Say: The Atlantic Story.* New York: Welcome Rain, 2001, p. 7.

5 Ibid.

CHAPTER FIVE

River Deep, Mountain High

B y 1960, rock 'n' roll was all but over. Its creators had abdicated or self-destructed, while those least concerned with its survival—Madison Avenue and industry profiteers—rushed in to scavenge what they could through such moronic trifles as "Itsy Bitsy Teeny Weeny Yellow Polka Dot Bikini" and a patronizing musical called *Bye Bye Birdie* that mocked rock 'n' roll as music barely fit to chew gum by. The TV and radio waves once dominated by Elvis, Little Richard, Chuck Berry, and Jerry Lee Lewis were now more often the province of *Bandstand* mannequins like Connie Francis and Frankie Avalon, and as label revenues continued to climb, skirmishes intensified over the music's origins and ownership.

Singer-songwriter Carl Perkins (whose "Blue Suede Shoes" became an early standard for Elvis; other Perkins tunes appeared later on Beatles albums) considered himself living proof that rock 'n' roll was a hybrid of black rhythm and white hillbilly styles. In *A Change Is Gonna Come*, author Craig Werner writes that as a child, Perkins used to spend hours on the porch of a black sharecropper named Uncle John Westbrook just to pick up guitar licks. "I put a little speed and rhythm to what Uncle John had slowed down. That's all," Perkins explained. "That's what rockabilly music or rock 'n' roll was to begin with: a countryman's song with a black man's rhythm."[1]

Louis Jordan scoffed at such insinuations. "That's white publicity," he informed *Honkers and Shouters* author Arnold Shaw in 1973. "Rock 'n' roll was just a white imitation, a white adaptation of Negro rhythm and blues. What the white artist has done— and they started it fifteen or twenty years ago—they started the publicity and eliminating talk of the black artist. They eliminated talking about who did what and how good it was, and they started talking about white artists."[2]

Jordan's gripes echoed those of his predecessors in jazz, ragtime, and spirituals. He wanted to know when black people were going to get their due for creating this cross-cultural phenomenon. "I lived in New York for twelve years," he complained to Shaw, "and I've had white musicians hang around me twenty-four hours if I would let 'em, hang around until they learned something from me. *And then* [because of segregation] *I couldn't go hear them play!*"[3]

Little Richard soon joined the chorus: "I was there at the beginning, and when I started, there was no soul, no doo-wop, no nothing. I am the originator and the emancipator, and the architect, and I'm telling you there ain't nothing new under the sun, baby. Rock 'n' roll's only rhythm and blues played up-tempo."

Many of the artists concluded that enough was enough. It might still be legal in many parts of the country to harass and bully black Americans, but they would not endure their abuse quietly anymore. By 1960, a full six years had passed since the Supreme Court's decision in *Brown vs. the Topeka Board of Education* rejected separate-but-equal schooling and ended segregation. It had been five years since a black woman named Rosa Parks defied the law by refusing to surrender her seat at the front of a bus in Montgomery, Alabama. Her arrest instigated a successful boycott led by Dr. Martin Luther King, Jr. and signaled the beginning of the modern civil rights movement, but every advance threatened to rouse America's sleeping giant of segregationist opposition. In Mississippi that same year, a fourteen-year-old boy named Emmett Till was beaten and shot to death after he supposedly whistled his approval at a white woman.

Down South, "equal treatment under the law" meant that even the most famous blacks were second-class citizens by white standards. B.B. King always took extra precautions below the Mason-Dixon Line. "I had fears for my safety, sure, because I grew up in the South and I knew how segregation rules were," he says. "We knew there were certain places we couldn't go, and if you didn't want any trouble, you didn't go there. You didn't drink out of certain fountains at certain times and you didn't use rest rooms that were marked 'For Whites Only.' So to stay out of trouble, you'd have to abide by their system. That's the only way you could make it. Sometimes we got paid and sometimes we didn't. In the South, we couldn't stay in hotels, so it's like (the black stand-up comic) Moms Mabley said, 'What good old days?' *These* are the good old days."

Civil rights activists took hope, however, in the passing of presidential power from the Eisenhower administration to the Kennedys. When Martin Luther King was arrested in Georgia on charges of driving with an out-of-state license just weeks before the 1960 presidential election, Robert Kennedy intervened on behalf of his brother Jack to secure King's safe release. The pastor's father immediately issued a grateful endorsement that served to quell anti-Catholic (meaning anti-Kennedy) sentiment and bolster black support. "I've got all my votes," the senior King declaimed, "and I've got a suitcase, and I'm going to take them up there and dump them in (Kennedy's) lap."

The budding alliance between King and the Kennedys helped JFK slip past Richard Nixon and into the White House. Although blacks were not yet able to eat, drink, or sit among whites in many parts of the nation and images of *Amos 'n' Andy* and Sambo's restaurant mascot continued to flicker unhindered across the country, a palpable optimism wafted in the air. Cataclysm chased triumph through the rest of the decade, and although producer Phil Spector wrote "River Deep, Mountain High" without any political agenda, his title proved eerily prescient.

PEOPLE GET READY

Within days of John Kennedy's victory, nearly a thousand white New Orleanians showed up to prevent black six year olds from entering an all-white grade school, and Martin Luther King found himself back behind bars after participating in an Atlanta sit-in. Casual observers dismissed the arrest as business as usual, and it might have been just that— except that many activists considered Kennedy's election the sign they had been waiting for, and that the time had come to press their case.

If integration had to be won on every street corner, at every dime-store lunch counter, and in every bus station throughout the nation, a broad alliance of black and white equal-rights groups wanted it known they were up to the task. Dr. King said as much in *Stride Toward Freedom*, his 1958 account of the Montgomery bus boycott. "We will soon wear you down by our capacity to suffer," he wrote, "and in winning our freedom we will so appeal to your heart and conscience that we will win you in the process."

Music and nonviolence became synonymous with the civil rights movement, especially for those watching from the sidelines. Witnesses who saw the demonstrators file past recall hearing an assortment of gospel favorites and contemporary protest tunes, many borrowed from the bohemians in New York's Greenwich Village. Such Peter, Paul, and Mary hits as "If I Had a Hammer," and "Blowin' in the Wind" (the latter written by a young folk artist calling himself Bob Dylan) were commonplace, as were "Go Tell It on the Mountain," "Ain't Gonna Let Nobody Turn Me 'Round," and the inevitable "We Shall Overcome."

These anthems bridged the reality gap between the disparate marchers, who were now older as well as younger, not always local or even Southern, and increasingly white and Jewish. After-hours, however, there remained little race mixing between them. Northern liberals retreated to the comforts of their Pete Seeger, Joan Baez, and Dylan records, while black marchers flicked on the radio to hear Ruby and the Romantics vow that "Our Day Will Come" or imagine a cool summer night spent "Up on the Roof" with The Drifters.

Acoustic blues was the one place where the tastes of both groups overlapped. White student activists so revered Robert Johnson that an album of his newly rediscovered tunes called *King of the Delta Blues* might as well have been on the Ivy League's recommended list of school supplies. Their devotion betrayed a view of blacks as cosmically fated to suffer, with the downtrodden bluesman offered up as Exhibit A. During this time, even Muddy Waters, the father of Chicago's electric blues, was recast as a "folk" artist. Buddy Guy was mystified. "I made a record with Muddy when they were calling it 'folk music,'" he says through the slightest of smiles. "Somehow blues got in the colleges in the '60s, and I don't know how it got started; maybe because you could play it with an acoustic guitar. But a guitar is just a guitar. I could unplug mine right now, but does that make me a folk singer?"

Bob Dylan cemented the folk/blues alliance by adding a number of blues standards to his acoustic debut. Dylan's record included Blind Lemon Jefferson's "See That My Grave Is Kept Clean," Willie Johnson's "In My Time of Dyin'," and "House of the Rising Sun." Eventually, these were supplanted both in the singer's repertoire and on the front lines by newer originals, including Dylan's own "Ballad of Emmett Till," "A Hard Rain's a-Gonna Fall," and "The Times They Are a-Changin'."

Protesters sang as they were cursed, kicked, punched, clubbed, and spat upon. They sang while they were cuffed and hauled away from the scene. They sang and their voices trailed off into the distance as paddywagons carted them off to jail. Nightly appearances on the network news raised their profile and sparked a short-lived interest in the movement's music and speeches, released under such titles as *Freedom in the Air—Albany, Georgia, Songs of the Selma-Montgomery March* and *The Story of Greenwood, Mississippi.* Observing the struggle had a galvanizing effect on the young Bonnie Raitt: "I was bitten by the folk music bug through being raised as a Quaker and my family's interest in the civil rights and peace movement," she recalls. "There was a marriage of social action and populist music with Woody Guthrie, Joan Baez, and Bob Dylan. They're all part of a tradition that I caught onto when I was about eight or nine."

Raitt spent many a school break at summer camp, learning folk tunes from older counselors swept up in the cultural zeitgeist. "There was a revival that started in the main populace with the Kingston Trio and Peter, Paul, and Mary," Raitt says, "which actually began in Greenwich Village in the folk and beat centers and out west at Berkeley where social progressive movements converged with folk music."

A chain reaction of demonstrations, racist reprisals, and media exposure nudged the movement toward critical mass. Backed into a political corner by Dr. King, the Freedom Riders, and the loose coalition of groups around them—the Southern Christian Leadership Conference (SCLC), the Congress of Racial Equality (CORE), the National Association for the Advancement of Colored People (NAACP), and the Student Nonviolent Coordinating Committee (SNCC)—the Kennedy administration reluctantly shouldered the burden thrust upon it by history.

On June 11, 1963, JFK gave a prime-time address throwing the weight of his administration behind the civil rights struggle. Blacks had been too long denied equality, he said, restating the same argument posed to him. "Who among us would then be content with the counsels of patience and delay? One hundred years of delay have passed since President Lincoln freed the slaves, yet their heirs, their grandsons, are not fully free." Segregationists in Mississippi responded within hours of Kennedy's plea for justice by killing the state's most visible NAACP activist, Medgar Evers.

By summer, the blood, sweat, and tears shed over racism crested into a tsunami. The August 28 March on Washington featured Mahalia Jackson, Peter, Paul, and Mary, black folksinger Odetta ("the only person," in the words of one observer, "who could sing 'Kumbaya' without sounding ridiculous"), Bob Dylan, Lena Horne, Bobby Darin, Harry Belafonte, Joan Baez, and the great Marian Anderson—reprising her 1939 appearance— and Martin Luther King, Jr. Also present were 250,000 onlookers, some sixty percent of whom the media identified as white.

In years to come, King would rhapsodize about "the mountaintop," but the emotional peak of the civil rights movement took place that day in August 1963. Mary Travers of Peter, Paul, and Mary recalls her experience to author Joe Smith in *Off the Record*: "If I had to pick one song, my softest spot, it would be 'Blowin' in the Wind,'" she says. "If you could imagine the March on Washington with Martin Luther King and singing that song in front of a quarter million people, black and white, who believed they could make America more generous and compassionate in a nonviolent way, you begin to know how incredible that belief was."[4]

The rally called for an end to discrimination at every level: in voting, housing, transportation, education, and employment. Justice and the U.S. Constitution demanded no less, but they might never have resulted in the Civil Rights Acts of 1964 and 1965 had John Kennedy lived to face reelection. His murder in November 1963 left Lyndon B. Johnson in charge, and as former Senate majority leader and the nation's most skilled manipulator of legislative flesh, LBJ positioned his civil rights agenda as a valedictory to the slain president. Johnson's experience at cajoling and calling in favors paid off with the passage of the most sweeping civil rights reforms since Reconstruction. Poll taxes and other vestiges of Jim Crow law crumbled overnight, leaving segregationists terrified they'd face the wrath of those they once subjugated.

Victory at the federal level may have been sealed with John Kennedy's blood, but those who cheered the president's assassination as "good riddance to that nigger-loving son-of-a-bitch" were far from finished. Even before Kennedy's trip to Dallas, radical segregationists were determined to foment a counteroffensive in Birmingham—nicknamed "Bombingham" because of the 50 bombings carried out in the city between 1947 and 1965.

On September 15, 1963, a black singing duo from Florida visited the city. Sam Moore and Dave Prater had taken parallel paths as gospel singers, but they joined forces as Sam and Dave in hopes of crossing over to pop. In a few years, they would reach fame at Stax Records with songs custom fit to them by Isaac Hayes and David Porter, including "Soul Man," "Hold On, I'm Comin'," and "I Thank You." But in the early hours of this morning, they had long finished their show and were basking in the afterglow of a little clandestine Southern hospitality.

That's when all hell broke loose: A bomb ripped through the 16th Street Baptist Church, killing four schoolgirls. "Dave and I were there, across the street at a hotel," Moore recalls. "We couldn't afford our own rooms, so we were there together, and believe it or not, we had two white girls in the room with us—in Birmingham, Alabama. We were lying up with these young white women, talking and carrying on, and we heard this BOOM, and it shook us! I mean, we jumped up, and we ran to the window, and people were just *staring*, then they started running. And I remember we went downstairs, and Dave asked what was going on, and the guy at the desk kinda drawled something about 'trubble at th' nigger church. You niggers need to stay where you are now.' He wouldn't let us outside!

"Then," Moore says, "the police started checking the neighborhood, including the hotel rooms. Dave was in a panic. And of course, they came banging up on our door— so hard they splintered it, and I'm not going to lie to you: we put those girls up under our bed, pulled the sheets out over them and tried to act normal. Next thing you know, these white fellas barge in, all guts-hanging-over-their-belt and one says, 'Who is you niggers?' I said, 'Sam, and this is Dave.' 'Sammy Davis?' he said. He thought we were putting him on. We told him we were entertainers, and we sang church music. I swear to God, we were so scared our shirts were drenched. Naturally the clerk told them about the girls, and the cop wants to know where they are, but we're not talking. So he says, 'Why don't we have a look around, and if we find them, we cut your dicks off.' Then, for some reason, he backs off and says, 'We're gonna go downstairs, but we will be back, you understand what I'm saying, *boy?*' And we got those girls outta there and left up outta there as fast as two people ever did anything."

The true cost of defying racists on their home turf became apparent a few weeks after the disappearance of activists Michael Schwerner, Andrew Goodman, and James Chaney on June 21, 1964. The trio had been ambushed and murdered by nearly two dozen Klansmen abetted by a county deputy sheriff in Philadelphia, Mississippi. Overnight incarceration and bruises were tolerable risks in the minds of many idealists, but martyrdom was something else again. Rumors began to circulate that many whites in the movement were losing faith and had privately consigned black people to their fate. The SNCC began a purge of its white members lest their pessimism become contagious.

Black activists withdrew into church music and soul, leaving folk to the coffeehouse cognoscenti. White kids, in turn, abandoned their Southern crusade for the insulated calm of academia, but something had changed in their absence. Their transistor radios had become a musical hall of mirrors with a dozen Bob Dylan wanna-bes banging on as many guitars—each one with a prettier voice, a slicker arrangement, and a less strident social agenda than the last.

Idealists saw firsthand how cutting-edge music becomes passé as soon as the record industry identifies a trend and starts to churn out copycats in the mold of the prototype. The Weavers, a Caucasian folk combo consisting of Pete Seeger and a few other left-of-center pals, unintentionally provided a blueprint in the 1950s with their straightforward readings of Leadbelly's "Goodnight Irene" and a tune of African origin they called "Wimoweh," which became an international hit in 1952.

Journalist Rian Malan traced the song back to its roots in a 2000 article for *Rolling Stone*. As it turns out, black South African vocalist Solomon Linda improvised the original melodic line in 1939 when he recorded "M'Bube" (or "the lion" in Zulu) with a group called the Evening Birds. By the time the lily-white Tokens took it to #1 in the United States at the end of 1961, its title was "The Lion Sleeps Tonight," and Solomon Linda's name was missing from both the record and the sheet music.

CUPID

Black singing sensation Sam Cooke wasn't about to share Linda's fate—not if he could help it, anyway. Cooke and Ray Charles were among the first singer-songwriters to demand control of their intellectual property, and, just as Charles left Atlantic Records in 1960 because another label promised him more money and ownership of his master tapes, Sam Cooke passed on a contract offer from Jerry Wexler and the Ertegun brothers for the same reason. Wexler never missed an opportunity to call Sam "the best singer who ever lived," but when it came down to granting Sam his own publishing, Atlantic balked, and Cooke ended up on the RCA roster with Elvis Presley.

Sam Cook (later to be spelled with an "e") was born in Mississippi in 1931 to an itinerant preacher who relocated to Chicago's largely black suburb of Bronzeville while the family was still young. There, Sam was brought up in the gospel community, where he performed with his siblings and opened for his father as one of the Singing Children. In his spare time, Sam read voraciously and sang tunes from the Hit Parade on the corner with his friends to earn spending money. By the time Sam was 18, he was set to tour with a group of his own, the Highway Q.C.s, and had apprenticed himself to R.B. Robinson of the world-famous gospel group the Soul Stirrers.

Despite intense criticism, the charismatic Sam Cooke abandoned a gospel career with the Soul Stirrers to embark on a quest for crossover stardom. "You Send Me," "Cupid," and "Chain Gang" began a run of chart successes that allowed Cooke to form his own production company. His posthumous hit, "A Change Is Gonna Come," looked beyond the dance party hits into a future where soul music reflected the turbulence of the 1960s. (Star File)

Cook was also impressed by the secular world, where Nat "King" Cole, Johnny Mathis, and Sammy Davis, Jr. had an abundance of everything the boy found most desirable—music, women, riches, and fame. Sam's devotion to scripture and his drive for crossover success were at odds throughout the remainder of his life. Nevertheless, when the Soul Stirrers lost their lead vocalist to retirement in 1950, they turned to twenty-year-old Sam Cook, who appreciated the enormity of leading gospel music's premiere male attraction. He threw himself into the work and grew a moustache that barely reached both ends of his smile. Even so, his first outing as a Soul Stirrer, "Jesus Gave Me Water," sways with confidence and offers hints at the vocal acrobatics to come. The record sold better than many Stirrers classics, and the group spent the next five years barnstorming across the country, winning converts and rousing the nascent libidos of young female congregants. But to remain a gospel singer forever would have marginalized Sam's talent, and he knew it.

In 1956, Specialty Records delivered a blatant rewrite of the Soul Stirrers' "Wonderful" to Top 40 radio. "Loveable," as it was now called, was attributed to one Dale Cook. Its middling chart performance only strengthened Sam's resolve. He added an "e" to his last name, took the masters that Specialty deemed "too pop" for rhythm and blues (R&B), and left the studio. It was their loss. The next single, "You Send Me," sold an estimated 1.7 million copies.

The elements of a hit record were all there—a hummable tune sung with originality by a handsome star—except that the single's original A-side was Sam's cover of "Summertime" by George Gershwin. On a hunch, a young Detroit disc jockey flipped the 45 to play Sam's self-penned confection. "The producer, Bumps Blackwell, had been fired by Specialty because he put white singers in the background," radio pioneer Casey Kasem recalled later. "I was the first one to turn that record over. I was working at WJLB, a black radio station, as a newsman and a board operator in 1954, so I was exposed to a lot of that music. During the 1950s, I always watched the black charts very carefully, and I was very conscious of what was happening there. In those days, disc jockeys made their reputations by finding records, and if you could take a song that had already proven itself on the black charts and play it, your chances of getting a hit were pretty strong. A couple of years later, when I was doing my own show, I broke 'You Send Me.'"

Cooke soon became a fixture on the pop charts with such hits as "Only Sixteen," "(What a) Wonderful World," "Chain Gang," "Cupid," and "Twistin' the Night Away." Biographer Daniel Wolff spoke to Herb Alpert (who led the Tijuana Brass in the 1960s and later cofounded A&M Records) about Sam's knack for transforming study hall chitchat into the stuff of classic soul. "Sam used to come in with a loose-leaf folder of lyrics," he tells Wolff. "On sight, the lyrics just looked like . . . eh! You just didn't get any tremendous feeling from the words on the page. But then you asked him to pick up the guitar and play the song; it turned into a magical experience . . . . I'd look over his shoulder and say, 'Is that the same song you just showed me?'"[5]

Onstage, Cooke worked the Chitlin Circuit much as he had the churches, except that women no longer had any qualms about throwing themselves at him while he wooed them through song. His aspirations were decidedly loftier. Cooke was desperate to shine in the Rat Pack world of casinos and nightclubs—those places where Nat, Sammy, and Mathis could command thousands for extended engagements. The dichotomy between the soulful Sam and Cooke the cabaret singer is well documented on record: during his life, he released a live album recorded at New York's Copacabana club that includes such shopworn standards as "Bill Bailey, Won't You Please Come Home" and "Frankie and Johnny."

But more than two decades later, tapes of Sam at a Miami hot spot called the Harlem Square Club surfaced to show how gruff and loose and sexual Sam could be in a less stodgy (white) environment. Women in the crowd are captured in midswoon as Cooke offers up "Chain Gang," "Cupid," and a gospel-drenched rendition of "Bring It on Home to Me." While most live albums are little more than greatest hits collections distinguished by moments of self-indulgence and ambient noise, *Live at the Harlem Square Club* showcases Cooke at his most irresistible and charismatic. He sings rings around anyone who's ever held a microphone, and infuses his pop melodies with a raspy grit that singers ever since have failed to surpass. And that was just the *music*. Joined by sax virtuoso King Curtis and a taut group of road-seasoned professionals, Cooke turns in a bravura performance, with the band and the crowd goading each other from one climax to another—communicating entirely through Sam.

The fireworks are real, but nothing new to Cooke, who was reaching for something on a different plane altogether. On *Live at the Copa*, he covered Bob Dylan's "Blowin' in the Wind," and he set about writing a bookend piece from the black perspective. His inspiration became the brilliant "A Change Is Gonna Come," a song both pop and gospel and yet neither. Sam's original became an instant classic. Spike Lee uses Cooke's version in *Malcolm X* (whom Sam also knew) to transport his audience back to the calamitous 1960s. The song unfolds with a quick bio of the narrator, "born by the river in a little tent," who then describes the yoke of his life as "too hard livin', but I'm afraid to die." Next comes something of a surprise from a preacher's son: "I don't know what's up there beyond the sky." I don't know much, he testifies, but something tells him "A change is gonna come." At the bridge, Sam makes his timeless tale contemporary when he reports being harassed at the movies and downtown. The song ends as it began, elliptical and yearning with an undertow of conflicting emotions. However things turn out, he concludes with restraint, they cannot remain as they are. "A change is gonna come," he assures us, and himself. "Yes, it will."

The changes Cooke wrought in the music business were many. By 1964, he was a performing songwriter and an icon in both the sacred and secular communities who oversaw his own management firm, a publishing concern, and a record label. But Cooke saw only a glimmer of the influence he'd have. He missed hearing the many artists he inspired. Sam never caught Aretha Franklin sauntering through "You Send Me" or saw Otis Redding bellowing "Shake!" to the delight of audiences from Paris to Monterey. Sam might have been chagrined by Cat Stevens' take on "Another Saturday Night" or Rod Stewart's sloppy-rock reading of "Twistin' the Night Away." And it's easy to picture him shaking his head at Journey frontman Steve Perry, the 1980s singer who took Sam's signature yodel and made it his own. "You make me we-e-yeep," Perry yelps at the opening of "Lovin', Touchin', Squeezin'"—as if he'd just invented it.

Sam Cooke died December 11, 1964 under suspicious circumstances. After checking into a Los Angeles motel with a woman who was not his wife, Cooke came beating on the door of the motel manager wearing nothing but his sport coat—because his "guest" had fled with the rest of his clothes. The singer charged her, she testified, and she first beat him away, then pulled a gun on him and fired. When asked if she knew she'd hit him, she said yes, because Sam told her, "Lady, you shot me."

In 2000, RCA issued a box set dedicated to Cooke's legacy, calling it *The Man Who Invented Soul.* In hindsight, it seems soul music had more in common with rock 'n' roll than their common bloodline. With Ray Charles performing only cover material and Sam Cooke now dead, the medium's greatest pioneers were no longer making new music.

NIGHT TRAIN

Cooke and Charles shared a desire to market themselves on both sides of the color line. Neither would ever be mistaken for white, but Cooke kept the arrangements trend friendly and curtailed his vocal acrobatics, while Ray Charles broadened his appeal with familiar favorites and something else: an album called *Modern Sounds in Country Music.* Not only was it Charles' first full LP to explore white roots music (after his 1959 dalliance with Hank Snow's "I'm Movin' On"); it was the first time most Grand Ole Opry fans heard their music performed with soul. "All it did was legitimize country music," Willie Nelson says matter-of-factly. "Before that record, people thought country music meant songs written by hobos, recorded by hayseeds, and sold to hillbillies. Ray Charles put country music in a tuxedo."

In an era when no one defied convention, Charles did the unthinkable. At a time when white singers sang country and black men kept to the blues, Ray revealed that these genres were separated by nuance, not by color. Some of the album tracks were songs he remembered from childhood, while others he'd overheard in clubs, at parties, or on the radio. With tunes like "Worried Mind," "Born to Lose," and "I Can't Stop Lovin' You," the record built a bridge between generations. Michael McDonald, the burry-voiced former Doobie Brother, recalls: "My Dad was a singer, and one of his favorites was Ray Charles. One of my earliest memories was when I was hardly old enough to see over the dashboard of our '57 Ford Fairlane and watching my Dad crank the radio whenever Ray Charles came on. I think his favorite was *Modern Sounds in Country & Western,* so that became my introduction to pop music, too. Even now, Ray still takes me back, and I only need to hear the sound of his voice to feel good again. That music was something my Dad and I really shared in a relationship that really didn't have a lot of other commonalities."

Charles and Sam Cooke led the crossover charge through the mid-1960s, joined on occasion by such female singers as Barbara Lewis ("Baby, I'm Yours"), Barbara Mason ("Yes, I'm Ready"), and Doris Troy ("Just One Look"), but the nation's juke joints were concurrently stuffed to the rafters with road acts better known for their shows than their hits.

McDonald grew up in the late 1950s and early 1960s in St. Louis, Missouri, a city that "may not have appeared to be segregated on the surface," he says. "But it was underneath. And it was sad for us, because all the bands we considered the best—our idols growing up in St. Louis—were the bands with the black rhythm sections. For example, Ike Turner's band was always great, even before Tina. But in order to see those bands, you had to go over to East St. Louis for the most part. In fact, it was Ike Turner who kind of broke that barrier by playing on the other side of the river at the Club Imperial, one of the nicer dance clubs for people our age. They really played to a much larger audience than many black groups were allowed to."

No one worked the Chitlin Circuit harder or better than James Brown, born in 1933 and raised on both sides of the Savannah River in South Carolina and Georgia. Brown grew up hard; his mother deserted him and his father sent him to live with relatives in

Augusta, where he picked cotton and peanuts, cut sugarcane, and put his instinct for showbiz to work in creating a flashy shoe shine for passersby. He quickly picked up licks on the drums, piano, and guitar, and learned to sing gospel in church. But, like Sam Cooke and Ray Charles, Brown also had a sweet spot for pop. He liked everything from Sinatra and Crosby to Glenn Miller and Count Basie and especially loved the Louis Jordan film shorts featured at the Lenox Theater. Sitting there in the dark, watching Jordan yelp out "Cal-done-Ya!" Brown heard a sound he would later transform into squeals that conveyed anguish, delight, and innumerable emotions in between.

After showing early promise in sports as well as in music, Brown demonstrated that he had a knack for stealing, too. At 16, he was convicted on a charge of armed robbery. He served a three-year sentence without incident, but adversity imbued his grunts and growls with depth and resonance—those wordless exhortations not far removed from the cries of African slaves. Once paroled, Brown returned to the gospel and pop he loved, dissolved one band and set up another: the Famous Flames. Within another three years, he was second in stature only to the Georgia Peach himself, Little Richard. And when Richard's career took off, it fell to Brown and the Famous Flames to fill the same halls, which they did with a driving sound that had none of the salacious freneticism of their predecessor. In its place were rhythms slick as well-waxed linoleum, and out front a man dancing—or was it skating?—in four directions at once, a blur of passion, precision, and economy. Over and over, he'd scream, "Please . . . Please . . . *PLEASE* . . ."

Unlike Charles and Cooke, though, Brown's crossover to pop success was delayed for years by label missteps and lack of faith in the raw R&B that the Famous Flames had now stoked into an inferno. At the zenith of Presleymania in the winter of 1956, Brown and his band were signed to King Records in Cincinnati. Label president Syd Nathan didn't like "Please, Please, Please," and agreed to issue the single only under duress and, one suspects, a half-hearted attempt to recoup what he could from a bad investment. As a businessman, he never really understood why fans adored this gutbucket R&B sound, but once the record sold a million copies, Nathan had to admit that Brown had something worth keeping.

Every few weeks a new routine for the show materialized. Brown did splits, shimmies, and the "mashed potatoes" (a hot dance at the time), and dropped to his knees so often they were swollen and sometimes bleeding by the encore. Rumor had it that he lost seven pounds a night in performance. At the show's conclusion, his emcee would drape Brown's crumpled body in a cape and lead him off, supposedly drained—until the band's irresistible rhythms summoned him back to center stage. A hundred years before, Charles Dickens wrote of the black dancer billed as Juba, famous for "snapping his fingers, rolling his eyes, turning in his knees, presenting the backs of his legs in front, spinning about on his toes and heels, dancing with two left legs—all sorts of legs and no legs" at all. Whatever polyrhythmic demons Juba was exorcising had clearly found a new host in the soul of James Brown.

His hits on the R&B charts continued unabated, from "Try Me" (1957), "I'll Go Crazy" and "Think" (1960), to "Night Train" (1962), with Brown providing the material and Nathan providing the mechanism—a typical arrangement between artist and label at the time. Still, Brown strained at his tether every moment. Nathan thought him capricious, but his creative brainstorms often resulted in dance hits that consistently appealed to young black record buyers. Predictably, when Brown met with his boss in 1962 to discuss making a live album in Harlem, Nathan quashed the idea. Brown recalls pitching the concept in his autobiography, *James Brown: The Godfather of Soul*. Brown tried to explain how his songs took on a new life in a concert setting. "You ought to hear the way the audience hollers," he told the label chief.

Nathan was unmoved "I'm not going to spend money on something where a lot of people are going to be screaming," he said. "Who wants a lot of noise over the songs?"[6]

Ultimately, Brown slapped down $5,700 of his own money to finance the project. Certainly there had been live albums before, including such recent R&B hits as Ray Charles' own live record, *In Person*, but the sonic boom of *James Brown Live at the Apollo* reverberated throughout the music world. Recorded in October 1962 at the world-famous Harlem nightspot on a bitterly cold Wednesday (traditionally the Apollo's amateur night to ensure a raucous crowd), Brown got everything he could have hoped for. The atmosphere is electric, the Famous Flames turn on a rhythmic dime, and Brown sets a standard for recorded frenzy that would stand for decades to come. The LP became the centerpiece of every James Brown fan's collection, even for those who had bought all the studio versions of the songs—which had been Brown's original intent. But the sizzle that stretched over both sides of the record (actually less than a half hour long from start to finish) also won millions of new converts who barely knew him until the LP took off in the spring of 1963. Owning the master tapes also gave Brown enough leverage to block the release of any singles from the album. Professional suicide, some thought, but Brown was once again vindicated when R&B stations fielded scores of requests to play an entire side of the record rather than any one song, and the album went on to become a million seller.

The following year, Brown agreed to appear on a TV program called *The T.A.M.I. Show* alongside such acts as the Rolling Stones, Bo Diddley, the Supremes, Marvin Gaye, Chuck Berry, and white pop performers Leslie Gore and Gerry and the Pacemakers. In a studio full of stars, Brown's shone brightest as he committed the same magic to film that he put down on vinyl the year before. He spent the next phase of his career chiseling songs down to a few core ingredients—jabbing horns, paint-peeling screeches, and the choked scratch of electric guitars driving a ferocious rhythm.

In 1965, with white America finally ready to hear such voices as Bob Dylan and Mick Jagger, James Brown had a pair of pop-soul tunes that gleamed like matching cuff links on Top 40 radio. "Papa's Got a Brand New Bag" (#1 R&B and #8 pop hits) and "I Got You" (#1 R&B and #3 pop hits) paved the way for the sonic lathe in voices from Wilson Pickett and Tina Turner to the parade of white blues belters that would soon follow, including Led Zeppelin's Robert Plant, Janis Joplin, and Paul Rodgers of Bad Company. Not that James Brown worried about the competition. The man introduced as the "hardest working man in show business . . . Mr. Dynamite . . . the Godfather of Soul" and "Soul Brother Number One" finally stripped his music of everything that wasn't either rhythm or emotion. The recipe yielded hits in "Cold Sweat" (#1 R&B and #8 pop hits, 1967) and "Get Up, (I Feel Like Being a) Sex Machine" (recorded in 1970 with a brand new group, the J.B.s), and, later, "Get on the Good Foot" and "Get Up Offa That Thing."

Brown's dance moves created a blueprint for R&B stagecraft copied by everyone from Michael Jackson and Prince to Vanilla Ice and 'N Sync. He was also among the first artists to address race pride directly through music, and, as such, his heirs include George

Clinton, Bob Marley, Public Enemy, the Fugees, Mos Def, the Roots, and many others. Add to that the likelihood that Brown is the most widely sampled artist of all time, and that his beats laid the foundation for everything that would become funk and much of what would become hip-hop.

James Brown broke through the race barrier in 1964 when he lip-synched his way onto the big screen in a Frankie Avalon picture called *Ski Party*. The costumers dressed him in a preposterous snow bunny outfit, but at that moment, even an avalanche couldn't have frosted the funk he laid down. In the few minutes of film time allotted him, Brown took a group of Hollywood extras straight to the ghetto.

PAINT IT BLACK

Halfway through the 1960s, many of the R&B pioneers who couldn't crack the Top 40 at home discovered they were worshipped by white teens overseas. "I really don't know what it was that made black American music mean so much to white working-class English kids," puzzles English blues singer Joe Cocker. "I grew up on the left side of the tracks, so I guess maybe that created some relative connection in being able to identify with what we call black music."

Raised in the debris of bombed out Britain, English youngsters had firsthand experience of deprivation, squalor, and uncertainty—and all the attendant responses that spawned the blues to begin with. Some liked to sneak transistor radios into bed, where they could scan the dial for American rock and blues broadcasts from Radio Luxembourg or the BBC. Signals were sometimes faint and constantly shifting, so in a very real way they were secret radio operators only a generation removed from the underground resistance of occupied Europe.

"Radio Luxembourg would come on about 11 o'clock at night," Cocker recalls, "and I remember 'What'd I Say' as the first real R&B record for me. I mean, we used to listen to Little Richard, Chuck Berry, and Jerry Lee Lewis, but Ray Charles' 'What'd I Say' was the revelation for me. I remember hearing 'Whole Lotta Shakin'' by Jerry Lee when I was about 12 and just being in disbelief. I remember the record label on the jukebox and thinking it was Jerry Lewis, the comedian, and thinking, 'Wow!' These records were coming at you from right and left in those days, and I think that's why they stand up today; there was no fixed mode of making them, and every one was just a guessing game and that's why a few of them were absolute gems."

As a teenager, Mick Jagger mail-ordered records by Chicago bluesmen and anxiously waited to see how many would arrive from the States intact. Before long, he connected with a guitar player named Keith Richards, who spied him on a train with a copy of *The Best of Muddy Waters* tucked under one arm. Like so many English adolescents, Jagger and Richards freed themselves from the bleak sameness of postwar English life by delving deep into mystical Americana—resplendent in the sunshine with its open spaces, fast cars, and pretty girls, and entrancing in the moonlight with its black masters of hoodoo and the blues. Decoding the records of Muddy Waters, Lightnin' Hopkins, and John Lee Hooker became a national pastime.

Eric Burdon was a folk fan years before he and the Animals stormed the charts with "House of the Rising Sun" in 1964. "It was a trickle down effect," he explains, "when Lonnie Donnegan joined the Chris Barber Traditional Jazz Band, and then suddenly there was skiffle (an upbeat offshoot of folk, typified by Donnegan's "Rock Island Line"). Then you put a backbeat to skiffle, and suddenly it became rock 'n' roll. Suddenly Elvis Presley came along, and we all wondered, 'Where the fuck did this guy come from? Is he male or is he female for a start, and what's he singing? Is it, 'Since my baby left me, I been in a lonely Hell,' or is it . . . ? And we'd have competitions to find out who would be the first to translate the lyrics into English we could understand."

What's clear is that once they got it, they got it like a virus. Burdon refers to Chuck Berry as "the Poet Laureate of America," and considers Berry responsible for "putting Bob Dylan on the right track. Bob knew what to say and what must be said and was plugged in directly to the folk roots, but Chuck Berry took the sexuality—and it was an innocent, high school sexuality, pre–pill sexuality, which made it a lot more innocent—but I think that for the time that Chuck made his statements, I thought they were as hard-core, as deep blue as Muddy Waters."

Fandom inevitably led to emulation, with bands like the Animals and the Rolling Stones attracting throngs who not only cheered for their favorite Howlin' Wolf and Willie Dixon tunes, but for the peculiarly English way in which the bands re-created what they heard. Early on, there were hardly enough devotees to support a group, Cocker says. "Oh, we did some teen dances, but we really played in a lot of workingman's clubs. We wore the suits and ties, and we played this one place where a machine with a lightbulb would come on if you played over 10 decibels. They were very stiff kinds of places where they were used to hearing Frankie Laine soundalikes, you know."

Disaffected youngsters embraced them, but the English mainstream media considered British blues something of an oxymoron. In a 1964 *Melody Maker* column labeled "RUB-BISH," British columnist Bob Dawbarn sniffed, "My chief complaint against The Rolling Stones—and against virtually all of the so-called British R&B movement—is its utter lack of originality. There are dozens of Americans doing the same thing, only better."

While those in the previous generation "sandpapered their epiglottis and tried to sing like Louis Armstrong," Britain was now plagued by "painful imitations of the Chicago Negro singers—listen to Mick Jagger on 'Walking the Dog,' for a typical example." Dawbarn concluded, "To me, it is still farcical to hear the accents, sentiments, and experiences of an American Negro coming out of a white-faced London lad"—a mirror image of barbs hurled at the Fisk Jubilee Singers a hundred years earlier when they dared to show up in evening dress to sing their program of original spirituals.

British rock and blues gathered momentum until groups finally began to clamber out of their hovels and into larger venues in 1962. Billy Preston, touring Europe as a second keyboardist with Little Richard's band, watched the momentum build: "The Beatles were the opening act on that tour," he says. "We met when they played Liverpool, and then they spent two weeks opening for us at the Star Club in Germany. I used to get free Cokes and steaks and pass them onto the band, because I could get whatever I wanted since I was in the headliner's group."

By late 1963, even Americans were taking notice. The *CBS Evening News* marked the Beatles' American TV debut, according to Walter Cronkite. One of the network's more straight-laced and serious correspondents had seen the moptops in England and filed a story on the gathering storm. "We all remarked on their long hair," Cronkite laughs, "and it just barely touched the top of their ears, but that was really long for the time. And they

Briton Eric Burdon led two bands to fame in the 1960s. With the Animals, he helped reintroduce the sound of the blues to young America. When he left War (pictured surrounding Burdon) in 1971, the band soldiered on, scoring a string of pop and R&B hits that included the graphic urban landscapes "Slipping Into Darkness" and "The World Is a Ghetto." (Frank Driggs Collection)

were packing in the music hall there with young ladies who were screaming and yelling, and apparently these guys were the hottest thing happening in the Midlands. And our reporter Alexander Kendrick did a little short about them and their popularity. We had the story kicking around in the shop there for several weeks and never used it because it was just a feature, filler really. The night we finally did run it, we weren't even off the air when Ed Sullivan called and said, 'Hey, tell me about those kids—The Bugs, or whatever they call themselves. How do I find them?' So I helped him find Kendrick, who led him to the Beatles. He recognized their appeal and flew them immediately to America, where they were on his show the following Sunday."

The Beatles' appearance with Ed Sullivan in February 1964 triggered an obsession with all things English and put the British Invasion into high gear. Bands from the Rolling Stones to the Animals, on down to the Dave Clark Five and Herman's Hermits found that overnight they had become teen idols, even though American parents had no more use for them than for their black mentors. When Mick Jagger and company found their way onto the American airwaves via *The Hollywood Palace* in 1964, they got something less than the warm welcome Ed Sullivan extended the Beatles. Host Dean Martin repeatedly taunted the quintet, chuckling that their hair wasn't as long as it seemed, "it's just smaller heads and higher eyebrows."

The most vapid British imports were no worse than their domestic counterparts, while the best were able to bring the blues back home in a way that made sense to American youth. But for those who already had a deep affinity for R&B and expectations for how it should be played, the English had a lot to learn. "I went to see the Stones," Michael McDonald winces, "and frankly I didn't get it. To me, the whole experience was a strange spectacle. Now I really appreciate the Rolling Stones and I love their book of songs and what they do, but it took me a while to get it, because to me it just didn't translate—a bunch of white guys up there playin' R&B. Their guitars were always out of tune, and the drummer was kinda funky, but they didn't have a lot of ability going on up there that I could see. It's not that I didn't like white soul bands, but I really was used to a band like Mitch Ryder's, where the playing was a lot better."

The Stones, the Beatles, and the rest of the British bluesmen engendered a new appreciation of R&B, McDonald says, and popularized songs the masses might have otherwise overlooked. "The British also had a greater understanding of the older blues artists than I did," he admits. "I wouldn't have said, 'You gotta listen to this old blues record,' someone whose teeth are all out mumbling and whose guitar is really out of tune. That's just not the school of music I came from. Now I realize it's an acquired taste, and the Rolling Stones uncovered something in those records that not only inspired them, but inspired the generations who grew up listening to them."

In Britian, a rift developed between pop blues bands and their more doctrinaire counterparts. Purist outfits like the Graham Bond Organisation (who also evinced traces of jazz) and John Mayall's Bluesbreakers developed a fiercely loyal following by playing their blues without artistic license or pandering. By definition, this limited the groups' commercial prospects, but there was an underground cachet to being in the group or its fan base that British teens loved. One of those was Eric Clapton, a fiery young guitarist who walked away from the Yardbirds on the eve of their first pop blues hit, "For Your Love."

A mutual respect developed fast between Delta bluesman B.B. King and English wunderkind Eric Clapton. While King never altered his fluid, direct style during the psychedelic era, Clapton pushed the blues into uncharted territory with wild flights of improvisation. Hippies at the Fillmore and Winterland ballrooms embraced them both. (DP/MO/Star File)

Clapton took to practicing more than five hours a day in solitude, then emerged from seclusion as the featured attraction of Mayall's Bluesbreakers. The Yardbirds never had a steady lead guitarist again. Clapton was first replaced by Jeff Beck, then by Jimmy Page. Beck departed in 1966 to work with Rod Stewart in the Jeff Beck Group and left Page to fulfill the group's live obligations with "The New Yardbirds," a band that morphed within a few months into Led Zeppelin. The end of the 1960s would see the stream of British guitar virtuosos continue with Procol Harum's Robin Trower, Fleetwood Mac's Peter Green, and Humble Pie's young prodigy, Peter Frampton.

American musicians caught in the riptide of Beatlemania "went electric" as well. Bob Dylan, the Byrds, and the Grateful Dead launched the folk rock movement with extended solos and more adventurous arrangements. Many of these groups had no idea what the blues were, and learned everything they knew from British Invasion records. When Jack Bruce and Ginger Baker (who had played together with Graham Bond) joined Eric Clapton (who had worked with both of them separately) to form Cream, the trio flaunted their pedigree as well-schooled practitioners of the blues. Even their name was meant to telegraph that they were the "Cream" of the English blues elite.

When the band toured America in 1967, they were stunned at what their love for the blues had wrought. Once venues like the Fillmore and Avalon ballrooms opened their doors, Eric Clapton told a reporter for the British television series *South Bank*, "we were up against people like the Jefferson Airplane, the Grateful Dead, and Big Brother and the Holding Company. And they really were struggling. It didn't seem to me like any of them had really listened to any of the proper records. It was like they were all influenced by the Kingston Trio or something. So we walked in and cleaned the place up."

For a blues purist like Bonnie Raitt, psychedelia wasn't exactly the Golden Era she had been hoping for: "I was aghast at the success of the psychedelic and acid blues stuff that was going on," she recalls. "It's always been very problematic for me that people like Johnny Winter were getting fifteen times what Buddy Guy was making, but that's the way it's always been. Eric Clapton gets a lot more than Buddy does now, and some of that is that he's not only doing blues, but incorporating blues into rock and pop."

While Clapton, Jagger and the rest were clearly getting rich off music they did not invent, Raitt maintains that "the Rolling Stones did more to publicize the blues in America than any other group. They and Eric Clapton were very vocal about their influences and cast a lot of attention on people like Muddy, Lightnin' Hopkins, John Lee Hooker, and Howlin' Wolf. And you have to remember; all of the great blues-rock that we love came about as a direct result of what was created in the Mississippi Delta. They're all streams from the same tributary."

Rock 'n' roll began its transformation into rock when car-and-surfboard ditties were supplanted by elements of blues and soul. During that transition, it was commonplace to see British hitmakers on the same bill as one of the blues veterans who inspired them. "In the long run," Burdon says, "my early friends, the guys like Mick Jagger, Keith Richards, and John Steele out of the Animals, and John Lennon and Paul McCartney were responsible for saving rhythm and blues, for saving American music, pulling it out of the trash can, dusting it off and saying, 'What is this? It's fucking magic!' I mean the people at Decca (Records) were about to trash this stuff. They were about to burn their catalogs to make more room for pop."

COMMERCIAL BREAKS

Indeed, American folk music seemed to be following the same route the Clampetts took in *The Beverly Hillbillies*' opening credits—bounding out of the backwoods and into the heavy traffic of pop culture. Unlike the Clampetts, though, these folkies were quick to assimilate into the urban marketplace. Hits by the Highwaymen ("Cotton Fields"), the New Christy Minstrels ("Green Green"), and the Kingston Trio ("M.T.A.") paved the way for others trying to exploit the acoustic craze, among them Burl Ives, the Journeymen, the Chad Mitchell Trio, and a national organization called Up With People!

In the same way Paul Whiteman once sought to legitimize jazz, a new generation of songwriters prettified R&B for mass consumption. These tunesmiths were the spiritual descendants of Tin Pan Alley—some artful craftsmen, others shameless hacks. Many worked under the same roof at 1619 Broadway in New York's Brill Building, where Burt Bacharach and Hal David were breaking away from white schmaltz (they were already well known for such trifles as Perry Como's "Magic Moments" and "Blue on Blue" for Bobby Vinton) to create a kind of cabaret soul for a slate of black performers. What they began with the Shirelles' "Baby It's You" and Jerry Butler's "Make It Easy on Yourself" reached a peak by the time Dionne Warwick sashayed into the limelight with "Walk on By" in 1964.

Likewise, Carole King and partner Jerry Goffin composed in as many styles as they could conceive—including "Will You Still Love Me Tomorrow?"—a hit for the (black) Shirelles; "Don't Bring Me Down," a hit for the (white) British R&B band the Animals; and "I'm into Something Good," by the whiter-than-white U.K. pop group Herman's Hermits and, later still, the Monkees' "Pleasant Valley Sunday." Also on the staff roster: Neil Sedaka and collaborator Howard Greenfield, Barry Mann and his partner Cynthia Weil (the composers of Paul Revere and the Raiders' "Kicks" and "Hungry"), superstar-to-be Neil Diamond, and, preceding him, a Bronx wunderkind named Phil Spector.

Spector remains a mystery to many around him (at this writing he's under indictment for murder), but his reputation as a songwriter and arranger is unassailable. Under his Napoleonic rule, black artists were placed center stage in songs of nursery rhyme simplicity to create the era's first crossover hits. There was no mistaking his girls were black, but somehow it didn't matter—which was significant in and of itself. Sam Cooke had gone pop as had the Drifters and others before, but they always kept a bit of themselves in reserve in order to maximize their appeal. With Spector's groups, ethnicity was never sacrificed at the altar of opportunity.

Barely more than five feet tall and not even legally an adult, Spector exuded such an air of confidence that he could flaunt his Austin Powers fashion sense years before it became popular. Cuban heels mitigated his stature, and as Brill Building colleague and singer Tony Orlando recalled, "His hair was shoulder length, in what we call a pageboy, flipped up this way, both sides and in the back . . . and when a guy walked into a room with long hair in '61 (predating the Beatles by some three years) he was really a freak. You think there are freaks walking around now? That was really being freaky."[7]

Spector finessed his way into an apprenticeship with Jerry Leiber and Mike Stoller, the composers of such Elvis hits as "Jailhouse Rock" and "Trouble." Then, in collaboration with Leiber, Spector wrote "Spanish Harlem," a 1961 smash that launched a solo career for former Drifters frontman Ben E. King. Spector popped up next in the mix of the reconstituted Drifters' "On Broadway," playing the guitar break.

That same year, Spector formed Philles Records and began to develop a production technique hailed by session players as "The Wall of Sound." A combination of overdubs and overkill, his approach called for a studio crammed to the rafters with instruments (multiple pianos were commonplace), all to be recorded live simultaneously. The session tape was then repeatedly layered on top of itself until the track was sonically splitting at the seams. "A Wagnerian approach to rock 'n' roll," he called it. "Little symphonies for the kids."

A millionaire at 21, Spector headed west, where he assembled such disparate Los Angeles session stalwarts as Glen Campbell and Sonny Bono, future Joe Cocker sideman Leon Russell, and studio drummer Hal Blaine. Comedian Lenny Bruce played percussion on at least one date, and Herb Alpert, Harry Nilsson, and Mac Rebennack (a.k.a. Dr. John) all lent their talents as well. Spector's legions created a monumental body of work and began the cult of the "studio genius"—a title subsequently conferred on perfectionists from both sides of the color line.

Largely through the influence of music critics, artists since have been placed in one of two categories: those who catch fire before a live audience (Charlie Parker, James Brown, Bruce Springsteen, and Stevie Ray Vaughan all fit the bill), and those whose talents find fullest expression in the studio. Reviews in the mid-1960s began with praise for the audio experiments of the Beach Boys' Brian Wilson and the Beatles. That, in turn, ushered in the era of the studio auteur, with Jimi Hendrix, Steely Dan, Stevie Wonder, and Fleetwood Mac's Lindsey Buckingham all honored members of that exclusive club. In the late 1970s, the architects of disco (Donna Summer producer Georgio Moroder, for example) achieved celebrity nearly equal to the performers they lofted to stardom, while Brian Eno and Trevor Horn, and the team of Stock, Aitken, and Waterman (David Bowie, U2, Bananarama, and Seal) helped pave the way for contemporary electronica, today's club mixes, and the obsessive knob twiddling of such diverse acts as Prince, Beck, and Radiohead.

Spector's stock-in-trade was girl group bombast (with "Be My Baby" and "Baby, I Love You" for the Ronettes and "Da Doo Ron Ron" and "Then He Kissed Me" for the Crystals, both black female trios), but he could also work a song up from a whisper into a soulful roar, as he did with the (white) Righteous Brothers' hits, "You've Lost That Lovin' Feelin'" and "Unchained Melody" in 1964 and 1965, respectively. Spector sank a fortune into "River Deep, Mountain High," a 1966 high-stakes production featuring Tina Turner. Ike Turner was banned from the studio, where Tina sang the song until she thought her lungs would burst. "River Deep" was for Spector what *Citizen Kane* had been for Orson Welles—bigger in conception, grander in style, and more brilliantly executed than anything he'd done before. The British loved it, but the single stiffed in America, and Spector retreated into his mansion amid rumors of madness.

HITSVILLE U.S.A.

In Detroit, a black entrepreneur named Berry Gordy, Jr. tinkered with all the same components and came up with an entirely different invention. By applying his knowledge of the auto assembly line (where he once pulled down $86.40 a week) to record making, Gordy created a hit factory. By the time he founded Motown Records in 1959 with less than $1,000 in borrowed cash, Gordy had already carved out a niche for himself in the

1950s, progressing from failed boxer and record retailer into the composer of two major hits for Jackie Wilson, "Reet Petite" and "Lonely Teardrops." Over the next decade, Gordy watched his company grow into the largest black-owned business in America.

His timing couldn't have been better. The first wave of rock 'n' roll was over, with Elvis in Hollywood, Chuck Berry in jail, Little Richard at the pulpit, and Jerry Lee Lewis in exile. And, while Philadelphia, New York, and Los Angeles all had competitive music scenes, Motown faced few rivals in Detroit. Under cover of obscurity, Gordy prospected for composers who could write catchy tunes, then tapped into the local talent pool for unknown gospel singers who could record them. Such a plan increased the odds for success, but would have meant little without Gordy's unerring sense of what Americans—black *and* white—wanted to hear.

One Detroit hopeful who didn't make the cut was Billy Levise, who later rose to stardom as Mitch Ryder, fronting a band called the Detroit Wheels. "They loved my voice," the white singer recalls, "but I got turned down solely for the fact that I didn't write enough material. Motown was more sophisticated rhythm and blues, more pop-oriented, polished and accessible," he says. "They used to bring in the Detroit Symphony Orchestra and do a lot of string overdubs. Berry had a brilliant idea, obviously, and it sold and sold and sold, but it was a watered down version of what we used to call rhythm and blues."

With one eye trained on the bottom line and the other fixed on commercial trends, Gordy's instincts guided everything Motown and its ancillary labels released during the 1960s. All told, it was a staggering feat of micromanagement. His commitment was infectious too, filtering down through the ranks from raw studio recruits to the outer office help. Gordy put his entire company in service to each song rolling off the production line, as one track after another was meticulously readied for vinyl. Simplicity was the key. In the early years, from 1960 to 1962, Motown records were sock hop soap operas, running the gamut from parental advice (the Miracles' "Shop Around") to long distance love ("Mr. Postman" by the Marvelettes) and dancing (the Contours' "Do You Love Me?").

Melodic hooks were repeated frequently to ensure quick recognition; lyrics were innocuous by decree. Syncopation was verboten. More often, drum tracks were simplified, then amplified, lest any of Motown's more rhythmically challenged fans be left by the wayside. Hand claps and tambourines were common overdubs, but Gordy and company were not above enlisting the services of wood blocks, cowbells, footstomps, or clicking ballpoint pens to make their records more dance friendly. During the recording of "Dancing in the Street" in 1964, a session man beat the floor with snow chains to hammer home its 4/4 beat. It wasn't all that funky, groused a competitor, "but it sure sold."

For Gordy, that was enough—making hits and keeping the people who made the hits happy enough to make more hits. And, at the dawn of the decade, that challenge was daunting enough. Gordy surrounded himself with loyalists who understood that the upstarts at Motown would sink or swim together, and dual emphasis was placed on quality control and camaraderie. Four Tops lead singer Levi Stubbs maintains that "Motown was responsible for black and white music merging. The people there were concerned with excellence and there was a concerted effort to create music for a certain purpose," he says. "They wanted to reach everybody. I've never seen a company come together with such a common purpose and a kind of love—that's what made Motown."

Motown artists appeared so often on the Top 40 charts that it seemed the label's writers and arrangers had decoded exactly what elements comprised a hit record and could knock one off at will. Not so, says Stubbs: "Take 'I Can't Help Myself' (Sugar Pie, Honey Bunch), for example. I thought it was the worst song I'd ever heard. Eddie Holland said to go ahead and just put it on tape, and because we had respect for the writers and producers, that's what we did, and it became a huge hit. 'Reach Out (I'll Be There)' was also a little different for that time, and I didn't hear that, either, and it probably became our biggest success. These guys would call you on the phone at 2 A.M. and say, 'I've got something great for you. Are you up?' We came down at 3:30 in the morning and recorded 'Baby, I Need Your Lovin'.' That's the way it worked."

"The Motown Sound" remained an identifiable commodity throughout the 1960s while adapting to a rapidly evolving pop market. The talent pool included proven songwriters (Gordy and William "Smokey" Robinson), the hitmaking triumvirate of Eddie and Brian Holland and Lamont Dozier, and, later, Marvin Gaye, Stevie Wonder, and at least a half dozen others. There, at the label's Detroit studio on 2648 West Grand Boulevard, each melody was lavished with care by a group of studio musicians who earned their stripes as "the Funk Brothers." They included bassist James Jamerson, drummer Benny Benjamin, keyboard player Earl Van Dyke, and guitarists Marv Tarplin, Joe Messina, and Robert White. In 2002, the surviving members were paid belated tribute in a documentary called *Standing in the Shadows of Motown.* Berry Gordy was nowhere to be seen, and his absence went unmentioned.

Gordy seemed to regard selling to whites as a marketing strategy rather than a roadmap to integration and harbored few illusions of fostering racial unity through music. Perhaps he felt that guiding a black-owned company from inception to major-label status in less than five years was statement enough. Martin Luther King was the one with the dream: Gordy had a *plan*. Unfortunately, if providing his stable of artists more autonomy or a larger wedge of the royalty pie was ever part of that plan, those notions went quickly by the wayside.

"Everything was done to satisfy Berry," Martha Reeves of the Vandellas told author Joe Smith in *Off the Record.* "Whatever he said was right. During the early days, when we'd be rehearsing, he would sit in the audience and critique us and give us pointers, things I still use today. The man did know what he was doing. Everybody who did well at Motown owes it to Berry Gordy and his taste."[8]

Rough-hewn artists signed to the label were provided charm school lessons encompassing everything from diction and walking to which utensil went with what course at a formal dinner. But Gordy's goals for his artists were a double-edged sword. Tuxedos, evening gowns, and etiquette vaulted Motown's stable of stars out of the chicken-wire venues of the Chitlin Circuit, but many were so heavily programmed that they became blathering marionettes. Consider the live album that documents the Supremes' farewell concert in Las Vegas. Midway through "Someday We'll Be Together," Diana Ross weighs in on current events: "I'd like to see today, tomorrow, or in the coming year, let's bring all of our boys home from Vietnam," she coos. "And by all means, let's *do* try and put black and white together."

Little was left to chance. Like Phil Spector, Gordy made his fortune by controlling as many variables as possible, irrespective of obstacles or objections, and the veneer of Motown as all-for-one and one-for-all wore thin as the 1960s waned. While many competing record labels renegotiated contracts to reward their top breadwinners, Motown became known as one shop where the owner's interests superceded all others. Writers and performers were obliged to sign with Motown's Jobette music publishers, and the label established legal ownership of group names whenever possible. Furthermore, artists on tour typically received allowances rather than the entirety of their earnings on demand, because they were represented by Gordy's International Talent Management Incorporated.

"Motown had signed us to ironclad contracts and turned us into international stars," Reeves recalls. "Yet after several years of million-selling records and sold-out concerts, in 1969 I realized that my personal income was but a fraction of what it should have been."[9]

Nothing was above exploitation—not even Martin Luther King's "I Have a Dream" speech. In June 1963, King agreed to have Motown record his remarks at Detroit's Cobo Hall, but by the March on Washington at the end of August, the album had yet to see daylight. Yet when King's popularity soared after the Washington oration, the Motown LP suddenly appeared under the coy title *The Great March to Freedom*, with part of the Cobo Hall text subtitled "I have a dream." Soon King decided to sue Motown, 20th Century Fox, and Mr. Maestro Records for including the Washington address on albums that siphoned money away from the official release—profits of which were earmarked solely for the movement. In October, a federal judge in New York issued an injunction against all three labels. Then, for reasons unknown, King dropped Motown from the suit, but proceeded against the others. Finally in December, a New York federal court decreed that King's work was protected intellectual property, which opened the door for damages to be paid for the unsanctioned recordings.

Such naked greed contradicts Motown's carefully manicured image as a community participant. Certainly the label began in an atmosphere of cooperation, with Gordy and Smokey Robinson cast as the company's benevolent mentors. And when Motown releases began getting airplay, dozens of fresh-faced locals appeared at the studio pleading to audition. Among them were the Primettes, comprised of Barbara Martin, Florence Ballard, Mary Wilson, and the coquettish Diane (later Diana) Ross. "We would open for the touring acts that would come through," Wilson remembers. "We tried out, and Berry Gordy said he'd rather we finish high school first because we were just sophomores. After he turned us down, we started hitchhiking to Motown every day after school just to do hand claps and sing backgrounds."

Ultimately Barbara Martin dropped out and the girls did get their contract. They also racked up eleven flop singles in a row as an act that company insiders dejectedly called "the no-hit Supremes." Even Motown's most dependable songwriter, Smokey Robinson, couldn't get an angle on them, Wilson says. "Flo had an Aretha/Billie Holiday kind of style; Diane (as Ross was known pre-divadom) was pop, and I always sang the ballads. When we hooked up with Holland/Dozier/Holland, they captured our sound and it was like having a good tailor. They made the songs suit us completely." The next five Supremes records all reached #1 on the pop charts in the months between August 1964 and June 1965. They included "Where Did Our Love Go?," "Baby Love," "Come See About Me," "Stop! In the Name of Love," and "Back in My Arms Again."

Overlapping that period, crossover hits became so commonplace that *Billboard* magazine suspended publication of its R&B charts entirely from November 1963 until January of 1965, and the dawn of Beatlemania in the early months of 1964 further ob-

First nicknamed by their fellow Motown artists as the "no-hit Supremes," Florence Ballard, Mary Wilson, and Diana Ross saw nearly a dozen singles flop before they scored four #1 hit singles in a row in the mid-1960s. They became the template of R&B girl groups to come, influencing acts from the Pointer Sisters to En Vogue and Destiny's Child. (Frank Driggs Collection)

scured the picture. By the week of April 4, 1964, the Fab Four held all five of the top positions on the Top 40, and for the next year, only Motown and the Beach Boys could offer much competition.

For the Beatles, the rivalry with Gordy was a friendly one in which they regularly covered such Motown standards as "Money (That's What I Want)," "You've Really Got a Hold On Me," and "Please Mr. Postman." The moptops also provided some historical context for their younger fans by recording tributes to black rockers Larry Williams ("Slow Down" and "Dizzy Miss Lizzy"), the Isley Brothers ("Twist and Shout"), and Wilbert Harrison ("Kansas City"). It's impossible to overestimate the value of those endorsements, according to Temptations vocalist Otis Williams: "The Beatles gave credit to Bo Diddley, Chuck Berry, Frankie Lymon and the Teenagers—all of that brought attention to black music that had been around for ten years. People who had been buying covers by Pat Boone and the McGuire Sisters discovered that those songs had originally been done by Little Richard and the Moonglows."

Disc jockey Casey Kassem calls crossover "a recurring pattern." In the absence of a craze (think Elvis, the Beatles, new wave, grunge, rap, metal), when the pop charts stagnate, the public always turns to dance and rhythm-based music. "It's always there to fill the void," he says. "In the '60s, once Motown had that opportunity, they were on their way, especially with the girl groups. The records started pouring out of Philadelphia and New York and Phil Spector's label, and when the Beatles and the British Invasion came along, they didn't push Motown off the charts, because Motown *became* the pop charts."

During its peak years from 1964 to 1967, Motown's dominion extended from the upper reaches of pop culture with the Beatles down into fraternity parties and urban ghettos, from the Playboy Club to the juke joints of the South. In retrospect, according to Mary Wilson, Motown had vital impact on society as a whole. "Our sound transcended color," she says. "It brought all kinds of people together, made them aware of blackness and the enjoyment of music a universal thing. Some people have to march and scream and yell, but I think Motown did it through music. Not once did any of us think we were doing that. We didn't realize what we had done until much later, when we were all adults."

TRUE GRITS

A day's bus ride to the South, a string of small labels pieced together an alternative to Gordy's paint-by-numbers soul. The Stax label, followed by Fame Studios in Muscle Shoals, Alabama and later American (the Memphis company where Elvis Presley chose to record "Suspicious Minds") and Hi (the home of Al Green) kept closer to blues traditions and earned a reputation as blacker in inspiration and execution. In truth, though, there were usually more white musicians in the studios than were ever commonplace at Motown.

While Gordy's label was taking flight in Detroit, a variety of talents crossed paths in Memphis until they coalesced around a white country fiddler named Jim Stewart. The company began as Satellite Records in 1958 (partly inspired by Sam Phillips' Sun label) as a showcase for pop and country acts, but one release after another failed to click with the public. Something, Stewart knew, had to change. After recording at a variety of locales in and around the city, he finally settled into an old movie house in South Memphis.

To cut costs, he kept the sloping floor as his studio, modified the stage into a control room, and replaced the concession stand with an in-house record store. In the summer of 1960, Stewart agreed to record a Memphis radio personality named Rufus Thomas and his daughter, Carla. The resulting tune, "'Cause I Love You" turned out to be the hit he was looking for—only it was an R&B tune by a black duo.

For Stewart, there was no looking back. He told Stax historian Rob Bowman in retrospect, "prior to that, I had no knowledge of what black music was about. Never heard black music and never even had an inkling of what it was all about. It was like a blind man who suddenly gained his sight."[10]

"'Cause I Love You" caught the attention of New York record executive Jerry Wexler, who struck a deal for Atlantic Records to distribute the Stax tunes that seemed likely to catch on nationally. The Mar-Keys had just delivered on that promise in 1961 with an instrumental piece called "Last Night" (#2 R&B and #3 pop hits), when a preexisting Satellite Records asserted its ownership of the company name. Stewart and his sister Estelle Axton were forced to rechristen their label Stax (taking a syllable apiece from *St*ewart and *Ax*ton). Amid the ruckus, the complexion of the neighborhood was also changing, with blacks moving in while whites relocated to the suburbs. It was during this gestation that the Stax lobby shop evolved into a community center where musicians and R&B fans gathered to argue which records hit and why. A select few in this slow parade of unknowns drifted through the record store and into the Stax studio where, for the better part of the decade, they came to define Southern soul.

By 1962, the label had a house band, which included a black keyboardist and drummer (Booker T. Jones and Al Jackson, respectively) and a white guitarist named Steve Cropper. Black bassist Lewis Steinberg withdrew a few years later, leaving room for a young white player named Donald "Duck" Dunn. As Booker T. and the MGs, they struck gold with an instrumental called "Green Onions" (#1 R&B and #3 pop hits) in the fall of 1962. Singer-songwriters William Bell ("You Don't Miss Your Water") and Eddie Floyd ("Knock on Wood") joined soon after. Jim Stewart recognized his company had promise, but as a man who never leapt before looking, he kept his banking job until 1964.

Stewart's reservations may have stemmed from Stax's lack of consistency in and out of the studio. Stax records could shift wildly in tempo and players missed entrances, hit the occasional "clam" (bum note), and confused breaks with a bridge or chorus. Most of the horn parts were "head arranged," meaning that players improvised their roles while rehearsing and rarely had charts written out for them beforehand. Stax was anomalous in other ways, too: in New York, for example, studio musicians were paid by the three-hour session. Stax paid its players per completed master—allowing the songs to gel organically until everyone felt ready to roll tape. Not the most lucrative way to work, many later sighed, but then no one was getting rich at their expense, either.

Perhaps comparisons between Stax and Motown are unavoidable now, since both labels worked primarily in R&B with black artists and nipped at each other's heels on the singles charts throughout the 1960s. But by every measurable standard, from sales reports to chart positions, Motown ran rings around Stax—and it was easy enough to see why. Each camp made its mission clear with a slogan posted outside. While Gordy set a sales goal by hanging his "Hitsville U.S.A." shingle in front of Motown's Detroit address, the marquee outside Stax's renovated cinema emphasized quality over quantity. It read "Soulsville, U.S.A." Stax refused to smooth its rough edges for crossover success, and its staff thrived on interdependence rather than on the friendly competition Gordy liked to engender at Motown. In 1969, Stax became fully integrated when a black promotions and marketing executive named Al Bell bought out Estelle Axton.

Hits and stardom often translate to estrangement between those involved, but the nuclear family at Stax actually closed ranks during their peak years. This was not some photo opportunity concocted for the pages of *Ebony* or *The Saturday Evening Post*, but a camaraderie that began with Jim and Estelle, then grew exponentially with the arrival of the label's greatest talent, Otis Redding.

Redding's ascendance at Stax would have seemed miraculous to anyone but him. He was a man who lived, breathed, and pursued music his entire life. His first hit was a fluke, recorded at the end of an abortive session by Johnny Jenkins and the Pinetoppers in October 1962. There, as Steve Cropper remembers, Redding had been pestering people throughout the day for an opportunity to sing. Many present mistook him as either the band's valet or roadie, and when he began with a Little Richard knockoff called "Shout Bamalama," none of them were particularly agog. But Redding had another song he wanted to try, and in the time remaining, he led the players through "These Arms of Mine," a yearning plea that showed just how well Otis could write and sell a song. It was another year before he became a fixture at Stax, but once aboard, he became the spiritual patriarch of the company.

In 1965, Redding recorded perhaps his finest album, *Otis Blue*, in less than two days. "We went ten to six on a Saturday," Duck Dunn told author Peter Guralnick in *Sweet Soul Music*, "and then we all went and played our gigs until about two . . . and then we all came back to finish cutting, from about two 'till eight in the morning. Otis just had so much to do with the feeling at Stax, that was one reason it held together so long. See, you'd go along six weeks, say, cutting nothing but blues sessions—Johnny Taylor, Albert King—and it got so bad guys wouldn't even show up, and you'd have to put the session off. We finally quit playing Mondays altogether," Dunn said. No one was ever late for an Otis Redding date. "With Otis, you'd feel like you accomplished something. And that'd pick you up for a few weeks, and then you'd slump back off."[11]

Otis Blue contained some of Redding's most soulful work, alternating between his own compositions (including "I've Been Loving You Too Long" and "Respect," the song that would ignite Aretha Franklin's career) and daring reinterpretations of the Rolling Stones' "Satisfaction" and the Temptations' "My Girl." Plastered across the cardboard jacket of *Otis Blue* is a seductive portrait—not of the singer, but of an unidentified blonde whose head tilts to one side, apparently transported by the sensual sounds contained within. Is this white ingenue aroused by Otis, or is the photo a subtle hint to white singles that *Otis Blue* is make out music of the highest order? More importantly, where the hell is Otis Redding, and why is he absent from the cover of his own album? No one seems sure where the idea originated, but it reoccurs on the Booker T. and the MGs LP, *Hip Hug-Her*, where white girls in low-rise slacks pose in a layout typical of fashion photography of the day. Who made these marketing decisions and why? And if Motown watered down its music, did Stax try to camouflage black artists behind comely anglo faces to make whites feel more comfortable about buying their product?

"You might be trying to read something into that when there wasn't really anything underhanded going on," says Duck Dunn. "I don't know who was responsible, but it wasn't anything overtly racial. If you ask me, it was simply a case of 'sex sells.'" Whatever the motive, the decision may have been made not at Stax, but by the marketing department at Atlantic, which had used a similar strategy to launch a white East Coast soul group called the Rascals. Rascals drummer Dino Danelli says that Atlantic consciously tried to keep his band's color a secret during its early days on the label. "Atlantic Records was very aware that to some people, we sounded black," Danelli says. "And they actually helped open up the market for us by keeping our pictures off the record sleeves for the first couple of singles. They knew what to do in order to cross us over into an R&B market as well as the white pop market, so they intentionally stayed away from promoting us with photos."

Along with the Righteous Brothers, the Rascals—Felix Cavaliere, Gene Cornish, Eddie Brigatti, and Dino Danelli—pioneered what critics came to call "blue-eyed soul." Atlantic Records sensed that their music would sell just as well on both sides of the color line, and initially kept audiences guessing whether they were white or black. (Frank Driggs Collection)

Although Atlantic may have been the culprit behind such ignominies, the label made a good faith effort to ensure Stax enjoyed the fruits of its success. In mid-1965, engineer Tom Dowd visited Memphis to oversee renovations on the antiquated Stax control room. Next, Wexler flew in with Wilson Pickett and helped record the singer's first hit, "In the Midnight Hour." The germ of the song belonged to Steve Cropper, who came up with the title after listening to live recordings of Pickett testifying about "late in the midnight hour." During the recording, Wexler had a sudden epiphany: he dashed into the studio to demonstrate how the beat of the song could be fit to a nightclub dance called the Jerk. Cropper and MGs drummer Al Jackson tried to follow Wexler's moves (the visual alone is priceless), and came up with the delayed backbeat that gives "Midnight Hour" its swagger. As Cropper remembers it, "we'd got so involved watching Jerry dance around the place that he really pulled us into it, and that produced the rhythm on 'Midnight Hour.' It felt so good when we went and listened to it that we kept it that way."[12]

Wexler also assigned Sam and Dave to the Memphis studio, where they established instant rapport with house composers Isaac Hayes and David Porter. Within a short time, Sam and Dave were the biggest hitmakers at Stax, with three chart-topping singles— "Hold On, I'm Comin'" (#1 R&B and #21 pop hits, 1966), "Soul Man" (#1 R&B and #2 pop hits, 1967), and "I Thank You" (#4 R&B and #9 pop hits, 1968)—as well as a repertoire of classic soul, ranging from such up-tempo numbers as "You Don't Know Like I Know" and "Wrap It Up" to showstopping ballads like "When Something Is Wrong With My Baby" and "I Can't Stand Up for Falling Down."

Years later, Sam and Dave were cited as the unlikely inspiration for *Layla and Other Assorted Love Songs*, the blues-rock bible recorded by Derek & the Dominos in 1970. The Derek in question was, of course, Eric Clapton. His songwriting collaborator was fellow Domino Bobby Whitlock, who later revealed how most of the songs on *Layla* "just evolved, like they did with Isaac Hayes and David Porter." In the liner notes to the 20th-anniversary edition of the *Layla* album, Whitlock told Gene Santoro that he and Clapton "approached singing like Sam and Dave did; he sings a line, I sing a line, we sing together." That same approach would surface in a variety of rock and soul records—most notably in a fusion of both created by Sly and the Family Stone.

MS. 'REE

As the distribution deal between Atlantic and Stax wore on, relations between the two labels began to sour over contract disagreements. Undeterred, Jerry Wexler set his sights on Fame Studios in Muscle Shoals, Alabama, where he found another integrated house band to back Wilson Pickett on "Land of 1,000 Dances" (#1 R&B and #6 pop hits, 1966). During the flurry of sessions, Wexler heard that Columbia Records was releasing a young singer who could never find her niche there: Aretha Franklin. John Hammond, the man who once championed Billie Holiday and Charlie Christian, had signed Franklin to Columbia in 1961, but later lamented that as good as Aretha's records were, Columbia remained a largely white outfit that "misunderstood her genius."

Wexler signed the future Queen of Soul to Atlantic in a whirlwind deal sealed with a handshake. Unlike Gordy's protégés at Motown, Aretha was no ingenue. She'd spent half a decade as a recording artist and was well used to the spotlight as a daughter of one of the most recorded preachers in gospel history, C.L. Franklin. "My first instinct was to offer her to Stax's Jim Stewart and have the Stax team produce her," Wexler says in the liner notes to Aretha's 1992 retrospective box set. "They were flaming hot and I figured no one would produce Aretha any better than the folks in Memphis. I told Jim (Stewart) that if he paid the $25,000 advance, Aretha could be a Stax artist with Atlantic promotion and distribution, the same arrangement we had with Otis, Sam and Dave, and others. Stewart passed. Thank you Jesus."

Clinging to his belief that Franklin had to record in the South, Wexler took Aretha to Fame Studios in Muscle Shoals, where the players added fuel to her gospel fire. Those called to the session were white almost to a man, but Aretha took no apparent notice. She sat down at the piano and connected with her sidemen instantly. A few hours later, "I Never Loved a Man (the Way I Love You)"—a record of remarkable nuance in which Aretha coos, wails, moans, and shouts, forcing her microphone to overmodulate as it practically wilts from exposure to the blast furnace of her voice—provided incontrovertible evidence of her talent and Wexler's intuition. Up in the booth, the console showed meters peaking because they couldn't accommodate Aretha's dynamic range.

"You try to capture a performance in what I call 'white heat,'" Wexler explains. "Usually when you're doing the vocals there comes a certain point when that happens, and then it's like a therapist-and-patient relationship. There's an understanding there that no one else is getting. I never had any problems with Aretha once we got in the studio. There's no anger in her. There's self-doubt and confusion, but no meanness, and once the session starts, she's unique; a completely brilliant female vocalist."

There were dramas aplenty, including Aretha's flight from Muscle Shoals the next day after her husband scuffled with a session player. Wexler reunited Franklin with most of the Fame musicians in New York and elsewhere, and together they made a series of jaw-dropping classics, including "Think," "Chain of Fools," the transcendent "Do Right Woman, Do Right Man" (written by Fame regulars Dann Penn and Chips Moman), and, of course, "Respect."

"When Otis heard it," Wexler recalls, "he said, 'that girl done stole my song!' He loved it, and it became her signature tune. But it's kind of a strange one to have. People talk about it as a kind of feminist statement, but it's also a sexual invitation with its 'give me respect when I get home'—then 'sock it to me, sock it to me, sock it to me.' I mean the logic is *Alice in Wonderland*, but it works."

HEAT OF THE NIGHT

In the spring of 1967, Stax decided to send its stable of artists abroad. Bottom to top, the bill featured the Mar-Keys horn section, with Booker T. and the MGs providing the instrumental firepower for Arthur Conley (then riding the crest of his hit, "Sweet Soul Music"), Eddie "Knock on Wood" Floyd, Sam and Dave, and headliner Otis Redding.

The studio musicians who went along were stunned to discover they were instant celebrities, since many of them only gigged around Memphis when they weren't recording. Booker T. Jones and his bandmates were inundated with press requests from professionals and collegians who had studied the Stax oeuvre and now wanted to discuss the label's significance in depth.

Otis, on the other hand, was already well known to Britons, in part because The Temptations' "My Girl" was never released in the UK as a single, and Otis' version is the one recalled by most English fans. At home, the disparity between Redding's R&B chart success and his Top 40 performance was becoming worrisome. In 1965, his singles included "Mr. Pitiful" (#10 R&B and #41 pop hits) and "I've Been Loving You Too Long" (#2 R&B and #21 pop hits), leading to "Respect" (# 4 R&B and # 35 pop hits) and "I Can't Turn You Loose" (#11 R&B hit). Overseas, Redding was in the top tier of soul singers, mentioned in the same breath as James Brown, Marvin Gaye, and Smokey Robinson.

The stage was well set, with ticketbuyers primed by Motown tours and Redding's recent appearance on the British pop TV show, *Ready, Steady, Go!* British fans also shared a fondness for Otis' take on "Satisfaction." It was a daring raid on Redding's part, poaching on the sacred turf of their beloved Rolling Stones, pinching their best rock riff, and turning Mick Jagger's laundry list of grievances inside out. In Redding's hands it became a juggernaut of black angst, and having a "man come on the radio, telling me how white my shirts can be" bore implications its creators never foresaw. More interesting still is that "Satisfaction" began as a song created in the mold of R&B by foreign white men. Redding retooled the song the way an Indie 500 crew tweaks everything under the hood: at his direction, horns blared the Richards riff, the tempo raced, and the lyrics were blown out like so much exhaust. "Satisfaction" emerged instantly recognizable yet unmistakably altered, and it bounced back out onto the streets as a prowling black muscle car.

Another part of the cycle appeared complete. Three hundred years before, white Europeans subjugated black Africans and brought them to the New World, where their music forms began to recombine. Blues, jazz, movies, technology, and transportation accelerated the exposure and creative cross-pollination, leading early 1960s British blues fans to put their own spin on the sounds of Chicago and the Delta and bring their music to America. Now Otis Redding was bringing "Satisfaction" home to the UK.

But Redding was merely the brightest spot in a twinkling constellation of stars. Widely circulated video bootlegs of the Stax revue depict what happened when the curtain rose on the tour as it barnstormed across Europe. From the stage, beaming black faces look out onto a sea of white smiles in the audience. This is no throng of screaming bobbysoxers. Everyone is behaving impeccably, sitting politely, keeping time by tapping a foot or patting a rolled-up souvenir program against a thigh. But by the look on their faces, they've died and gone to heaven. The tour was an unqualified success, and the company returned home triumphant, with one commitment remaining, a mid-June appearance in California at the Monterey Pop Festival.

Nearly 40 years on, it's clear that the organizers behind Monterey hoped to declare rock music had come of age as an art form in 1967. It was, after all, the summer of the Beatles' *Sgt. Pepper's Lonely Hearts Club Band*, the Jefferson Airplane's *Surrealistic Pillow*, and The Doors debut album. San Francisco's Haight/Ashbury district was in full flower, and musicians from the Bay Area were anxious to prove they were every bit as talented as Hollywood's pricey session hands. Monterey's Board of Governors included Paul McCartney and Mick Jagger, Los Angeles folkies Roger McGuinn and John Phillips (of the Byrds and the Mamas and Papas, respectively), Berry Gordy and Smokey Robinson of Motown, Paul Simon, and Brian Wilson of the Beach Boys.

Gordy and Robinson appeared in name only, as "they never returned phone calls," according to organizer John Phillips, and no Motown stars were booked. Chuck Berry also declined to appear, since no one was being paid, which meant black acts would be limited to supper club singer Lou Rawls, a South African trumpeter named Hugh Masekela, Otis Redding, and a complete unknown named Jimi Hendrix.

Otherwise, the lineup suggested a friendly exhibition match between Los Angeles and Bay Area bands to see who curried public favor. "We knew we weren't the most proficient musicians," says Sam Andrew, lead guitarist for San Francisco's Big Brother and the Holding Company. "But we also knew that with our stage experience, we could incite a party. A lot of the bands from Los Angeles were more used to playing in the studio than in front of people."

It was a weekend of highlights, almost none of them expected. Janis Joplin tore into her set with Big Brother with such gusto that the filmmakers documenting the event requested an additional show they could shoot. The Who imploded in a maelstrom of power chords, overturned amps, smoke, and double-bass drum fills, while such groups as the Association and Simon & Garfunkel leavened the proceedings with feel-good harmonies and radio pop hits.

Jimi Hendrix Experience drummer Mitch Mitchell remembers that Monterey was strategically important to cracking the American market, but believes the trio had played better elsewhere. Hendrix, a Seattle native, was discovered in New York by Chas Chandler, the Animals' white bass player. Chandler spirited Hendrix off to London and recast him as a psychedelic Wild Man of Borneo. "I guess the Experience started off in late '66," Mitchell muses, "and we played Monterey the following June. It was actually the only gig we had lined up in the States when we came over. And it was a very fun thing, you know. Lots of nice people everywhere, and we put on what I thought was a nervous but good show."

Jitters notwithstanding, Hendrix and his bandmates managed to upstage the calamitous Who. Hendrix played while somersaulting across the stage, picking with his teeth, tongue-lashing his fretboard, humping the guitar into his amp, and finally setting his instrument on fire in a staged sacrifice. That weekend, he and the Who helped inaugurate "hard rock," the bone-crunching sound later labeled "acid rock" until "heavy metal" settled in as the catchall term sometime in the '80s. But by becoming the axe-wielding guitarist of every kid's dream, Hendrix also acquired a minstrel patina that he never shed completely in life or death. In him, white teenagers found the same anti-authoritarianism and sexuality that once lured their great-grandparents to blacken up and attempt the hambone. *Monterey Pop* was roundly praised when it hit the big screen in 1968, but it also threatened to permanently fix Hendrix in the public mind as a novelty act.

Rolling Stones guitarist Brian Jones was another luminary roaming the festival grounds, stoking rumors of an impromptu Beatles or Stones appearance, although both groups had retired from the road to focus on studio work. Toward the end of the second day, Booker T. and the MGs launched into their instrumental vamp and Otis Redding strode out. The stage was set for a clash of cultures—a sleepy audience of well-rocked flower children spread across the fairground, and at the microphone, a half dozen black and white Memphis country boys whose specialty was soul music. Within moments, Otis had them up and on their feet, where many remained for the rest of the set. It was the beginning and the end for Redding. Far from being indolent and spoiled, he found them refreshingly open. Otis spent part of the remaining summer on a houseboat in Sausalito, reexamining his musical direction while poring over Bob Dylan and Beatles albums. He returned to Stax with a new tune, "(Sittin' On) The Dock of the Bay," and finished recording it days before he died in a December plane crash.

Like Sam Cooke, Otis was only beginning to see beyond the confines of his stardom as a soul singer. Just weeks before his own death in 2003, Maurice Gibb remembered Otis as so much larger than life that he immediately inspired a song, which ultimately became one of the Bee Gees early hits. "That was 'To Love Somebody,'" said Gibb. "We just got signed to Atlantic, and the powers-that-be suggested it. Barry came back from New York with (manager) Robert Stigwood and said we needed to get a song together, and 'To Love Somebody' was sort of implanted, the idea of it being more soulful like Otis and sounding like Memphis or Muscle Shoals. Barry and Robin wrote that one. Otis loved it, but never actually recorded it. The arrangement and the way we did it was sort of as a tribute to him."

Overnight, Otis was gone, and with him went much of the peace and harmony that he engendered at Stax. The August before he was killed, Otis threw an opulent house party for the R&B industry rank and file who were gathering in Atlanta at the annual National Association of Television and Radio Announcers (NATRA) meeting. Some 500 guests attended, label executives mingling with artists and deejays, with Otis as the glue holding it all together—black and white.

A year later, NATRA held its convention in Miami. Jesse Jackson and Julian Bond were present, along with the recently widowed Coretta Scott King. But the spirit of cooperation Otis championed was long gone. The record industry was denounced from the podium as a modern-day plantation system, and Jerry Wexler, the white Jew who took Ray Charles, Aretha Franklin, and Wilson Pickett to the top of the charts, was hung in effigy. A white R&B businessman named Marshall Sehorn was pistol-whipped while in the shower. And Phil Walden, Otis' white manager, was accused of complicity in his friend's death.

"You know," Walden explained to Peter Guralnick, "if I was a young black, I'd probably have been the most militant sonofabitch in the black race. But I just got tired of being called whitey and honky, because I knew in my heart what I had done and I knew in my heart I was right." After that, Walden said ruefully, "I just decided to get into white rock 'n' roll, and that's what I did."[13]

NOTES

1 Werner, Craig. *A Change Is Gonna Come: Music, Race & the Soul of America.* New York: Plume/Penguin Putnam, 1998, p. 59.

2 Shaw, Arnold. *Honkers and Shouters.* New York: Collier, 1978, p. 73.

3 Shaw, Arnold. *Honkers and Shouters.* New York: Collier, 1978, p. 74.

4 Smith, Joe. *Off the Record: An Oral History of Pop Music.* New York: Warner Books, 1988, p. 161.

5 Wolff, Daniel. *You Send Me: The Life and Times of Sam Cooke.* New York: William Morrow and Company, 1995, p. 193.

6 Brown, James with Bruce Tucker. *James Brown: The Godfather of Soul.* New York: Thunder's Mouth Press, 1990, p. 130.

7 Ward, Ed, Geoffrey Stokes, and Ken Tucker. *Rock of Ages: The Rolling Stone History of Rock and Roll.* New York: Simon & Schuster, 1986, p. 227.

8 Smith, Joe. *Off the Record: An Oral History of Pop Music.* New York: Warner Books, 1988, p. 173.

9 Williams, Otis, with Patricia Romanowski. *Temptations.* New York: Cooper Square, 2002, pp. 136–7.

10 Bowman, Rob. "The Soul Saga of Stax Records. Soul Spectacular: The Greatest Soul Hits of All Time." Rhino Entertainment Co., 2000, p. 9, liner notes.

11 Guralnick, Peter. *Sweet Soul Music: Rhythm and Blues and the Southern Dream of Freedom.* New York: Harper & Row, 1986, p. 173–174.

12 Ertegun, Ahmet. *What'd I Say: The Atlantic Story.* New York: Welcome Rain, 2001, p. 167.

13 Guralnick, Peter. *Sweet Soul Music: Rhythm and Blues and the Southern Dream of Freedom.* New York: Harper & Row, 1986, p. 384.

CHAPTER SIX

Time Has Come Today

The United States burst into polarized shards in 1968. Americans separated into black and white on civil rights issues, hawks and doves on Vietnam, and young and old on almost every cultural tradition. In effect, two factions were locked in a battle for the ideological soul of the republic. One was the generation who beat back the Depression, defeated fascism, and split the atom. Opposing them were their well-educated offspring—handed a world they considered immoral, and a national conversation reduced to the bumper sticker logic of "AMERICA: Love It or Leave It" that defined the peace sign as the "Footprint of the American Chicken." Politicians pled for unity while vilifying anyone who dared dissent. Today's historians attempt to recapture the era by tallying its Vietnam body counts and domestic turmoil, but none truly capture the apprehension of a society teetering on implosion. Once social unrest became a fever, militants and pacifists alike were on constant alert, ready for a skirmish to break out at a courthouse, on a college campus, or over the family breakfast table.

The mass media tried to caulk the void growing between the factions. General interest magazines illustrated the disconnect in glossy pictorials—gaudy Day-Glo color layouts for fashion, music, and movies, with current events relegated to grainy black-and-white treatments reminiscent of crime scene photos. Television propped up the status quo, providing simple solutions to complex times via the tough-on-crime *Dragnet '67* and Diahann Carroll's *Julia*, the first sitcom to feature a black lead. The kids were only a room or two away, but they might as well have occupied a parallel universe.

A growing rift was invisible and inescapable, but present on the nation's airwaves as music. In particular, AM radio offered a haven where all of the country's most disparate forces tussled in glorious cacophony. *Billboard*'s pop charts mapped out a turf war between classes, races, and generations. In August 1964, Dean Martin ousted the Beatles' "A Hard Day's Night" from the #1 slot with "Everybody Loves Somebody Sometime." Soon after, television host Art Linkletter gave youngsters a tongue-lashing in an "Open

Letter to My Teenaged Son," and Staff Sergeant Barry Sadler scored a major hit with "The Ballad of the Green Berets." But while Frank Sinatra, Barbra Streisand, and Wayne Newton remained strong sellers, they were increasingly swamped by psychedelia and soul. The 1960s burned down to a fiery conclusion, with John F. Kennedy's New Frontier and its nonviolent pleas for change displaced by increasingly angry singers who used music as a rallying cry to storm the gates of an uncaring, entrenched establishment. In "Street Fighting Man," the Rolling Stones rallied the young and disaffected. "Ev'rywhere I hear the sounds of marching, charging feet, boys," yelled Mick Jagger, "'cause summer's here and the time is right for fighting in the streets, boys . . ."

The state of a besieged nation played out over the radio, as much during the songs as in the hourly newsbreaks. January 1968 brought the Vietcong's Tet Offensive and CBS anchorman Walter Cronkite's assessment that Vietnam was a quagmire that Lyndon B. Johnson's generals were nowhere near winning. A month later, the president was staggered by political challenges from within his own party: a surprising showing by Senator Eugene McCarthy in the New Hampshire primary, and, in March, the entry of Johnson's archrival, Robert Kennedy, into the presidential race.

In April, Martin Luther King, Jr. visited Memphis to organize a garbage workers' strike and was murdered as he stood on a motel balcony. Rioters across the country set their neighborhoods ablaze, and National Guardsmen were called out in Washington, D.C. to protect the halls of government from its own citizens. Johnson was aghast. In an interview with Jeff Shesol, the author of *Mutual Contempt: Lyndon Johnson, Robert Kennedy, and the Feud That Defined a Decade*, LBJ aide Roger Wilkins describes Johnson as a man who "never understood black consciousness. He did not understand that generations of heaping inferiority into our souls needed to be purged, and you're going to put that awful stuff into people, when people begin to expel it, it's not coming out pretty."[1]

In Boston, fearful local officials, whose first impulse was to cancel a James Brown appearance the Friday after King's murder, decided they might actually be inviting violence should ticketholders arrive to find the Boston Gardens' doors padlocked. Instead, the civic leaders opted to televise the event. In doing so, they hoped to placate ticketholders and keep potential malcontents at home with the promise of a free James Brown concert. Brown went on as promised, with the crowd in a volatile state. Repeatedly they surged toward the stage, seeking something, but what? Solace? Protection? Comraderie? Archival video shows Brown calming them with reminders of brotherhood and nonviolence— then tearing down the house with a performance that rattled the paint from the plaster.

At the end of March, LBJ opted out of the presidential race. Richard Nixon was by then the odds-on favorite to win the Republican nomination, and Hubert Humphrey scrambled to collect the Democratic delegates shaken loose by Johnson's abdication. In June, Robert Kennedy, who had marched in Martin Luther King's funeral procession to surrounding chants of "Yes, Bobby, Bobby," was gunned down after winning the California primary. The twin murders staggered everyone, including the Rascals' Felix Cavaliere. "There had been so much hope and promise," the songwriter said ruefully, "and it all . . . well, it just vanished. All within a couple of months." Cavaliere responded to the assassinations by composing "People Got to Be Free," easily the most potent equal rights anthem ever to scale the Top Forty. His tribute is textbook pop-soul, from its

Memphis-driven horn arrangement and Dino Danelli's funk-fortified drum attack to the Rascals' irresistible melody. "Shout it from the mountains and on out to the sea," they chime with gospel fervor, "it's a natural situation for a man to be free." Shortly after the single's release, Cavaliere told a *Cashbox* reporter that "the Rascals have decided not to appear in any concert unless half the acts on the bill are black. We can't control the audience, but we can be sure the show is integrated. So from now on, half the acts will be white and half will be black, or we stay home." Popular headliners started to equate sales and airplay with influence and began to push their agendas, first in front of an audience, then in backstage negotiations with promoters.

James Brown remained at the forefront of the cause. While he declined Otis Redding's call for a black performers' union to break the hammerlock of segregationist promoters, in all likelihood it was because he was his own entertainment powerhouse by now. He bought up a string of radio stations from Knoxville to Baltimore and kept a Lear jet at his beck and call emblazoned with the inscription "Out of Sight." His records were also among the most daring to receive international airplay. Just as "Black Is Beautiful" was becoming a national catchphrase, Brown played his trump card alongside a chorus of inner city youths. In 1960, the song on everyone's lips was Frank Sinatra's "High Hopes" (also the JFK campaign jingle), with Ol' Blue Eyes leading schoolchildren in a sing-along about perseverance, ants, and rubber tree plants. Eight years later, James Brown surrounded himself with inner-city kids, and in one voice they chanted, "Say It Loud! I'm Black and I'm Proud!!"

For the first time, black suffrage was not something suggested in metaphor or indicated by musical dissonances. Brown roared what few had dared to say only a few years earlier. Because this was so, black parents and teens—the same ones who walked picket lines and ducked nightsticks, police dogs, and firehoses—regarded Brown's declamatory lyric as a mantra. Conversely, many of Richard Nixon's law-and-order constituency grew increasingly apprehensive. If this record truly represented the majority opinion of black Americans, did it mean revolution was next? Militant black activists like Huey Newton, H. Rap Brown, and Stokely Charmichael fanned the flames. Charmichael in particular maintained a barrage of invective directed at the entrenched white power structure, prodding blacks to "stand up and take over. We have to do what every group in this country did," he told them. "We got to take over the community where we outnumber people so we can have decent jobs, so we can have decent houses, so we can have decent roads, so we can have decent schools . . . So we can have decent justice."

OFF THE CHARTS

On the pop charts at least, white artists amplified the call for racial equality, with Elvis Presley's "In the Ghetto" keeping company with Phil Spector's homage to a simple housekeeper ("Black Pearl, precious little girl/ Let me put you up where you belong"), and Jackie DeShannon's "Put a Little Love in Your Heart." In country and western, blacks all but disappeared when Ray Charles returned to his rhythm and blues (R&B) roots via such hits as "Let's Go Get Stoned" and "In the Heat of the Night." But in 1965, a twenty-three-year-old black native of Sledge, Mississippi named Charley Pride appeared to fill the void. Chet Atkins signed him to RCA in 1965 and a year later pressed his first single, "The Snakes Crawl at Night," above the name "Country Charley Pride"—neglecting to issue the customary publicity photo. Nashville's Music Row seemed to hold its collective breath, waiting to see if a black country singer could find acceptance from an audience largely comprised of white conservatives. They needn't have worried. Pride clearly felt the country impulse, identified with its fans, and considered himself a product of its traditions. Moreover, he did exactly what Hank Williams, Sr. had done so effectively a quarter century before—he took an expressive voice and used it to tell stories of love, loss, joy, and triumph. And, like Johnny Mathis, he publicly skirted hot-button issues (including race) rather than alienate his already-skeptical audience of down-home folks.

Asleep at the Wheel's Ray Benson says it's fairly easy to understand why country music hasn't produced any major black country acts since Pride's heyday. "There's this idea that Ray Charles broke down racial barriers for black people in country, and I loved *Modern Sounds in Country & Western*, just like everybody else," he says. "But Ray Charles didn't really *do* country music. He did country and western tunes, but he did them in his style. And country music is still a personality-driven business where the fans want to be able to identify with the artist, which is why so few performers of color, like Freddy Fender and Charley Pride, break through."

In country music, Benson explains, "You have to sing 'white' to make it. Charley Pride was the first black country performer to sound like a hillbilly, and people had no idea he was black. Our country has become a lot less racist as years go by, but until recently, country music has been pretty much a Southern white demographic. And country music fans regarded Charley as one of their own—their boy, with all that it implies. When a redneck calls another redneck 'boy,' it means one thing, and when he calls a black fellow that, it may mean something else."

Lyle Lovett, whose Large Band features both black and white musicians playing a mélange of American roots music, agrees. Why hasn't there been a successor to Charley Pride? "You mean aside from the fact that black people are way too cool to sing country?" he says with a wary chuckle. "I suppose it speaks to what people are exposed to. It's not easy, if you're looking to be inspired by something unfamiliar. You've got to wade through the weeds to find the stuff that speaks to you. I'm not sure what would attract an outsider, really. I consider myself on the outside of the world of country music. I've been marketed as a country artist, but I've never felt embraced as part of the country music business, and I am white. I think it would be that much harder if you were black."

"In the late '60s, I was the first one to put Charley Pride on a festival bill in Texas," recalls Willie Nelson. "I had him open for me, and I remember being a little jittery about it because I felt kind of protective since I was the one who invited him. He went out onstage, and just took the bull by the horns, you know. He said, 'I bet ya'll are wondering what this guy with the permanent tan is doing onstage, but if you'll give us a chance we'd like to show you what we do.' And he just went into his set, I guess maybe 'Snakes Crawl' and 'Is Anybody Goin' to San Antone,' and he had them in the palm of his hand in no time. They loved every song. Loved him so much, in fact," he says with a chuckle, "that I never let him open for me again."

BITCHES' BROOD

Jazz, on the other hand, had fallen so commercially fallow as to become a kind of intellectual exercise for grad schoolers and middlebrow aesthetes. "If you listened to jazz in the mid-to-late '60s," said one collegian at the time, "you were considered barely to the cool side of weird. Jazz was not where the national dialogue was taking place. Because of the Beatles and Dylan, pop and rock were becoming very politically focused, very dynamic, and in the face of all that, jazz was becoming almost defiantly abstract."

Ornette Coleman was both prime offender and high priest of the new jazz. Just as the boppers had turned their backs on swing, Coleman challenged the supposition that solos could work only within the framework of a firm musical structure. Instead, Coleman used melodic themes as a port of call from which he could sail in any direction. Without chord progressions, key signatures, or catchy choruses, Coleman and crew (who were often white) set the jazz world ablaze. Was it audacious or the Emperor's New Clothes set to music? Coleman's work proved arguably older than jazz itself, since his concepts were perfectly in keeping with the free-form cries, shouts, and calls of ancient Africa—although hearing them played on a sax in a contemporary context continually startled his audience.

Coleman's devotees began to call it "free jazz"—that is, jazz untethered from any rules, including those of time and melody. And, just as bop broke from the white-dominated world of swing, free jazz sought to promote black consciousness through a similar exclusivity. This music would not submit itself to the approval of white critics or black musicians who put assimilation ahead of artistry. Free jazz subdivided the already-fragmented jazz community. In the fall of 1964, a four-day concert series billed as "The October Revolution" was held at New York's Cellar Cafe. Some twenty groups participated, including ensembles led by Ornette Coleman, Cecil Taylor, and John Coltrane, but they did little to quell the furor.

From the Depression through the end of World War II, jazz remained at the apex of its influence because it was a melting pot of Americana, employing performers regardless of color or creed. When bop came into vogue, it was certainly more self-referential, but never snubbed its passionately devoted audience. Looking back, it's clear that free jazz offered a fresh approach in a medium where innovation is held in the highest regard. But the ideas were so radical they put free jazz practitioners at odds with what should have been their core audience.

Only rarely did jazz artists of the '60s cross over into the pop market. Occasional hits included the first jazz million seller, "Take Five," by the Dave Brubeck Quartet, and Miles Davis' modal masterpiece "So What," both recorded in 1959. Neither conforms to the rules of hard bop or West Coast sentimentality—Brubeck's smoky ramble (written by the band's sax player, Paul Desmond) is in 5/4 time, while Davis' deceptively simple meditation is based on a single chord. Virtuosity was in vogue again, as Jimmy Smith developed a vocabulary for jazz organ and guitarist Wes Montgomery picked up where Charlie Christian had left off to record numerous successful covers of Beatles and Top 40 tunes. Stan Getz' "The Girl from Impanema" ushered in a mid-1960s fascination with Brazilian rhythms, and from out of left field, Bay Area pianist Vince Guraldi created a string of pop-jazz confections for TV's animated *Peanuts* specials.

Race ceased to be a defining characteristic in jazz during the 1960s, and while consumers were largely distracted by rock and soul, jazz artists worked in an insular environment where they were more often judged on fealty to tradition than on their ethnicity. Audiences dwindled and became increasingly white, while Miles Davis, Charles Mingus, and John Coltrane continued to press the artistic envelope. Davis in particular was disgusted by convention, whether that meant critical and crowd expectations or the demands of contemporaries who considered rock-leaning records like 1969's *Bitches Brew* something akin to blasphemy. His horn parts became increasingly brittle and removed from the proceedings, not unlike the trumpet master himself. Instead, the band would develop a theme, then head for parts unknown, with Davis providing color commentary or nudging the ensemble toward some new possibility. Despite naysayers bent on preserving jazz tradition, *Bitches Brew* was a hugely successful record (in both sales figures and chart position) and became even more influential when former Miles sidemen John McLaughlin, Wayne Shorter, and Joe Zawinul formed a series of fusion bands including The Mahavishnu Orchestra and Weather Report in the 1970s.

Detachment worked for Davis; he had blown hot in the 1940s and cool in the 1950s and left the 1960s as an ally of Jimi Hendrix and Sly Stone. Neither Mingus nor Coltrane could be so aloof. Mingus, among the most restless and irascible figures in American music, addressed bigotry ("Fables of Faubus" is a typically pointed example), incorporated elements of gospel and R&B ("Better Get Hit in Yo Soul" has sass to spare), and was as adept behind the bass as he was as a pianist and composer. Mingus may have been a roiling cauldron of contradictions, but he was always fully engaged in his moment, and with "Good-Bye Pork Pie Hat," he even enjoyed a brief taste of mainstream success.

Coltrane, by contrast, left the physical world long before illness claimed him in 1967. After stints with both Dizzy Gillespie and Miles Davis, Coltrane embarked on his own musical odyssey. Jazz critic Ira Gitler coined the phrase "sheets of sound" to describe Coltrane's ability to suggest entire chords with a single shotgun blast from his sax. The practice left many early fans disgruntled, as did his eighty-plus choruses of "Chasin' the Trane." But if it can be said that one of music's grandest purposes is to provide insights into the psyche of an artist, Coltrane succeeds as few others. Much like staring at a computerized op-art piece until the image hidden within is revealed, Coltrane's sheets of sound eventually outline a dynamic personality in search of the ecstatic. In 1960, Coltrane had a hit of his own in "My Favorite Things," which clocked in on his album at close to fourteen minutes. As Coltrane's ambitions soared, his commercial prospects plummeted, and it wasn't until well into the 1970s that Carlos Santana and John McLaughlin began to show how his approach could be incorporated into more linear music in records like Santana's *Caravansarai* and The Mahavishnu Orchestra's *Birds of Fire* as well as their collaboration, *Love, Devotion, & Surrender.*

Davis, Mingus, and Coltrane preached to the converted while the fan base for straight-ahead jazz continued to shrink. Someone had to take the blame, and the white man made a convenient target. The confrontational mood that saw Jerry Wexler burned in effigy at the Miami National Association of Television and Radio Announcers convention crept into jazz, where in 1969, it became easy to attribute jazz's commercial woes to race. And jazz had its own scapegoats—including the icon who discovered and once dated Billie Holiday. In a collection of essays called *Rhythm & Business: The Political Economy of Black Music*, writer Frank Kofsky vilifies John Hammond, the late Columbia Records executive. The essay wipes clean a long and laudable slate of accomplishments (discovering Aretha Franklin among them) so that the writer can deconstruct Hammond's offhand remarks at a conference on black music. Kofsky first suggests Hammond falsified his account of Bessie Smith's death in a car accident (a recurring accusation by her fans), although the essay never explains how, or what possible motive Hammond might have for such doings. Then he rips Hammond apart for suggesting that any genre of music *ought* to pay for itself through sales. Hammond may have been guilty of talking in generalities, but Kofsky sees something more sinister. The essay snipes that western classical music is never held to such a sales standard, then concludes that jazz gets short shrift because Hammond must have considered it "nigger music," to use Kofsky's phrase. "Oh, to be sure," he opines, "it isn't played in whorehouses any more, and now there are some white misfits who are involved in it. But when push comes to shove, it is still nigger music, and never mind if some of the niggers happen to be white. Subsidize nigger music? What an absurd notion!"

During all the infighting, *Bitches Brew* (with Miles fronting an interracial band that included Chick Corea as well as future members of the Mahavishnu Orchestra and Weather Report) not only continued to sell, but to turn the heads of aspiring young musicians throughout the spheres of rock and jazz. Pop bands like the Rascals began to take their flirtations with jazz (already apparent in "Groovin'" and "It's a Beautiful Morning") seriously. The British Jeff Beck Group ditched psychedelia for a set list of flashy instrumentals staged over a bed of syncopation and synthesizers. Beck's *Blow by Blow*, released in 1973, reached out to both rock and jazz audiences with a hybrid dubbed as "fusion"— an ironic label, considering how divisive it became. *Bitches Brew* and *Blow by Blow* shepherded many a rock fan down the path to jazz, but apparently the road led one way only, as jazz diehards dismissed fusion as a simplification of the music they held dear.

Wynton Marsalis insists that jazz derives from the blues, and that all that has arisen in popular culture after jazz fell from commercial grace is dumbed-down music. His history is short, direct, and rife with absolutes. "You have the early New Orleans style," he told writer Lolis Eric Elie in 1990, "then you have swing era jazz, in which the musicians play a lot of blues. And then you have R&B, which is a much more watered-down version of what the older jazz musicians were playing. The cycle just keeps going on, the original music keeps getting watered down more and more and more until you get to fusion or funk. Each generation of that style becomes less sophisticated. The arrangements are simpler. The harmonies are simpler. The musicians are less accomplished. The level of social statement is much simpler."

But simple doesn't necessarily mean simplistic, and complexity for its own sake can result in a pretentious muddle. The blues may be full of nuance, but it is not a complex music. To insist that R&B, fusion, and funk are somehow "jazz lite" belittles their power to communicate (and often that message is a call to the dance floor) and ignores the cycles that folk music and pop music follow. Innovations start simply, often as a rejection of the previous generation's music, and the new music becomes increasingly diverse until it collapses under the weight of that complexity, inspiring artists to wander off in a new direction.

The sins of fusion go far beyond lightweight musicality, Marsalis goes on to say. "What fusion does is it relieves us, our country, of the problem of dealing with jazz and the contribution of the Negro to the mythology of America." In his view, most black artists backed away from dealing with race through music and sold their souls for a meal ticket. "So what they did is just become rock musicians," he says. "This is the most popular form of 'jazz' today . . . the reason these people want to be called jazz musicians is for longevity. So what they can constantly do is play these jazz festivals for fifteen, twenty years, playing basically pop music. Whereas in pop music, gigs are almost always based on a steady stream of hits, especially for black groups. You can't name a black group like the Rolling Stones or the Who who can sell out stadiums twenty years after their most potent hits. You go to jazz festivals in Europe and there's almost nobody playing jazz."

BALL OF CONFUSION

Upheaval struck the commercial mainstream in 1968, as the Summer of Love declared by hippies just a year before went from bacchanalia to bust. "Time Has Come Today," the Chambers Brothers proclaimed, but were they heralds of an Aquarian Age or Armageddon? A shellshocked plurality of voters abandoned LBJ's Great Society and elected Richard Nixon president. Anarchists pressed for revolt, but Americans had little stomach for it after seeing their cities gutted, their leaders assassinated, and their kids battle cops at the 1968 Democratic Convention. Many were simply overwhelmed by the epic tragedy of national life, bookended the following year by America's landing on the moon and the Manson family murders. Liberals deserted the radicals en masse; music industry professionals were no exception. The hit parade offered proof in such pablum as "Yummy, Yummy, Yummy" and "Little Green Apples." Even the mighty Motown machine began to sputter.

In his autobiography, *To Be Loved,* Berry Gordy recounts the departure of his hit-writing triumvirate—Brian Holland, Lamont Dozier, and Eddie Holland. "Signs of trouble had sparked several months before," he writes, "when their productions began to drop on the charts. After their Supremes' 'Reflections' went to #2 in September of 1967, the next release, 'In and Out of Love,' only made it to #9. Then I was told H-D-H had stopped recording and were on some sort of strike." In an effort to persuade the team to "come to their senses," Gordy initiated a $4 million lawsuit, alleging breach of contract. The trio quickly countersued, asserting they were owed $22 million for unpaid earnings. (Most of the issues in the case were resolved in a 1972 settlement that netted the composers $799,000. Late in the 1980s, Holland/Dozier/Holland began another round of suits as individuals, claiming that Gordy was more than a million dollars behind in payments. At the turn of the century, there was still no final disposition in the case.)

"Everyone in the company rallied around me," Gordy's memoir asserts. "When Smokey got the news, he came into my office burning, 'Berry, how can they do that? After all you've done for them, for all of us. But don't worry man, we'll keep it going. Me and Whit (composer Norman Whitfield) and the others will get plenty of smashes. We can handle it. You'll see.'" Considering Gordy's penchant for varnishing over unflattering moments until they read like press releases, this seems hyperbolic at best. More likely, it's either the way Gordy would like to remember their exit or the way he thought it would be best to spin their departure. No matter: Holland/Dozier/Holland were gone for good, along with Mary Wells, the Isley Brothers, and soon, the Spinners and Gladys Knight and the Pips.

Defections were only part of the problem. Rancorous disagreements over who deserved star treatment within the Temptations would eventually lead to original members David Ruffin and Eddie Kendricks quitting the group. The Supremes were similarly miserable.

Florence Ballard, unhappy in her role as window dressing for Diana Ross, began to eat and drink to such an extent that her weight ballooned and she could no longer be depended on as a stage performer. "One of our biggest qualms is that we could never be soul singers," Mary Wilson laments. "We wanted some songs like Martha and the Vandellas had. Had Florence been the lead singer, we could have sounded like that. People would come up to us and accuse us of selling out to white audiences, and we kept asking our writers for something like 'Dancing in the Street.'"

Wilson believes the Diana Ross-era Supremes were finished soon after Gordy replaced Ballard with Cindy Birdsong, who had been singing alongside Patti LaBelle. "We all knew that Diana was leaving about a year before it happened," Wilson says. "We were all growing apart and Diana was dating Berry, so the only time we saw each other was on-stage." The group's name was expanded to "Diana Ross and the Supremes," and Gordy mapped out a strategy to split the Supremes' stock, launching Ross into movies and di-vadom while maintaining the Supremes as viable artists under their own banner. Motown issued "Someday We'll Be Together" in 1969 as their final release. The single was intended as a heart-tugging send-off for Ross as she set out on her own. For those who knew the truth, it had a mean and ironic twist, as neither Wilson nor Birdsong were brought to the studio to record the song with her.

THE FREAK FLAG FLIES

At the decade's end, Berry Gordy was presiding over the most lucrative black-owned business in America, but how long could it remain so? His premiere hit writers were in mutiny and the very acceptance of Motown acts in Chicago supperclubs and the show-rooms of Vegas threatened the label's claim as "The Sound of Young America." In a world shifting from black tie to tie-dye, the Motown stable had become a black Rat Pack with an air of Hugh Hefner savoir-faire. More worrisome still, competitors from the Atlantic and Stax labels had established beachheads in the marketplace and ended the misconception that Motown and soul music were one and the same.

On the West Coast, a black disc jockey and record producer was turning Gordy's formula inside out. Sylvester Stewart first renamed himself Sly Stone, then defied the prevailing notions of rock and soul by assembling a group that flouted conventions of both race and gender: "It was deliberate," the group's white sax player, Jerry Martini, told journalist Joel Selvin. "He knew exactly what he was doing. He was so far ahead of his time . . . . He intentionally wanted a white drummer. There was a shit pot full of black drummers that could kick Gregg (Errico's) ass and there were a lot of black saxophone players that could kick mine. He knew exactly what he was doing: Boys, girls; black, white."

Even as a disc jockey at KSOL in San Francisco, Stone's appeal crossed the color line. Emilio Castillo, then on the verge of forming an integrated soul band called Tower of Power, remembers that "Sly was nuts, but there wasn't anybody who didn't listen to him. Even people who didn't like soul music listened to Sly, because he was hilarious." And Stone wasn't the only element in the show from left field. He programmed Bob Dylan and the Beatles alongside soul singles, and his San Francisco listeners became addicted. Naturally, a band bearing his name would carry expectations of greatness. But lacking focus, Stone's first steps faltered and the first Sly and the Family Stone album, *A Whole New Thing*, collected more dust than fans. A second LP, *Dance to the Music*, appeared to

Black and white, boys and girls, and rock and soul—all roads met in the Day-Glo world of Sylvester Stewart, the leader of Sly and the Family Stone. Long after their heyday, his songs became sitcom titles (*Diff'rent Strokes*) and TV commercials ("I Am Everyday People!"). Generations of musicians have followed in his footsteps since, including the Temptations and O'Jays, Prince and Madonna, and Lenny Kravitz and Janet Jackson. (Bob Gruen/Star File)

be a momentary flash of genius, particularly when their third effort again failed to make any kind of dent with radio programmers. But the release of *Stand!* in the early months of 1969 made it clear that Sly had assimilated the sounds of the 1960s and provided a beacon for the next phase of the century's music.

Every track on the record breaks artistic ground—not only for Sly and the Family Stone—but for rock and soul and everything that would follow in their wake. It is as soulful an album as any recorded by Aretha, Otis, or James Brown, yet remains an essential record for pop fans and jazz musicians alike. Over time, its wealth of material yielded hits for Sly protégés Little Sister, followed later by Ike and Tina Turner, Aretha Franklin, and Arrested Development. Sadly, in the thirty years since *Stand!* hit the charts, its hand-tooled undercarriage of grooves and gospel have been stripped for parts like some loaded sportscar abandoned on the worst side of town. Sly himself first betrayed the album's egalitarian ideals with a long slide into drug dependence. Next, Hollywood plundered its lyrics to coin a sitcom title (*Diff'rent Strokes*), and Madison Avenue executives coopted its melodies for commercial jingles (Toyota's "I Am Everyday People!" campaign). Yet somehow, *Stand!* has withstood every assault on its brilliance. Equal parts musical revelation and social manifesto, it meets race questions head-on, then moves beyond stereotypes to address a common humanity.

The title track was conceived as a campus call-to-arms, and works for succeeding generations as a declaration of self-reliance. "Stand," Sly exhorts his audience, "don't you know that you are free . . . Well, at least in your mind, if you want to be." Then, as if to undercut his own proselytizing, the following cut is "Don't Call Me Nigger, Whitey," a six-minute name-calling stalemate. "I Want to Take You Higher" serves as the Family Stone's over-the-top encore and remains a highlight of the *Woodstock* film. When the fringe-clad Sly thrusts his arm skyward to exclaim, "Throw the peace sign in the air and it will do you no harm," he dances across any line separating preacher from pimp and rock star from politician. Certainly this vision of utopia was diffuse, but for the moment it seemed as if Sly was simply mulling over the details.

The seeds of funk are also scattered throughout the *Stand!* album, often more evident in the band's attack than in the tunes themselves. (A year later, Larry Graham would virtually reinvent bass playing with his thumb-popping technique on "Thank You Falettinme Be Mice Elf Agin.") The group leaves pop behind for a 16-minute instrumental workout on "Sex Machine," embracing Jimi Hendrix and fueling the jazz experiments that would lead Miles Davis to his most daring records, including *Bitches Brew*. This is not the stripped down roots-and-horns funk James Brown was pioneering with "Cold Sweat." This was something darker, neither as buoyant nor rhythmic, born in late night jam sessions where guitars crossed paths with drugs and psychedelia.

"Dance to the Music" and "Everyday People" endeared the group to AM radio fans, while the Family Stone's diverse makeup, politics, and musical adventurism earned street cachet with hippies and black radicals, including the Black Panthers. Three decades on, "Everyday People" survives as the band's definitive statement, perhaps because listeners can still project their own interpretations onto its nursery rhyme simplicity. "I can be right, and I can be wrong, my own beliefs are in my song," Sly intones, suggesting that everyone wants and deserves dignity—even if they have yet to fulfill their own aspirations. "I am no better, and neither are you, we are the same whatever we do . . ."

The sound of Sly and the Family Stone is a perfectly preserved composite of black and white music at the turn of the decade. Everything that pop represented—in terms of its threatening appearance to an older generation and its representation of idealism to the young—is there. The beat is more than propulsive; it wells up from someplace primordial and impels the listener to move in the same way a Saturday night fairground revival might. The tunes are undeniably melodic and their lyrics thoughtful and playful, jaded and innocent, scolding and all embracing. In music and lyrical content, Sly's apparent contradictions reflected the same ones taking place in American society during the hippie heyday—the newfound bond between blacks and whites finally hearing and playing with the same musical palette, and the growing rift between the races over a broad range of political and social issues.

In Detroit, Norman Whitfield and his Motown writing partner Barrett Strong memorized the Sly formula verbatim. The duo considered "You Can Make It If You Try" and "Sing a Simple Song" more than songs to emulate; as compositions, they foretold new directions in writing and arranging. In short order, Whitfield and Strong internalized Sly's ideas and created new works in their image. The Temptations ditched the naïveté of "My Girl" to score a handful of Whitfield/Strong hits traced from the Sly schematic. "Psychedelic Shack" borrowed the Family Stone's custom of passing lead vocals from one band member to another and Sly's counterculture posture—which in this case meant slipping into an underground discotheque where "the music's so high, you can't get over it; so low, you can't get under it." On "Cloud Nine," the "trip" offered temporary respite from ghetto life. By the time the Temptations scored with "Ball of Confusion" and "I Can't Get Next to You," Whitfield and Strong were working the Sly style as well as the master.

The Temptations' Otis Williams remembers how seriously the top brass at Motown took the Sly Stone challenge. "We were very conscious of what we were doing at the time," he recalls, "what was going on in the world—and things that were happening around us. We collaborated with Norman Whitfield and those songs just came tumbling out. Sly was the forerunner of that kind of sound, but we jumped on it right after that, very early on, really, before a lot of people knew what Sly was doing."

The notion of multiple lead singers ricocheting off one another occurred simultaneously to a Los Angeles trio, all veterans of the club and studio scene. Three Dog Night's vocalists included Danny Hutton, a mellow baritone; blue-eyed soul shouter Cory Wells; and the high tenor of Chuck Negron, a singer of pop-operatic sensitivity.

"People used to come up and congratulate Floyd Sneed, our (black) drummer for singing the songs, because people thought we were a black group at first," says Wells. Without a visionary songwriter like Sly to guide them, the group settled on a simple plan: they would split up, unearth old records, review material they'd done in previous bands, and solicit demos from unknown composers. Then they'd reconvene and debate which songs worked best for the group.

"Oh, each one of us wrote," Wells maintains, "but we were always a democracy, and if I wrote the song and the others didn't, there was always somebody saying it wasn't good enough. Consequently, we had to find stuff on our own to sing. So we would find material from other writers we admired. Chuck found 'One' by Harry Nilsson, which we originally tried to record in waltz time the way he did it. One day we did it with the full band, and the song just clicked right away. That's on the first album, which was pretty much taken from our stage show at the time, and we brought in things we had done from groups before Three Dog Night, too. I did Sam Cooke's 'A Change Is Gonna Come' and a couple of Randy Newman things, including 'Mama Told Me Not to Come.' By then, we were finding demos and songs all over the place; that's when we got 'Eli's Comin'' from Laura Nyro and a couple from Elton John, including 'Your Song,' which he hadn't put out himself yet."

The summer of 1969 ended with the Family Stone basking in the acclaim of their Woodstock performance and enjoying an even warmer reception for their next singles—"Hot Fun in the Summertime" and "Thank You Falettinme Be Mice Elf Agin"—which together lofted Sly to the pinnacle of pop music. Closer inspection of "Thank You" reveals an inner strain percolating deep in the grooves, as various factions attempted to hijack the Family Stone worldview. Black nationalists adopted "Stand" and "Don't Call Me Nigger, Whitey" as talismans of Afro-American pride and chided Sly to write more militant music, going so far as to issue threats of assassination. Conversely, record executives envisioned Sly's band as a crossover hit factory whose multiracial appeal was simply another selling point. For Sylvester Stewart and/or Sly Stone, the result may have been a nervous breakdown. Onetime manager David Kapralik described the schism to *Rolling Stone* writer Timothy Crouse, calling Sylvester Stewart "creative, rational, and responsible . . . representative of everything that is life affirming and healthful in our society." Sly Stone, on the other hand, was a "street cat, the hustler, the pimp, the conniver, sly as a fox and cold as a stone." You can take Sly Stone, Kapralik said, "and shove him up the nearest narc's ass. But Slyvester Stewart—I love him."

Whatever his emotional burdens, Sly's legacy proved to be a musical wishbook so full of ideas that artists today still evoke his spirit as a resource when their own muses falter. Family Stone acolytes on the sunny side embrace Kool & the Gang's "Hollywood Swinging" and the unabashed Afro optimism of Earth, Wind & Fire. Others—the Temptations and War paramount among them—adopted the grittier expressions of "Somebody's Watching You" as a point of departure. Sly himself launched something of a cottage industry in paranoid hits. Among them were the O'Jays' "Backstabbers" and the Undisputed Truth's "Smiling Faces," who sometimes don't tell the truth. "What'cha See Is What'cha Get" with these miscreants, according to the Dramatics, who explained that "some people are made of plastic/ some people are made of wood." Elsewhere, blacks were exiled far from America's economic Eden in a funky slum that Parliament christened "Chocolate City."

Canceled concert dates and a series of late appearances in the early 1970s made it clear that drugs were gnawing away at Sly's talent. Future Chic bandleader Nile Rodgers recalls that as a kid, he loved the group, "but half the fun of going to a Sly concert was wondering if he was going to show or not." Money, cocaine, and pressure yielded the Family Stone's grim masterwork, *There's a Riot Goin' On*, and a pair of hits ("Family Affair" and "Runnin' Away"), but the record was the band's last gasp creatively. It fell to Whitfield and Strong to graft Sly's approach onto a disco beat in 1972. "Papa Was a Rolling Stone" was the lushly appointed coffin in which the Family Stone's social commentary and baton-passing vocals were finally buried.

Those who have worked with Sly since his fall from the Top 40 contend that his genius remains intact. "Sly was a phenomenon," grants Parliament/Funkadelic ringmaster

George Clinton, who briefly had Sly in the band. "But when you do (the funk) with that intensity, it's hard for anyone to stay around. There were so many people trying to make him do this or that and he just rebelled against all of it. They told him he was a star, and soon as he believed it, he was out there on his ass."

But no formula with profit potential goes unexploited for long. A second generation of Stone acolytes appeared at the dawn of the MTV age, with Human League offering a nod to Sly in the basso profundo "Hey hey hey hey" asides on "Keep Feeling (Fascination)." Madonna performed "Family Affair" in the encore of her *Blond Ambition* tour, and cites Sly as one inspiration behind "Express Yourself." Janet Jackson's "Rhythm Nation" simply superimposed a new lyric over the recurring riff of "Thank You Falettinme Be Mice Elf Agin." At the turn of the millennium, Janet Jackson told a *Rolling Stone* reporter that "one of the biggest musical influences in my life . . . was Sly and the Family Stone's 'Hot Fun in the Summertime.' I was only three years old when that song had me jumping up and down."

In 1991, Lenny Kravitz borrowed elements from "Thank U" for his own track, "Always on the Run." Since then, vocal groups from New Edition and New Kids on the Block to Run-D.M.C., En Vogue, and the Backstreet Boys have updated the Sly method of tag-team lead vocalists to create their own signature sounds.

Those most musically indebted to Sly have been instrumental in keeping his name before the public since his hit-making days. Producer Nile Rodgers recalls, "When I was working with Power Station back in the '80s, we'd be in the studio jamming on a track that still wasn't funky enough, and we'd start yelling at each other to 'Sly it up!'" Prince, in particular, has been a Family Stone booster with a trail of Sly-like hits twice as long as the chart history of the original group. Both "1999" and "Little Red Corvette" trade off vocals with other band members, several of whom were white women, while "Kiss" and "Alphabet St." are directly descended from the Sly school of guitar funk. By the late 1990s, the Prince entourage expanded to include original Family Stone bassist Larry Graham. Years later, Sly would only mumble quixotically, "I don't know whether they have been influenced by my stuff or not, but I think they were at least encouraged. There was a lot of funky stuff that came out in those records of ours. I think I would have been influenced myself."

In the overlapping rock world, Jimi Hendrix found himself facing a fate similar to Sly's—trapped between militants, management, and his meal ticket. Hendrix may have become a black icon in death, but while he was actively recording, no one doubted that his fan base was primarily white. Yet after two years of constant touring and recording, Hendrix had tired of his role as the musical Mandingo who showed up to hump his guitar, pick a solo with his teeth, and set his equipment on fire. Mitch Mitchell, who rejoined Hendrix on drums months before his death, thought that "Jimi may have frightened some people, being one of the first black performers to use sexuality in a very overt sort of straightforward way. I think the sex thing became kind of a trap for him after a while, and he would try to steer away from it in the shows." Instead, Hendrix was anxious to explore blues and funk, free jazz, and advancements in recording technology. But many businessmen in his retinue believed the real cash cow remained the Jimi Hendrix Experience—two white Brits and a freaky Super Spade—and that what was really needed was another single like "Foxy Lady," something to both titillate and startle white America.

Jimi Hendrix burst onto the American music scene at the 1967 Monterey Pop Festival, simulating coitus with his guitar and fronting a trio that included two white Englishmen. Three years and three albums later, he died, suffocating on his own vomit after ingesting sleeping pills. In life, his audiences were mostly white, although in the years since his passing, black artists have come to claim him as an inspiration as well. (Barrie Wentzell/Star File)

Publicly, Hendrix spoke of independence. "When the last American tour finished," he told the press, "I started thinking about the future, thinking this era of music sparked by the Beatles had come to an end. Something new has to come and Jimi Hendrix will be there . . . I want a big band. I don't mean three harps and 14 violins. I mean a big band full of competent musicians that I can conduct and write for. And with the music we will paint pictures of Earth and space so that the listener can be taken somewhere."

While his imagination scoured the heavens, Hendrix' mind was very often on the business at hand, according to Mitchell. "These days a lot of people like to talk about how cosmic he was, and I don't think that was what was really going through his mind," he cautions. "Oh, we had some bizarre, strange experiences in our travels, but I never thought of him in terms of spiritualism much. He was just a very good musician who was getting better and better all the time." Privately, however, Hendrix may have capitulated to the wishes of those leash holders who insisted Jimi was a rock artist—which meant, fairly transparently, that most of the fans spending money on him were young, male, and white. Hendrix' efforts to break free of his past led to experiments with a large aggregate (his band at Woodstock, for example) and a power trio comprised of two black players, bassist Billy Cox (whom Hendrix had known in the Air Force), and Buddy Miles, once the drummer of an integrated blues band called Electric Flag. As the Band of Gypsys, the trio played only a few gigs before Hendrix pulled the plug, allegedly on the advice of a manager who believed Jimi's fans wouldn't support a black power trio. "He said his manager thought it would be a bad idea to have three blacks in a group," Miles later recalled bitterly, "that Jimi would be alienating his white audience. I wasn't completely surprised, though, because as creative as he was, Hendrix was set to self-destruct from the time I met him."

On September 17, 1970, the last night of his life, Hendrix was expected at a London club, where he planned to jam with ex-Cream drummer Ginger Baker. "I went over to see Ginger," recalls Mitch Mitchell. "I didn't hang out much with drummers, but Ginger and I were friends, and I recall that Sly Stone was coming in, and we were all supposed to meet later at this club to sort of have a play. Jimi never missed an opportunity to do that; he was always up to play with whoever was in town. Ginger and I went out and we waited and waited for Jimi to show, but he never did. I guess I got home to my place in the country about four in the morning, and I got a call about seven that he was gone."

Black guitarslingers did not rush in to fill the void created by Hendrix' death, in stark contrast to the ubiquity of black and white Sly imitators over the airwaves. Hendrix was an inspiration to many (think Ernie Isley's solo on "Who's That Lady," Stevie Ray Vaughan's reverential "Voodoo Chile," or Vernon Reid's soundscapes while fronting Living Colour), but re-creating Hendrix' incursion into the rock world would prove formidable, because his conquest of the (white) rock festival world became regarded as one more feat only Hendrix could manage. No one looked like him or matched his manipulation of sound on stage and in the studio; and when the press began its deification of Hendrix immediately after his death, it seemed no black rock guitarist dared follow in his footsteps without the risk of appearing a usurper.

Conversely, enterprising white players may have had a tough time deciphering the dexterous Hendrix style, but felt no racial imperative against doing so. Several, in the grand minstrel tradition, have learned his catalog, had their hair afro-permed, and taken their tributes on the road. The Hendrix appeal remains tricky to unravel, because in addition to his instrumental prowess and his songwriting talent was his reputation as an iconoclast—a commitment, in his own words, to "let my freak flag fly." Hendrix still commands fascination for those who dream of rejecting convention to embrace a more salacious renegade persona. (To hear some of them tell it, Hendrix was the natural man, while showing up at work to put out fires for the boss was considered a façade.)

Although voracious sexual energy and impressive fretwork remain Hendrix hallmarks, white kids in garage bands thoroughly plundered the guitarist's image in search of their own identities, appropriating everything from stage theatrics—playing Stratocasters with their teeth or slung behind their backs—to penning pretentiously cosmic lyrics and tying bandannas around their heads.

These suburban whites grew up half a decade behind the teens who discovered the blues of American blacks from British groups like the Rolling Stones, the Yardbirds, Cream, and Fleetwood Mac. In this short timespan, fashion and flash supplanted allegiance to the rigid structure that traditional blues playing demands. When headbangers like Grand Funk Railroad and Black Oak Arkansas strode into the limelight, the blues were trampled beneath power chords, fuzzed-up bass lines, and ham-fisted drum attacks. Some outfits, like the Climax Blues Band, were blues in name only.

These teens also adored Led Zeppelin, a band that thought nothing of giving a blues classic like "Killing Floor" a transparent rewrite in order to claim the copyright for themselves. "Whole Lotta Love," the first Zeppelin single to earn international attention, owed "deep down inside . . . woman, you need love," entirely to Willie Dixon's "You Need Love." Only after extended legal wrangling did Dixon receive any notice for his contribution—when "Whole Lotta Love" appeared on the concert anthology *How the West Was Won* in 2003. Another classic on the live disc, "Bring It on Home to Me" (from *Led Zeppelin II*) reduces the Plant/Page credit to a footnote, while Willie Dixon appears as the main source.

Most of the group's fans had no idea. Adolescents of the era didn't pore over Robert Johnson records or steep themselves in the music of the Chicago blues masters, as had Eric Clapton. Kids first picking up guitars in 1970 had little interest in tracking down "I'm So Glad" by its creator, Skip James—they wanted to re-create the incendiary Cream version.

Clapton retired such affectations long ago, dispatching them along with his *Disraeli Gears* afro, paisley pirate shirts, and stacks of Marshall amps. In the June 2004 issue of *Guitar One* magazine, he scoffed at the 1968 Cream version of Johnson's "Crossroads"— a much beloved artifact of the Woodstock generation. Some of today's purists (and Clapton is one) liken the arrangement to a cat with its tail set on fire. "I actually have about zero tolerance for most of my old material," he told the press, "especially 'Crossroads.' The popularity of that song with Cream has always been mystifying to me. I don't think it's very good. Apart from that, I'm convinced that I get on the wrong beat in the middle of the song, which happened often with Cream. It drives me crazy that there's this performance of me where I'm floating around out there; I'm supposed to be on the 'one,' when, really, I'm on the 'two.' So, I never really revisit my old stuff. I won't even go there."

Just as baby boomers' parents had transmuted the jazz of their youth into big band, bebop, and West Coast cool jazz, adolescents of the Vietnam era codified the electrified blues of British Invasion bands like the Animals and morphed them first into hard rock, and then into a southern-based spinoff known as "boogie." The Paul Butterfield Blues Band, Canned Heat, and the Allman Brothers added their own regional shadings to the concept, which combined blues structures with the freedom of jazz improvisation.

THE MEDIUM MEETS THE MESSAGE

Coincidence lofted a new generation of white rock groups and their black inspirations into the American consciousness. First, pop music was cut loose from the tyranny of the two-minute, thirty-second single when FM radio caught on in the late 1960s. On FM, programmers were finally permitted to spin longer, more exploratory album tracks (in hi-fidelity stereo) rather than Top 40 hits. The other watershed occurred in the summer of 1967, when the Beatles achieved conventional acceptance via *Sgt Pepper's Lonely Hearts Club Band.* In tandem, these events suggested that albums could be an art form unto themselves, and that audiences would indulge attempts to stretch pop beyond danceable melodies. Label talent scouts were suddenly on the hunt for "serious artists" who could move LPs as well as singles.

Few fit that mold better than Van Morrison, the Celtic soul star who arose from the ashes of a Belfast R&B band, Them, to become one of the preeminent singer-songwriters of the early 1970s. Fronting a shifting roster of Them members on the road, Morrison tore through raucous performances fueled in equal parts by booze and devotion to soul luminaries Bobby "Blue" Bland and Ray Charles. Them's hits—"Here Comes the Night" and "Gloria"—barely hinted at the abandon Morrison unleashed onstage, and, much like his mentors, he never gave the same performance twice. In one of the few surviving video clips of the era, Van lip-synchs his first solo hit, "Brown-Eyed Girl" on *American Bandstand* with such contempt for the charade that he doesn't even attempt to stay in time with the prerecorded track. Producers of the show might have been miffed, but in retrospect, it's both hilarious and revealing of Morrison's volatility.

"Brown-Eyed Girl" had been a fluke anyway, a happy accident born of Morrison's intent to compose a calypso song and producer Bert Berns' desire to create a pop hit. Berns was an American, and in addition to producing, he had written a couple of chart smashes himself, including "Twist and Shout" for the Isleys and the McCoys' "Hang on Sloopy" (which Them rejected). Indifferent to his own pop stardom, Morrison allowed himself to be managed during sessions for "Brown-Eyed Girl" and the accompanying album tracks, then turned surly when the single took off and a full-length LP was issued. Tacked on were the expected R&B covers and a handful of iconoclastic originals (a gloomy ramble about tuberculosis called "TB Sheets," for one) that set the stage for one of the great interracial cross-pollinations in pop—a folk "song cycle" by a white soul singer featuring black jazz session players.

Berns' fatal heart attack in December of 1967 helped spring Morrison from his contract, and he signed a two-record deal with Warner Brothers. By this time, Van had become a hippie, moved to Cambridge, Massachusetts, and dispatched his electric band for a looser acoustic group. In an effort to save money on studio time, a crew of studio veterans was recruited to translate Van's sketchy compositions to vinyl. The producers contracted Modern Jazz Quartet drummer Connie Kay; Richard Davis, the bassist and onetime sideman to Miles Davis; and Jay Berliner, a guitarist whose credits included a stint opposite Charles Mingus. The resulting album, *Astral Weeks*, is unlike anything Morrison or pop has seen since. The music runs seamlessly between folk, jazz, and blues idioms to create a shimmering backdrop for Morrison's ruminations on spirituality, love, and loss. In only a few hours—and with very little discussion, according to those present at the sessions—the musicians wove a delicate latticework of mood. Every rise and fall in Van's restless tenor gets its perfect complement, and the gentle sway of the band pushes Morrison's intensely personal lyrics to the fore. Despite nearly unanimous praise from the rock press, *Astral Weeks* stiffed when Warner Brothers could not find a potential single anywhere on the album.

Morrison quickly abandoned the poetics of *Astral Weeks* to embrace the glossier soul sound in vogue with bands like the Rascals, Joe Cocker, and Delaney and Bonnie and Friends. That meant concise songs with a well-defined melodic hook and a punchy horn section. On *Moondance*, Morrison finally found a comfortable juncture between commercial appeal and artistic integrity. The title track is supper club soul of the first order, pliant and restrained with swing to spare, with just enough schmaltz to tempt aging crooners like Sinatra into covering it. "Into the Mystic" distills Morrison balladry to its signature elements—romance, mysticism, and a keening melody. Several R&B trifles are tossed in as well—"And It Stoned Me," "Crazy Love," and the first single, "Come Running." But the most enduring cut of the record turns out to be "Caravan," a gypsy folk yarn that jumps to life when Van sneaks in behind a sax chorus, entreating his followers to "turn up your radio; just enough so you know it's got soul."

Moondance fixed Morrison's course for much of the 1970s, as he delivered one record after another of what became known as "Caledonia Soul." Half the tracks would find Van sketching epic valentines to lady love and the metaphysical (both *Tupelo Honey* and *St. Dominic's Preview* excel) while the remainder catch him wrestling the soul shaman within. Clearly "I've Been Working" finds its mojo through Muddy Waters and John Lee Hooker, while "Moonshine Whiskey" and "Street Choir" stroll the backroads of revisionist folk-country alongside the Band and light a path for pilgrims to come, including Dexy's Midnight Runners and the Thrills. And while no one was looking, Morrison also became a prosperous singles artist, slipping into the *Billboard* Top 40 with "Domino," "Blue Money," "Wild Night," and "Jackie Wilson Said."

Morrison's AM successes proved that even living legends benefit from a radio-ready single. But in the new climate of the 1970s, where poetics met bravura technique, many other artists found themselves suddenly obsolete. "When psychedelics started to happen," Rascals' drummer Dino Danelli recalled, "the music was changing and we weren't changing with it, and that's when the hits quit coming and that was the beginning of the end."

BAYOU COUNTRY

Still, a variety of groups thrived in the anything-goes climate of the early 1970s, paramount among them Creedence Clearwater Revival (CCR), a band famed for its blue-collar roots and regarded as the forerunner of "roots" rockers Bruce Springsteen and Tom Petty. Even though the group never landed a #1 hit single, their records were often at the upper reaches of the pop charts from 1969 until the band's dissolution in 1972. During CCR's heyday, composer/vocalist John Fogerty forged such a bond between his songs and the swamplands of the South that many concluded that Creedence had to be black. "I think that was a big misconception for some time," Fogerty says, looking back. "I was still only about twenty-six, and some guy came and knocked on the door of our office. He came in and met me doing an interview, and when he was leaving he told one of our business guys in the office, 'I thought John was this thirty-seven-year-old black guy.' To me, it was like a huge compliment. I thought, 'I got some barnacles on me. All right!'"

Although the band rose to prominence in the California Bay Area during the late 1960s, Fogerty's brilliance was not in experimentation, but in synthesis. At a time when most rock bands were saturating their songs in tape loops, echo, and random sound collages, Fogerty kept his songs so simple that an average garage band could play them after a few hours' practice. He recaptured the elegant simplicity of Chuck Berry's guitar hooks without sounding derivative, updated the ringing clarity of vintage Sun Records (check out CCR's take on the Roy Orbison classic, "Ooby Dooby"), and used psychedelic touches like feedback and fuzztone as a tool rather than as a crutch. And, instead of pushing rock 'n' roll into a new direction, Fogerty revisited the Memphis glory days of Elvis, Jerry Lee Lewis, and Johnny Cash, then set about creating new works within the same framework. In turn, Fogerty's work (along with that of the Band) inspired a return to minimalism.

Talking with writer Craig Werner for a CCR oral history called *Up Around the Bend*, Fogerty explained, "Our sound was a bit different (from San Francisco contemporaries Jefferson Airplane and the Grateful Dead) because I grew up in the East Bay and rock 'n' roll radio and R&B radio were my teachers . . ." And while the Dead and Airplane consisted of folk musicians who followed the Beatles and Dylan when they "went electric," Fogerty stayed true to the country twang of Scotty Moore (Elvis Presley's original guitarist) and Steve Cropper. On the other hand, "My singing doesn't have one source," Fogerty would say. "I'd certainly have to tip my hat to Little Richard. But it's sort of a composite guy, because I love Wilson Pickett, and there are a few guys who have that sort of high, edgy thing, Little Richard being the best and the most famous."

Fogerty may be the first American rock artist to mine the R&B vein without calling his own legitimacy into question. Certainly Leiber and Stoller had done it, along with a host of writers in the mid-1950s, but none of them were performing stars; in that regard Fogerty fulfills the promise of his forbearers. The miracle of his singing and CCR's playing is that neither sounds forced, whether plowing through new originals or a soulful oldie. When Creedence tackles an R&B classic, their influences seem so internalized that they capture a song's essence without artifice and often take their version to new heights. Fogerty opens his throat full throttle in "I Put a Spell on You," the song that gave "Screamin'" Jay Hawkins his name, and one album later rips into Little Richard's "Good Golly Miss Molly" with the same ferocity that Paul McCartney used to shred Richard's "Long Tall Sally." (Also like McCartney, Fogerty couldn't resist "writing a Little Richard song." McCartney's "I'm Down" was served up opposite "Help" in 1965 and Fogerty's "Travelin' Band" was issued on the flip side of "Who'll Stop the Rain" in 1970.)

The group waded into country music with the same dexterity. They draped "Cotton Fields" and Leadbelly's "Midnight Special" in homespun harmonies, and took a Stetson-sized glee in covering Rick Nelson's "Hello, Mary Lou." Fogerty also crafted a slew of his own country standards, including "Bad Moon Rising," "Lodi," and "Lookin' Out My Back Door." Under his guidance, CCR surveyed the broadest vistas of American popular songcraft—all of which Fogerty derived from an unerring blues instinct. He and the band did belly flop from time to time, most spectacularly in their rendition of "I Heard It Through the Grapevine," which provides the usual 3:30 of Creedence greatness doled out over an excruciating 11 minutes. "Grapevine" hardly tarnishes the magnitude of their achievement, though, considering they are the first major American rock act to never break stride in many raids across the borders of R&B, country, pop, and hard rock. Diverse as their music was, it remained heartfelt rather than stilted and at every moment uniquely Creedence.

The depth and diversity of CCR's catalog reaffirms the notion that good music need not be complex in order to communicate. Folk, blues, and country all wended their way into Fogerty's sound because he commingled them over a lifetime—unlike the generation of kids who bought his records and showed as much affinity for rock stardom as they did for the music. The Byrds explained it all on their 1967 single, "So You Wanna Be a Rock 'n' Roll Star," when they sang, "in a week or two if you make the charts, the girls will tear you apart."

Record jackets, concert posters, and the *Monterey Pop* film helped fix the guitar hero in teenage fantasies as a Colossus of Rhodes with a Stratocaster slung at crotch level. By the time of the Woodstock Festival in August 1969, jam bands like Mountain, the Grateful Dead, Jefferson Airplane, Fleetwood Mac, and Santana were everywhere. The *Woodstock* movie immortalizes that image, lingering on Ten Years After's Alvin Lee as he meanders through ten minutes of "I'm Going Home." Long loud solos showcasing dexterity over imagination became a blueprint for 1970s arena rock. Carloads of *Woodstock* filmgoers sat at drive-ins transfixed by the flailing figure of Alvin Lee, and imagined all the while how cool it would be to move your fingers that fast, shake the sweat off your long hair, and bellow, "I—Gon'—Home / Mah—Bay—Beh / I—Gon'—Home!"

Anything that smacked remotely of blues rock, from Alice Cooper to Grand Funk, was rewarded with sales comparable to the Allmans and the inheritor of Cream's English blues pedigree, Led Zeppelin. Jimmy Page, the guitar wizard bandleader, used his band as a springboard to reinvent the blues he studied. Young apprentices who followed in his wake would hear the bombast and the tangled runs Page wrung from his Les Paul, but discover little about the blues in the process. White kids picked elements à la carte from the blues handbook, mirroring the oral tradition that gave birth to the blues in the first place. Creative mutations could electrify, accelerate, and psychedelicize the blues, but its basic components survive even as they change hands with each succeeding generation— although they frequently morph in transmission.

Woodstock alumnus Joe Cocker was one who took the blues as a starting point. But by finding new talents (Page was a session player on his first LP) and creatively mixing such classics as "Bye Bye Blackbird" with contemporary material by the Beatles, Dylan, and Ray Charles, the British Cocker created a music that was uniquely his—as funky and compelling as the best in soul, and as wildly adventurous as any rock band on the scene.

Cocker, a native of working-class England, has built his career in a mainly black milieu without ever having to defend his motives. "Maybe I'm wrong to say so," shrugged Ray Charles, "but I do hear a lot of myself in Joe Cocker and his music. You ask where that comes from, and I couldn't say whether he's purposely trying to do that or it comes natural, but I can hear a lot of me in his singing."

Although Charles hedges a bit on what he hears, Cocker is absolutely clear about his inspiration. "I got the arrangement of 'A Little Help from My Friends' out of my love for Ray Charles and those waltzes he used to do—'Drown in My Own Tears,' and the really slowed down 'What Will I Do Without You?' I got to the point where I just heard it in my head one day while doing 'Bye Bye Blackbird.' I can't remember who wrote 'Bye Bye Blackbird,' it's such a great classic, but ours was very removed from the original. And I just kept thinking on those lines, and I came up with 'A Little Help from My Friends,' and I could hear the girl parts in my head and the pattern of it. And we worked it up one afternoon while rehearsing at a cinema in London with the Grease Band."

When Cocker's sassy-fat version of "A Little Help from My Friends" hit the top of the English charts, the singer received a congratulatory telegram from the Beatles, who were delighted with the liberties he'd taken. "I think they were a bit surprised by that," Cocker says, "so I got a meeting with Paul and George over at the Apple offices, where they played me a few songs each, and George gave me 'Something,' and then I got 'She Came in Through the Bathroom Window,' so by the time we were done, they were still working on *Abbey Road*, and I think we had ours out a couple of months ahead of them."

The late-1960s boom in blues meant that opportunists prospered alongside doctrinaire practitioners and the legends who inspired them. The same era that saw B.B. King land his only real hit single, "The Thrill Is Gone," found Frijid Pink hitting paydirt with a sledgehammer reading of "House of the Rising Sun." "It was unfortunate when blues became a fad and some of the great blues artists who got rediscovered in the '60s were forgotten again," laments Bonnie Raitt. Her devotion to the music was such that Raitt not only apprenticed herself to the blues masters of the day—she became a lifelong friend to many of them as well. In the late 1980s, she took a pivotal role in launching the Rhythm and Blues Foundation, an organization dedicated to helping musicians ease the financial burdens of their later years. Raitt does not claim credit for her work on this issue; but those behind the scenes say she works tirelessly on behalf of those who tutored her when she was young.

Some rockers happened onto blues simply because it was in vogue and 12-bar progressions were easy to write. Others—Californian Lowell George, for example—were utterly smitten with the bluesy rhythms of black music. At the helm of the Los Angeles-based Little Feat, George and bandmate Paul Barrere sketched out a Mississippi Delta landscape overrun with dissipated suitors ("Time Loves a Hero") and their magnolia-scented floozies ("Dixie Chicken"). George's blues-drenched baritone and slide guitar mastery, coupled with Bill Payne's jazzy keyboard fills, were enough to set the band apart from the mainstream. Despite changes in direction and membership every few records, Little Feat became a must-see concert attraction with a deep well of FM album staples to their credit. At the decade's end, George broke up the band for good, then died while touring to promote his solo debut.

George wore his Bourbon-to-Beale Street influences without the slightest irony, confident that at least in spirit, he was a true Son of the South. At the same time, in the humid nightclubs of Louisiana half a continent away, Mac Rebennack emerged from a chrysalis of studio work to become Dr. John the Night Tripper, the bayou's psychedelic high priest of gris-gris, whose ascension raised new questions about where reverence ends and parody begins. Rebennack, who turned out to be the genuine article, chalked up a

Top 10 single, "Right Place, Wrong Time," followed by "Such a Night" and decades of smaller hits and successful productions for other artists.

Radio became the expense-free trip that took John Fogerty and Lowell George to Beale Street in Memphis, allowed them to hear blues from Chicago, and helped them explore New Orleans' French Quarter behind Dr. John. Individually they had wildly disparate childhoods, but after radio baptized them, they were reborn kindred spirits in music and their assimilation of Southern styles helped to ensure that pop would remain a mongrel sound in which any instrument, scale, or production technique could be tapped in the service of making a tastier record.

NAME YOUR FAVE RAVE

On the FM airwaves, Clapton and Hendrix sparkled brightly as the morning and the evening stars, but only a flip of the switch away on AM radio a sizable number of listeners had little or no idea who they were. Instead, younger adolescents were caught up in the battle between two new groups—one that resembled Frankie Lymon and the Teenagers decked out like Sly and the Family Stone, and the other a white mirror image. The Jackson 5 and the Osmonds fought out their good-natured skirmishes on 45s, Saturday morning TV, and the backs of cereal boxes.

Berry Gordy launched the Gary, Indiana-bred Jackson 5 with his usual blend of hoopla and half-truths. After having the group brought to him by Bobby Taylor of the Vancouvers and Gladys Knight, he decided his protégés would capture more attention had they been discovered by the newly solo Diana Ross. Accordingly, their first LP was titled *Diana Ross Presents the Jackson 5*, and Ed Sullivan played along with the whole charade by singling her out in the studio audience when the group made its TV debut on his program.

"Having Diana Ross introducing us to the public was just a good public relations idea," Marlon Jackson shrugs. "At the time, we didn't think about what was happening very much, because we were still so young. We didn't think about, say, 'What was it like to have a #1?' After our first album, we were always the stars of the show; we always headlined and we just accepted that. We didn't try to figure out things like crossover or how much of the audience was white or black. They were an *audience.*"

Conversely, the Osmonds had established their marquee value while the Jacksons were still sleeping multiple kids to a bed in Gary. Now this well-scrubbed group of Mormon boys from Salt Lake City were working their way through adolescence under the watchful eye of Andy Williams. When the barbershop group admitted young Donny and added pop to their repertoire, preteen girls went apoplectic. "We left barbershop, and I added that fifth voice so that we could start singing rock and roll and more close harmonies. It just kind of evolved from where it was," Osmond attests. Soon, the two camps were locked in fierce competition for the braces-and-training bra crowd. The Jacksons' first batch of singles, "I Want You Back," "ABC," and "The Love You Save" (all of which reached #1 on the pop singles charts in 1970) were answered by a number of estimable hits from the Osmonds, "One Bad Apple" (which spent five weeks at #1 in 1971), "Down by the Lazy River," "Crazy Horses," and "Hold Her Tight," all of which landed in the *Billboard* Top Twenty. When Michael went solo with "Rockin' Robin" and "Ben," Donny stayed in the hunt with "Puppy Love" and "Go Away, Little Girl."

Teen magazines kept the playing field level for a few months, pitting Donny against Michael on weighty issues like first kisses and favorite junk foods. "A lot of people thought we copied the Jacksons," Osmond says, "and even Michael told me this: he said that when they were little, they used to sit down and watch us on *The Andy Williams Show*. Their dad, Joe Jackson, used to make them. He'd say, 'I want you guys to study this.' About three to six months after 'ABC,' we did come out with 'One Bad Apple,' which a lot of people thought was the Jacksons'. There were definitely some concoctions there, in terms of saying 'Let's use Donny. Let's push him out in front, because Michael's being pushed out in the limelight with the Jacksons, and it's a perfect white-Jacksons group.' The timing was perfect, so I would imagine that those powers-that-be who were running the record company, running the management firm—sure, they were looking at that. Absolutely."

In terms of record sales, the competition was over before it began. While the Osmonds enjoyed weekly exposure on *The Andy Williams Show*, the Jacksons had Motown's peerless songwriting, publicity, and grooming teams behind them. "We worked on 'I Want You Back' for three weeks at least before being finished with it," Marlon recalls. "I think we rerecorded it four or five times because the producers were all looking for a certain

Bubblegum soul made its debut in the early 1970s with the Jackson 5, left, and the Osmond Brothers. The Osmonds were a barbershop quartet featured on *The Andy Williams Show* who added little brother Donny (front and center) to compete with Motown's Jackson 5. Donny says that the brothers' management and record label clearly hoped to position the Osmonds as "a perfect white Jacksons group." (Frank Driggs Collection)

sound. They wanted to be sure it sounded just the way they had it in their minds because it was our first record and they knew that would be the only thing the public would have to identify us with."

Osmond reflects, "I look back at some of the music I recorded as a fourteen- or fifteen-year-old kid, and now it's a little bit different because kids are much more mature at that age. But back then, I was really at the whim of a lot of producers. Mike Curb was directing a lot of things, and I'm not going to complain about him because he gave me 'Puppy Love' and 'Go Away, Little Girl' and a lot of hits. But if you listen to the music on the albums I did, it was very much 'music by the pound,' I call it. Everything I did turned to gold because there was a base out there and little girls were just buying it up. So it was, 'let's just hurry and pump an album out.' With my brothers, we'd spend hours and days and weeks in the studio perfecting a sound. As Donny Osmond the soloist, I'd go into the studio and someone would hand me a cassette. I'd listen to it three, four, maybe five times, record it once, and get a gold record out of it. The whole teenybopper machine was so powerful that my career overshadowed the music of the Osmond Brothers, and their music means a lot more to me than a record like 'Too Young,' which I liked because it was a hit. But I only sang it once."

His counterpart, Michael Jackson, was the find of a lifetime and Berry Gordy knew it. In phrasing and intonation, the eleven year old was seasoned far beyond his years (a result, he says, of turning the wings of every stage into a private classroom where he studied and dissected the performances of James Brown, Sam and Dave, and Jackie Wilson), and he was cuddly and cute as need be. But while Gordy was indoctrinating his newest charges into the Motown Method, his grip on several others suddenly slipped.

SIGNED, SEALED, DELIVERED

At 21, Stevie Wonder quit being "Little" forever. He disavowed the contracts he had signed with Gordy as a minor, and demanded treatment commensurate with his true market value—historically an act of suicidal proportions at Motown. But Wonder orchestrated his moment with nothing left to chance. Gordy later recalled his protégé's birthday celebration in Detroit, just as the company was moving its entire base of operations to Los Angeles. "We laughed and told stories as the party went on until the wee hours of the morning," Gordy's biography states. "The following day, tired but in great spirits, I flew back to L.A. Waiting for me at the office was a letter from a lawyer I'd never heard of disaffirming every contract Stevie had with us—effective upon his turning 21."

Wonder held every ace and played his hand like a pro. He wisely honored not only the letter, but the spirit of his apprentice/mentor relationship with Gordy until his contract was nearly completed, incurring no enmity along the way. Wonder's name also appeared with escalating frequency on Motown records as co-composer—a fact camouflaged by pseudonyms as far back as "Uptight." Then, on the verge of his emancipation from the label, he stepped into the studio as composer, arranger, and producer to construct the 1971 Spinners' hit, "It's a Shame." At the same time, Wonder quietly readied an album of his own (*The Music of My Mind*) showcasing his prodigious skills as a singer and composer and featuring him on nearly every instrument. Gordy received all the evidence he'd need to justify loosening the reins, and a compelling argument for keeping Wonder aboard with his demands met.

As soon as Gordy agreed to new contract terms, Stevie returned to his characteristic equanimity. He shrugged off his tactical victory and fell just short of calling the whole episode a bluff to secure a raise and artistic autonomy. "I'm staying at Motown because it is the only viable surviving black-owned company in the record industry," Stevie told a reporter. "If it were not for Motown, many of us just wouldn't have had the chance we've had at success and fulfillment. It is vital in our business—particularly the black creative community, including artists, writers, and producers—to make sure that Motown stays emotionally stable, spiritually strong, and economically healthy."

With no one holding a leash on him, Stevie Wonder blossomed. His music, more protean and adventurous than ever, was suddenly everywhere. Easy listening stations embraced "You Are the Sunshine of My Life" and "Isn't She Lovely," rock programmers latched onto "Superstition," and pop and R&B jocks simply added each release as it became available.

"Stevie was truly amazing in those days," recalled Bee Gee Maurice Gibb. "Absolutely at the top of his game. I fell in love with Stevie Wonder's music while he was doing 'Superstition' in L.A. at the Record Plant. He'd done the drums already, and we didn't really know what he was doing, but we popped in and Steve McQueen was sitting there in the hallway on his motorcycle. Stevie's the kind of guy who'll yell out, 'I know that voice . . . it's a Gibb!' He showed us ways to take our songs to another level; at the time he was very jazz influenced, kind of how Sting is in his own way. It's slightly more sophisticated than pop, but there's pop in there. There's always a hook there that grabs you, and he was doing the keyboards when we came in and it had such an incredible groove to it, you know? To this day, when I hear it on the radio, I still love it because it's got such a great feel to it. And that was back in the days when Stevie was doing all of his own instruments, and he taught me as an individual, 'Wow, we could do that.' So he was a huge inspiration."

In 1972, Wonder agreed to open for the Rolling Stones on their tour of America. The Stones garnered their usual headlines with bad boy behavior and blue collar appeal, but Wonder generated much of the tour's real heat through sheer charisma and musicianship. More importantly, though, Stevie won the respect of an overwhelmingly white rock audience. Black acts before and since have opened for the Stones, but none with Wonder's degree of success. (Early on, Jagger and company recognized the value in having a black opening act—a strategy that buttressed the Stones' street credibility in the face of their evermore lavish lifestyles. The same gambit backfired with Prince when he was booed off the stage opening for the Stones in 1981, but paradoxically worked again when Living Colour took a spot on the mammoth *Steel Wheels* tour.)

Wonder survived a horrific car wreck in 1973 and recovered to create a virtual template for 1970s soul with such albums as *Talking Book, Innervisions, Fulfillingness' First Finale*, and *Songs in the Key of Life*. He spiked the punchy choruses of "You Haven't Done Nothing" and "Living for the City" with pointed social commentary, and his explorations of funk, reggae, and synthesizers expanded the medium as a whole. For a time, Wonder was the envy of every musician—black or white—in the industry. He dashed off songs that became career highlights for other artists ("Tell Me Something Good" did it for Rufus, and an old album track, " 'Till You Come Back to Me," clicked for Aretha). He launched a ground-breaking hit single of his own every few months, and three Stevie Wonder LPs in a row earned a Grammy for Album of the Year. Finally, in 1975, *Still Crazy After All These Years* won, prompting Paul Simon to quip in his acceptance speech, "I'd like to thank Stevie Wonder for not making an album this year."

By contrast, Marvin Gaye did everything the hard way. His marriage to Berry Gordy's sister, Anna (17 years older than the singer) may have cemented a connection to his boss in the early 1960s, but their dealings never became routine. Gaye remained the temperamental artiste, Gordy the bottom-line pragmatist, and the two came to an impasse over *What's Going On*, Gaye's deeply personal 1971 manifesto documenting society's ills— completed at the boiling point of the antiwar/pro-ecology movement. As an artist on AM radio, Gaye's track record was beyond reproach, and his 1969 hit with "I Heard It Through the Grapevine" provided Motown with its biggest single ever. But his albums were stuck in the Hitsville rut—Top 10 tunes garnished with filler—and Gordy saw no reason to change. The follow-up to "Grapevine" was, in fact, a jaunty confection called "Too Busy Thinkin' About My Baby."

Marvin had a broader vision, and even though he spent his life careering wildly between the sacred and the profane, *What's Going On* evinced Gaye's moment of Zen clarity. Music for the title track was actually penned by the Four Tops' Renaldo "Obie" Benson and his friend Al Cleveland, but, according to biographer David Ritz, Marvin himself did "the major work" of the album. Gaye adopted an alter ego for the project, a barely fictionalized rendering of his brother Frankie, who had recently completed a tour of duty in Vietnam. Through him, Gaye depicted a society ravaged by malice and neglect.

The resulting record is unlike any other in the annals of R&B. Most of the day's political rock albums were as self-righteous as they were leftist—with records like the Jefferson Airplane's *Volunteers* crying, "Up against the wall, Motherfucker!" and Steppenwolf's 1969 LP denouncing America as a bloated, out-of-control *Monster*. Edwin Starr's "War" aside, soul music expressed only a vague disappointment in presidents Johnson and Nixon. If their administrations were truly culpable in consigning young people (particularly blacks) to quick slaughter in Asia or a lingering economic death in the urban ghetto, soul music was not exactly giving voice to their rage.

Sly's *Stand!* was an exception to the rule, but its party atmosphere tended to camouflage the record's proactive agenda. By contrast, *What's Going On* is a detached lament, more lyrically akin to Pete Seeger than to Motown or the Family Stone. (Similar differences emerge two decades later between Public Enemy and N.W.A. and less strident albums from Arrested Development and Lauryn Hill.) Place a lyric sheet for Gaye's "Mercy, Mercy Me (The Ecology Song)" alongside Seeger's "Where Have All the Flowers Gone," and the composers, separated by time and culture, are outlining the same universal truths. Incorporating protest ideals into an R&B context was clever; joining them with such spellbinding music made *What's Going On* immortal. Gaye's arrangements are loose and jazz inflected, often with triple-stacked Marvins singing in three different registers, tonalities, and rhythms.

"From Jump Street, Motown fought *What's Going On*," Marvin later told biographer David Ritz. "They didn't like it, didn't understand it, and didn't trust it. Management said the songs were too long, too formless, and would get lost on a public looking for three-minute stories. For months they wouldn't release it. My attitude had to be firm. Basically I said, 'Put it out or I'll never record for you again.' That was my ace in the hole, and I had to play it."

Whether they knew it or not, the Gaye–Gordy–Wonder showdowns at Motown began a dialogue about the expectations performers have of their record companies, and vice versa. When the multifaceted Prince appeared in 1977, executives at Warner Brothers convinced themselves they had "the next Stevie Wonder," and when Prince displayed his virtuosic command of a variety of instruments, a three-octave voice, and skills as both a composer and producer, the label allowed him to self-produce. Free agency has yet to become commonplace in the industry, but Wonder's stewardship of his own career, including control of his own master recordings, proved that an artist could negotiate for autonomy and ally himself with a major company to the benefit of both.

PLIGHT OF THE NATURAL WOMAN

In the early 1970s, black women—with Aretha Franklin as the lone exception—were relegated to one role and one role only: romantic partner. They could pine (as Gladys Knight and Roberta Flack demonstrated in "If I Were Your Woman" and "The First Time Ever I Saw Your Face," respectively), act the seductress (pick any one of a dozen Tina Turner classics), or gripe about their men's failings—a common theme for a number of early 1970s hits. Betty Wright stewed over the "Clean Up Woman," who gets "all the love we girls leave behind," while Shirley Brown placed a call to the tramp who had snagged her man and politely told her to back off in "Woman to Woman."

There were signs, though, that women—particularly black women—were emerging in song as three-dimensional human beings. In "Love Child," and "I'm Livin' in Shame," the Supremes navigated premarital sex and single motherhood. Freda Payne groused about a husband who shirked his marital duties in "Band of Gold," and the Honey Cone (produced by Motown's estranged hitwriters, Holland, Dozier, and Holland) advertised in "Want Ads" that they were swearing off playboys once and for all: "Wanted, young man, single and free/ experience in love preferred, but will accept a young trainee . . ."

The news that women of color were rejecting subjugation wasn't exactly met with enthusiasm on either side of the color line. In 1969, Johnny Taylor sounded an alarm heard by cheaters the world over when he mused, "Who's making love to your old lady, while you were out making love?" Suddenly it was open season on the unfaithful. The Persuaders' "A Thin Line Between Love and Hate" tells the story of a carouser who returns home at 3 AM to his sweetheart, a woman who's only apparent concern is for his comfort. "Are you hungry?" she asks in the lyric. "Did you eat yet?" He's king of the castle—that is, until he wakes up in the hospital, "bandaged from foot to head."

Compared with Aretha Franklin's pronouncements on romance and equality, though, such songs remain grade-school primers. Profiles from the time delve into Franklin's tumultuous relationships with lovers, sidemen, and handlers, but musically she remains unassailable. Again and again, Aretha surrenders her heart, but never her dignity. In one of her best early hits, she puts her detractors on notice: "You'd better *think* about what you're trying to do to me!" For women, Franklin drew an unmistakable line in the sand. No longer would she sit quietly and take whatever men chose to offer. Aretha represented independence, and "Respect" became to Women's Lib what Kate Smith's "God Bless America" had been to patriotism during the war years of the 1940s.

Franklin wore her mantle as soul's female emancipator right into the new decade, when it dovetailed into the black consciousness movement. There were catchy, even great records between early hits like "Baby, I Love You" and "Natural Woman" and her gospel-infused take on "Bridge Over Troubled Water." But with the release of *This Girl's in Love With You* in January 1970, Franklin caught an artistic second wind, plunging deep into collective and personal reservoirs for inspiration. Her voice swathed "Dark End of the Street" in a deep indigo and infused "Call Me" with schoolgirl delight. With nary a dissenting voice, critics and audiences alike crowned her Queen of Soul, and she regularly placed in polls as the best female singer in contemporary music (she was a perennial honoree of the annual *Playboy* music poll, for example), a feat she has continued to duplicate nearly at will into the next millennium.

Franklin's greatest recorded triumphs arrived at the onset of the 1970s. *Spirit in the Dark* and *Young, Gifted, and Black* showed her moving beyond the boy-meets-girl sides that marked her breakthrough as a singles artist. In tandem, these records capture the zenith of an amazing career. They're sure-footed strides from a woman who knows precisely what she wants to say and how to say it, supported by a symbiotic group of musicians. She rolls at the piano; they rumble in time. Her voice rises to a shout, and the band matches her in a whipcrack. Together, they uncover a swing hidden in the grooves of Ben E. King's "Don't Play That Song" and converge on "Spirit in the Dark" to fuse gospel solemnity with the delirium of secular soul. Still, there's never a doubt as to who's in charge here, as Aretha latches onto B.B. King's "The Thrill Is Gone" and "Why I Sing the Blues" and tailors each to express her personal anguish. The nucleus of *Young, Gifted, and Black* contains Aretha's most sophisticated original work, including "Day Dreaming" and "Rock Steady." In addition, she expropriates the best material from her rivals in pop—Lulu's "(Oh Me, Oh My) I'm a Fool for You, Baby" and Dusty Springfield's "A Brand New Me"—drenching them with passion enough to eclipse their better-known counterparts. Nothing is too great a challenge for Aretha, as she claims the Beatles' "The Long and Winding Road" and Elton John's "Border Song" for her own.

Womens' Liberation ushered in notions of gender parity—a broad umbrella encompassing everything from equal pay for equal work to bra burning and open sexuality. Songs celebrating women's self-esteem also ran the gamut in the world of white pop, from the vapid Helen Reddy anthem "I Am Woman" to Gayle McCormack's tough-but-tender remake of "Baby It's You," fronting a band called Smith.

Among them, Janis Joplin remained the great white aberration; a puffy-faced little girl hidden behind a bird's nest of feather plumes and upturned Jack Daniels bottles. In August of 1968, she acquiesced to the sycophants who told her that Big Brother and the Holding Company were sloppy and beneath her talents. What nearly everyone aside from Janis could see was that Big Brother *worked*. The loose arrangements and sometimes slipshod playing perfectly reflected the band's hippie constituency. Janis wanted a razorsharp ensemble like the Muscle Shoals players who backed Aretha Franklin. With little foresight, Joplin assembled the Kozmic Blues Band, requesting that Big Brother guitarist Sam Andrew join her for the sake of continuity and moral support.

Andrew was much more than a sideman. In every sense, romance excepted, he was Joplin's partner. He wrote with her, kept her confidences, and shared both her visions and her heroin kit. What people still fail to understand about Janis, he says, is that "she really wanted to be Aretha."

"Every day, she talked about it," Andrew says. "She wanted to be like Tina Turner, she wanted to be like Aretha, and she was impatient about it. Janis really wasn't ready to leave Big Brother, but the guys in the band wouldn't let her have horns or keyboards; they wouldn't let her add these modular elements. Six months or a year more, and she'd have had the confidence to be a real bandleader. But so much of the time with Kozmic Blues, there were ten people standing around not knowing what to do, and Janis didn't know what to tell them."

In December of 1968, Joplin was enticed to debut the group at a Memphis show billed as "The Stax/Volt Yuletide Thing." Her band would headline over a constellation of local favorites, including the Staple Singers, Carla Thomas, Eddie "Knock on Wood" Floyd, blues guitarist Albert King, and Booker T. and the MGs.

According to Stax historian Rob Bowman, Kozmic Blues first rehearsed for the make-or-break date on December 18, four days before their scheduled Saturday performance. That Friday night, Janis and her entourage made themselves unwelcome at the mansion of Stax founder Jim Stewart, where a drunken Joplin dropped lit cigarettes onto the new carpet and snuffed them out underfoot. She was asked to leave.

When showtime finally arrived, Janis tore through her set with the usual fervor, but the band's lack of rehearsal and Joplin's misreading of the crowd left her backstage

Like Jimi Hendrix, Janis Joplin struggled to free herself from the image she established at Monterey Pop. Although she had a much greater following among white fans as a swaggering blues mama, she yearned to be an R&B singer. Her guitarist and confidante Sam Andrew would say later, "she really wanted to be Aretha." (Frank Driggs Collection)

waiting for encore cheers that never materialized. With reporters from *Rolling Stone* and the national music press in attendance, the underwhelming launch of Kozmic Blues made overnight headlines, and Joplin's confidence was profoundly shaken.

According to Andrew, the real problem was that at the core, the group was hobbled by addiction. "Kozmic Blues could have been called the heroin band," the guitarist shrugs. "It was just a doomed enterprise. I was doing a lot of heroin and so was Janis. There's even some book that claims I was stealing heroin from her. I think it wasn't true, but I wouldn't deny it in a court of law; it's entirely possible. One day, she called me into her room and asked me if I wanted a hit. We both got high, and then she said, 'we're not going to be needing your services anymore.' Then she had me stay on for a little while to train my replacement."

The band's only album, *I Got Dem Ol' Kozmic Blues Again Mama!*, added little to Joplin's reputation, although cuts like "Try" and the title track attest that at least conceptually, the group had merit. "I don't think it was bad reviews that killed Kozmic Blues," Andrew says. "I think she kind of gave it a bad review in her mind. That band really hit it for a while, but that phase went unrecorded. It worked well when we did things live like 'Raise Your Hand'; some of those were really barnburners."

Joplin rebuilt her ensemble from the inside out and rechristened them the Full-Tilt Boogie Band. It was this group that entered Sunset Sound in September of 1970 to record what would become the *Pearl* LP. For the first time, Joplin embraced her Texas roots. Joplin's largely unheard twang debuted on "Me and Bobby McGee" (her only #1 pop single), and her sense of humor led to an a cappella throwaway called "Mercedes Benz." Paring back the blues banshee wails, Janis left room for a more mature voice to emerge with the old vulnerabilities intact. On the night of October 3, 1970, with most of the major work on *Pearl* complete, she went back to her Hollywood hotel room and shot up for the last time. Janis was found dead the next day.

She knew that junkies overdosed from time to time, according to Andrew, but Joplin considered herself invulnerable. "Janis said to me several times, 'I come from pioneer stock; they were all really strong people and nothing's gonna happen to me.' Every time she'd say that, I'd get a chill down my back."

Joplin's reduction in death to swaggering blues mama sells her short, but ensures that succeeding generations have a timeless (if incomplete) image of her to embrace. Today, she remains more celebrated in the rock pantheon than in the R&B circles from whom she so sought acceptance. Mainstream black audiences never embraced her as whites did Jimi Hendrix. "I think a black person could listen to (the white soul revue) Delaney and Bonnie more easily than Janis," Andrew muses, "because Janis was always kind of her own thing. She expressed herself in very original and colorful ways. She was completely herself and couldn't be anything else. She was also a musician, and a real good one. I've worked with a lot of women singers since Janis died, and none of them had the range she had in sheer musical ability. I didn't realize that until long after she was dead."

WHAT YOU SEE IS WHAT YOU GET

The passage of time has fixed Brown, Sly, Hendrix, Gaye, and Franklin as lodestars in the music firmament, illuminating a course for pioneers from heavy metal to hip-hop. During the weekday rush hours of the early 1970s, though, relief from introspection was only the punch of a button away. Hits by Van Morrison, Joplin, and Creedence had to share airtime alongside vapid smashes like "Love Grows (Where My Rosemary Goes)" and horn-driven hits by Chase and the Ides of March. The singer-songwriter craze spawned denizens of clones, each one less substantial than its predecessor. Morris Albert scored with "Feelings"; "Snowbird" sent Anne Murray to the top of the charts; and Sammy Davis, Jr. gave the world a collective toothache crooning "The Candy Man."

With Hendrix and Joplin dead, Sly stoned, and Motown in decline, record companies simply churned out more of what had been working for the past few years. Listeners found their options limited to FM stations broadcasting more fuzzed-up guitars and keyboard solos or mindless hours listening to the peppy hit singles reflexively added by AM programmers. Prevailing critical opinion holds the pre-Watergate 1970s as the last hurrah of the 45 record—an era that bounced from Rod Stewart's "Maggie May" to *Jesus Christ Superstar* and Neil Diamond's quasi-African "Soolaimon." In truth, the pop charts leaned on R&B for inspiration, daring, and danceability. Nightclubs couldn't fill a dance floor with tracks from Led Zeppelin, Chicago, or America. The R&B charts were more daring and diverse, making room for Billy Preston's pop-synthesizer instrumentals alongside the finger-popping funk of Tower of Power, tuneful confessions from Bill Withers, and an assortment of vocal group performances still getting airplay today—The Chi-Lites' "Have You Seen Her?," The Stylistics' "I'm Stone in Love With You," and The Hues Corporation's "Rock the Boat." All of these songs crossed over, enlivening an industry mired in James Taylor and James Gang clones.

Americans used the years between Woodstock and Watergate to convalesce from the epic violence that had touched everyone old enough to remember John F. Kennedy's inauguration. In 1972, a "Now More Than Ever" campaign returned Richard Nixon to office with the most decisive popular vote victory in U.S. history. But when the administration brokered a peace treaty with Hanoi the following year, no ticker tape celebrations marked the event. Instead, people returned to the business of running their own lives, and the country enjoyed an idyllic *American Bandstand* summer several years too long, in which the detritus of the previous decade became fodder for the pop market. Protest and peace curried favor in Hollywood, where Keith Partridge batted his eyelashes and tossed his feathered hair weekly on one network while Archie Bunker defended his beloved president, "Richard E. Nixon," on another. Across the drive-in screens of America, viewers warmed up to soundtrack homilies like *The Poseidon Adventure*'s hit, "There's Got to Be a Morning After," and "One Tin Soldier" from Billy Jack: "Go ahead and hate your neighbor; go ahead and cheat a friend," chirp the singers, "do it in the name of heaven, you can justify it in the end." Americans had come to believe Vietnam was a mistake, and now indulged its appetite for repentance. "There won't be any trumpets blowing, come the judgment day," the song concludes, "on the bloody morning after . . . one tin soldier rides away . . ."

Watergate ended all of that, of course. And the idealism of the Woodstock Nation melted away into a decade-long club crawl—rife with cynics, hard drugs, narcissism, orgies, and an obsession with celebrity culture. Music was ready for a change, too, and if weather vanes could measure such shifts, they would have been spinning wildly in different directions.

NOTE

1 Shesol, Jeff. *Mutual Contempt: Lyndon Johnson, Robert Kennedy, and the Feud That Defined a Decade.* New York: W.W. Norton, 1998, p. 448.

CHAPTER SEVEN

Play That
Funky Music

Grassroots activism rattled the United States to its moral core throughout the 1960s, fueling the greatest transformation of social order since Reconstruction. As a result, blacks could now depend on their right to vote and rely on federal courts to ensure their access to public facilities, including the one trophy essential for a brighter future: the schoolhouse. But, as the 1970s unfurled, was America really any closer to realizing Martin Luther King's "beloved community," that colorblind society where members of both races were judged "not on the color of their skin, but the content of their character"?

Success depended largely on who was keeping score. With the civil rights movement sufficiently established to begin bringing Dr. King's ambitions to fruition, several former aides-de-camp became trustees of The Dream. (Jesse Jackson, for example, oversaw Operation Breadbasket, the "economic arm" of the Southern Christian Leadership Conference.) But with a potpourri of disparate causes ranging from women's and gay liberation to environmental concerns and a growing "Jesus Freak" craze, civil rights activists were difficult to spot among the gathering throng. Worse, America's bloody trail of assassinations left the civil rights movement leaderless. And with none of the heirs apparent able to satisfy every faction, a very pragmatic question emerged—whether to press on while circumstances remained fluid, or to accept and consolidate the gains won through years at the battlements.

By the 1970s, *Billboard*'s rhythm and blues (R&B) charts were fast becoming a bulletin board that listed the possibilities. The normally reserved Fifth Dimension weighed in with "Save the Country" by white soulsmith Laura Nyro. "I Don't Know What the World Is Coming To," the Soul Children lamented, while Curtis Mayfield thought it best to "Keep on Pushing," to which the Philadelphia International All-Stars added, "Let's Clean Up the Ghetto" and the Chi-Lites pleaded, "(For God's Sake) Give More Power to the People."

On the pop side, Ten Years After gave the stoner response. "I'd Love to Change the World," shrugged Alvin Lee, "but I don't know what to do." John Lennon offered up his own more strident "Power to the People," and even comedian Ray Stevens issued a call for tolerance via a pair of singles, "Everything Is Beautiful" and "America, Communicate With Me." Everyone, it seemed, had something relevant to say. But with everyone talking, who was listening?

EYES ON THE BOOBY PRIZE

By the 1970s, Motown had become the largest black-owned business enterprise in the country, but now four of the company's eight vice presidents were white. And with a shrinking disparity between black and white middle incomes (a National Research Council survey found that by the end of the decade, black men aged 25 to 34 with college experience would earn from 80 to 85 percent of their white counterparts), more blacks were living below the poverty line. Public records show that by 1980, only one percent of blacks held elective office in the United States, although they represented more than eleven percent of the populace.

Whites did not rise up en masse to challenge the Civil Rights Acts of 1964 and 1965; on the contrary, most appeared to endorse integration, at least in the abstract. As institutionalized racism fell by the wayside, pop culture was there to bear witness, and whites paid more than attention—they paid money. "Society's Child," a tale of interracial romance by fifteen-year-old Janis Ian, climbed into the Top 20 in 1967—the same year Spencer Tracy and Katherine Hepburn asked moviegoers to *Guess Who's Coming to Dinner?* (Answer: a white ingénue's black suitor). Clarence Williams III became a soulful third of *The Mod Squad* in 1968, and in 1970, Bill Cosby graduated from television's *I Spy* to a sitcom bearing his own name. Comedian Flip Wilson began hosting a variety show the following year, and in 1972, Congresswoman Shirley Chisholm became the first woman of color to run for the Democratic Party's presidential nomination.

At the same time, Los Angeles and Detroit both elected black mayors (Tom Bradley and Coleman Young, respectively), joining an ever-growing crowd that eventually included Cleveland's Carl Stokes, Atlanta's Maynard Jackson, and Richard Hatcher in Gary, Indiana. Their cities were no urban theme parks, but were some of the same urban slums torched by rioters a few years earlier—breeding grounds for ignorance, poverty, and crime. Whites abandoned them in droves for the suburbs, leaving blacks to wonder whether they'd been awarded keys to the cities or left to sort through the rubble created by years of neglect. "Don't you know that it's true," ran the rueful 1972 hit by the interracial band War, "that for me and for you . . . The World Is a Ghetto."

It seemed there were more ways to thwart the beloved community than Dr. King ever dreamed; that somehow privileged whites would always find a way to keep America's bounty just out of reach. Reporters in the 1960s coined the phrase "credibility gap" to convey the gulf between real progress in fighting the Vietnam war and the spin manufactured by the White House, and now black artists like Wilson Pickett were viewing questions of color with a similarly jaundiced eye. In conversation with author Gerri Hershey, Pickett fumed that nothing trumps race in America, not even celebrity. The idea that blacks were better respected than they had been before the civil rights movement was a "big lie," as far as he could tell, and most blacks were still regarded as curiosities, not people. "I should have known," Pickett told Hershey in *Nowhere to Run*, "even a motherfuckin' monkey make it to the Johnny Carson show."

AIN'T NO SUNSHINE

Although those who survived the crucible of the 1960s faced fewer impediments to decent jobs, schools, and housing, common civility remained elusive nonetheless. The dichotomy made a lasting imprint on Bill Withers, the singer-songwriter of "Lean on Me" fame. "I grew up," says Withers, a native of Slab Fork, West Virginia, "and from the first day of my life, there was a concentrated effort made to convince me that I was genetically stupid, ugly, and something was wrong with my damned hair. That was very organized, and it was concentrated. So there were a lot of things to overcome just to exist. If you put the profile of an abused child up next to the profile of the average black man of my age . . . . What's an abused child told? He has low self-esteem because he was told he wasn't this, he wasn't that . . . . It's almost identical."

While most of his contemporaries worked their way up the food chain of the music industry through coffee houses, road gigs, and showcases, Withers spent nine years as an adult in the Navy, followed by several more as a blue collar worker. At thirty-two years of age when his career took off, he was considered over-the-hill by pop standards. "And," he contends, "I give absolutely no credit to the little integrating that's always occurred underground around rock 'n' roll music, jazz in its time, or whatever, because it ain't got a damned thing to do with reality." For Withers, the world *is* black and white, in terms of morality as much as skin color. His rural upbringing and his no-nonsense approach to music making and the music business have left him financially comfortable, but utterly without illusions.

Withers considers desegregation equal parts cosmetics and real progress, and believes odes to brotherly love are inconsequential in a world where bigots still wield power. "I don't think music changed anything," Withers says flatly. "It's not like everybody follows the rules just because you pass a law."

Beverly Hills has been Withers' home for nearly three decades, and he's spent most of it in private. "This is serious shit, and I have no illusions, man," he intones. "I know where the racial divides are. When I first moved into my house thirty years ago, I would get stopped in my car. I know that if I go buy a house tomorrow—and I can do it—say I want to go buy a house tomorrow, and a house costs $3 million. I can get in there, okay? The first thing I'm going to have to deal with is somebody asking me what I am doing there. What do I want and why am I there, until they find out that I own it. Then they're going to be relieved that I'm an entertainer, because that's more palatable . . . there's always been room for a black person who can sing and dance, and if you can clown, well, oh my God!"

Fame and fortune are woven deeply into the American dream of success, and African Americans have spent four hundred years biding their time for a fair share. They've strummed banjos, sawed at fiddles, and painted themselves black—essentially shucking and jiving—and for what? Passive or militant, they remained second-class citizens in the 1970s. How could they secure true social and economic freedom? For Withers, educating his children proved the most satisfying answer. College degrees and high-paying professions don't guarantee respect, the singer concedes, but they provide the best buffers.

"At some point I realized, this is cool," he admits. "I get to make some bucks and change my life. But I'm not breaking any ground here by being another black guy entertaining. You're another nigger with a hit record. So what? What's changed? Nothing." Far more valuable, he says, are the opportunities he's been able to secure for his children. "If I can take this gift I've been given and turn it over to some descendants of mine who got to go to some good schools and got to pursue law or medicine or whatever, then I've done something worthwhile," Withers says. "Overall, I am much more proud of my children's education. Maybe I broke some ground with that."

LOVE AND HAPPINESS

Despite the sturm and drang of the times, a wave of recently single performers trooped up and down the charts throughout the early 1970s—a field crowded by solo Beatles and ex-Temptations, Diana Ross, Rod Stewart, Curtis Mayfield, and Brill Building songwriter Carole King. Add to that list newcomers Roberta Flack (the soft rock songstress who wrote "Killing Me Softly With His Song" after watching Don McLean sing "American Pie") and Al Green, a black transplant from Flint, Michigan torn by the same hedonistic and religious impulses that brought Sam Cooke to an untimely death.

Like Bill Withers, Green sprang from country origins, but artistically, they were worlds apart. Where Withers' homespun narratives ("Lean on Me," "Use Me," and "Grandma's Hands" are fairly representative) often doubled as morality plays, Green burnished his gospel-trained voice into a tool of seduction. He and Hi Records producer Willie Mitchell dropped the tempos of proven chart toppers ("I Can't Get Next to You," "For the Good Times," and "How Can You Mend a Broken Heart," all recorded at Hi Records in Memphis between 1971 and 1977), and pushed Green's voice up into its highest register, with Mitchell insisting that Green keep his gutsy tenor tightly under wraps.

Consequently, each record pulsed with emotion seeking release. When the Green/Mitchell version of "How Can You Mend a Broken Heart" got back to the Bee Gees—who wrote it—they were stunned. "Oh, we knew of Al Green," Maurice Gibb remembered, "but when I heard it, I was taken aback. I thought, 'Wow, he's really feeling it; it's so slow, but done with so much emotion.' Only Al Green could have done it that way. It's completely his stamp, with so much soul—the kind of thing you'd hope and dream that Elvis would do."

The impact on white singers was as immediate as it was apparent. Boz Scaggs, who began playing blues in West Coast rocker Steve Miller's band, set his jeans and guitar aside to re-create himself as an R&B crooner draped in silk scarves and designer suits. The transformation was complete by the time of *Silk Degrees*, Scaggs' 1976 breakthrough LP. The album yielded a bevy of FM favorites ("Georgia," "What Do You Want the Girl to Do," and "It's Over") and a pair of classic singles in "Lowdown" (#3 pop on the *Billboard* charts) and "Lido Shuffle" (#11 on the survey in 1977). With free-form radio at its zenith, listeners could choose for themselves whether they preferred Green to Scaggs, or Bill Withers to the unaffectedly soulful—and unmistakably white—James Taylor. By mid-decade, it was commonplace to find listeners of every stripe who cherished albums by all of them.

Musicians found nothing unusual about this, since they had been cherry-picking from black and white records since they could remember. Trekking down to the local record shop on Tuesdays—the day stores stocked their new arrivals—became a ritual for Harry Wayne Casey while growing up in Hileah, Florida. "Most of the time, I was the odd man out," says Casey, who made a name for himself as "KC" in the Sunshine Band. "My friends were all into the Beatles, and I was into Motown and Memphis and Stax records. What attracted me to Motown was that they always had that sound—that beat and rhythm that always made me feel good inside. But I also liked (the white) Blood, Sweat & Tears; I thought they were soulful, too. I think soul is soul, and I don't think there's any color to it."

Oakland-based Tower of Power has a similarly color-blind appeal. Over the years, the group has featured black and white performers as vocalists and soloists on the horn line. Their run of hits began in the early 1970s with "You're Still a Young Man" (#29 pop and #24 R&B hits, 1972), "So Very Hard to Go" (#17 pop and #11 R&B hits, 1973), and "What Is Hip?" (#91 pop and #39 R&B hits, 1973). Despite gushing acclaim from jazz enthusiasts—and the fact that their material was almost exclusively written by two non-black core members, Emilio Castillo and Stephen "Doc" Kupka, Tower of Power always maintained that they were primarily "a soul band." Rock impresario Bill Graham took them on as manager; their first real gig saw them open for Jimi Hendrix, and in 1973, the group hit its stride with their eponymous LP, *Tower of Power*.

Perhaps because their music withstood easy categorization, hippies embraced them as the funk band of the Fillmore era. While radio-friendly album tracks like "Soul Vaccination" and "This Time It's Real" kept them in demand as a concert attraction, the horn section slipped into the studio and revolutionized rock music. First, they worked out a head arrangement (with no charts, just general guidelines agreed upon by the players) to Santana's third-encore showstopper, "Everybody's Everything." Then, in 1974, they fit Elton John's "The Bitch Is Back" with a sleek brass undercarriage that made it pounce off the starting line. "Before that," says Castillo, "there weren't a lot of session calls for horn players—not rock players, anyway. Usually, if someone wanted horns, they'd hire session players who weren't rock 'n' roll players at all."

In their second decade, they backed up everyone from Huey Lewis and the News to Phish to the *Late Night With David Letterman* house band. "They were the first thing in the R&B mold that really knocked me out," recalls the Time's keyboard player Monte Moir, who later went on to write for Janet Jackson. His bandmate Morris Day agrees: "Actually, the Minneapolis Sound evolved from us all liking things like the Ohio Players and especially Tower of Power, which was one of my personal favorites with David Garibaldi and Lenny Pickett. We didn't have horns in the Time, but we decided to use keyboards to do the horn lines instead. And really, with some of the other influences, having the keyboards do the horn lines is what became known as the Minneapolis Sound—essentially the Oberheim synthesizer."

Black performers fuzzed up the bass and freaked out on guitar. White rockers challenged the limits of rhythmic elasticity, and once inviolable dictums of formatted radio chipped away like so much old paint. Divisions in race and music dissolved, and it seemed to be only a matter of time before this new contagion of brotherly love filtered out into society at large. It was America-as-Melting-Pot, wrestled into a mind-blowing variety of styles and sounds that couldn't easily be catalogued according to race.

Yvette Stevens, who took the name Chaka Khan while performing social work with the Black Panthers in the early 1970s, concurs. "I've been dealing with the label of being a soul singer ever since I opened my mouth for the first time," she says. "People looked at the color of my skin and decided I was an R&B artist. But from the time I was old enough to listen to the kind of music I wanted to hear, I was into Ray Charles and Dionne Warwick, and then in high school, Led Zeppelin, the Stones, and Roger Daltrey. But they didn't necessarily affect my phrasing or anything, because I think I'm me first."

Not all black artists began with such self-confidence. Rock was the music of the day, and its most visible accessory—long hair—excluded blacks. Nile Rodgers, who co-founded the black dance band Chic, remembers his late partner Bernard Edwards confiding how he'd take his father's underwear and put them on his head so the shorts "would drape down to his shoulders and it would give him the appearance of having really long hair. And then, finally, he could visualize himself as a star. To think of himself in the normal physical image of a black man, he couldn't down that. And I don't think it was a whole psychological thing, it was purely visual and instinctual. He said to himself, '*Real* stars look like *this*.'"

DREAMS TO REMEMBER

It was a classic case of perception versus reality. Civil rights leaders spent the 1960s challenging the white power structure to look beyond racial stereotypes, but what did that portend? If blacks really were more than janitors and maids, bus drivers and cooks, who were they? Their identity crisis set off a wave of Afrocentrism under a banner that terrified the status quo: Black Power. For many African Americans, the slogan implied racial pride and solidarity. Across the racial divide, however, the slightest suggestion of Black Power called to mind Muhammad Ali refusing induction, storefront shootouts with the Black Panthers, and footage of black radical Angela Davis led from court in handcuffs.

Scarier still, black power repudiated the 1960s rhetoric of pacifism. The magnanimous Great Society Lyndon Johnson legislated, the beloved community Dr. King envisioned— both seemed like smoke and mirrors and empty promises now. This country of immigrants was never going to be a melting pot, where each ingredient complemented a harmonious whole. There were never going to be enough hair-straightening products or leisure suits to turn black folks into white folks. Spurned once more by the nation that transplanted them, black Americans sought to rediscover themselves.

Curiosity about African culture skyrocketed. Turtlenecks, trenchcoats, Ray-Bans, and berets gave way to dashikis and turbans or blown-out natural Afros. In 1968, a Chicago television sportscaster named Don Cornelius sank $400 of his own money into the pilot for an after-school dance show highlighting black music—in effect reclaiming the teenage pastime *American Bandstand* had tried to scrub lily white—and *Soul Train* became a local sensation. After attracting investors ranging from Sears Roebuck to the black-owned Johnson Products, Cornelius relocated the program to Southern California and began broadcasting nationwide in October 1971. For the next two decades, landing a *Soul Train* guest shot was tantamount to winning amateur night at Harlem's Apollo Theater. In the years preceding MTV and BET, *Soul Train* became the one appearance every R&B act had to make, and, eventually, all the single-name celebrities showed up, including Aretha, Marvin, Diana, Smokey, and Tina.

America also went to the movies, where a gritty realism slithered through the nation's cineplexes in the early 1970s. There, for the first time, the disaffected finally saw themselves depicted onscreen—transformed into anti-authoritarian avengers. Many movies were plotless bloodbaths of situational ethics, rife with corrupt cops and dope dealers flaunting their trappings of excess. In *Shaft* and *Superfly*, just as in *Billy Jack* and Charles Bronson's *Death Wish*, justice was meted out by vigilantes who answered only to themselves.

GOOD MORNING HEARTACHE

Black artists had been a recurring presence in the Top 40 for more than twenty years, but movies were another matter. Sidney Poitier remained the film industry's lone black icon, and many Hollywood insiders dismissed the new Afro-aware cinema as nothing more than "Blaxploitation." Berry Gordy, having revolutionized pop and soul, sensed a niche for quality films with black story lines, and suddenly Motown's relocation to Los Angeles made sense. As Gordy tells it, all his dreams and opportunities converged in *Lady Sings the Blues*. Here he finally saw a way to immortalize his idol Billie Holiday, a strategy to become a movie mogul, and a business plan to make his hottest commodity—Diana Ross—even hotter. Paramount Pictures agreed to the working title *Berry Gordy Presents Diana Ross as Billie Holiday in Lady Sings the Blues*. With typical hubris, Gordy put his money where his mouth was, then put his mouth where his money was. When cost overruns led to a half-finished film with 95 percent of its budget spent, Gordy met with studio boss Frank Yablans (who was concurrently overseeing *The Godfather* and *Save the Tiger*) to suggest they "rework" the budget. Yablans balked, and Gordy offered to preview a few scenes to bolster the executive's confidence.

Yablans didn't budge. In his autobiography, *To Be Loved*, Gordy remembers the studio chief explaining, "The biggest budget for other black films is $500,000, tops. We're giving you two million dollars. You understand what that means, two million dollars for a black film? You should be happy." To his everlasting credit, Gordy replied, "This is not a *black* film. This is a film with black stars." The next day, Gordy returned with a check for two million dollars, and only then did Yablans take him seriously. The studio kept control, but the showdown emboldened Gordy to haunt the set and attempt to "try different approaches" with actors Ross and Billie Dee Williams—far overstepping his role as financier with director Sidney Furie. Gordy's detractors were certain that this time ego would be his undoing.

Besides, the naysayers felt, Ross was all wrong for Billie Holiday; her voice was thinner than her figure, she displayed none of the tragic grandeur that made Holiday a legend (in performance, Ross grinned through most Supremes hits, no matter how sorrowful the lyric), and she had no acting experience beyond the occasional TV appearance. But when the film opened in October 1972 and earned nearly $10 million in its initial run, Ross and Gordy emerged triumphant. There were grumbles about historical accuracy, and many doubted that Ross had really brought Billie to the silver screen, but whoever was up there was captivating. To an unexpected degree, Ross lost herself in the role and allowed herself to be captured looking not only unglamorous, but battered and heroin addicted as well. She was nominated for an Oscar—one of the picture's five nominations, although Ross lost to Liza Minelli's performance in *Cabaret*, and the film went home empty-handed.

Jazz fans hated the idea, but Motown founder Berry Gordy was determined to see protégé Diana Ross play Billie Holiday on the big screen. *Lady Sings the Blues* was released in 1972 at the height of the "Blaxploitation" movie craze. The film lost in every Oscar category where it was nominated, but proved that audiences of all colors would pay to see quality movies with black themes. (Frank Driggs Collection)

Jazz aficionados objected, but it's hard to imagine who could have satisfied them. *Lady Sings the Blues* may not have been a faithful representation of Billie Holiday, but there were ameliorating factors. The film proved Ross could act (although she'd never again be so challenged), that supporting actors Billie Dee Williams and Richard Pryor were on the cusp of stardom, and, most importantly, that a black cast could carry a mainstream motion picture that all America would want to see. Ross and Williams reunited for *Mahogany* two years later, but Gordy and Ross fought with each other, and then turned on English director Tony Richardson. Gordy fired him to complete the picture himself, and the film fared poorly at the box office. A similar fate befell *The Wiz* in 1978, with Ross (now approaching middle age) cast as Dorothy. Here, the subplot—which took place off-screen—was more interesting than the final film. Between takes, a loose-limbed adolescent playing the Scarecrow tossed around ideas for a solo album with the film's music supervisor. Less than two years later, Michael Jackson and Quincy Jones would launch *Off the Wall*, the album heralded as the dawn of the 1980s.

MAJORS MALFUNCTION

Motown would never again enjoy such power and prestige, but at least the doors remained open. Stax, by contrast, had its offices shuttered permanently halfway through the decade. Leaving aside hard work and faith, Stax came together through happenstance, thrived with good luck, and was finally crushed between business miscalculations and the very disco music its stars helped to launch.

When the distribution deal between Atlantic and Stax fell apart at the end of the 1960s, label chief Jim Stewart learned that the contract he had signed included a clause ceding the Stax back catalog—including masters that should have been the company's nest egg—to Atlantic Records. Jerry Wexler has said that the Atlantic brass was as surprised to learn of the clause as Stewart, but their relationship never recovered.

Stax was still mourning the losses of Otis Redding and Dr. King when an enterprising songwriter and ex-deejay named Al Bell became company vice president in 1970. Bell was a public relations natural who took every opportunity to remind the press that Stax had long been integrated, and that the house band, Booker T. and the MGs (comprised of a black keyboard player and drummer and a white guitarist and bass player), provided incontrovertible evidence to that effect. Behind the scenes, though, the studio's neighborhood was becoming dangerous, with guns in the studio and gangs alternately threatening and playing bodyguard for visiting session players. Rumors circulated that underworld connections to Stax led from the offices out, not the other way around. In short order, Booker T. and his bandmates scattered to session work on the coasts, hitmakers Sam and Dave fell apart, and house composer Isaac Hayes moved on to stardom on his own.

In 1969, Stax issued Hayes' first solo project, *Hot Buttered Soul.* Having written "Soul Man," and "Hold On, I'm Comin'" for Sam and Dave, as well as "B-A-B-Y" for Carla Thomas, Hayes well understood the constraints of the Top 40. Hayes took Glen Campbell's pop country hit, "By the Time I Get to Phoenix," downshifted its tempo, and extended it into an eighteen-minute dissertation on love gone cold—years ahead of disco and the "Quiet Storm" R&B radio format that would later showcase singers Anita Baker and Al Jarreau. By the time Hayes' *Shaft* score put him on the Oscars telecast—the bald and bearded singer draped in a shirt constructed entirely of chains—he was a superstar.

Bouyed by Hayes' success, the embattled Bell soldiered on with a new slate of artists that included the Staple Singers ("I'll Take You There," "Respect Yourself," and "Heavy Makes You Happy"), the Dramatics ("What You See Is What You Get" and "In the Rain"), and Mel & Tim ("Starting All Over Again"). But in 1972, Bell dragged the label into a boondoggle called WattStax, an R&B festival intended to commemorate the Watts riots half a decade earlier.

The connection between Stax—still based in Memphis—and the Los Angeles suburb of Watts was never fully explained. Jesse Jackson hosted the concerts, which later yielded a film and multidisc record, with all proceeds allocated to either national black charities (the Sickle Cell Anemia Foundation was one) or programs designed to benefit the city of Watts, including a summer festival. The Memphis black community was mystified. Why should Watts be the beneficiary of such generosity when there was so much privation at home? Stax struck another distribution deal, this time with CBS and Gulf+Western—which resulted in a cash infusion of $6 million arranged by CBS label chief Clive Davis—but Bell was a better promoter than manager, and in December 1975, the courts honored a creditors' petition to have the label declared bankrupt.

Meanwhile, Atlantic quietly eased away from soul and into the rock arena. Corporate-sounding commodities like Crosby, Stills, Nash & Young sold well, as did the blues-based Allman Brothers and a group of Northeastern white funksters called the J. Geils Band. Aretha Franklin left the label in 1979 after a string of commercial disappointments. Small wonder. Midway through the decade, Atlantic held contracts on the biggest-selling acts in the rock world—all white British bands, from the Rolling Stones to Led Zeppelin, Eric Clapton, Bad Company, AC/DC, and Foreigner. The label continued to tout a cadre of influential black jazz stars, including Yusef Lateef, the Modern Jazz Quartet, and fusion drummer Billy Cobham, suggesting that if the embers of commercial jazz could ever be fanned back to flame, Atlantic had plenty to offer.

With so many caught up in the political and social causes of the moment, few noticed as Atlantic packed up and moved from juke joint cool into the gilded parlors of the Zeppelins, Stones, Bee Gees, and Scandinavian hitmakers ABBA. In the transition, the company lost something intangible. Rock album sales were filling the corporate coffers, but the "Sweet Soul Music" Arthur Conley sang about in 1967 had become an anachronism. No more Otis. No more Aretha. No more Drifters singing about being "Up on the Roof," or walking "On Broadway." Atlantic lost its soul, and would spend the next two decades trying to find it again.

THE HARVARD EXPERIMENT

Columbia wasn't doing much better. On May 11, 1972, the Harvard Business School released a report on black music commissioned by the Columbia Records Group (CRG) —now a part of the Sony label. In what was widely circulated as "the Harvard Report," six masters students took six months and five thousand dollars to study the economics of black music and determine how the largely white-oriented Columbia could more effectively penetrate the record market with African American artists.

The students first found what had been evident for some time—that black music fans were above all else radio lovers, that they were predisposed toward singles rather than albums, and that disc jockeys were an essential component to success. They also found that

Columbia executives failed to recognize the company's best resources, even when they were presented on the proverbial silver platter. The company had to face mishandling Aretha Franklin—whom they had promoted as a cabaret singer, only to see her crowned Queen of Soul after departing for Atlantic records. Slowly, and largely due to the crossover phenomenon of Sly and the Family Stone, Columbia's brass came to grasp the earning potential of black music.

Under its original title, "A Study of the Soul Music Environment Prepared for Columbia Records Group," the 1972 report estimated the genre's annual revenue at $60 million—translating into sales of twelve million LPs and sixty million 45 rpm singles. Harvard's researchers blamed failure to exploit the market on CRG personnel who were acclimated to the industry in a way "that differs fundamentally from soul music in the critical factors required for success." As a remedy, the students recommended that Columbia establish an in-house soul music department focused on improving the quality of records and the company's visibility within the black community.

Of course, hiring Harvard grads to analyze soul music was not unlike asking a team of physicists to quantify the taste of pie. Soul music, the researchers decided, was best described as a "raw, driving beat that is as much viscerally as aurally experienced," as well as music produced and appreciated predominantly by African Americans. The study is rife with deficiencies and betrays an ignorance of Columbia's historic connection to black artists—knowledge that even a hobbyist might possess. For example, the Ivy Leaguers seemed oblivious to the label's long-standing ties to black music, reaching back to the first blues hit in 1920 with Mamie Smith's "Crazy Blues" as well as the race-barrier-breaking work of John Hammond, or to Columbia's successes with Billie Holiday and Miles Davis.

Omissions and generalizations aside, the report did render a few insights. Most notably, the researchers found that black audiences relied primarily on radio for their music, meaning the song—and, therefore, the single—still came first for them. There were hints that this pattern was changing, however, as evinced by such successful albums as Marvin Gaye's *What's Going' On* and Sly and the Family Stone's *There's a Riot Goin' On*. Largely in response to the grandiosity of such pop albums as *Sgt. Pepper's Lonely Hearts Club Band* and the Who's *Tommy*, along with Broadway's embrace of both *Hair* and *Jesus Christ Superstar*, black artists began thinking beyond standard song structure—Isaac Hayes' *Hot Buttered Soul* being the prime example.

Harvard's report also reaffirmed the value of black disc jockeys in crossing songs over from R&B to pop—something Otis Redding had known for years. If a song received enough airplay and popularity on black-oriented radio, its chances of going pop increased accordingly. The pop market welcomed soul, too. The early 1970s ushered in a black pop renaissance on AM radio with confections like Blue Magic's "Sideshow," "Be Thankful for What You've Got" by William De Vaughan, and the Pointer Sisters' "Yes We Can Can." Over the next few years, entire record companies grew up around producers who replaced the organic sounds of real instruments played by human beings with the gadgetry that drove disco.

Although Columbia label executive Clive Davis maintains he never read the Harvard report (and no remedies were publicly attributed to its conclusions), the study forced CBS to revamp its approach to recording and marketing black artists. Within three years,

CBS/Columbia became a major player in the field, with a stable of artists that included Earth, Wind & Fire, the Isley Brothers, and a subsidiary label that defined soul music for the early 1970s—Philadelphia International Records (PIR).

LOVE TRAIN

In hindsight, it's clear that PIR deserves much of the credit or blame for transforming soul from dance-and-romance 1960s music into the fashionable fascism of disco. On their watch, a maelstrom of strings and synthesizers supplanted the happy-go-lucky horn charts, rhythms twitched nervously into the foreground, and the ubiquitous wah-wah pedal created a percussive undertow just short of lethal. The funny thing is, PIR began as life-affirming near-religious music intended to uplift listeners of every creed and color.

The principals behind PIR were a trio of black artist-entrepreneurs—Kenny Gamble, Leon Huff, and Thom Bell, all of whom came of age in Philly and had worked in various combinations previously. Gamble, and Huff in particular, were already proven hitmakers by 1970, having composed "Expressway to Your Heart," a brilliant slice of blue-eyed soul for the (white) Soul Survivors in 1967, as well as the 1968 musical summit meeting "I'm Gonna Make You Love Me" for the Supremes and the Temptations, the Intruders' "Cowboys to Girls" (also from 1968), and "There's Gonna Be a Showdown" for Archie Bell and the Drells in 1969.

In 1971, the Philly reign began with "You Are Everything," a Thom Bell track hand-crafted for the Stylistics. The elements Bell chose to emphasize—a lovesick falsetto married to greeting card sentiment—created a signature sound for the group instantly recognized by anyone who listened to radio. Accordingly, "Betcha By Golly, Wow," "I'm Stone in Love With You," and "Break Up to Make Up" all went Top 10 R&B and pop in the early 1970s, and Bell began to work the same magic with a group of Motown ex-patriates, the Spinners. Through a loose application of the same formula, the Spinners had a similarly amazing run with "I'll Be Around," "Could It Be I'm Falling in Love," and "Then Came You," each a single that landed in the Top 10 or better on both the R&B and pop charts.

At the same time, Gamble and Huff were organizing Philadelphia International, and in 1971, they struck a distribution deal with CBS/Columbia and set up shop recording at Sigma Studios. Within nine months of signing, they sold ten million singles. Billy Paul's "Me and Mrs. Jones" (#1 hit on the R&B and pop charts) led the way in 1972, followed by PIR main attractions the O'Jays and Harold Melvin and the Blue Notes, featuring the suave frontman Teddy Pendergrass on lead vocals. There were even hits for the studio backup singers the Three Degrees ("When Will I See You Again") and the PIR house band (whose tune, "The Sound of Philadelphia," or "T.S.O.P.," was credited to MFSB—Mother/Father/Sister/Brother, and is best remembered as the *Soul Train* theme).

Overnight, everyone who made records wanted them to sound as though they were recorded at Sigma Studios. Elton John wrote "Philadelphia Freedom" in the PIR mold, and later recorded an entire album, *The Bell Sessions* (which featured another Philly homage, "Mama Can't Buy You Love") with producer Thom Bell at the controls. Caught up in the middle of Phillymania was a white session singer with a special affinity for soul: Daryl Hall.

Chart histories now acknowledge Hall and his partner John Oates as the best-selling duo of all time, eclipsing the Everlys and Simon & Garfunkel—a feat Hall credits to

Philly, where he learned how to weld beat to melody. "My influences? That's easy," he says. "Because it was all the Philly scene and Motown. Going back to 1966, my first audiences were all black crowds, and that's what I started with." When psychedelics and long jams replaced soul as the music of American youth, Hall worried that his moment in the sun might never come. "By the '70s," he says, "it was considered cheesy to be singles oriented, because the flavor of the moment was FM radio and tracks that would take up a whole album side."

Hall and Oates were initially signed to Atlantic, but were dropped after a few lushly produced R&B albums. ("Daryl Hall has so much taste," one critic sniped, "that if he'd written *Moby Dick*, he'd have made the whale off-white.") They cranked out occasional hits for Atlantic and RCA during the 1970s—"She's Gone," "Sarah Smile," and "Rich Girl" rank among the best—but the duo caught a major career break when MTV put their videos into heavy rotation in the early 1980s, once again bringing a nonthreatening variant of R&B to mass attention via white artists. "There's always talk about how black and white people influence each other," Hall allows, "but maybe that's why people look to America for inspiration. There's some kind of exchange that goes down between the different groups. That's why places like Philly and New York mean so much to me—people are thrown together, joined socially and musically."

To many minds, Philadelphia was heir to the R&B throne Detroit abdicated when Berry Gordy pulled up stakes for Los Angeles. But there were substantial differences. For one, the Philly Sound was constructed by adults for adults, whereas Gordy regularly clipped his artists' musical wings in order to attract whites and teenagers. In addition, Gamble and Huff followed Gordy's example in public statements that claimed the Philly label was a "family" as well as a business, but PIR's principles were largely set aside as the company lost ground to disco. Gordy was also careful to give his talent top billing, but with the exception of Harold Melvin and the Blue Notes and the O'Jays, many in the PIR fold took a backseat to Gamble and Huff's star billing as producers. The producer-as-artist mentality may have begun with Phil Spector and Brian Wilson, but with disco, producers let it be known that the artists were all but interchangeable.

No one could have foreseen that PIR's production techniques would become a Frankenstein's monster that ultimately turned on its creators. Because the Philly soul scene began in such a rush of optimism, camaraderie, and musical adventure, it didn't matter that the artists weren't particularly distinguishable. The producers were. While Thom Bell's work with the Stylistics ran from ornate to mawkish, Gamble and Huff sandwiched social commentary between pop-friendly melodies and the slickest dance grooves of the day. The first PIR smash, "Me and Mrs. Jones," was uncharacteristically amoral in presenting a cheating husband's weak defense ("we both know that it's wrong, but it's much too strong to let it go now"). More often, the topics dealt in moral imperatives. The O'Jays' "Ship Ahoy" described the Middle Passage of slavery; "For the Love of Money" dealt with greed (at this writing, it serves as theme music for Donald Trump's TV series, *The Apprentice*); and "Wake Up, Everybody" testified that utopian goals could be achieved through communal commitment.

Philadelphia International's parent company CBS also signed Earth, Wind & Fire, another group with compatible views on race pride, although they also dabbled in African folklore and Egyptology. Spiritual proclivities notwithstanding, the band quickly found a multiracial fan base that has continued to grow since the mid-1970s. Led by former session man Maurice White (the drummer on "Rescue Me" by Fontella Bass), EWF spent ten years on the pop and R&B charts without compromising musicality or ideals. What was it that attracted blacks and whites in equal measure? Critics pointed to the extravagant stage shows (some with illusions created by magician Doug Henning) and the danceable melodies that propelled "Shining Star," "That's the Way of the World," "Get Away," "Sing a Song," and "September" into the upper reaches of both the R&B and pop charts throughout the latter part of the decade. It's also worth mentioning that of all the acts to appear in the ill-conceived *Sgt. Pepper* film, only EWF emerged unscathed—turning fiasco to glory with their finger-popping version of "Got to Get You into My Life" in 1978.

"We just did our part, and that was the end of it," says Philip Bailey, who remains EWF's distinctive falsetto virtuoso. "Somehow we didn't catch any flak for it. We were also an all-black band with audiences that were sixty-to-eighty-percent white. Maybe it's because Earth, Wind & Fire has always been a very message-oriented band; it's all about love and higher consciousness, and that translates across all kinds of boundaries."

When black music splintered into warring factions over disco and funk, Earth, Wind & Fire stood its ground well into the 1980s. "There was some disco that was very cleverly put together," Bailey will grant, "but most of it I found very predictable. It seemed like there was a formula for everything." Instead, the band had its own small group of imitators—among them Con Funk Shun (listen to "Ffun") and Jeffrey Osborne's band, LTD ("[Every Time I Turn Around] Back in Love Again"). While Earth, Wind & Fire temporarily succumbed to the times (along with their mostly white counterparts, Tower of Power), by relegating the horn section into a secondary role behind synthesizers, they returned to form in the late 1980s and continue to tour.

Firm grounding in a pop sensibility and Philly-bred vocal styles and arrangements helped create a template for the singers of the 1980s and beyond—approaches that would soon become known as much for showboating as for soul. It's not too far a stretch to hear Luther Vandross and Whitney Houston tackling the PIR songbook, and, in turn, the Boyz II Men, En Vogues, and Backstreet Boys who would follow.

HOUSE OF FUNKENSTEIN

Just as rock reinvented itself through *Sgt. Pepper* and *Tommy*, old notions of what constituted R&B were under review. Soul still referred to the intersection of gospel and R&B, but not all R&B qualified as soul. Motown staff writer George Clinton read the signals long before the label's move to California. Clinton understood that he and his band, the Parliaments (who hit #20 pop and #3 R&B on the charts in 1967 with "[I Wanna] Testify"), would never reach full potential in a world of matching suits and polished dance steps. He disappeared after a contract dispute, only to resurface as the leader of Parliament/Funkadelic, an aggregate of funky freaks whose mission statement spoofed a plaque found in the office of a Nixon appointee: "When you have them by the balls, their hearts and minds will follow." Clinton made it simpler: "Free Your Mind, and Your Ass Will Follow."

Embracing acid rock was the practical choice according to Clinton, since that niche in black music was wide open. "We were coming up on the East Coast," he recalls, "and loved the Temptations, but it was hard getting Motown to notice us. Our all-time favorites were the Pips; nobody could outdo them in terms of class. They were *it*. Once Motown signed them, that meant the whole routine-oriented thing was played out, so all we could do was try a whole new thing. We started looking around, and it seemed that Muddy Waters and the Chicago players could never break through, even though they were basically playing electric blues. Then all of a sudden, there was this new style of blues with Jimi Hendrix. Pop music was becoming psychedelic, and rock 'n' roll was still there, but ultimately, I have to say that if we hadn't seen Hendrix, it might not even have occurred to us. I mean, we liked Ten Years After and a bunch of groups playing in that style, but until we saw Hendrix, it didn't seem there was room for blacks to do it."

In concert and on record, Clinton and Co. whipped up an alternately pointed and incoherent mélange of politics, mythology, rhythm, and screaming guitar. "At Motown, everything was planned," Clinton explains. "But I wanted the musicians in charge, where you trust them to play what they feel. And if they leave, they leave, and when they come back, they're there again. So it's kind of free-form, but it works. Everybody gets together and learns the basic song, and then onstage after that I'm sort of the traffic cop for the personalities."

P-Funk, as they are known to their fans, often shot wide of the mark, but when they boiled a message down to its basics, its effect was undeniable. In fact, not many ransom notes get to the point as well as the chant from *Let's Take It to the Stage*. "SHIT . . . GODDAMN . . . Get off your ass and JAM!" The band actually enjoyed a substantial hit in 1976 with "Tear the Roof Off the Sucker" (best known by its chorus, "We want the funk!"), which went to #15 pop and #5 R&B on the charts, and staged one of the most memorable tours of the decade behind the 1976 album, *Mothership Connection*, which featured a spaceship descending from a gigantic denim cap.

Numerous Clinton-inspired outfits brought his ideas back to Earth by pruning back the guitar solos, setting the songs to more dance-friendly rhythms, and replacing his sci-fi poetics with sexy innuendo. And when the beats and melodies matched up, a band like the Ohio Players could hit the top of both the pop and R&B charts, as they did with "Fire" in 1974 and "Love Rollercoaster" in 1976. Album covers resembled centerfolds, costumes recalled *Battlestar Gallactica*, and basses rumbled deep enough to shake sheetrock from the wall. Case in point: "You Dropped a Bomb on Me," the Gap Band's air raid set to music, sure to tax even the most expensive set of woofers. There was female funk, too—as evinced by the cover of Labelle's *Nightbirds*, the 1975 album sporting their lone pop hit, "Lady Marmalade." The LP cover presents the ladies as extraterrestrial love goddesses in platform shoes and sexy silver "spacesuits." Even the Commodores, well remembered for the treacly ballads "I'm Easy" and "Three Times a Lady," laid down a few slabs of funk, including a synthesizer-clavinet showdown called "Machine Gun," and the titanic "Brick House."

Determined not to be outdone, P-Funk tried zanier shows (where diapers passed for stage apparel) and less structure, as Clinton turned the band into a *Love Boat* for wayward funksters, including James Brown expatriates Maceo Parker and Boosty Collins, as well as the increasingly erratic Sly Stone. Musicians particularly gravitated to the P-Funk sound, and Clinton's idiosyncrasies can be heard down through the years in such rock/funk hybrids as the black Living Colour and the white Red Hot Chili Peppers. "The music is starting to get some respect now," says Clinton, who appeared on the 2004 Grammy Awards alongside Earth, Wind & Fire and Outkast. "In the early days, most people didn't think it was worth anything, and that goes for some of the musicians, too. They just thought they were jamming, and now they sort of stick their chests out because they've been part of something great. Now that the music has some history behind it, people are recognizing that it's cool in the same way as live jazz."

BYE BYE BLACKBIRD

Live or recorded, jazz fell on fewer ears as the 1970s ticked by. The Olympians who showed the world how to swing departed the world stage with an atypically soft tread. When Louis Armstrong died in 1971, he was remembered by Duke Ellington as a man who "was born poor, died rich, and never hurt anyone on the way." The Duke followed suit less than five years later. Armstrong and Ellington, better than anyone before or since, demonstrated how music could reach into once-hardened hearts, expunge bigotry from the deepest nooks and crannies of ignorance, and unite the races in a frenzy of dance floor exhultation.

Armstrong and Ellington lived long enough to see that jazz would outlast them and return to its roots as regional music. No longer the American preoccupation, jazz in the 1970s remained vital in the dizzying maze of New York's loft scene. There musicians were able to take greater control of their careers and book their own shows outside of the club circuit. Jazz also rebounded in the Midwest, where Chicago's Association for the Advancement of Creative Music (AACM) fused avant-garde sounds with the politics of the New Left. The first music to break through the color barrier to mass acceptance was also the first to see segregation vanish from the venues and the bandstand.

Much of the remaining decade was spent responding to or building upon Miles Davis' *Bitches Brew*, with many traditionalists left marginalized by the rising popularity of jazz-rock fusion. Davis himself went AWOL from the stage in 1975, returning six years later to serve notice that jazz was "dead." Boppers, moldy figs, and neoclassicists alike agreed that promising players were being siphoned away by fusion, not because the music had generational relevance, but because it carried the prospect of high-dollar gigs at rock palaces. Jazzbos had no trouble affixing blame to an old scapegoat—the white hacks who first stole the blues, and then the audiences and paychecks that full houses guaranteed.

Defections from within further inflamed the situation. It was easy enough to scorn Chick Corea for going electric when he had no black heritage to protect. Hell, it made sense in a world where white swinger Woody Herman was now covering Steely Dan tunes to turn a buck. No, the barbs that festered deep in the flesh belonged to Miles Davis and his former bandmate Herbie Hancock, who were finding new listeners, encouraging notices from the rock world, and earning enough money to live in style. In 1973, Hancock's *Head Hunters* LP finally trounced *Bitches Brew* to become the best-selling jazz album of the genre. Hancock then hit his adversaries where it hurt most—in the ego— by implying that jazz performers weren't the only ones who could actually play. "Rather than work with jazz musicians who could play funk," he told a reporter blithely, "I worked with funk musicians who could play jazz."

In the absence of mainstream airplay, artists scrambled for a niche or a gimmick. Drummer Billy Cobham and keyboardist George Duke edged closer to the funk of Stevie

Wonder, and Wayne Shorter and Joe Zawinul's group, Weather Report, yielded middling results as a band bent on ensemble improvisation. Eventually the group added the astonishing (and self-destructive) Jaco Pastorius, who did for jazz bass what Larry Graham had done for funk. Pastorius played wildly intricate melodies and cleared a path for the electronic aerialists of fusion who would appear in the 1980s and beyond.

Somewhere out in the margins was Herman "Sonny" Blount, known to the world since the 1950s as Sun Ra, resident alien from the planet Saturn. After beginning his recording career as a hard bopper, Sun Ra set a course for the stars and pioneered the use of synthesizers and multimedia presentations to counter the otherwise staid jazz shows of the period. By rejecting nearly every convention jazz traditionalists held dear, Sun Ra influenced artists ranging from George Clinton to Pink Floyd and Sonic Youth. Almost gleefully subversive, Sun Ra practiced what Duke Ellington recommended so many decades before: find the rules, then break them.

In an essay headlined "Kind of Blue: Jazz Competes with Its Past, Settles for the Hard Sell," Michael Cuscuna tells *Village Voice* writer Richard Woodward that "'when (a new artist like) Joe Lovano puts out a new record, he's not only competing with his contemporaries for sales. He's also up against Gene Amons and Coltrane and every record ever made. The whole history of music is now available on CD, and that's a problem for anyone who hopes to break through."

It's also worth noting that such heritage artists as Bird, Miles, and Coltrane have a higher cool quotient than any of the more recent arrivals. Unlike pop, where a contemporary group like Maroon 5 can become (however temporarily) more hip than the Beatles or Stones, the opposite assumption is often made about jazz artists. Not many trumpet players (or aficionados, for that matter) find Wynton Marsalis as compelling a figure as Armstrong or Miles Davis—an assessment that even Marsalis would find tough to dispute.

Marsalis has himself to blame, because his constant harangues against musical adventurism have left him a dapper mortician presiding over a hall where jazz lies in state. By persecuting those who have sought to enliven jazz by introducing elements of rock, hip-hop, and electronica, Marsalis and his stalwarts have convinced young people that jazz welcomes only those creative thinkers willing to practice tunnel vision and recuse themselves from the influences that swirl around them in today's culture. Just as many of the jazz faithful turned their noses up at bop in the 1940s, Marsalis and his latter-day moldy figs have decreed that if it isn't *their* jazz, it can't be real jazz at all. Jazz, once the most immediate of music forms, has become to most Americans a decrepit wax museum stuffed with the melting figures of Armstrong, Ellington, Basie, Monk, and Gillespie.

The mistake—granting that the pro-Marsalis forces have good intentions—is in thinking that if jazz can't be handed down the way it was, it will fail to thrive or even survive. But this has not proven true of the blues, even though no one came to its rescue in 1964 when the Rolling Stones and Animals radically reimagined it, and certainly not at the end of the decade when wah-wah pedals and power chords took the music in directions that W.C. Handy, Bessie Smith, and Robert Johnson never envisioned.

NO STATIC AT ALL

The roads between rock, soul, and jazz all fed into a roundabout where artists could detour anywhere inspiration led. Steely Dan, for example, began as a straight-ahead rock band. But the group dwindled into a duo after the first few albums once founders Donald Fagen and Walter Becker permitted their early infatuation with blues and jazz to lead from flirtation into heavy petting. At first, says onetime Steely Dan member Michael McDonald, "Walter and Donald dug the Hollies and that Crosby, Stills & Nash sound, so I got the gig because I was recommended and inadvertently because I reminded them of Graham Nash." But Becker and Fagen's quirky material quickly challenged rock players who were used to charging the beat rather than swinging inside it. "You notice they don't hire me now," McDonald laughs. "That was back when I was all they could afford. They really weren't impressed by my playing, although Donald figured he could teach me the parts well enough to make it work."

Steely Dan dared to drape jazz chords over blues structures (in "Chain Lightning"), take soulful laments to the Top 40 ("Rikki, Don't Lose That Number," "Deacon Blues," and "Babylon Sisters"), and occasionally dabble in the kind of pop-jazz fusion that yielded their 1977 masterpiece, *Aja*. Despite the unmistakable scent of jazz wafting from the rock section in record stores across the nation, *Aja* instantly garnered heavy rotation on FM radio, then went Top Five within three weeks of release and was later certified platinum.

Aja posed the age-old riddle in a sleek new package: is the public more fond of black-inflected music when its emissaries are white? "Ah," Fagen says sardonically, "that's been the secret of our success." A moment later, he reconsiders. "Honestly, people love black music, the rhythm and the creativity, but there are a lot of people uncomfortable with their clash with black culture and there's just a general xenophobia. So (our music is) coming from someone who's more familiar to them and they get the same musical thrill from it, so it's just easier to accept. And it's too bad, because a lot of black artists have been exploited, but it's really hard to control. In our case, we don't really play black music, but there are certainly a lot of elements that we do combine—all kinds of things, really, including literature and a lot of European music."

But nonconformist cool—a trait long ascribed to blacks—is a Steely Dan hallmark, seeping up through the lyrics and thrumming deep in the grooves. Chatting with journalist Greg Tate, Living Colour guitarist Vernon Reid says he believes that Becker and Fagen genuflect before the same altar of black hipness that seduced "Mezz" Mezzrow during the swing era. In *Everything But the Burden: What White People Are Taking from Black Culture*, Reid cites the chorus of "Deacon Blues," in which the subject "learned to work the saxophone," but plays just what he feels, and drinks scotch whiskey all night long, only to "die behind the wheel"—a fate befitting the terminally cool. Becker and Fagen have "synthesized a certain idea of the jazz life," Reid says. "They project a certain archetypal and stereotypical idea of the jazz musician's life circa the 1950s, 1940s . . . this whole romanticized life of the music and the notion that the discipline of learning the saxophone will lead to unimagined hedonistic pleasures."

By setting the lyrics of "Deacon Blues" in the first person, Becker and Fagen imply oneness with their protagonist—no longer identified as black, no longer a bedraggled Jim Crow figure, but a struggling musician obviously transformed by talent into a Chandler-esque hero who may yet "die behind the wheel." The song deftly liberates this Jim Crow from associations with anything black—other than jazz—focusing instead on the universal theme of being cast as a pair of brown loafers in a tuxedo world, to paraphrase comedian George Jessel.

Think of "Deacon Blues" as *My Fair Lady* with a racial twist. And just as Steely Dan unhitched their dissipated sax player from the minstrel image of Jim Crow, English glam rocker David Bowie took Zip Coon to the finest tailors in London. Bowie, who had been touring with the latest variant of his Ziggy Stardust persona, fell under the spell of Philly Soul in 1974. He immediately jettisoned all the production elements of his show, including props, dancers, and his costumes, morphing overnight from carrot-haired glam rocker into Thin White Duke to record an R&B album called *Young Americans*. Like Zip Coon, Bowie was a foppish dandy given to outrageousness (wife notwithstanding, he informed the press he was gay) and excess. Bowie's new "plastic soul" image went over so well that he and fellow Brit Elton John rank among the few white performers ever to appear on *Soul Train*—Bowie performing his Philly Soul tribute, "Fame" (#1 on the pop charts in 1975), and John offering up "Bennie and the Jets."

Bowie and Elton John treated soul music as a way station. For Michael McDonald, it was a way of life. Temp work with Steely Dan and Bonnie Raitt led McDonald into his highest profile gig yet—a stint with the Doobie Brothers, another band ready to push the limits of standard rock fare. When Doobies frontman Tom Johnston fell ill on the road, McDonald found himself leading one of America's top rock attractions. The band could have kept him in the background and leaned more on Patrick Simmons, the Doobie who composed "Black Water" and "South City Midnight Lady." Instead, they allowed McDonald to present his own material.

"When I joined the Doobies, I was notorious for leaving tunes unfinished," McDonald attests. "'Takin' It to the Streets' and 'It Keeps You Running' were songs like that. I was always very conscious of drawing from the past; sometimes it was the memory of learning to play something by ear that I'd heard on the radio, usually some R&B or gospel stuff that I'd hear in passing while sitting at the piano at my mother's house." Under pressure, McDonald discovered himself as a composer. "You learn," he says, "that if you put a diminished chord here, it has a moving effect, and I love that kind of unashamed drama. So it kind of became a style for the band, borrowing heavily from gospel."

The Doobie Brothers never renounced their reputation as a biker's band. Instead, they fortified their sound to become the most successful white American soul outfit since the Rascals. Their 1978 album *Minute by Minute* sold in the millions and took McDonald's syncopated soul to the Grammy Awards, where the Doobie Brothers won Record of the Year for "What a Fool Believes." The band split in 1982, only to reunite a few years later with most of its pre-McDonald roster. McDonald, on the other hand, enjoyed a handful of solo hits and a career resurgence in the new millennium with a pair of albums covering Motown classics of yesteryear.

Satiny soul was the order of the day, meaning that the raw sounds of Aretha and James Brown sounded unpolished by comparison. Meanwhile, the young artists who had idolized them were now sprinting into the limelight. A white Scottish group called Average White Band enjoyed worldwide success with "Pick Up the Pieces" and "Cut the Cake" (both Top 10 hits on the American R&B and pop charts), and a rock band named Wild Cherry covered the Commodores' "I Feel Sanctified," then logged one of the most unlikely hits of the decade with "Play That Funky Music (White Boy)."

In 1975, Harry Wayne Casey became the funkiest white boy in the land. The Florida native who raced to the record stores as a kid started his music career as a retailer, then a distributor. That's when he met Rick Finch, with whom he formed a songwriting partnership that soon yielded a hit for George McCrae, "Rock Your Baby" (#1 on both the pop and R&B charts), in 1974. A year later, the Sunshine Band emerged as a nine-piece band fronted by Finch and Casey—now KC—who were the only white members. "I started out in the Church of God," says Casey, "which was basically all white. But people would clap and shout and speak in tongues, and when you sing, you sing from the spirit. It's not something that's taught; it's something that comes from the gut."

With "Get Down Tonight" in 1975, KC and the Sunshine Band embarked on a hit-making spree that landed them six Top Five singles in two years—four of them ending up at #1 on both the pop and R&B charts. "When I wrote those songs, I was thinking commercial, #1. When we started out, the general mood was depressed over Watergate and the gas shortage, things like that. I think we brought some light back into the country. The band had the same effect that the sun has on people, very much high energy and percussive, using lots of brass. We geared all the production to being able to reproduce the record onstage, even down to the ad-libs. The first three minutes and six seconds were exactly what we played in the studio, and then we'd have fun."

But trouble was brewing. "True," he says, "we didn't pay much attention to the music business with our competitors and contemporaries. We were setting the trend."

That trend turned out to be disco.

BOOGIE FEVER

Disco music, with its 120 beat-per-minute pulse, began much as rock 'n' roll—in scattered bits of pop and fashion ephemera that swirled together into a scene and then a phenomenon before collapsing under the weight of its own pretensions. Polka, accordion, and bagpipe music have each had their share of detractors, but only disco provoked enough loathing to require a public execution.

On July 12, 1979, 47,795 attendees gathered at Comisky Park in Chicago for what was billed as a "disco demolition" staged by Steve Dahl of local station WLUP-FM. Dahl actually despised the music so much he quit his job across town at WDAI when management switched to a disco format in 1978. In his new gig, Dahl made a running gag of ripping the needle of his record player across disco tunes, followed by the sound of the record "exploding," and climaxing with Dahl smashing the record over the air.

"The whole 'Disco Sucks' movement was rooted in racism and homophobia," says Nile Rodgers of Chic, "and a lot of music people saw that for what it was, but it didn't matter. Once it set in, people quit taking our calls. In this industry, it's all about the latest trends, and one day we just stopped being cool. We went from having "Le Freak" be the biggest-selling single in the history of Atlantic Records to being a couple of guys who were yesterday's news. That's the reason we disbanded Chic. We weren't a disco group, but we were pigeonholed as that, and that's all that mattered to most of the industry."

The disco movement began in the black and gay nightclubs of New York, where disc jockeys found the longest and most danceable songs possible, then began toying with ways in which to stretch them further or otherwise distinguish them. One enterprising deejay beat-matched Led Zeppelin's "Whole Lotta Love" to the percussion break from Chicago's "I'm a Man" to come up with a way to make both records something that neither was by itself—gay and dance friendly. Early on, the mix included European and African obscurities from artists like Manu Dibango, Osibisa, and Cymande.

"That's when deejays started mixing things in and out and enjoyed playing around with the records," says Harry Wayne Casey, "and that's how they started to become stars themselves. They'd only have two 45s, and they were only two-and-a-half-minutes long apiece, so they'd segue back and forth from one to the other to make them longer." Demand for "extended" versions increased to the point where record companies began issuing elongated mixes for club play, and later for release to the general public. By this time, deejays were counting beats per minute (some labels printed the track's BPM as a courtesy) and segueing seamlessly from one tune to the next—establishing both the hypnotic and monotonous effect of dance club music, which continues uninterrupted to this day.

Disco began as a lark, subsisting on novelties ("Disco Duck") and mildly risqué tunes like "Disco Lady" ("move it in, move it out . . .") or "Do It 'Til You're Satisfied." And the craze might have spun itself out, except for a sitcom actor, a white English trio steeped in R&B, and a script based on a 1976 *New York Magazine* article.

In 1977, John Travolta, the Bee Gees, and *Saturday Night Fever* (based on "Tribal Rites of Saturday Night" by Nik Cohn) broke disco into the mainstream. The resulting album is still the biggest-selling soundtrack of all time, having spent twenty-four weeks at the top of the charts and responsible for four #1 singles for the Bee Gees: "How Deep Is Your Love," "Night Fever," "Stayin' Alive," and "If I Can't Have You" (recorded by Yvonne Elliman).

Bee Gees producer Robert Stigwood—also the man behind the movie version of *Tommy*—may have expected *Saturday Night Fever* to become the 800-pound gorilla of 1970s pop, but no one else did. In fact, the Bee Gees tracks on the album were more or less donated to the film at Stigwood's request. The Bee Gees were more concerned with retaining the new converts they'd recently won with their biggest album in years, the 1975 melding of Gibb brothers harmony to urban R&B called *Main Course*.

In a 1979 *Village Voice* essay called "The Dialectic of Disco," Andrew Kopkind wrote that by the end of the decade, nightclub artists had finally vaulted from dance floor novelty acts to radio favorites, "bringing the music out of the subcultural ghettos into mainstream life. The Bee Gees were crucial to that passage; they made disco safe for white, straight, male, young, and middle-class America. What Elvis Presley did for black rhythm and blues . . . the Brothers Gibb have done for disco."

"But Atlantic Records thought it would totally ruin the Bee Gees," according to Maurice Gibb, "so *Main Course* was first sent to radio on a blank label, with no words on it to give our identity away. When we were doing the album, there were four tracks we did that (Atlantic exec) Ahmet Ertegun wasn't too mad about, because he thought we should be going in another direction. It was Stigwood who kept saying, 'You've gotta keep doing songs like "Fanny, (Be Tender With My Love)."' When 'Nights on Broadway' was brought up, it was Robert who suggested, 'Why don't you put a slow part in the middle?' And we said, well, the song's finished, we'd have to re-record it completely, and he said, 'No, just record it separately, and we'll edit it in.' And that was 'Nights on Broadway,' which was originally 'Lights on Broadway.' Robert thought we should make it seedy."

Sixteen minutes of orgasmic groaning lofted Donna Summer to the top of the charts with "Love to Love You, Baby" in 1975. An unabashed pop singer, Summer was one of the few artists associated with disco to pull free from its commercial death spiral at the end of the decade. (Frank Driggs Collection)

Gibb insisted the brothers always preferred sensuality to dance rhythms, and never aspired to become the standard-bearers of disco. "To us, disco meant 'party,'" he said, "people singing along and dancing in the clubs to things like KC and the Village People, and we never set out to make those kinds of records. The only song we had at the time that was even close was 'You Should Be Dancing,' which we only considered as a dance song, not as something disco—and we did that two years before *Fever*, so we really weren't even thinking along those lines at the time. We never went out to the clubs and we didn't really try to fit into the culture, because when we wrote those songs, disco really wasn't that big. It became disco after the film. If it hadn't been for that, I don't know what the album would have been called. To us, 'Stayin' Alive' and 'Night Fever' were more about the underground nightclub scene at the time in New York, very black and very R&B; it was sensuality with an edge to it."

There didn't seem to be a downside. For the first time since the swing era, black America's music was the music of all America. Disco empress Donna Summer recalls wondering if disco foretold a cultural renaissance in which white acts could incorporate black influences and vice-versa. "For a time, crossover in the '70s really worked in the opposite direction," she says. "I think things eased up, with black stations playing the Bee Gees and KC, and that started to open doors in other areas. I know I was fortunate. You know, I'm not a rhythm and blues singer like Aretha Franklin. I have a straighter voice. But just because I don't sing like her or Chaka Khan doesn't mean I'm not soulful. I could shuck and jive with the best of them, but that's not my life. I'm more of a pop singer, like Diana Ross. She doesn't sing all over the place, either. She sticks with the melody, and that leads me to believe that there are as many kinds of soul as there are colors in the rainbow."

SATURDAY NIGHT MASSACRE

Soon there were disco versions of movie themes and TV shows (*Star Wars*, *Close Encounters of the Third Kind*, and *I Love Lucy* all got the treatment), Ethel Merman released a disco album, Percy Faith discofied "Hava Nagila," and Sly Stone reconfigured his hits to a drum machine in hopes of a comeback. Most rock artists shunned disco, although there were a few one-night stands, including "Da Ya Think I'm Sexy?" (Rod Stewart), "Miss You" (the Rolling Stones), and "Goodnight Tonight" (Paul McCartney & Wings).

Very quickly, though, the music and the scene diverged. Isolated songs from the era stand up as well as any pop music—KC's uptempo romps, Donna Summer's erotic thrillers (including the techno masterpiece "I Feel Love"), Amii Stewart's sizzling remake of "Knock on Wood," and Chic's dance floor throwdowns "Dance, Dance, Dance (Yowsah, Yowsah, Yowsah)," "I Want Your Love," and their monstrous #1 R&B and pop smash, "Le Freak."

The lifestyle, on the other hand, sucked participants into a vortex of decadence marked by endless parties that everyone absolutely had to attend—not to enjoy, but to be seen. Less than a year elapsed from the genre's peak with the Christmas 1977 launch of *Saturday Night Fever* and the Internal Revenue Service raid on New York's notorious Studio 54 nightclub that proved emblematic of the movement as a whole. Worse, radio programmers and rock audiences alike agreed that the music was not just juvenile (like 1960s bubblegum), but that it represented a malignance that warranted intervention.

"You could sense a backlash coming," Casey remembers. "Pop stations didn't want me and neither did soul stations, because I'm white. We'd play someplace where we'd have more people than had ever showed up there before, then the critics would tear us down. I finally had to stop reading the reviews because the writers would all be into Led Zeppelin or something like that and couldn't relate to us at all."

After the Comisky Park debacle, Bee Gees records had less value than a drawer full of used mood rings. "I remember hearing about radio stations having Bee Gees–free weekends," Maurice Gibb sighs, "and I suppose that anything as successful as we were during that period reaches a saturation level. Blowing up disco records was a bit ridiculous, but that's America for you. Everything is over the top and done in a big way. In England and in Europe, they didn't burn disco records; they just stopped buying them and they just decided to go somewhere else—and fortunately, our fans didn't."

It's unfortunate that the forces united against disco didn't liberate club dancers from their 120 BPM trance. They didn't stem the flow of banal Top 40 disco with artists making more adventurous dance music, or even help self-important record producers rethink the rut they'd gotten themselves into. No, the death-to-disco movement did to black music what Watergate did to the GOP. Every black artist stood accused of the crime of disco, and when the music was banished from the airwaves in the early 1980s, scores of black performers were swept away with it—whether they were doing disco, funk, or R&B. The lone exception: reggae and its acknowledged figurehead, Robert Nesta Marley.

Reggae, and Bob Marley in particular, symbolized the kind of black music that rockers could get behind. Never mind that the rhythms had no more variety than most disco. On the surface, reggae's Rasta artists closely mirrored white American youth culture in their denim clothes and penchant for stirring up trouble with songs about brotherly love (strictly the platonic variety). There were no intricate disco dance moves to master, no doormen to bribe, and no worries about dressing to fit in alongside Warhol, Liza, or Bianca.

Marley and reggae did benefit from the shared antipathy for disco, although it was never by design. In fact, Marley was everything an American rock fan looked for—a pot-smoking pacifist who sought to unite the world under a banner of groove and ganja. "One love, one heart," he liked to sing, "let's get together, and feel all right." With a career that began in Jamaica with the 1963 single "Judge Not," Marley built a fan base through domestic shows that led to international exposure. By the early 1970s, his foothold in America solidified after two of his songs, "Stir It Up" and "I Shot the Sheriff," became hits for Johnny Nash and Eric Clapton. Under his own name, Marley scored only twice on the U.S. singles chart, first with "Roots, Rock, Reggae" (which peaked at #51 in 1976), and again with "Could You Be Loved," which landed at #56 on the R&B charts in 1980. But his impact continues to resound across all boundaries of color and nationality, largely due to his egalitarian politics and the anthems that won over audiences that nearly doubled in size with each successive tour. For many, he was the promise of Bob Dylan made manifest in black form—a poet laureate who actually rocked

In his homeland, however, Marley was a lightning rod, and in 1976 he survived an assassination attempt after trying to broker a deal between warring political factions. Instead he succumbed to cancer in 1981, mere months after the murder of John Lennon, and like the ex-Beatle quickly ascended to near-diety status. A quarter-century after his

With disco ruling the AM charts, reggae and English punk began to infiltrate the FM airwaves during the latter 1970s. Audiences who grew up on the Beatles and Rolling Stones had an easier time identifying with the proletarian, peace-loving, ganja-smoking Bob Marley than the glitterati who danced the night away at the discos of Manhattan. (Bob Gruen/Star File)

passing, Marley's son Ziggy still works to keep an identity separate from his father, despite a handful of hits on his own. "Still, being a child of Bob Marley is a blessing," he says. "It's not a burden. Some people find it hard to open up enough to accept the things I do because of their expectations about me. Because of my heritage, we tried to fit (the Marley legacy) into Ziggy Marley and the Melody Makers, but now I'm just trying to let the music come out naturally and be what it is. But in terms of a burden, for me it's not."

Reggae made a comfortable fit for rock audiences. Surely this had something to do with the Rastafarian social agenda of unity and brotherhood, but it also referenced a culture as far removed from most Americans as the scenery of television's *Fantasy Island.* Jamaican rockers were exotic, rustic, and peace loving—not down the street and threatening. Furthermore, reggae was also heartfelt proletariat music, unlike disco's shallow soundtrack for social climbing. Throughout the decade, Jamaican artists Jimmy Cliff ("Wonderful World, Beautiful People" and "The Harder They Come"), Toots and the Maytalls ("Pressure Drop"), and Bob Marley sidemen Peter Tosh and Bunny Wailer made steady inroads with American audiences, but, for the most part, their influence echoed in the music they inspired rather than the records they released. A few stateside acts toyed with reggae, most notably Paul Simon—whose 1972 single, "Mother and Child Reunion," prefigured a world music sojourn that culminated in 1985 with *Graceland*—and the new wave band Blondie, who took "The Tide Is High" to the top of the charts in 1980.

AM I BLUE?

In 1980, just as President Jimmy Carter was slipping in the polls to Ronald Reagan, rock—a music based on commingled African American styles—attempted to purge itself of black influences. Armed with three screaming chords and an urgent rhythmic simplicity, punks revolted against the banality of corporate rock and disco's zombielike monotony, all the while treating the blues as if it were some ugly family secret. At the same time, radio teetered between the manicured sounds of Boston and Billy Joel and new wave novelties like the Knack ("My Sharona") and the Vapors ("Turning Japanese"). The titans of soul were relegated to nightclub dates, and the only ones who seemed to notice were a pair of comedians from the Midwest.

"Talk to Aretha Franklin or James Brown," says film director John Landis. "Ask them and they'll tell you—they weren't working. When we started putting together *The Blues Brothers*, everywhere you turned it was all about the Bee Gees and ABBA. Dan Aykroyd and John Belushi were instrumental in turning that around, and it was because they had a reverence and a passion for the blues, and a real love for the artists who were going unnoticed at the time."

Belushi and Aykroyd had been friends years before they became part of the Not Ready for Prime Time Players on NBC's *Saturday Night Live* (also the title of a short-lived Howard Cosell TV series). Both were core members of the Second City comedy troupes, Belushi in Chicago and Aykroyd in Toronto, where Danny also spent time running a blues spot called the 505 Club. According to those present, the pair bonded as much through music as through comedy, and Aykroyd had no trouble leading Belushi from the headbanging sounds of Grand Funk and Led Zeppelin into the more subtle pleasures of Floyd Dixon, the Chips, and the Stax/Volt stable of stars.

On the set of *The Blues Brothers* in 1980, Aretha Franklin posed with the film's stars, John Belushi and Dan Aykroyd. Critics called them a modern-day minstrel act, but the pair helped to refocus attention on such R&B veterans as James Brown, Ray Charles, and Franklin. (Courtesy John Landis © Universal Pictures)

According to Landis, Ackroyd and Belushi began piecing together the Blues Brothers mythology in Toronto. "At first, they just wore the dark glasses and had porkpie hats because they wanted to look like John Lee Hooker," he laughs. "It was interesting, because they performed with Delbert McClinton's band and all kinds of people in New York for fun. Basically, Danny turned John onto rhythm and blues while we were shooting *Animal House* in Eugene, Oregon, and John really got into it, like a born-again convert."

Landis was something of an R&B aficionado as well. The *Animal House* soundtrack is sprinkled with tracks from Sam Cooke and a band called Otis Day and the Knights, whose cover of the Isley Brothers' "Shout!" became one of the few R&B tunes that white rock clubs would play. "Otis Day and the Knights was based on two real groups who used to tour frat houses all throughout the Northwest," says Landis, "the Hot Nuts and a group called Five Screaming Niggers. So Otis Day was our version of them, and he was played by Duane Jesse—a very fine actor. A guy named Mark Davis recorded the stuff in L.A. and then we had to hire local guys in Eugene to be the Knights. So we got African American students to play the band, and we had to process their hair and all of that. One of those guys, the bass player if you look closely, is Robert Cray."

By 1977, Chevy Chase had left *SNL*, leaving Aykroyd and Belushi as the cast's main attractions. Separately, they had distinctive enough identities—Belushi had a collection of blustery ethnic characters (the Samurai and the Cheeseburger Chef to name but two), while Aykroyd's strengths lay more in sardonic impressions of President Jimmy Carter and Tom Snyder, the host of NBC's late-night show, *Tomorrow*. While series producer Lorne Michaels had endorsed the pair performing Slim Harpo's "I'm a King Bee" dressed in bee suits, the Blues Brothers routine was entirely musical and required no input from any of the other cast members.

Not seeing how it could cause any harm, Michaels agreed to have the Blues Brothers—shades, suits, and hats included—warm up the audience before the series tapings began. Audiences swallowed it whole. Michaels promptly put them in front of the cameras in April of 1978, where, in Paul Shaffer's introduction, the Blues Brothers were introduced as "no longer an authentic blues act, but . . . a viable commercial product." By the time *Animal House* hit at the box office, Belushi and Aykroyd had turned Jake and Elwood Blues into recurring TV characters. Comedian Steve Martin was so impressed he asked them to open the show during his September residence at the Universal Amphitheatre. Those shows yielded a record, Landis recalls, "and *Briefcase Full of Blues* became the best-selling blues album of all time. It did a huge amount to call attention to this kind of music." (Eventually that title would go to bluesman Eric Clapton, whose 1994 album, *From the Cradle*, went double-platinum.)

Not everyone was pleased. Rock critic Dave Marsh writes in his book, *Fortunate Son*, that "as soul music in its classic form began to be swept aside by newer styles, it was picked up by exploitationists, the contemporary equivalents of blackface minstrels. The difference between John Belushi yowling 'Soul Man' as a patronizing parody of Sam and Dave, and Al Jolson yowling 'Mammy,' as a patronizing parody of some ex-slave whose name we don't know isn't wide enough to spit through."[1]

Cruel perhaps, but Marsh makes a valid point—several, in fact. If donning the clothes, mimicking the movements, and approximating the vocal and instrumental styles of black artists is minstrelsy, then the Blues Brothers stand rightly indicted. Cork excepted, the

Blues Brothers act embodies every element associated with blackface. It's clear from watching this comic duo that they're genuinely transported in the moment, but so were the mayors and city councilmen who blacked up and strummed their banjos a century before. It's impossible to watch Belushi and Aykroyd in character without seeing them slough off their Midwest whiteness to bask for just a moment in the possibility of Black Cool. If it's a tribute, then the same can be said of *Amos 'n' Andy*.

Marsh next tries to cushion the blow, but adds insult to injury when he writes that the difference between Jolson and Belushi lies in the fact that Jolson was "sentimental and old fashioned, while Belushi was hip and up-to-date. Neither man meant to be racist, I'm sure. Both men were." His 1979 piece concludes by observing that the comics managed to enroll both Steve Cropper and Donald "Duck" Dunn of Booker T. and the MGs to record the Blues Brothers' cover of Sam and Dave's "Soul Man" (Cropper and Dunn played on the original) and perform on show dates in what constituted a tacit endorsement of the act. Meanwhile, the real Sam Moore and Dave Prater were appearing in relative obscurity on a Sunday night in New York before a small crowd backed by a shabby band that understood nothing of their magnitude.

The Blues Brothers belong somewhere in a continuum that begins with shameless opportunists (Thomas Rice, the original Jim Crow? Al Jolson? Pat Boone? Michael Bolton? Marky Mark?) and ends with the most respected acolytes, including Elvis, Van Morrison, Janis Joplin, and Bonnie Raitt.

Where the Blues Brothers fall in that continuum is unclear. Few would call Dan Aykroyd's love for the music into question. He's the best-known face behind the House of Blues bar and restaurant chain, which continues to book blues and R&B artists into House of Blues venues across the country. In a very practical way, Aykroyd ensures that blues performers have a decent place to be seen and heard, and that they're well compensated for their efforts. And if that wasn't contrition enough, he also hosts a weekly syndicated radio program dedicated to keeping the past, present, and future of the blues alive and vital on the airwaves. Had he been born a rich unknown and squandered his inheritance on blues promotion in the face of disco, the House of Blues might be bankrupt and Aykroyd penniless today. But because Belushi and Aykroyd donned those costumes, the blues received a much-needed reintroduction to popular culture. So does the preservation of a black art form justify an act some consider racist?

Motive has to be taken into account, Bonnie Raitt insists. "At every turn," she says, "I believe that white mainstream musicians' embracing of black musical forms and then making them more commercial wasn't really a question of unethical practices as much as it was just popular at the time. A flawed system doesn't necessarily indict the participants. And I don't believe the intent was to rip off the originators. Over and over, whether it's Pat Boone and Little Richard or Eric Clapton and myself covering R&B hits, the (black) originators never make the money that the (white) people covering it later do."

The final twist is that no two people agree on what makes an artist legitimate in incorporating black influences. Clapton and Raitt make the cut; Al Jolson and Marky Mark do not. In between, there's a sea of gray. One of the great melodists of the era was asked to describe the nature of soul and what separates a Van Morrison from a Michael Bolton. "Well, for one thing, Michael Bolton can sing," he said dryly. "Don't say it came from me, but I've never been able to stand Van Morrison's voice. Whatever else you say about Bolton, at least you can find the tune in there somewhere."

NIGHT OF DELIGHT

One night in 1979, Nile Rodgers dropped into one of his favorite dance spots in New York, a bar called Leviticus. "I loved going there," he recalls, "because the deejays there were really great. They used to rap over what we would call 'breakbeats.' All of the cool bands would have great breakbeats that just went on and on, and the deejays would get up and start dropping their rhymes over the beats. So this one night, I heard the best rapper dropping rhymes over beats that felt like ours. And I thought, 'Man, this is crazy,' because that's what Bernard and I used to do to make extra money."

Flashback to five years earlier—before "Le Freak" and "We Are Family" made Nile Rodgers and Bernard Edwards the hottest producers in the industry. For spending money, they'd huddle up in a studio, figure out the patterns and instruments on a tune like MFSB's "Love Is the Message" or "Get Away," by Earth, Wind & Fire, and then copy and record the instrumental vamp, turning a four-minute single into an extended mix that could run on as long as a deejay might want. They'd press a small number on blank labels and sell them to nightclubs on a small scale. Nobody got hurt, much.

Rodgers strolled though the bar, liking what he heard. "I thought another band had taken 'Good Times' and done what we used to do," he says. "Then I looked up and I could see the deejay wasn't rapping it, he was *playing* it. I asked the bartender, who told me the deejay bought the record a couple of days ago up in Harlem. I said, 'Wait a minute, now. We'd sell our records, but never in a record store. I went up to the booth, and I couldn't believe it. Our song, with another label that says 'Sugarhill Records.' Here I strive all my life to be original, and somebody's gonna take my stuff? Of course we sued, and they settled out of court. But that was the first time I heard 'Rapper's Delight.'"

Melody had been losing ground to rhythm ever since the first Africans arrived in the Americas and began playing music alongside white Europeans. Now for the first time, melody was being shunted aside entirely to make room for a new sound from the street. Rap was angry, urban, insistent, and, most frightening of all, unrepentantly, unapologetically, unmistakably black. But with none of the performers singing or playing, and backing tracks ripped from preexisting records, how could it even call itself music? Rap was perceived as a menace from the instant it drifted out over the din of city traffic. It threatened not only the family values so cherished by the religious right, but rock 'n' rollers, a record industry wounded in the collapse of disco, and the plan for a cable channel to establish a lasting union between rock and television. "I Want My MTV" ushered in the 1980s mania for music on video. But by the end of the decade, the network was headed in another direction entirely. "Yo," their hit series declared. "MTV Raps!"

NOTE

1 Marsh, Dave. *Fortunate Son: The Best of Dave Marsh; Criticism and Journalism by America's Best-Known Rock Writer.* New York: Random House, 1985, p. 275.

CHAPTER EIGHT

Controversy

A merica nursed its disco-induced hangover in the lingering months separating Jimmy Carter from Ronald Reagan, and in the interim the cash cow of American pop music gave but grudgingly. After reaping unprecedented profits through most of the 1970s with revenues doubling in just five years, the record industry suffered its first recession in more than a quarter century. The numbers said it all: between 1978 and 1979, revenues slid eleven percent, tumbling from $4.1 billion to $3.7 billion. Some seven hundred jobs were lost in the waning months of 1979, and downsizing continued through much of the 1980s. CBS alone cut seven thousand jobs in the years from 1980 through 1986.

Billboard talent editor Paul Grein says the industry had one collective scapegoat for their misfortune. "The more specific reason for the slump in crossover," he explained, "was that disco had such a negative association for white people that any kind of black music would remind people of the dreaded disco phenomenon. That's the reason a lot of people blamed the record slump on disco itself."

Conversely, music critic Ed Ward saw the downturn as a microcosm of a larger economic process at work. "It's something you see in American business in general," he said in 1985. "When expansion stops happening at a rate that seems to indicate growth, people start to scream. They call it a slump or a depression, which is not really true. There was a lot of dead wood in the industry, and people suddenly saw their jobs being threatened. They expected to sell millions and millions every time out of the box."

Panic set in. During the 1970s, it had been simple enough to gauge public interest because given previous buying trends, what music buyers really wanted was more: more tuneful pop from relative newcomers Boston and Billy Joel, and more classics on demand from the titans of the 1960s—Bob Dylan, Diana Ross, Barbra Streisand, and Jefferson (Airplane) Starship. They wanted more roots rock from Bruce Springsteen, Linda Ronstadt, and The Eagles, and more quirky new wave music from the likes of The Cars, Blondie, Elvis Costello, and Devo. And, of course, the public wanted more and more and more disco . . . until suddenly, they didn't.

While big band swing took nearly half a decade to disappear from the airwaves, disco vanished like a gaudy new superstore caught in a flash fire. In the first half of 1979, almost half the pop records tracked by *Billboard* registered on the R&B charts, too. But six months into 1980, that number had fallen to twenty-one percent, and by the winter of 1982, the trend bottomed out at seventeen percent black, urban, or R&B in origin. In October of 1982, just as Michael Jackson's *Thriller* was shipping to stores, not a single black artist was represented among *Billboard*'s Top 20 singles or albums.

It seemed no one wanted to remember anything about the decade just ended: not the leisure suits or the smiley faces; not *Roots* or school busing; and neither urban decay nor the victory of the Viet Cong. In the aftermath of disco, the humiliation of the Iranian hostage crisis, and the emergence of a strange new disease communicated by sex, Americans joined together in penitence and a shared longing for someone who could tell them how everything would be all right and that society as a whole could ease back into an imagined past of moral certitude.

Ronald Reagan agreed to do that, and more. As the GOP's 1980 candidate for president, he told supporters that the country's problems stemmed not from too little compassion, but from too much money wasted being compassionate. According to the Reagan scenario, "trickle-down economics" guaranteed eventual prosperity for all, if only his plan could be given time to work. As Nelson George writes in *The Death of Rhythm and Blues*, "Reagannomics—more guns, less butter, and the failure to enforce civil rights legislation—just stone cold stopped black progress in this country. For the first time since the New Deal, the government, including Congress and the Supreme Court, didn't support the civil rights agenda, and, in fact, did much to dismantle the laws on the books and encourage a resurgence of racism."[1]

Urban blue-collar workers found themselves competing in a shrinking market as local businesses yielded to national companies and those companies mushroomed into international corporations that outsourced jobs to the lowest bidder. The proliferation of crack and angel dust were decimating the inner cities, leaving many families short not only a principal wage earner, but also an indispensable role model.

"Hard times for healing," Craig Werner echoed in *A Change Is Gonna Come: Music, Race & the Soul of America*, "the worst period in race relations since the 1890s." Werner cites the murder of Yusef Hawkins in Bensonhurst—killed for walking with a white woman—and the Ku Klux Klan murders of five participants in a North Carolina anti-Klan rally in 1979. Incredibly, candidate Reagan began his presidential quest in the same Mississippi county where civil rights workers Michael Schwerner, Andrew Goodman, and James Chaney were murdered in 1964. With contenders seeking the nation's highest office either unconscionably callous or shockingly oblivious, how could anyone even think that singing and dancing together might bridge the racial divide?

So many changes, observed semiretired songwriter Bill Withers; yet so little change. "Those are things that really make people stop and think," he intones. "A lot of people have never seen that real hate. I've *seen* it. It was all over me, Jack. When you're in Mississippi, man, and you see that kind of hate. I remember seeing that, and looking at that, and seeing those faces, and thinking, *Man*. That hate look. They ain't even listening to no music you made. How in the hell you gonna change their minds with music?"

The unblinking eye of cable TV put the country on 24-hour alert with calamities instantly available via satellite hookups from CNN. And the news never failed to disappoint. By the end of summer in 1981, audiences had witnessed attempts to fell a Pope and a president, as well as the killings of John Lennon and Egyptian peace advocate Anwar Sadat. Network television programmers conversely set about reinforcing middle class mythology through *The Cosby Show* and *Family Ties*.

What did any of that have to do with life in what Hollywood now calls "the flyover states"—that vast expanse of America between the high-rises of Manhattan and Los Angeles? Not much, concluded the kids growing up in New York area ghettos at the turn of the decade. Just as punk and new wave provided respite from the ear candy of REO Speedwagon, Styx, and Supertramp, black youth from the boroughs devised an alternative to the trashy flash of disco. Out of the detritus of crack dens, hock shops, and rehab centers, hip-hop culture was born, bringing with it a graffiti style known for its color and braggadocio called "tagging," the whirligig athleticism of breakdancing, and rap. Once again, black Americans were taking twenty-five cents and making it look like a dollar.

THE BREAKS

When a power blackout plunged New York City into darkness in 1977, hundreds of area businesses were sacked by the same regulars who had shopped there for years. After nearly a decade of neglect and middle-class flight, residents of the South Bronx accepted that their home had become emblematic of every failure and vice attributed to city life. They even had a nickname for it: "Vietnam." Moralists ready to pass judgment on the failings of modern society could always point to New York in general—the city President Ford refused to bail out with federal assistance in the mid-1970s—and the South Bronx in particular, as the nadir of civilization. But deep in the heart of the ghetto, something was rising up through the grates that eluded statisticians, doomsayers, and Hollywood's myth machine.

In the 1981 film *Fort Apache, the Bronx*, filmmakers somehow managed to wade hip deep through the community's lawlessness and devastation without stumbling over the creative impulses of the youth culture taking root there. The hip-hop renaissance coalesced in relative obscurity even as decay enveloped the scene's pioneers. As early as 1973, youngsters interested in urban art began to gravitate toward the Youth Organization at Adlai Stevenson High School. Under the supervision of Afrika Bambaataa, an ex-gang leader familiar with the teachings of Malcolm X, these kids and their associates—mostly black, Puerto Rican, and Jamaican—began to explore new ways to express themselves. Some chose creative application of magic markers and spray paint, others drifted behind the turntables to spin records, while the most daring grabbed a microphone to lead the revelers in chants. The playlists at these gatherings typically depended on funk staples from James Brown, Wilson Pickett, and Rick James, but were recombined with samples cannibalized from anywhere, often lifting a riff or vocal hook from the hits of yesteryear. Frequent targets included bands which first appealed almost exclusively to white youth: Grand Funk, the Monkees, Chicago, and Led Zeppelin.

These were unconventional choices perhaps, but they paled by comparison to the liberties deejays took with the mechanics of record playing. Where disco mixmasters sought to segue seamlessly from one vinyl source into the next, hip-hop deejays grew fixated on "the break," that optimal moment containing a track's percussion breakdown, guitar solo, or horn fanfare. With two turntables and twin copies of the same track, "spinners" (as they became known) could sustain their breaks indefinitely. Rhythmic accents were added by rapidly tugging the vinyl back and forth beneath the stylus—all while the song continued to play over the speakers. "Scratching," they called it. In disrespecting the record and the turntables (neither was made to weather such abuse), deejays not only found a new way to present music, they discovered an uncharted universe of sound locked within. This "break-beat" music quickly attracted adventurous dancers who dubbed themselves b-boys and b-girls, who responded by inventing an entirely new dance lexicon. They developed the rudiments of breakdance, which eventually included popping and locking (moves in which various body parts appear to "lock" into position before "popping" out again).

Nothing like it had been seen or heard before. Still, breakdancers had to depend on music provided by the deejays, and in turn the deejays received second billing to the records they played. But when various "MCs" (from "emcee") began taking turns at the microphone either to exhort the dancers or to demonstrate their own rhyming skills, the result was an immediate and visceral connection to the audience. And, whether they knew it or not, these MCs were revisiting practices that predated slavery.

As far back as the 1600s, explorer Richard Jobson logs journal entries that describe the griots as a roving assortment of West African troubadours renowned for their storytelling skill. Rap has early American roots, too. In the 19th century, the practice of "patting juba" (or the hambone) was often accompanied by a vocalist who would repeat an existing rhyme or invent verses on the spot. Antecedents of rap are strewn about black culture, in fact, from the hepcat jive of Cab Calloway and Shirley Ellis' word-warping novelty, "The Name Game," to the social commentaries of performance artist Gil Scott-Heron.

But rap's most obvious precursor is the venerated black tradition called "playing the dozens," an informal competition where players inflate their own assets while denigrating those of an opponent. Whites have engaged in similar games for years. Consider the "tall tales" of America's frontier days, including Davy Crockett's boast that he could swallow a black man whole—if he was buttered and had his ears pinned back. Antecedents are strewn throughout the blues ("I'm a back door man," Willie Dixon told the world. "The men don't know . . . but the little girls understand."), and then white rock 'n' roll arrived, and with it came Elvis Presley's warning, "I'm evil, so don't you mess around with me." Of course, no one played the dozens like Muhammad Ali, the boxing legend whose grandstanding raised trash talk to a sport all its own. (Before his upcoming 1974 bout with George Foreman, Ali told reporters he'd "float like a butterfly, sting like a bee, his hands can't hit what his eyes can't see. Now you see me, now you don't. George thinks he will, but I know he won't.") Even 1970s folkie James Taylor dabbled in the dozens, jokingly referring to himself in "Steamroller" as "a napalm bomb, stone guaranteed to blow your mind."

Like rap, hip-hop culture also claims international origins. When the Jamaican government refused to air politically charged reggae on its stations in the early 1970s, fans of the music took to the streets with sound systems assembled on flatbed trucks. Inevitably, crowds would gather around for a spontaneous party, where "dub" versions (in which songs are tweaked to elongate and enhance their rhythmic qualities, while other melodic elements weave in and out of the mix) of current favorites would leave plenty of room for MCs to engage in oral cutting contests, typically for bragging rights, and sometimes for prizes or cash. Because these battles (known by the locals as "toasting") escalated back and forth to the triumph of a winner, dual turntables and records were used to draw out the drama. And, as immigrants made their way into the United States, many of their techniques survived largely intact. Several of hip-hop's original deejays hailed from Jamaica, including Grandmaster Flash (whose given name was Joseph Saddler) and DJ Kool Herc (born Clive Campbell), who arrived in the Bronx from the Jamaican capital of Kingston at the age of twelve.

In October 1979, rap first demonstrated commercial potential when the Sugarhill Gang's "Rapper's Delight," a disco/rap hybrid with no political axe to grind, began shipping 75,000 copies a day. Eventually, it slipped into the Top 40 pop charts and sold two million copies. Major record labels still feeling the sting of disco's spectacular flameout took notice, but no action. Meanwhile, as rap gathered momentum in Harlem and then moved into Manhattan's downtown scene through the Danceteria, Peppermint Lounge, Ritz, and Roxy nightclubs, MCs began to diversify in topics and style. Just as rock 'n' roll marked a departure from the swing and crooner eras that went before, rap now drew a line between the music of baby boomers and generations X and Y. Everything about rap—its sound, its dances, its politics, its fashion—telegraphed one overarching message: *This Is Not Your Parents' Music.*

Everything about hip-hop sprang from the street. Pop, rock, and the burgeoning heavy metal scene belonged to big business; it had become the stuff of arena shows for the fans and life behind limo glass for its stars. Punk had more attitude, but less music. Rhythm and blues was tainted by association with disco, and besides, the idea that there "Ain't No Stoppin' Us Now" or that we'd board a "Love Train" seemed absurdly naïve for inner city adolescents growing up in the Reagan Age.

Todd Boyd's 2003 book, *H.N.I.C.: The Death of Civil Rights and the Reign of Hip Hop* opens with a preface attributed to "The Notorious D.O.C." (H.N.I.C., by the way, refers to "Head Niggas in Charge.") "Hip-hop has rejected and now replaced the pious, sanctimonious nature of civil rights as the defining moment of blackness. In turn, it offers new ways of seeing and understanding what it means to be black at this pivotal time in history."[2]

By the time Grandmaster Flash and the Furious Five issued a manifesto of their own called "The Message" in 1982, it was also clear that this music had unique identifiers setting it apart from disco and that hip-hop wasn't going to be some momentary diversion on the way to something else. Where "Rapper's Delight" really was a novelty record—albeit a key one for introducing hip-hop into the mainstream—"The Message" was seeded with the same dread and menace that would eventually typify the most confrontational rap music. Rapper Melle Mel's assortment of urban terrorscapes run the gamut, from repossessed cars and bill collectors who "scare my wife when I'm not home" to people pissing on the stairs and baseball bat–wielding junkies crouched in the alleys nearby. To it all, he adds his own chilling admonitions, "It's like a jungle sometimes, it makes me wonder how I keep from going under." Just as Stevie Wonder's "Living for the City" showed the bigotry directed at America's working poor, "The Message" visits the same territory and concludes with a staged police–artist altercation reminiscent of Wonder's classic.

With conditions substantially worse and a hip-hop generation coiled to strike back, Mel says he's reached the point of no return. "Don't push me," he warns, "'cause I'm close to the edge."

Harsh as it may seem, rap's rejection of the civil rights mentality was essential to the creation of a new identity for the young and disaffected. They knew better than anyone how the brilliant sunshine of Dr. King's vision refused to penetrate the places they slept, played, and went to school.

British musicians embraced their dissident expressions long before hip-hop earned notice stateside, and, just as predictably, they helped America get comfortable with its own music. By 1981, the Police had already scored several Top 40 hits with their Jamaican-tinged pop (the group's album *Regatta de Blanc* translates to "White Reggae") and England's ska-influenced agitprop band the Clash had Grandmaster Flash and the Furious Five open for them the same year, when they appeared at a New York city club called Bond's. Unfortunately, the crowd still held the opinion that if it wasn't rock, it wasn't right. Long before the end of their set, Flash and crew fled the stage under a hail of plastic cups.

CROSSING OVER

Black rockers received even less respect than black rappers. In the 1970s, it had become commonplace for white rock artists to appropriate elements of the black burden (witness John Lennon's "Woman Is the Nigger of the World," Lou Reed's "I Wanna Be Black" or his drag queen opus, "Walk on the Wild Side," and Patti Smith's "Rock 'n' Roll Nigger"), so long as the lyrics implied solidarity. Mick Jagger made himself an exception when he groused on "Some Girls" in 1978 that black girls "only want to get fucked all night," adding sourly, "I don't have that much jam." Even though his jibe was equal parts satire and satyr, the comment kindled a firestorm in the media. For months Jesse Jackson publicly lobbied Atlantic, the band's parent label, to have the song banned and the Stones sanctioned. True to their image as jet-set reprobates, the Stones refused to capitulate to either Jackson or Atlantic. "I've always been opposed to censorship of any kind," Jagger demurred, "especially from conglomerates. I've always said, 'If you can't take a joke, it's too fucking bad.'"

White artists could claim immunity from African-American approval by invoking freedom of expression. Conversely, either by choice or by playing to the lowest common commercial denominator, black artists continued to write from a palate limited to dance, romance, or oppression. One Los Angeles outfit, the Bus Boys, managed to work against those conventions. With an assortment of tunes lampooning black stereotypes, the group (who charted with "The Boys Are Back in Town" from the 1983 film *48 Hrs.*) pointed out how blacks remained marginalized in a genre that wouldn't exist without them. The cover of their 1980 LP *Minimum Wage Rock & Roll* presents a Norman Rockwell-esque rendering of an Afro-wearing waiter rushing toward a customer with serving tray held high in hand. Call it Steppin Fetchit meets Ike Turner. Among the tracks were "There Goes the Neighborhood" ("the whites are moving in, they'll bring their next of kin, oh boy"), "Johnny Soul'd Out" ("he's into rock and roll and he's given up the rhythm and blues"), and "KKK," in which the singer longs to "be an All-American man . . . join the Ku Klux Klan and play in a rock 'n' roll band."

Through the Bus Boys, Los Angelinos had some experience with contemporary rock music played from a black perspective. But they were caught unawares on Friday, October 9, 1981, when a young black artist from one of the flyover states appeared to open two shows on the Los Angeles leg of the Rolling Stones tour. Jagger himself handpicked the Minneapolis-bred Prince Rogers Nelson to warm up the L.A. Memorial Coliseum, and it made perfect sense—in theory. Prince freely told reporters he wished his band could become a "black Rolling Stones." He and his sidemen grew up loving and recycling everything they heard on the radio, from psychedelic Temptations and Sly and the Family Stone hits to the gospel according to Al Green and the Staple Singers. They were as likely to turn out to see Black Sabbath as Tower of Power or Weather Report. But for Warner Brothers Records, Prince's talented and eye-catching band was mere icing on the cake. The label wanted Prince, knowing he was a studio prodigy and multi-instrumentalist, and as such he was granted the rare opportunity to produce himself from the outset.

Trouble was, neither of his first two records made much of an impact on the hit parade, although the early singles "Soft and Wet" (#92 pop and #12 R&B hits in 1978) and "I Wanna Be Your Lover" (#11 pop and #1 R&B hits, 1979) are now regarded among his first great songs. His third LP, *Dirty Mind*, was considered a freak show—the front cover presenting Prince in androgynous drag, and the back peddling such aural delights as "Head," "Do It All Night," and a zippy ode to incest called "Sister." The tune provides a good indicator of the album's direction: "I was only sixteen but I guess that's no excuse," coos the narrator, who describes his sister as "thirty-two, lovely and loose." Then it gets nasty. "She don't wear no underwear," he tattles, "she says it only gets in her hair." Synthesizers race the giddy vocal to cross paths at the punchline: "and it's got a funny way of stopping the juice."

Not that this was anything new. Josephine Baker danced in a skirt made of bananas and T-Bone Walker had his table-in-teeth twirling routine. Little Richard piled his perm high and wore three times as much makeup as most hookers twice his age, and Jimi Hendrix liked to dry-hump his amplifier. All were exemplary talents, but they understood, as did Prince, that the First Commandment of show business is to captivate the public. Love him or hate him, no one was going to ignore Prince.

Percussionist Sheila Escovedo recalled meeting Prince around this time. "I heard about this kid from Minneapolis doing all his own writing, playing, and producing," she reflected in 1987, "and even now record people won't let anybody do something like that. I saw him backstage; it was at an Al Jarreau concert. He turned and saw me; I knew it was him, and then I saw him a couple of months later onstage in San Francisco wearing a pair of bikini bottoms and leg warmers."

It was this incarnation of Prince who strolled out to greet the Rolling Stones' throng of Los Angeles diehards. Guitarist Dez Dickerson recalled the gig in an interview with Dave Hill for the British journalist's 1989 book, *Prince: A Pop Life*. They opened with the title track from the about-to-be released album, *Controversy*. Next, according to Dickerson, the group launched into "a fairly metallic" rendering of "Why You Wanna Treat Me So Bad."

A roar of approval washed across the stage, Dickerson remembers. "I'd never heard so huge an ovation in my life. But the next song we played—I don't remember what it was—was a bit too black for that part of the audience that harbored ill feelings toward

Prince Rogers Nelson was booed off the stage when he opened for the Rolling Stones in 1981. Four years later, he ruled the music world with the #1 film and best-selling soundtrack to *Purple Rain*, and had a constellation of protégés and imitators riding his purple coattails to glory. (Richard A. Aaron/Star File)

black people." Objects, cups mostly, began landing on the stage. "I had seen many, many shows where the headlining act got pelted with things out of admiration," the guitarist tells Hill. "That's rock 'n' roll. Culturally, it's a different thing. Black audiences generally don't throw things unless they don't like what's going on." Prince left the arena, left the city, and ultimately had to be coaxed back to California from Minneapolis to fulfill his contract two days later.

After the Friday set, promoter Bill Graham lectured the Stones' fans about treating others with respect. The crowd responded with catcalls, and word spread that Prince was a prima donna poseur who'd been booed from the stage, although that wasn't the case. By the time he returned, Los Angeles was primed to give this Prince the royal treatment. The band was pelted with spoiled chicken parts, shoes, and a full bottle of Jack Daniels. Dickerson recalls that their newfound bassist, still in his teens, was hit by "a half-gallon jug of orange juice. It was pretty wild."[3]

In less than five years, Prince would have many of those same Stones fans paying top dollar to buy his records, watch him onscreen, or see him perform live. The performer they jeered that night in Los Angeles was simply sketching out his formula for stardom— a wedding of pop melodies to James Brown funk and Hendrixian theatrics with just enough Little Richard sexual ambiguity to titillate. And, by adding claims of mixed race parentage to the mix, Prince soon set an image translucent enough for every music lover to project upon regardless of color.

DANCING MACHINE

Few black artists scaled enough racial barricades to land atop the *Billboard* Hot 100 in the early 1980s. Among them were the one-hit-wonder Lipps, Inc. (also from Minneapolis), who scored in April 1980 with "Funkytown" and a pair of wedding reception perennials, Kool & the Gang's "Celebration" (unavoidable throughout the winter of 1981), and "Endless Love," the Diana Ross/Lionel Richie duet which arrived the following fall. Interestingly, in an era when "soul" had become a commercial four-letter word— too close to disco for whites and too white for blacks who had moved on to hip-hop— Ross' album, *diana*, and Michael Jackson's *Off the Wall* were somehow inoculated.

Veteran disc jockey Casey Kasem has an explanation. "I think what happens in the biggest crossover periods is that whenever there's no particular craze like the British Invasion or hard rock, or whenever the pop charts get dull, dance and/or rhythm-based music seems to do better," he suggests. "It always fills the void. In the early '80s, you had acts like Michael Jackson, Prince, and Lionel Richie, whose music is black, but whose basis is in pop, a combination of what we remember as rock 'n' roll and country from back in the '50s. So by the mid-'80s, when that style of black music came around again, pop and black seemed almost synonymous and records started crossing over again."

Among the anomalies were a surprisingly resilient pair of singles from Diana Ross, "Upside Down" and "I'm Comin' Out." Both were written by Nile Rodgers and Bernard Edwards, whose band Chic fell victim to the Death-to-Disco mob. That Chic became so closely identified with disco was purely accidental, says Rodgers, and can be traced directly to the band's selection of strings to augment their records instead of the brass sections favored by most of their funk band contemporaries. That, compounded by Chic's elegant stage attire (with fashion inspiration provided by Brian Ferry of Roxy Music) and mannered commentaries on disco culture doomed the band and forced its leaders into exile, where they thrived in behind-the-scenes production. "I never really thought about it before," says Rodgers, "and maybe you're right. Maybe using strings was a way for critics to label us a disco band—that, and having the girls up front. So we did pour more time and energy into production, although that part of our career was well underway before Chic ended."

When the Atlantic execs offered Rodgers and Edwards their choice of the biggest artists on the label including the Rolling Stones and Bette Midler, they opted instead for a black vocal act with no chart history, Sister Sledge. (They reasoned that the industry rarely rewards producers for a superstar hit, whereas creating a monster record for an unknown could earn them cachet.) Their success with "He's the Greatest Dancer" and "We Are Family" earned Rodgers and Edwards an audience with Diana Ross, although she made the first move by dropping in on a Chic concert. "Diana lives in a very different world, and she hadn't really been touched by the underground dance scene, so when she heard an arena full of black and white people screaming, 'Chic! Chiiiic!!' I think she was impressed. When we got together with her, Bernard and I did what we always did with the artists we were producing back then. We'd sit down and do an interview, very in depth, almost like taking a legal deposition. And with the material we got, we'd go away and write an entire album."

The 1980 result, *diana*, aspired to be a daring LP that sprinkled the vaunted Ross glitter over a bed of slinky Chic grooves. But it was not to be. Still smarting from their box office disappointments with *The Wiz*, Motown and Ross grew skittish when they heard the mix Rodgers and Edwards delivered. The record sounded too . . . well, too *black*. According to journalist Brian Chin, Ross previewed the preliminary Chic mix for influential urban DJ Frankie Crocker, who told her flat out that the pair had "ruined her career." Gordy soon handed the multitracks over to Motown veteran mixer Russ Terrana, who had experience massaging Ross' material since her days with the Supremes. "Berry Gordy ignored the issue of creative control," Terrana explained to Chin. "That was his philosophy; you're competing, and you have to go out there with the best you can." Both mixes were assembled together for a 2003 CD reissue of *diana*, and the differences are startling. Motown's version finds Ross' singing aloof and disengaged, and the tracks themselves seem to tilt from Chic's bottom-heavy funk to a crisp and florid pop closer to listeners' expectations of radio and Ross.

The message was clear. If black music was going to claw its way back into the Top 40, it had to make records that white mainstream audiences would be willing to hear and buy. Other labels reached the same conclusion. "I remember going over songs for the album that became *I Feel for You*," says Chaka Khan. "Before that, I recorded Michael Jackson's 'Got to Be There,' even though it was against my better judgment. I did it because they just kept after me until I cut it, and it did pretty well. My producer Arif Mardin and I had been making albums that I thought were great, very interesting and fun. But the label thought it was about time we sold some records for them, and so we tried picking more contemporary material to try to connect with a younger audience, and maybe that's why it did so well."

At the other end of the spectrum, Michael Jackson never lost track of his ultimate goal to be the king of crossover, and pored over pop trends the way a day trader studies fluctuations in the stock market. Jackson spent much of his childhood internalizing anything that might set him apart or above other performers, and by 1979, his instincts were honed to prescience. Jackson's timing and stagecraft were cobbled together from observing the best—the James Brown skate, Sam and Dave's microphone interplay, Jackie Wilson's loose-limbed comfort onstage—all deconstructed with precision and care so that they could become part of the Michael Jackson persona he wanted to build. The process had been underway for some time, beginning with the Jacksons' departure from Motown, and culminating for Michael after success with his brothers at their new home on CBS/Epic and after the box office disappointment of *The Wiz.*

"When we left Motown in the mid-'70s," Marlon Jackson says, "we knew we needed a change. Our contract with them was up, and it was time to either renew or move on. We wanted to experience new things and go in different directions, and getting to work with Gamble and Huff was a real breath of fresh air. We hadn't had a big hit since 'Dancing Machine,' and to have our first record off Motown go gold—and that was 'Enjoy Yourself'—well, that felt great. The public had no idea where we were going to go, so it was an exciting time of experimentation. We had always wanted to play Vegas, and that was cool because whole families could come and see us. When we got tired of that, we went back to the one-nighters. And based on our success, we convinced CBS to let us produce ourselves, and things really took off in 1978 when *Destiny* came out."

In turn, the singles from *Destiny*—"Blame It on the Boogie" (# 54 pop and # 3 R&B hits) and "Shake Your Body Down to the Ground" (#7 pop and #3 R&B hits)—led to *Triumph,* and the Jacksons were back in vogue, courtesy of "Can You Feel It" and "Lovely One." Independence did have its price, however; the brothers never returned to the top of the *Billboard* charts after leaving Motown.

In his spare time, Michael hatched a new plan to establish himself as a solo act, one far removed from his childhood hits "Ben," "Rockin' Robin," and "Got to Be There." With producer Quincy Jones acting as a sounding board, Jackson constructed *Off the Wall,* a dance-driven pop record with rhythms as itchy as the melodies were light. "Don't Stop Till You Get Enough" and "Working Day and Night" were Jackson's own, distinguished by hiccupping vocals and in-the-pocket percussion. There were standout contributions from elsewhere, too—including the LP's title cut, "Off the Wall," "Rock With You" by Rod Temperton, and a Paul McCartney tune called "Girlfriend."

The album ultimately went multiplatinum and yielded four Top 10 singles, but Jackson's dreams of international acclaim and across-the-board appeal failed to materialize. He went back to work, rejoining his brothers on the road to promote the Jacksons' *Triumph* and compiling tracks for a live album. The tour grossed $5.5 million, and in its wake, Jackson began anew. Hints of what he had in mind materialized in songs he created for Diana Ross (the 1982 #10 pop entry, "Muscles") and in a song he wrote and produced for big sister Rebbie Jackson, "Centipede." CBS geared up to promote *Thriller* in the fall of 1982 with "The Girl Is Mine." The duet between Michael and Paul McCartney was easily the most calculating track on the LP, and not long on the heels of the former Beatle's saccharine ode to integration, "Ebony & Ivory," opposite Stevie Wonder. On the strength of its star power and feel-good atmosphere, "The Girl Is Mine" received a warm reception from a variety of radio formats.

Marlon Jackson recalls that *Off the Wall* had excellent songs and all these wonderful and original rhythms, but nothing prepared anyone for *Thriller.* "All of the songs were great, and to complement them, Michael put together videos that were more than that; they were short movies. Each one was different and yet none of them detracted from the music. I think *Thriller* would have been a huge hit anyway, but the videos helped to take it further. I put it this way: give the people what they want, and they'll buy it."

Among the first attempts to cross over were videos from Prince's *1999* and a trio of inspired visual bombshells conceived by Jackson to take *Thriller* over the threshold set by *Off the Wall* and beyond anything contemplated by a black artist in American music. There was only one problem. MTV, the one network dedicated to bringing contemporary music to cable subscribers, wasn't airing black artists. Like their record company counterparts, MTV's founders at Warner-Amex Communications held lingering antipathies based on the fallout from disco. Their halfhearted defense was that the network showcased rock acts, and blacks were by definition anything but.

It was widely reported that CBS/Columbia threatened to pull all their artists' clips in the fall of 1982 unless MTV added Jackson's "Beat It" to the video rotation. More than a year later, vice president of production and promotion John Sykes dismissed the story as "the biggest hoax of 1983. (CBS) never did any such thing," Sykes said at the time. "People who didn't understand music programming went after us, and by the time the rumor got started, it snowballed so quickly it was out of control. We were totally amazed because we play black artists whenever they play a rock 'n' roll song. But black artists do not always play rock music, so MTV does not always play them."

Given the ubiquity of Beyonce, 50 Cent, and *Cribs* on the network today, "people tend to forget that MTV wouldn't play black artists at first," says John Landis, "and that was corporate policy. Michael Jackson tore those walls down, and what does he have in common with Prince? They're both *light skinned*, and that's not a coincidence. With MTV these days, you wouldn't know that. Because of rap it's very black now or what they call 'urban,' with an audience of white suburbans."

WALKING ON THE MOON

From the moment MTV signed on with "Video Killed the Radio Star" in August of 1981, its programmers favored white pop rock, a disproportionately large amount of it imported from the English-speaking countries of Western Europe. Upon closer examination, a *Rolling Stone* report revealed that of the 750 videos shown by the network in its first 18 months on the air, less than two dozen showcased black performers.

Not that many stateside acts and or major labels had budgets for music videos anyway; but in those regional markets where subscribers could actually watch MTV, the artists in video rotation began racking up impressive sales. Labels quickly grasped how promotional videos—through MTV and other cable outlets—might have identified a new intersection between consumers and product, the likes of which had not been seen since the dawn of Top 40 radio. By the time CBS launched *Thriller* two years later, record companies observed a 10-to-15-percent bump in sales for artists whose videos debuted on MTV.

American audiences were exposed to Dexy's Midnight Runners from Ireland, the Aussie band Men at Work, and a flood of Britpop newcomers including Duran Duran, Culture Club, and the Eurythmics. These video clips provided more than a promotional shot in the arm; they inaugurated a new industry. By the close of 1982, artists with support on cable TV commanded seventeen of the Top 20 slots on *Billboard*'s album chart. Everyone won. Artists received more television exposure and had a say in the creation and exploitation of their likenesses. Record labels saw profits surge. Videos became a performer's live-action calling card, a modern parallel of the arty album jacket and magazine ad rolled into one. Fast-cut editing techniques, scantily clad women, violence, and a small fortune spent in rigging objects to explode on cue (mirrors were a favorite) fostered criticism from all quarters.

Reverend Jerry Fallwell's Moral Majority pronounced MTV just short of pornographic, and music lovers on the left believed the network's corporate caretakers were dumbing down rock for profit. Original MTV veejay Alan Hunter wasn't having any of it. "What gets me," he said, "is when people point their fingers at us and say we're glamorizing and squelching creativity. The only thing we've been selling out is record stores."

Overnight, the network became part of the cultural landscape. At start-up, only 2.5 million viewers could actually watch MTV, although subscriptions grew to 9.3 million as *Thriller* climbed the charts in 1983. Today, that viewership base is upwards of 375 million. "It's really the integration of two of the most powerful forces in youth culture during the past decade," Sykes concluded, "rock 'n' roll and television, which were never correctly integrated before. If you had to say any one thing, it would be that MTV was something whose time had come."

There was a downside, of course. MTV's reliance on Eurovideo and the de facto banishment of black music had the ancillary effect of chasing domestic music from its home turf. Instead, Dublin's U2 became a constant presence on FM radio, a sneering Billy Idol married punk to pop, and David Bowie was reborn through the synth funk of *Let's Dance*, an LP produced by Nile Rodgers and featuring a then-unknown Stevie Ray Vaughan on guitar.

This new troupe of U.K. artists had grown up a generation removed from the Beatles, Stones, Eric Clapton, and Bowie—too young to participate in the 1960s, but old enough to hear the echoes of American soul, psychedelia, and Phil Spector. The Brits, according to David Byrne, were among the first to embrace anything outside the norm in the world of pop. "When Talking Heads were first getting press attention here in the United States," he says, "very few people here picked up on where we were coming from, what our influences were. But as soon as we started playing London and other places, every article said, 'Oh, these people have been listening to this and they've been listening to that.'"

With MTV providing the transcontinental link, a full-fledged exchange program reinvigorated pop, and just as Talking Heads found fans abroad, British bands like Culture Club revisited sounds they heard from the Americas and shipped them back to the United States as breezy radio fare. Steel drums and reggae-tinged arrangements betray the group's infatuation with anything Caribbean, but closer listening reveals the profound influence of Motown's Smokey Robinson on Culture Club's front man, the überglamorous Boy George.

Given their disparate ages, upbringing, and sexual orientation, it's curious how much Boy George and Robinson share as vocalists and tunesmiths and that their racial disparity is, at least for musical purposes, inconsequential. Smokey would find Culture Club's "Do You Really Want to Hurt Me" or "I'll Tumble 4 Ya" as comfortable as a well-worn pair of loafers, just as Boy George could tackle Robinson's "Being With You," "The Tears of a Clown," or "I Second That Emotion" with similar finesse. However briefly or knowingly, Boy George worked with Smokey Robinson music in the same way John Fogerty delved into his beloved Sun Records catalog—creating music that breathes new life into a style thought to have run its course.

SAME AS IT EVER WAS

Black influences, suppressed but never completely expunged from pop, erupted again through the second British Invasion of MTV's Anglo imports. European videos were also artistically compelling. They could be nightmarish (as in Peter Gabriel's "Shock the Monkey"), silly (Thomas Dolby's comic turn in "She Blinded Me With Science"), or risqué (the British version of Duran Duran's "Girls on Film" has shots of bare breasts being rubbed with ice cubes). American acts who had come to fame before the ascendance of video—Fleetwood Mac, Tom Petty, and Bruce Springsteen, for example—angled for a way to project on television as effectively as they did from the concert stage. Conversely, newcomers Talking Heads plunged into the medium anxious to find something new to say musically and visually.

What made the band special? Was it the husband-and-wife rhythm section of Chris Franz and Tina Weymouth? Byrne's off-kilter songwriting and Jerry Harrison's minimalist keyboard shadings? Neither, says Byrne, who recalls his contemporaries on the club scene as obsessed with other areas of pop expression, from creating a "blanket of sound" to being driven by harmony and melody. (Both succinctly describe CBGB regulars the Ramones and Blondie.) "We were so heavily into the groove," Byrne attests, "that it made us kind of stick out. I don't think I really had my own voice for the longest time. I would go through other people's songbooks playing acoustic guitar at coffee houses. And maybe I did have a unique voice back then, but I was trying my damnedest to sound like whoever wrote the song I was singing."

Unorthodox rhythms, inscrutable lyrics, and bizarre covers earned Talking Heads a cult following among Manhattan's pocket-protector set. "There was a song on the first record, 'The Book I Read,' which I wrote to sound like KC and the Sunshine Band. Of course, we missed by a mile," he laughs, "so I was disappointed. They had a great groove, not just some drum machine formula for disco. And we liked disco. We didn't listen to it hours on end, but we all liked that you could occasionally hear really radical things being done with the mixes."

It took an obscure tune from soul crooner Al Green to introduce them to radio listeners. The group's live sets routinely ambled from Lou Reed covers to bubblegum classics like the Ohio Express' "1-2-3 Red Light," and Byrne says, "occasionally we'd do an Al Green song. At that point we did 'Love & Happiness,' although I can't imagine now how I must have butchered it. That's a song for a singer, you know? It seems so audacious for me to go after one of his songs."

Byrne recalls the band landed on Green's "Take Me to the River" one night, and it clicked. "I didn't hear until later that it was his show-closer, the big finale—and you wouldn't have guessed it from the record." Within a very short period of time, there were all these cover versions of it . . . Foghat, Annie Lennox, Delbert McClinton, all very different."

When Talking Heads finally made it to MTV, a pair of videos put a lock on their image as funk-loving nerds. One, "Once in a Lifetime," caught Byrne cuffing himself upside the head and demonstrating how a karate chop to the forearm might pass for modern dance. The other, "Burning Down the House," contained a potpourri of more disturbing images, including Byrne's lip-synching face projected from a moving vehicle onto a desolate highway.

As the 1980s unfolded, the group grew increasingly amorphous and distracted by outside interests; Tom Tom Club became Frantz and Weymouth's dance-oriented side project, while Byrne immersed himself in world music and dabbled in cinema with curiosities like *True Stories*. The band churned out albums of sporadic quality before dissolving altogether in 1990, but the best Talking Heads records remain as a kind of sonic library still raided today for hits from both sides of the color line. Any number of studio wizards offered advice for threading counterpoint and harmony into a track; Talking Heads sought ways to do the same with rhythms. Radiohead, Dr. Dre, Beck, Fatboy Slim, and N.E.R.D. toy with the same concepts today, building tracks lush with percussion rather than orchestral or pop instruments.

The band reached its zenith in 1983, when Talking Heads hit the road with an expanded roster of black and white virtuosos. Included were Adrian Belew, a former session guitarist who'd worked with David Bowie and Frank Zappa, an ex-Labelle vocalist named Nona Hendrix, and Bernie Worrell, a keyboard veteran from P-Funk. Director Jonathan Demme captured it all in *Stop Making Sense*, a documentary now lavished with the same praise once reserved for such rock classics as *Monterey Pop* and *Woodstock*. The film begins with David Byrne ambling out before the concert crowd to pop in a cassette of (what else?) percussion to accompany his acoustic reading of "Psycho Killer." As the show unfolds, the band introduces guest musicians to support their acrobatic leaps from pop hits ("Life During Wartime," better known by its chorus, "this ain't no party, this ain't no disco . . .") into arcana ("Slippery People") and on to the secular baptismal they made their own, "Take Me to the River." Techno, art school, white-hot funk, captivating cinema, and pure pop pleasure, *Stop Making Sense* may be the best single-artist concert film of the rock era, since the others depend largely on superstars performing their greatest hits of the moment.

AMERICA CHILLS OUT

While Demme and Byrne worked to push the envelope of mainstream cinema, others were cashing in. Once *Saturday Night Fever* and *Grease* demonstrated the cross-marketing potential in tying music to big budget films in the late 1970s, Hollywood producers understood soundtracks as more than incidental music—they had become a film's secret weapon and unseen co-star. On occasion, a commercial soundtrack (think *FM, Eddie and the Cruisers*, and *Streets of Fire*) could financially eclipse the movie it was intended to hype. Just as often, well-executed soundtracks gave some measure of artistic cover to such paint-by-numbers fluff as *Flashdance, Footloose*, and *Dirty Dancing*.

But until the arrival of *The Big Chill* in the summer of 1983, no one had seen a soundtrack album spawn an entire radio format. The tale of yuppies gathered for the weekend funeral of a friend who commits suicide struck a chord with the nation, and it took two volumes of *The Big Chill* soundtrack releases to slake the nation's thirst for nostalgia. Somehow it was "Morning in America" (Ronald Reagan's reelection slogan), and Americans allowed that the 1960s might now be upgraded from nightmarish to memorable—

provided the reminders didn't stray from fashion, movies, and music into Vietnam, assassinations, race riots, or generational warfare.

With its heavy reliance on Motown hits ("Ain't Too Proud to Beg," "I Second That Emotion," and "I Heard It Through the Grapevine"—each strategically placed to highlight dramatic moments), *The Big Chill* was lauded as the "feel-good movie of the summer," and it wasn't just for the soundtrack's comforting retro-rock favorites provided by the Band ("The Weight"), Procol Harum ("A Whiter Shade of Pale"), or Three Dog Night ("Joy to the World"). The film took the load off many, and put the weight right back where it had always been—on the poor, dispossessed, and black.

Looking back, *The Big Chill* mirrors public sentiment about not only the 1960s, but then-present-day America, providing absolution by proxy and "closure" for those bleeding hearts who canvassed in vain for Robert F. Kennedy, McCarthy, and McGovern. Jeff Goldbum's on-screen character once dreamed he'd teach reading to kids in Harlem; now he writes celebrity twaddle for *People* magazine. In her role, Mary Kay Place bemoans her work as a public defender, despairing that most of her clients are not political dissidents, but small-time hoods who deserve conviction rather than protection from The Man.

The intervening decades since the film's release have yet to make clear whether director/screenwriter Lawrence Kasdan is tweaking baby boomers for relinquishing their idealism or providing a tutorial on self-justification. It's arguable that *The Big Chill* mirrors the Reagan manifesto by asking the same question repeatedly posed by the Gipper himself: should the nation devote valuable resources and time to enable ungrateful wretches who will never become self-sufficient, or should we get on with the business of getting ahead? What goes unexplored are the consequences of discarding 1960s activism, doubtless more troublesome for those forsaken than for the deserters. (Gee, the film implies, dealing with all that yuppie guilt is going to be a real bitch.)

Just as the ensemble characters settled into the collective psyche, director Alan Parker found their polar opposite a few years later in Roddy Doyle's novel of rootless Irish kids, *The Commitments*. Here was a ragtag group who didn't play 1960s soul as background music for after-dinner cleanup in the comfort of a rambling suburban home. These working class misfits invested themselves in the music, and it saved them in return. When they started a band covering Stax and Atlantic classics, the music revitalized them; it gave them ambition and purpose. And rather than simply humming the melodies, they identified with their ethos. Parker's 1991 film makes certain to lift one line nearly verbatim from Doyle's book: "The Irish are the niggers of Europe. And Dubliners are the niggers of Ireland. And the Northside Dubliners are the niggers of Dublin. Say it loud. I'm black and I'm proud." *The Commitments* didn't fare nearly as well in the U.S. as *The Big Chill*, but its soundtrack of chestnuts by Otis Redding, Wilson Pickett, and others sold so well that Atlantic scoured its vaults to produce a sequel disc.

In commercial terms, *The Big Chill* was a glacier that rumbled across the country, etching an oldies radio station into every city, town, village, and hamlet. This format rapidly supplanted what had been called "easy listening"—selections from the Rat Pack, Connie Francis, and Henry Mancini, because quite literally the audience for such music was dying off. Just as those stations might play "In the Mood" without mentioning World War II or the Great Depression, retro-rock stations began to spin "Satisfaction" in between the Beatles' "Revolution" or Janis Ian's "Society's Child" without mentioning the context of circumstances behind any of them. Once MUZAK jumped aboard, shoppers could absently hum along with "Blowin' in the Wind" or "A Change Is Gonna Come," with only the occasional intercom interruption announcing the day's blue light special.

Motown answered the mania for oldies by releasing droves of budget compilations from its golden era, including not only superstars like the Supremes, Jackson 5, Temptations, and Four Tops, but such lesser known acts as Junior Walker and the All-Stars, Mary Wells, and Edwin Starr. Gordy's insistence in the 1960s that his releases demonstrate universal appeal paid huge dividends again, as oldies radio and dancefloor medleys from Stars On 45 (assorted studio players slavishly copying every note and vocal) helped resell tracks more than a quarter century old. As a testament to Gordy's quality control and his publicity machine, Motown became synonymous in popular culture with 1960s soul, although Aretha, Sly, Otis, James Brown, and Sam Cooke never recorded for Gordy or any of his Motown subsidiaries.

NEVER CAN SAY GOODBYE

Record executives dream of marketing a product with demographic roots spreading as deep and wide as *The Big Chill,* but the soundtrack was only one of Motown's twin triumphs in 1983. The other arrived on May 16, in the form of a two-hour television special called *Motown 25.* Many of the acts had long since left the company for greener contracts and greater autonomy, but on this one occasion they assembled in homage to Berry Gordy's irrefutable genius. Remaining Motown labelmates Stevie Wonder and Smokey Robinson were in attendance, appearing for the first time in decades alongside the Supremes (with Cindy Birdsong replacing the late Florence Ballard), Martha and the Vandellas, Lionel Richie, and a reconstituted Jackson 5. "The night we finished taping *Motown 25,* I remember feeling a little depressed," says the show's director, Don Mischer. "I thought all we had that was great was Michael Jackson doing 'Billie Jean' and the Temps and the Four Tops medley. Then I looked at the clips and realized, 'Hey, Marvin Gaye wasn't so bad and Smokey and the Miracles with Linda Ronstadt were pretty hot, too.'"

Then came the finale of "Someday We'll Be Together," in which Mary Wilson hoped to pull focus from Diana Ross by wearing an eye-popping red gown. Ross simply nudged her former partner aside and sashayed to center stage. Later Wilson dismissed the snub with practiced passive-aggressive charm. "Oh, that's just *Diane,*" she sighed, using the name Ross left back in Detroit thinking that it sounded too plain. "She performs very aggressively, and she was inspired by the moment, I guess. That sort of thing has been going on for years; it's just that the whole country got to see it this time."

So it went with the bittersweet *Motown 25,* an affair rife with happy memories and awkwardly staged reconciliations. Marvin Gaye, the label's former *enfant terrible,* left for CBS and was relishing his biggest hit in years with "Sexual Healing," Diana Ross was back on top at RCA with "Why Do Fools Fall in Love," "Mirror, Mirror," and "Muscles," but all loyally delivered only their Motown classics. Of course, Michael Jackson had other ideas. He'd appear with his brothers if—and only if—the producers agreed to air his performance of "Billie Jean," the program's only song not released under the auspices of Motown.

Once again, Jackson's flair for theatrics paid off. The televised Jackson 5 medley remains spectacular, with the brothers ripping through the same medley of "I Want You Back/ABC/The Love You Save" they perfected on the *Triumph* tour, only with departed brother Jermaine (who married Gordy's daughter and remained a Motown solo artist when the brothers left) added back into the fold. After nailing the campy old choreography and stopping on a dime in an iconic pose, the brothers slunk from the stage, leaving Michael alone in the spotlight. He's a man who understands his moment has arrived and plans to make the most of every nanosecond. As the backing track begins to play, Jackson is a tightly coiled mechanism ready to spring. When he does, he, the fedora, the glove, the moonwalk, all make history. And for him it would never be so good again.

DON'T MAKE IT BAD

Thriller earned Michael Jackson a dozen Grammys in 1983, and in order to capitalize on the hoopla (*TIME* commissioned Andy Warhol to paint him for their cover), the reunited Jackson brothers dashed off an album and set out on a tour buffeted between enthusiastic reviews and bad press over soaring ticket prices. In the meantime, *The Making of Thriller*, an in-depth look at Jackson's $300,000 film short, was on target to become one of the best-selling videos of all time—in 1984, the tape finished third, right behind *Jane Fonda's Workout* and Harrison Ford's *Raiders of the Lost Ark*.

Expecting to vault from one success to the next, Michael agreed to shoot *Captain Eo*, a 3-D short for the Disney theme parks, and surfaced the following January with "We Are the World," an all-star single with profits funneled to aid famine-stricken Africans.

On the advice of Paul McCartney, Jackson delved into music publishing and purchased the rights to Sly and the Family Stone's catalog; then he outbid the former Beatle and Yoko Ono on a host of Lennon/McCartney classics as well. By the time he resurfaced with a half-hour network special to promote his new album *Bad*, Jackson had become the tabloids' favorite whipping boy, with rumors floated that he slept in a hyperbaric chamber, preferred the company of chimps and children to adults, and once bid on the bones of a circus freak known in life as the Elephant Man. Martin Scorcese's video for the single "Bad" (originally conceived as a duel between Michael and Prince) made the singer look cream puff tough, and the rest of the rollout was spent making up for lost ground via state-of-the-art videos for "The Way You Make Me Feel," "Man in the Mirror," "Leave Me Alone," "Smooth Criminal," and "Dirty Diana." But by the end, Jackson had become a carnival attraction in his own right, more famous for bizarre behavior than his readily acknowledged talent.

In the consternation, music trends passed him by. The ensemble dancing taped for "Beat It" and "Thriller"—and repeated in videos by everyone from Lionel Richie to Madonna and Jackson sibling Janet—began to appear warmed over and prissy. Black pop remained profitable through easy-on-the-ears acts like Luther Vandross, Billy Ocean, and New Edition, but pop R&B was now just as often the province of white performers— George Michael, Huey Lewis and the News, and Hall and Oates.

Some, like Daryl Hall, claimed credit for the crossover renaissance. "In a way, I really feel vindicated by what's going on in music right now," he said in 1985. "For a long time we didn't have anyone to play off of, and it was sort of like working in a vacuum. I think it would be fair to say we were ahead of our time in that respect, because we saw the direction music was taking before it happened. I saw the combination of the two—dance and rock—a long time ago."

Hall's strategy yielded a string of hits that clung to the upper reaches of the mid-1980s pop and R&B charts, from "Kiss on My List" and "You Make My Dreams" to "Private Eyes," "One on One," "Maneater," and "I Can't Go for That." "We were interested in breaking down the barriers between white and black music in the '70s," Hall explained, "but nobody else was. Now there's so much talk about white musicians being influenced by black musicians and it's really the other way around. You have artists like Prince taking white influences and using them to create new things."

PURPLE REIGN

But there was a problem with that formula, and Prince seemed to know it. Those "new things" he created were being diluted by endless knockoffs and the unexpected staying power of rap music. His 1988 single, "Alphabet St.," prominently featured a rap in the middle and brought the question out into the open: should Prince pursue this new genre and appear to follow rather than lead, or remain the pop-funk demigod of a genre no longer considered cutting edge? His own 24-hour work ethic didn't help, since his many outside productions allowed the press to lump his work in with a growing list of synth funk imitators (Ready for the World and Nu Shooz), erroneously referring to it all as "The Minneapolis Sound."

There's no evidence that Prince resisted this assessment; in fact, he pursued it doggedly. He surrounded himself with yes-men and musical clones. Those loyal to the throne were rewarded with hits and some degree of fame and fortune, but the penalty for demonstrating individuality was exile from his court in Minneapolis. As far back as *1999*, even his touring partners were protégés. The 1983 Triple Threat Tour featured Prince's T&A act, Vanity 6, and a band comprised of player pals from his barroom days who were rechristened the Time. The group was fronted by ex-drummer Morris Day and included Jesse Johnson (one of the great unsung guitarists to emerge from the Ernie Isley/Jimi Hendrix school of funk rock), the bass and keyboard team of Terry Lewis and Jimmy Jam Harris, a piledriving funk drummer named Jellybean Johnson, and Monte Moir (the lone white member), who played keyboards and also wrote.

Any second-tier band could steal the drum machine settings and keyboard programs from Prince's records, but none of them shared his breadth of vision or ambition. Accepting that premise goes a long way toward explaining how Prince intended to conquer the entertainment world by being all things to all people—performer, producer, writer, satyr, savior. Unlike Little Richard, Sly Stone, Jimi Hendrix, or James Brown, Prince could rock out without reminding whites of his blackness and throw down enough serious jam to maintain street credibility with his urban audience. The plan worked perfectly. Almost.

According to Monte Moir, the Triple Threat Tour was well on track as *1999* continued to make inroads with urban audiences, and the crowds in attendance reflected as much. "But everything just went through the roof when the 'Little Red Corvette' video caught on with MTV," he says. "All of a sudden, more and more white faces started appearing in the crowd, and you could just tell things were going to break wide open for him. It was obvious."

But where Ray Charles, Sam Cooke, and Otis Redding attempted to control their circumstances, Prince sought to control people. "Things started to get ugly when *1999* came out," Morris Day recalls, "and we didn't know anything was going on. We were just doing our thing and happy to be there. At first, it was all about the music, and all the politics didn't come into play until money and management came into the picture. But all those outside influences came in and fucked everything up for everybody. Before you knew it, there was a lot of dissent going on and people who'd grown up in a small musical community together as friends all of a sudden had everything turn into a business. And the business took its toll on friendships, and I guess that's to be expected once it turns into a big money industry."

At what should have been its moment of triumph, the Minneapolis Sound atomized. The summer of 1984 offered up a flurry of releases from artists in the Prince orbit, including *The Glamorous Life* from Sheila E., the Time's *Ice Cream Castle* (featuring the eventual hits "Jungle Love" and "The Bird"), and *Purple Rain*, a soundtrack album from Prince and his new band, the Revolution. On May 16, Warner Brothers offered a preview by releasing "When Doves Cry" as the lead single. Perhaps the only R&B hit ever to have its bass track wiped completely from the final version, the tune received a rapturous welcome, spending five weeks atop the *Billboard* pop charts. In late June, the album shipped and raced to the number one position, where it perched unchallenged for a dozen weeks. Finally the motion picture *Purple Rain* arrived in theaters July 27, where it outperformed expectations and remained among the top box office draws of the season. Forgotten Prince tracks were now grist for the hit mill—"When You Were Mine" from *Dirty Mind* turned up on Cyndi Lauper's *She's So Unusual*, and Chaka Khan had her biggest hit in years with "I Feel for You," rediscovered from the 1979 *Prince* LP.

Late that year, Prince became the first artist since the Beatles to occupy simultaneously the #1 slot on the box office, singles, and album charts. Despite its plot holes, soap operatic script, and novice acting, *Purple Rain* delivered on the strength of its concert sequences and the antagonism between Prince and his comedic foil, Morris Day. But even as the film spread the gospel of crossover (set in stone by the rockers "Let's Go Crazy" and "Baby, I'm a Star"), few outside the inner circle knew the stultifying effects of what Minneapolis insiders call his "Napoleon syndrome."

According to Morris Day, "Prince wanted to rule the music world. He explicitly told me that. After I quit the Time, he called me up, before the *Purple Rain* stuff, and he was on such a roll. He was going to rule the world through his music and his sound, and he was so worried about people doing other projects that somehow this was all going to get diluted. That was his biggest beef with Terry and Jimmy."

With the filming of *Purple Rain* complete, Prince decided to make an example of Jimmy Jam Harris and Terry Lewis for missing a road gig (forgivable on its own until Prince learned they were secretly holed up in a studio producing another act, which was forbidden). Morris Day also quit after losing patience with the unremitting megalomania. Prince gave in to evermore eccentric behavior, an indulgence that began with the loopy psychedelicism of *Around the World in a Day*, which failed to consolidate the crossover success he'd labored for with *Purple Rain*. He challenged his audiences with sanctimony rather than music, and his focus grew scattered by the steady stream of women who caught his fancy, among them Scottish singer Sheena Easton (for whom he penned the salacious "Sugar Walls") and the Bangles' Susanna Hoffs, who scored a #2 pop hit in 1986 with his "Manic Monday."

Innumerable recoveries and reversals followed, to diminishing public interest. *Sign O' the Times, The Black Album,* and *Diamonds and Pearls* each provided flashes of brilliance, but misbegotten films (*Under the Cherry Moon* and *Graffiti Bridge*) and self-indulgent albums distanced him from the mainstream. He also broke faith with the Warner Brothers' brass, precipitating a feud that led to Prince appearing in public sporting the word "SLAVE" scrawled on his cheek, until he finally withdrew from his given name altogether and began referring to himself with an unpronounceable glyph. Did Prince have a legitimate reason for being discontented? Perhaps, but his actions were so grandiose that he lost all but his most ardent admirers. Since actual former slaves participated in the music industry only a few decades before, Prince's complaints appeared egocentric, insensitive, and reckless.

His next ten years were spent wandering the commercial wasteland; issuing records on the internet, making sporadic appearances, and insisting on a total lockout of the press. At the turn of the century Prince suddenly reclaimed his name, charged through a roof-raising duet with Beyonce at the 2004 Grammys, and released *Musicology,* his most lucid and successful album in a dozen years. Audiences responded in kind, welcoming him back as though he'd never left.

No one in contemporary music—not hip-hop record moguls P. Diddy and Russell Simmons, or stars like Whitney Houston and Mariah Carey—can claim the pervasive influence of Prince or Michael Jackson. But both have acted as agents of their own undoing, Jackson by flouting social mores (he maintains there's no harm in sharing his bed with preteens), and Prince by snubbing those who made him rich and famous. A spate of recent interviews suggest that Prince doesn't consider himself in the throes of a "comeback." On the contrary, he says, "I never went away." Jackson, on the other hand, has been pulled into court on child molestation charges, and no amount of money, charity, or surgery may be able to prevent him from going away.

DIVA-LUTION

The remainder of the 1980s can be seen through the lens of MTV, where careers were made and broken, pop stars introduced and bade farewell. Once the network deduced that middle-class Americans would watch black artists as well as white, "things suddenly got very exciting again," according to Philip Bailey of Earth, Wind & Fire. With his Phil Collins duet ("Easy Lover") still on the charts, Bailey explained that, for him, "the barriers in music are all dissolving. All you have to do is watch MTV or listen to the radio and you'll hear Madonna on every black station and Lionel Richie on every white station."

Dance music in the mid-1980s may have resembled disco, grants rock critic Dave Marsh, but an important distinction ought to be made. "Essentially," he says, "disco was to some extent a cult—it was historically self-conscious and made up of songs about dancing and aspects of disco life. Today's dance culture is a mass phenomenon. The music became more accommodating for singers, and as audiences became more sophisticated, they started asking for more rhythmic variety, too." Finally free of its guilt by association with disco, white and black dance edged back onto the charts. The Pointer Sisters, an act long associated with Las Vegas, scored four hits in a row with "Jump,"

"Automatic," "Neutron Dance," and "I'm So Excited." And up from the gritty discotheques of Manhattan came Madonna, a Detroit native who professed a deep love for 1960s soul and fanned her passion into a 20-year career as the penultimate dance floor diva.

Neither blacks nor whites were especially smitten by her first batch of singles, "Holiday," "Lucky Star," and "Borderline," but club deejays and dancers across the nation took a liking to her fat basslines, boy-toy hiccup, and moxie. (When Dick Clark inquired about her ambitions on *American Bandstand*, Madonna gazed into the camera and replied, "To rule the world.") Once MTV broadcast her orgasmic writhing-on-the floor rendering of "Like a Virgin" (in a chopped-up wedding dress, no less) during the annual music awards, all shades of teenage America fell at her feet. An uneven vocal performance at Live Aid in summer 1985 proved that she wasn't Aretha Franklin, and didn't need to be. Her songs were infectious, and the stage moves bawdy good fun. "Where's the Party?" she asked on the 1986 LP *True Blue*, and Madonna made sure anyone with a radio understood very quickly that she *was* the party. The music of her youth—the Supremes' "Love Child" and Sly and the Family Stone's egalitarian soul—served as blueprints for "Papa Don't Preach" ("I'm keepin' my baby," she vows) and her ode to feminism, "Express Yourself." That video opens with a gal-pal call to arms, followed by Madonna in a business suit and bustier grabbing her crotch, then prowling the floor on all fours chained at the neck for the amusement of a mysterious and wealthy letch. Finally, she's depicted ogling a shirtless slave who toils away in the factory below. (Carl Jung, pick up the white courtesy phone.)

The medium may have changed, according to the late Bee Gee Maurice Gibb, but not the message."Remember," he argued, "the Beatles were once considered clean-cut, even though they were classified by some as long-haired yobs. As it turned out, they were fairly harmless when compared with the Stones. So I think that's one of those things people find necessary in pop—you've got the rebel side, and then you have the more acceptable alternative. The good and the bad; the Whitneys and the Madonnas."

Music videos helped separate naughty from nice, younger from older, and black from white (Boy George may have *sounded* like Smokey Robinson, but no one with cable TV was going to confuse the two). MTV had a hand in resurrecting Aretha Franklin via "Freeway of Love" and "I Knew You Were Waiting for Me," and provided Tina Turner with a second career through videos for "What's Love Got to Do With It," "Private Dancer," and "We Don't Need Another Hero," all Top Ten hits in 1984–1985 and presaging her sweep of the Grammys, where "What's Love" won awards for best song and best record. (Turner's acclaim set a new course for the awards, too, as the association now regularly swoons over any music stalwart who demonstrates renewed commercial clout. In a few short years, the list has grown to include Bonnie Raitt, Eric Clapton, Carlos Santana, and Steely Dan.)

Radio success in the 1960s and 1970s was no guarantee of airplay on MTV, though, and both Franklin and Turner were lucky to make the cut. More often, the network preferred fresh faces and the enormous crossover potential of an artist like Whitney Houston. Her voice recalled Aretha's gospel fervor, her look nearly defined the 1980s black ingénue for a generation, and, finally, her choice of material (guided by record mogul Clive Davis) was unremittingly commercial—so much so that it sparked debate among her supporters. If living well is the best revenge, Houston showed them all as she

While other rockers turned in the 1970s to pop, disco, new wave, and punk, Bonnie Raitt continued to promote and sing the blues. Raitt vaulted into the limelight with *Nick of Time* in 1989. She swept the Grammys, winning four awards and new converts to her easy-on-the-ear amalgam of rock and blues. (Chuck Pulin/Star File)

posted eleven hits at the top of the pop charts in the decade between 1985 and 1995. Included among them is the nearly three-month record set by "I Will Always Love You" from *The Bodyguard*, the film that also launched her movie career. But even at the peak of her popularity, accusations of commercial sellout held fast. One guest touring the *Bodyguard* set volunteered between takes that Houston's remarkable voice was being squandered on pap. A fellow within earshot spun around and attempted to stare the blasphemer into a pillar of salt. "That," a member of the crew whispered to the visitor, "was Whitney's manager. You might want to keep your voice down."

So, after a half-decade in exile, dance music was alive and thriving on the U.S. pop charts. There were 12" extended versions (remix wizard Arthur Baker even gave Bruce Springsteen's "Dancin' in the Dark" a nightclub makeover in 1984), songs that crossed from the dance floor to the pop charts (Soft Cell's "Tainted Love" for one) and vice-versa, and an open competition to see who would be crowned the next high priestess of pop. Cyndi Lauper covered Prince, Gloria Estefan and the Miami Sound Machine added a Latin flair to the good-time Florida groove pioneered by KC and the Sunshine Band, and Madonna's hunger for dance beats led her back to the same kinds of places where disco was born—the gay and ethnic nightclubs of Manhattan. Out in Minneapolis, the careers of Jimmy Jam Harris and Terry Lewis were jump-started by a young divorcee named Janet Jackson.

Both Jackson and her producers had something to prove. Jackson, having dismissed both a husband (singer James DeBarge) and a manager (father Joe Jackson), wanted to show the world she wasn't just the baby sister of someone famous. Jimmy Jam and Terry Lewis were anxious to demonstrate that they didn't need Prince or any of his producer aliases (Jamie Starr, Alexander Nevermind, Camille) to get to the top. Together they created *Control*, an album of featherweight funk that yielded five Top Five singles as 1986 trailed into 1987. By 1989, Jackson was confident enough to move further afield to explore social consciousness on *Rhythm Nation*, where the title song had its melodic hook lifted verbatim from Sly Stone's "Thank You Falettin Me Be Mice Elf Agin."

BLAME IT...BLAME IT...BLAME IT...

Two years into the rebirth of dance on the charts, Madonna, Houston, and Jackson were awash in imitators, including Jackson's former choreographer, Paula Abdul, as well as the Miami Sound Machine-less Gloria Estefan, pubescent pinups Debbie Gibson and Tiffany, and showboat chanteuse Mariah Carey. As MTV eased into the second half of its first decade, the network grew in unforeseen directions. The prime directive to immortalize classic rockers Bruce Springsteen, the Rolling Stones, and the ex-Beatles remained in place and the network attempted to program a few actual shows (*Remote Control* was the first) while combing the English-speaking world for tomorrow's most telegenic rock stars. But whether by intention or happenstance, a large segment of the audience came to encompass latchkey kids. These viewers were typically sixth graders through early high schoolers who made MTV their daily afternoon indoctrination into young adulthood. They tuned in for the latest dance moves and music, took fashion cues from Madonna and Paula Abdul, and clamored for more from virginal (white) crooners Rick Astley and Richard Marx, who became the Donny Osmond and David Cassidy of the late 1980s.

Boston-based record impresario Maurice Starr had a feel for adolescent buying power, especially when it came to preteens who had no real incomes of their own but could easily nag their parents for the occasional new album. In 1981, Starr assembled New Edition, a black group who had a run of bubblegum hits through the middle of the decade, led by "Cool It Now" (#4 pop hit in 1985 and #1 R&B hit in 1984) and "Mr. Telephone Man" (#12 pop and #1 R&B hits in 1985). Starr was ousted in a contract dispute when the group moved from a small independent label to MCA Records. Evidently he concluded that if he could model a successful group after the Jackson 5, then copying their white counterpart—the Osmond Brothers—ought to be just as lucrative. In 1986, he launched New Kids on the Block, ostensibly a group of young white R&B singers discovered by Starr blocks away from the same Roxbury school once attended by New Edition.

Starr's idea proved that, like minstrelsy, swing, and disco, mainstream America will take its music black, thank you, as long as it's lightened with a little cream and sugar. By 1991, after searing a trail across the pop firmament with two #1 albums, *Hangin' Tough* and *Step by Step* (in 1988 and 1990, respectively), the New Kids topped *Forbes Magazine*'s list of best-paid American entertainers, eclipsing both Madonna and Michael Jackson. During the group's three-year reign, Starr apparently spent most of his time in merchandise meetings (the boys endorsed an untold number of products) and filling out deposit slips. The members publicly disputed accusations that they couldn't sing, appeared in concert miming to tapes most of the time, and were no more "authentic" than the Monkees.

If New Kids were faking it onstage, they were hardly alone. The decline of screaming guitar solos and incorporation of video elements into live concerts meant performers were expected to dance—and not only execute demanding choreography, but carry a tune memorably at the same time. Those who could, the Jacksons as a case in point, raised the bar so high that many newcomers literally couldn't keep up. The solution many artists found came through the use of "backing tracks"—prerecorded song elements played during shows to cover up musical deficiencies and allow performers to execute their moves without being bogged down by the pesky details of pitch and projection.

Madonna, Paula Abdul, and Janet Jackson fended off charges that backing tracks made up the majority of their shows. Few performers acknowledged their use until a black European twosome called Milli Vanilli ("Blame It on the Rain," "Girl You Know It's True," and "Baby Don't Forget My Number") was trapped onstage with a faulty backing track repeating the same vocal line over and over before a full house. The disgraced duo surrendered their 1989 "Best New Artist" Grammy Award and, although they made attempts to put the incident behind them, one drifted into obscurity and the other died of a drug overdose in 1998.

In the 1980s pop world, everyone had a gimmick, with only the angle and the quality of subterfuge remaining in question. Copying sounds, songs, and groups were smart strategies and, on the rare occasion, the results could rise above the contrivance. En Vogue was such an exception. The Supremes inspired their fashion-meets-passion template, and like New Kids, En Vogue was built one component at a time as if from a kit. Here the masterminds were producers Denzil Foster and Thomas McElroy, who cut their teeth with Timex Social Club (Think "Rumors" from 1986) and Tony! Toni! Toné! ("Feels Good" from 1990), then scored their biggest hit with a hip-hop remake of Bill Withers' "Lean on Me" as Club Nouveau in 1987.

En Vogue picked up the torch of glamorous girl groups formerly carried by the Supremes, Three Degrees, and Pointer Sisters. With their image as no-nonsense sexpots, they strode onto MTV with the videos "My Lovin' (You're Never Gonna Get It)" and "Free Your Mind," both culled from their 1992 multiplatinum album, *Funky Divas*. (Jeffrey Mayer/Star File)

En Vogue may have begun as a marketing scheme, but synergy between the recruits made them more than the sum of their parts. Their material—part of the late 1980s "New Jack Swing" movement, where R&B vocals were layered over hip-hop beats—seamlessly blended radio fare with strident demands for equality. The singers chide the men who take them for granted on "My Lovin' (You're Never Gonna Get It)," and "Free Your Mind" gives them a chance to rail at prejudice no matter the source. "So I'm a sister, buy things with cash," one line snarls over a blazing guitar, "that doesn't mean that all my credit's bad." And, according to another, "Might date another race or color, that doesn't mean I don't like my strong black brother. . . ." The video is more powerful still. The quartet is pictured strutting a high fashion runway dressed to kill and spitting out the lyrics with a ferocious glee. In the 1960s, the Supremes' last singles with Diana Ross all had to do with bigotry, too—but where "Love Child" and "I'm Livin' in Shame" plead to withhold judgment, En Vogue use "My Lovin' (You're Never Gonna Get It)" and "Free Your Mind" to remind listeners that assumptions are just that.

HARD TO BE

Away from the paintball world of MTV, entire music scenes seemed to emerge, thrive, and pass into memory—all without relying on music video. This was a universe populated not by stars, but by musicians. They weren't always pretty, prepped in television interview techniques, or sponsored to model the latest designer wear. These artists toured most of the year, worked with black and white players and promoters, sold records in the millions, and spent more time developing their craft than its promotion through video.

MTV made the contrast apparent, but given the number of bands that have made roadwork a livelihood over the last hundred years, only a precious few ever achieved the notoriety of a Fats Waller or an Allman Brothers, let alone the global ubiquity of a Madonna. So while the music network ruled the entertainment capitals of New York and Los Angeles and country music held sway in Nashville and in the resort town of Branson, Missouri, that left a nation full of venues to play, and scores of music fans in each one of them who had no use for records by Milli Vanilli, New Kids on the Block, or Tiffany. Scores of performers repulsed by the artifice in contemporary music carved out a path of their own.

Boston-born Susan Tedeschi grew up during the 1980s, the daughter of a supermarket grocer. Early on, she remembers being entranced by the uncluttered honesty of blues records, and their scarcity in record shops only galvanized her. "It was so tough for young people coming up to find those albums," she recalls. "I was searching for stuff, and I couldn't find Magic Sam, Cobra Records, T-Bone Walker, you name it. You just couldn't get your hands on those kinds of records in suburban America. You were lucky to find B.B. King and John Lee Hooker albums. You sure didn't have a resource like Tower Records or the Internet back when I was little. So I would hunt through record shops."

Every day in hundreds of cities just like Boston—Cincinnati, Spokane, Jacksonville, Tucson, and, of all places, the home of "cosmic cowboy" country music, Austin, Texas—music lovers were on pilgrimages of their own. In the 1970s, Austin became internationally known as a hippie enclave with its own Fillmore-esque venue, Armadillo World Headquarters. When Willie Nelson abandoned Nashville, he moved to Austin, and within five years, the pop charts saw country crossover hits for a handful of sometime Austinites, among them Jerry Jeff Walker ("Mr. Bojangles," and "L.A. Freeway"), Ray Wylie Hubbard ("Redneck Mother"), Michael Martin Murphy ("Wildfire" and "Geronimo's Cadillac"), and B.W. Stevenson ("My Maria" and "Shambala").

At the height of Austin's mid-1970s infatuation with outlaw country, a Louisiana entrepreneur named Clifford Antone opened a club to showcase blues artists. "I hadn't been to Austin in years," says Buddy Guy, "and I couldn't believe the love they had for the blues. Austin in the '70s reminded me of a little Chicago and that's when I met Jimmie and Stevie Ray Vaughan at Antone's. It got so good, I didn't even have to take my band down there, I could just call up some Austin guys and they could play it all."

Television producer Terry Lickona was launching a new television series at the time called *Austin City Limits*. In his memory, "the Austin music scene was growing and shifting and changing in a lot of ways. Antone's was an obvious contrast to the progressive country/cosmic cowboy movement that had already taken root around then, so you had a variety of different movements bumping up against each other. And it's hard to know if one would have happened without the other as a catalyst, but either way, what you ended up with was a unique homegrown hybrid."

Drummer Chris Layton arrived in Austin at the end of 1975, and quickly fell in with the simmering blues scene at Antone's. Like many of his cohorts, he was as comfortable playing Willie's brand of redneck rock as a Willie Dixon 12-bar blues. "A lot of us just weren't interested in making those distinctions," he says. "I think there are George Jones and Merle Haggard songs that are just as soulful as Muddy Waters. It's hard to pin down, like what makes a painting beautiful, but I do think everybody recognizes it when they hear it. It's a response that comes from within."

"There were a number of factors that contributed to the rise of the blues in Austin," Lickona explains, "but Antone's was probably the biggest. When Clifford Antone opened his place on Sixth Street and started bringing in blues acts, nothing like that had happened within the memory of people who were there at the time. Not to ignore what had happened on the East side of town with the Victory Grill and things like that that had gone on years and decades before, because Austin has long had an identity of its own as a music town."

Over time, Antone's earned international renown as "the Home of the Blues," but in Austin many struggling musicians looked to the shifting roster of blues legends as guest tutors in the genre. Muddy Waters, Buddy Guy, and John Lee Hooker were all happy to find paying gigs, a genuinely receptive audience, and their names leading the marquee once more. Meanwhile local bands opened for them and on the off-nights, they wrestled with their own interpretations of the blues.

One night, Layton agreed to see his roommate's band, the Cobras, at a crosstown bar called Soap Creek Saloon. "I remember walking up and I could hear the band playing from outside, since it was a little, thin-framed house," he recalls. "I heard this guitar that sounded like it was outside the building, even though it wasn't any louder than anybody else. It was just this tone, right? The moment you walked in the door, you turned around and the band was down at the end of the room, but instantly you were mesmerized. I never saw anybody play like Stevie Ray Vaughan. He could play the same lick over and over and it still had the

Perhaps the last of the "guitarslingers," Stevie Ray Vaughan came to personify the blues during the latter half of the 1980s. Vaughan honed his fiery and fluid style in Austin, Texas during years of woodshedding alongside such blues greats as Muddy Waters and Buddy Guy. After a session stint on David Bowie's *Let's Dance* launched his career, Vaughan and his band Double Trouble led a revival of the blues that continues today with such diverse players as Robert Cray, Vaughan's brother Jimmie, Tracy Chapman, and Susan Tedeschi. (Chuck Pulin/Star File)

same power. I went out and saw the band several more times and wound up sitting in one time when the drummer was late. So I wound up playing with him before we met. He was up stage left, turned to me and kinda winked, like saying, *'All right . . .'"*

When Layton and Vaughan finally talked, each recognized their interests were mutual. "We both grooved on jazz, Stevie Wonder, and Jimi Hendrix, and generally saw a lot of things the same way," according to Layton. They began playing together while prospecting for musicians to complete their chemistry. Stevie formed a brief alliance with Triple Threat, a group that included blues singer Lou Ann Barton. "But the whole scene was very much a purist kind of clique at the time," says the drummer. "Lou Ann would yell, 'What the hell are you playing all that Goddamned Hendrix rock shit for?' There was a whole attitude about the hair, the sharkskin suits, and the Brogan shoes, and the whole look. I thought, 'Well, that's all cool but it doesn't have anything to do with playing the blues.' And I don't think Stevie gave a crap about any of that."

Within a few months, the band splintered apart, ex-Johnny Winter bassist Tommy Shannon signed on, and the group became Stevie Ray Vaughan and Double Trouble. "From there, we were off to the races, just like that," Layton shrugs. "Stevie would say, 'Let's do some Jimmie Reed,' Sure! 'And let's do some Hendrix.' Okay, let's do that, too. It was kind of a done deal."

The endorsement of producer Jerry Wexler landed the as-yet-unsigned band on the bill of Switzerland's Montreux Jazz Festival in 1982. David Bowie caught the show and immediately enlisted Vaughan to play on the sessions that became the album *Let's Dance*. Singer/songwriter Jackson Browne was also in the crowd and offered free time at his studio to record. Vaughan declined an offer to join Bowie on the road, but his work on the album led legions back to the source. Legendary producer John Hammond (the man behind Billie Holiday, Aretha Franklin, Bob Dylan, and Bruce Springsteen) signed them, the Jackson Browne tapes were soon issued on Epic as the group's first record, *Texas Flood* in 1983.

More directly descended from Chicago blues than that other Texas trio, ZZ Top, Vaughan and company built an audience the old fashioned way: one gig at a time. "It's funny, though," says Layton, "because as much as we loved blues, we never had a black audience. Our audience was all blue-collar, working-class, white American males. At least that's the demographic we were told were buying our records. But I'm also happy to say that I never met many black people who didn't really like our stuff. And all those guys, Albert Collins, B.B. King—they all knew Stevie was the real deal. They didn't talk much about it, but you could tell by the way they made time for him personally; that spoke millions of words. They'd look at Stevie like he was some kind of adopted son."

To this day, Layton says he's not quite sure how Vaughan communicated blackness through white skin: "More than once, Stevie said, 'I'm prejudiced against white people.' If there was anybody who was more black, more imbued of the core black spirit and black sensibility, I don't know who it'd be. And the only reason I can speak about it intelligently is because a lot of black people who knew him felt the same way. They'd say, 'Yeah, he's just like a lot of black people I know.'"

The best shows transported Vaughan out of his skin entirely. "We'd have a really good show and come offstage," Layton remembers, "and Stevie would say to us, 'We sounded like niggas tonight,' which was the highest compliment possible. Some people would gasp at that, I know. But he meant that we were really getting deep into the grooves and the music was funky and it meant we were sounding more like black people than the white boys we were."

Vaughan became the world's most popular blues guitarist since Jimi Hendrix and Eric Clapton vied for the title in 1970. Unlike them, he wasn't trying to stretch the blues to say something new, but trying to stretch himself within its elastic framework. He never had a hit single, but his albums with Double Trouble, *Couldn't Stand the Weather* (1984), *Soul to Soul* (1985), and *Live Alive* (1986) sold in the millions. Many Chicago blues legends praised his talent. One assessed Vaughan's debt in a very tangible way. During the sessions for *In Step* in the late 1980s, Albert King dropped by ("and Stevie worshipped at the altar of Albert King," his bandmate says) asking to borrow money from the rising star. No one can recall the exact amount, but in Layton's words, "it wasn't chump change."

"And so we were about to leave. We're just about to go, and Stevie says, 'Well, we're about to leave, Albert . . .' And Albert says, 'Oh, well, good. Now that's all right. Okay.' Stevie asks him, 'I was wondering if I could get back the money that I loaned you . . .' Albert says, 'Money? Money? Come on now, son. You know you owe me, don't you?' And he left without ever paying. The back end of the story is that a good friend who heard what happened said later, 'Well, Stevie, with all the stuff you got from Albert, did you consider that a good deal?' Stevie thought for a second and said, 'Yeah, I did.' Now Albert King never sold two million records, and if you listen to Stevie, over and over again, you can say, 'There's Albert King. There's Albert King.' So I thought it was a pretty classy move that Stevie was fine with it."

Vaughan triumphed over drug and alcohol addiction, made a much-beloved record with his brother Jimmie called *Family Style*, and perished in a 1990 helicopter crash shortly after appearing at a Wisconsin blues summit alongside Eric Clapton, Jimmie, Buddy Guy, and Robert Cray.

"The night he died, we had our first conversation about the next album with Double Trouble," Layton remembers. "He was excited about going out with Jimmie to promote *Family Style*, but already getting worked up about playing with us again. And we were excited, too, because the more he played the more he became Stevie Ray Vaughan. Of course, he used to hear all the time how he was a world-class player and he didn't need us. And some years later, I told somebody else, 'you know what, I probably *wasn't* good enough to play with Stevie.' But in a way nobody was, and so it might as well have been me, because I loved him more than anybody else. We all cared about each other, and that whole chemistry and that family kind of thing translated to the music."

The blues resurgence occupied a universe parallel to the so-called "hair bands" of the late 1980s, a throng of headbangers led by the well-coiffed likes of Poison, Whitesnake, and Guns 'n' Roses. These groups used the blues in much the same way as Led Zeppelin and Van Halen before them—as a port of call before embarking on their forays into heavy metal. Like Hank Williams before him, the simplicity of Stevie Ray Vaughan's music ensures its timelessness for decades to come. And, although there were many music videos in the band's career (including clips for "Cold Shot," "Superstition," and "Crossfire") he and Double Trouble demonstrated that a rocking blues trio was still a viable commercial force around the country without genuflecting to MTV's *Total Request Live* fan base.

"The blues has remained a ghettoized music and the incomes of blues players have stayed steady but have never been great," Bonnie Raitt reflects. "There have been isolated crossover hits like 'The Thrill Is Gone,' and songs sometimes break through on their own strength, things like 'Smoking Gun' by Robert Cray and Tracy Chapman's 'Give Me Some Kind of Reason.' But breakthroughs like *The Healer* from John Lee [Hooker, in 1989] are few and far between. Sometimes I don't know how things like that happen. Maybe all the stars lined up to make that particular promotional campaign work."

Through its flavor-of-the-month process of selecting videos, MTV and its sister network VH 1 introduced and expelled artists across the spectrum of contemporary music. Acts like Bobby McFerrin (performance art), Lyle Lovett (alternative country), and Harry Connick, Jr. (jazz) might make a token few appearances, only to disappear—not into obscurity, but out into the real world, with gigs for the asking at college auditoriums, nightclubs, and theaters across the globe.

DIAMONDS ON THE SOUL

Some, like Paul Simon, were caught between authenticity and artifice. In 1986, Simon's *Graceland* was hailed as a major work from an artist with long established ties to world music. In truth, Simon contributed to the genre long before record stores had a section for it. His Peruvian-inflected "El Condor Pasa" appeared on the last Simon & Garfunkel LP, 1970's *Bridge Over Troubled Water*, and his first two solo singles, "Me & Julio Down By the Schoolyard" and "Mother and Child Reunion" brought international sounds to AM radio when few others dared try.

To create the mosaic of exotic rhythms and harmonies that became *Graceland*, Simon enrolled household names like Linda Ronstadt, the Everly Brothers, and Los Lobos alongside South Africans virtually unknown in America, including the Gaza Sisters, Ladysmith Black Mambazo, and a dozen more. At the time, Nelson Mandela remained imprisoned and the South African government still held its society together through the repressive policies of apartheid. Had Simon imported the artists of Soweto and the sounds of their township jive back to the States, he would have been accused of looting African culture. Instead, much of the album was recorded in Johannesburg, where Simon paid session musicians triple the union scale rates.

Graceland shipped in 1986 to nearly universal acclaim, but Simon was blacklisted by the United Nations and the African National Congress for flouting their cultural boycott. (The rebuke was withdrawn the next year when Simon agreed in writing to abide by terms of the boycott henceforth.) Casual listeners warmed to the record's happy-go-lucky hit, "You Can Call Me Al" and the globetrotting flavor woven so well into his signature sound.

But the album was a public relations minefield. For each of Simon's acts of magnanimity, an opposing factoid would surface to suggest he was exploiting his source of inspiration. The entertainment press described two opposing Paul Simons, each doing his best to outmaneuver the other. The good Paul lent his voice to U.S.A. for Africa in singing "We Are the World" just before leaving for Johannesburg to record. On *Graceland*, bad Paul showcased Linda Ronstadt, who had also just run the cultural blockade to perform in the South African resort town of Sun City. Good Paul refused to play Sun City personally, and shared the stage of his world tour with anti-apartheid African artists

Hugh Masekela, Miriam Makeba, and Ladysmith Black Mambazo. He also took repeated opportunities to publicly defend his motives as musical rather than political, and released a live *Graceland* video shot in Zimbabwe. Conversely, Bad Paul kept himself listed as the sole producer of *Graceland* and the holder of all its copyrights—ensuring that in an admittedly collaborative effort, he would remain the point man for awards and that royalty payments would tilt heavily in his favor.

PUSH IT

By definition, the music business is an uneasy alliance between creative forces and a capitalist agenda. Because that's true, artists and those who profit from their work are constantly renegotiating their loyalties. The process (dramatically simplified) works something like this: musical deviations from the norm (as bebop branched off from swing and rock 'n' roll diverged from R&B) are dismissed out of hand as fads. Once a movement earns cachet with the underground, though, it's quickly labeled as subversive, then grudgingly acknowledged to have artistic merit, until finally the most commercial aspects of the innovation are picked apart, diluted, and incorporated into the mainstream. MTV accelerated this chain reaction to a point where results were practically like a delivery from Fed Ex—absolutely positively overnight. What was avant-garde on Thursday could be bought online by Friday's lunchbreak The short attention span edits, Day-Glo spray-painted sets, and objectification of the sexes rapidly spread from one network into the others, then out into the magazine world and beyond.

By the late 1980s, the network was practically a demographic unto itself—an audience of immense discretionary income whose buying power would only grow over the ensuing decades. Big business wasted no time in cozying up to music icons (most major tours have corporate sponsors these days), and companies paid dearly to license baby boomer classics for their products. Michael Jackson was thrashed by the media for renting out the Beatles' "Revolution" to promote Nike, while everyone from Lionel Richie to Robert Plant hawked Pepsi and Diet Coke. Rock iconoclast Neil Young tweaked them all with "This Note's for You," a tune and music video where superstar pitchmen were caught *en flagrante* shilling for millions.

A small consolation: advertisers finally came to understand that licensing a track from the Rolling Stones or Muddy Waters offered more prestige than re-creating a cheaper imitation by the California Raisins. "Ad people were able to sell a lot of Levis and t-shirts, and trucks on TV, usually with white copies of black blues songs," says Bonnie Raitt. "I've heard more slide guitar on television than I have in mainstream radio over the last thirty years. Anytime you want to connote danger or sex and you have a truck driving over a dirt road, it's there, coopting that whole sense of foreboding. It's the same reason they use blues images in ads for cigarettes and alcohol; it's that devil side. So they play these slinky grooves to get people to give into their deep dark passions."

"What we're talking about is the difference between music and the music business," says Vernon Reid of the black rock band Living Colour. "We're talking about who controls the means of production, who ultimately profits from what is produced, and who is producing the thing that's being exploited."

But by 1990, the old certainties were disappearing. The sharecropper agreements between artists and their labels—practices that had been in place for nearly a century—were fraying at both ends. Labels played their game more conservatively, with fewer signings and more diligent searches for that artist who could write, play, perform, and look good on camera while doing so. Likewise, performers came to understand that the windfall advances and lavish parties they dreamed of were always charged back to them, and promptly retained high-powered lawyers to negotiate more favorable contracts. When hip-hop and the black slang called "Ebonics" became political footballs, the same record companies that defended protest music in the 1960s now left rappers to fend for themselves in the halls of Congress. And while no one was paying any attention, a mole called Napster quietly tunneled its way into the heart of the music business and began to feed.

NOTES

1 George, Nelson. *The Death of Rhythm & Blues.* New York: Penguin Books, 1988, p. 171.

2 Boyd, Todd. *H.N.I.C.: The Death of Civil Rights and the Reign of Hip Hop.* New York: New York University Press, 2003, p. xxi.

3 Hill, Dave. *Prince: A Pop Life.* New York: Harmony Books, 1989, pp. 108–109.

CHAPTER NINE

Wigga
Wonderland

efore hip-hop crept into the Top 40 during the second half of the 1980s, commuters could punch their FM buttons at random to find talents ranging from Garth Brooks to Anita Baker or Stevie Ray Vaughan—something for anyone trying to pass the time between daydreams and stoplights. Now hip-hop was everywhere. It swept through 1990s rhythm and blues like a tenement fire, leaving Whitney Houston a burned-out husk and innovators like Prince and Michael Jackson without a home. The phat beats and bravado of rap infiltrated Kurt Cobain's beloved grunge, too, corroding it from the inside out with headbanging choruses bracketed by rhymes from white bands like Faith No More, House of Pain, and Rage Against the Machine.

As the highest profile component of hip-hop culture, rap was easily the most radical (and the most black) detour from the mainstream since rock's arrival fifty years earlier, and in its wake, rap bashing became as fashionable in the halls of Congress as the music was on the streets outside. Throughout the 1990s and well into the new millennium, politicians assailed the music as a sewer of sound backing up into every home in suburban America. Vernon Reid, lead guitarist of the black rock group Living Colour, rattled them further by defending rap as "a vessel for the sound of black male rage." To the ears of protective parents and vigilantes, Reid might as well have claimed it causes cancer, too.

Former Reagan administration education secretary William Bennett spent much of the 1990s railing against the music industry, demanding that it protect children from morally bankrupt rappers and "stop its involvement with and support of gross, violent, offensive, and misogynistic lyrics." Among his supporters: Dr. C. Delores Tucker, an activist who once marched alongside Dr. Martin Luther King, Jr., then served as Pennsylvania's Secretary of State in the 1970s. She wasn't against rap per se, but felt that the gangsta strain undercut the respect that she and other blacks risked their lives for during the civil rights struggle. "Gangsta rap is a perverted form," she explained to reporter Erika Blount, "which had been encouraged by those who have always used the entertainment industry to exploit and project the negative stereotypical images to demean and depict African Americans as subhuman, which is the antithesis of what we as African American people are."

Many eyed hip-hop's appeal to young Americans with profound ambivalence. In one breath, proponents rejoiced that the nation was getting its ethnic music undiluted for the first time since the glory days of bebop in the 1940s; in another, detractors countered that rap glorified nearly every one of modern society's worst problems—gang violence, bigotry, materialism, and misogyny. More unsettling still was that this contagion wouldn't stay in its place—among inner city blacks.

To paraphrase a popular TV commercial of the day, it was all just a bit of history repeating. Hip-hop culture promised Adventure. Scorn. Danger. Sex. And, as always, white youth was beguiled by rap's possibilities of the unknown. A century before, youngsters followed ragtime's clatter from their parlors into across-the-tracks juke joints. Their children did the same when they slunk into dingy speakeasies to soak up the jazz and gin, just as their kids in turn answered the siren call of blues and rock 'n' roll. Now teenagers craved a new thrill, something to call their own. "Rock is old," one hip-hop impresario told *TIME* magazine in 1999. "It's old people's shit. The creative people who are great, who are talking about youth culture in a way that makes sense, happen to be rappers."

Rap's focus on alienation and disenfranchisement resonated clearly for adolescents, and although hip-hop culture hailed from the ghettos of urban America (not a circumstance to which the average teen in Anytown U.S.A. finds immediately relatable), it was also partially constructed of recycled rock melodies and beats snipped from 1970s funk bands. Those samples turned rap into a pop music Trojan horse, with enough recognizable elements to attract pop radio programmers and new listeners, while the lyrics within repeated a kind of me-first mantra that kids—both neglected and spoiled—found irresistible.

LADIES FIRST

Just as white men created *Playboy* in the 1950s to express their dreams and realities, rap began as a playground for the fantasies and frustrations of black males. And even though female rappers began to pop up in small clubs around the city at the end of the 1970s, their presence did little to change its Mens' Club mentality. Many women didn't find that ethically tricky at all. Since they had been raised in the same milieu as the creators of rap, breakdancing, tagging, and the rest, it made sense that hip-hop culture would reflect the values of its inventors. Besides, if rap was supposed to be locker-room talk for the boys, then girls could demand equal time to dish *their* dirt. And when the time came for toasting or playing the dozens, no one talked trash like the ladies.

The Bronx hip-hop scene was still in its infancy when women began assembling their own crews to perform at schools and parties throughout the neighborhood. There were all-female breakdancing troupes, girls publicizing their names and exploits in spray paint, and women making names for themselves as dancers or deejays. Just as often, they were involved behind the scenes, taking care of business.

Sylvia Robinson was the first entrepreneur to risk money to put rap on record. Robinson, a veteran R&B singer (who hit with "Love Is Strange" in 1957 as part of Mickey & Sylvia), was responsible for underwriting and distributing "Rapper's Delight" on the

Sugar Hill label in 1979. Initially, Sugar Hill was *the* rap label. But after signing and recording such rap progenitors as the Treacherous Three and Grandmaster Flash and the Furious Five, Robinson found her company caught in an industry crossfire.

In 1983, Grandmaster Flash quit the label in frustration, convinced that Robinson would never crack mainstream radio for her artists. Melle Mel and the other partners of Furious Five remained at Sugar Hill, while Flash was quickly snapped up by Elektra, a division of Warner/Elektra/Atlantic. In all likelihood, Robinson's misfortune had less to do with issues of black and white, and everything to do with the color of money. When Robinson faltered (she missed multiple opportunities to sign L.L. Cool J, for example), newer indie labels Def Jam, Tommy Boy, and Profile rushed in to fill the void. Sugar Hill entered its own distribution deal with MCA in the mid-1980s, but it was too little too late. Robinson and her label are now best remembered not only for staking money on the hunch that this music would sell, but for being first to release successful singles by female rappers, including a group called Sequence, who cut the disco–rap hybrids "Funk You Up" and "Monster Jam" in 1979.

There were other female trailblazers, of course, although most went woefully un-recorded. Of these, most were found alongside a deejay or a male rapping companion. Among them were Sweet & Sour (who worked with Grandmixer DST.), Little Lee (paired with Kool DJ AJ), and the Mercedes Ladies (who went uncredited on the regional hit, "Don's Groove," by Donald D.). The first rap track to feature a female lead was "To the Beat, Ya'll," recorded in 1980 by Lady B. In 1981, *Saturday Night Live* featured rap for the first time in showcasing Funky Four + One, in which female rapper Sha Rock was the "One" singled out.

As MC Lady "D" explained to *Vibe* reporter Laura Jamison, most women preferred the simplicity of rhyming to the responsibility of playing or producing an event, hard-ware included. A female rapper, she told Jamison, "didn't have to worry about getting her equipment ripped off, coming up with the cash to get it in the first place, or hauling it around on the subways to gigs—problems that kept a lot of other women out of rap in the early days."

Women remained among the best-kept secrets on the hip-hop scene throughout the early 1980s. They could be sexy, but unlike their contemporaries in pop, rock, or soul, they were never demure. Some were overtly political—like Lisa Lee, who went from work with Afrika Bambaataa's Zulu Nation to a triumverate called Us Girls, which featured the already well-known Debbie Dee of Mercedes Ladies and Sha Rock. But as rap moved out of the inner cities and into the suburbs, female rappers retreated into comical catfighting records that did little more than update the cutting contests of yesteryear with hip-hop beats.

One such shoutdown ushered in the first female group to cross over from rap to pop success. In 1986, part-time student Hurby "Luv Bug" Azor asked Cheryl James and Sandy Denton (a pair of his coworkers at the local Sears) to rap on a track for his audio production class at Queensborough College. And, since the fad *du jour* was dissing some-one else's record while proclaiming your own primacy, Azor decided to challenge a track called "The Show" by Doug E. Fresh and Slick Rick. The girls' response record, "The Show Stoppa," gamely scrambled to #46 on the R&B chart, and Azor took over manag-ing the duo. He added turntablist DJ Spinderella (first Pamela Greene, later Dee Dee Roper) to the mix, then changed the group's name from Super Nature to Salt-n-Pepa.

Their first album, *Hot, Cool & Vicious,* was released in 1987 on the independent label Next Plateau and featured three singles that buzzed around the R&B charts, "Chick on the Side," "My Mike Sounds Nice," and "Tramp." But when a San Francisco DJ named Cameron Paul remixed the B-side of "Tramp," the world heard Salt-n-Pepa as they came to love them—loud, sassy, and fearless—with "Push It." With its synthesized bass line and Kinks' quotes ("Boy, you really got me/ You got me so/I don't know what I'm doin'"), "Push It" (#19 pop hit) became the first huge female rap single in 1988. It also gave girls a role model alternative to Madonna and the tough as Press-On Nails Pat Benatar.

Salt-n-Pepa might have sailed through a respectable pop career unnoticed with forgettable reworkings of the Isley Brothers tunes "It's Your Thing" and "Twist and Shout" and punny albums like 1988's *A Salt With A Deadly Pepa.* But with the release of *Blacks' Magic* (#15 R&B and #38 pop hits) in 1990, the group took an Afrocentric turn that burnished their credibility with peers and fans alike. Some tracks were produced (again) by Azor, others by freelancer Steevee-O. But four tracks were produced by Cheryl "Salt" James, and her "Expression" spent eight weeks in the #1 slot of the R&B charts and went gold before going pop, where it topped out at #26. In addition, the group had another across-the-board pop smash in "Let's Talk About Sex" (#13 hit, 1991), which they rerecorded two years later as "Let's Talk about AIDS." The duo and Spinderella returned to pop after signing with a major label, London/PolyGram, and dismissing Azor, and continued to score the occasional hit, including "Shoop" (#3 R&B and #4 pop hits in 1993), a duet with En Vogue called "Whatta Man" in 1994 (#3 hit on both the R&B and pop charts), and "None of Your Business" (#57 R&B and #32 pop hits).

Blacks' Magic arrived just as the Native Tongues movement (represented in part by the Jungle Brothers, A Tribe Called Quest, and De La Soul) was attempting to supplant rap's growing emphasis on violence and avarice with a more positive Afrocentrism. The movement's most visible proponent was Queen Latifah (Dana Owens), who issued an album in 1989 called *All Hail the Queen* and a single, "Ladies First," that instantly announced her to the hip-hop community and beyond. At all of nineteen years of age, Latifah appeared as a contemporary Venus—fully formed in her African garb with a British ally (rapper Monie Love) in tow, and a supremely catchy pro-woman manifesto to chant. (Never mind that the tune was composed by Latifah's "homeboy," a fellow named Apache, who had earlier written a track called "Gangsta Bitch.") If hip-hop is about triumph over adversity, Latifah wore hers like a crown. Following the lackluster performance of her sophomore record, *Nature of a Sista'* (1991), she was dropped by Tommy Boy Records and picked up by Motown, who issued the acclaimed *Black Reign* in 1993. The disc not only went gold; it earned Latifah a Grammy award for another landmark single, "U.N.I.T.Y. (Who You Calling a Bitch?)."

With aspirations as big as her voice, Latifah branched out into a series of memorable acting roles. The Queen brought a much-needed spice to Spike Lee's 1991 film, *Jungle Fever,* subsequently starred for four seasons on the Fox sitcom *Living Single,* and turned an ancillary role in the 2002 film musical *Chicago* into enough industry buzz to generate an Oscar nomination. Although she's starred in a string of innocuous comedies since then, her ability to rise above unremarkable material and unpredictable circumstances demonstrates her value as rap's most authentic ambassador to Hollywood.

In a culture where thin was in and female rappers were either slinky sex kittens or curvier members of the b-boy crew, Latifah made it safe for women to rap with as much dignity as they did abandon. Her contemporaries were reluctant to follow, however. In the male-centric environment of hip-hop, men felt free to rap about TV, food, sports, or death. Once the genre became an industry, women were expected to dwell on topics related to sex and the sexes, and to do so cleverly enough that both genders would want to buy their records, see their shows, and listen to them on the radio. Many played the game well, and dared on occasion to violate musical boundaries (think of Neneh Cherry's "Buffalo Stance" blurring the lines between rap and new jack swing, as did Technotronic with "Pump Up the Jam"), but most kept to reactive rather than proactive roles throughout rap's early years. When rumors circulated that Salt-n-Pepa planned to record a rock/rap hybrid with Joan Jett, interest from both camps was fervent. The project was never realized, though, perhaps because all concerned deemed the idea too progressive for its time. After all, girls were supposed to wanna have *fun*.

RITE TO PARTY

In 1986, after years of jealous glances and fumbled overtures, rap and rock did finally discover common ground. That was the year a group from Queens called Run-D.M.C. tossed the Aerosmith FM staple "Walk This Way" into their hip-hop Cuisinart and poured out a rock/rap elixir more potent than frathouse punch. Since deejays had long poached on the preserve of classic rock to sample a drum riff here, a bass line there, and an encyclopedia of guitar hooks, it certainly wasn't the music that was different: it had to be the men in the mix.

Run-D.M.C. arrived on the scene when rap was still struggling for an identity separate from its influences. Through the group's principles, Run (Joey Simmons), D.M.C. (Darryl McDaniels), and turntable wizard Jam Master Jay (Jason Mizell), the music became irrevocably itself. Their beats were teeth rattling, their rhymes were lobbed like some fish market catch of the day between Run and his partner, and their topics embraced anything worthy of conversation, moving on from the polemics of "The Message" and the party-hardy vapidity in "Rapper's Delight." In addition, it was Run-D.M.C. who popularized rap's first identifiable gear—the fedoras, the goggle-eyed Cazal glasses, the ever-present but never tied Adidas sneakers, and a pirate's helping of gold chains and medallions.

Run's brother Russell Simmons masterminded the business end, serving as the band's co-producer, manager, and ultimately part owner of their label, Def Jam. The group's initial releases included the 1983 Top 20 R&B hit, "It's Like That"/"Sucker MCs," and in 1984, the Latin-tinged "Rock Box" landed them on the dance charts (being too coarse to pass for anything else). By 1985, Run-D.M.C. found themselves on the Philly bill at Live Aid alongside Hall & Oates, Madonna, and Bob Dylan. They had catapulted rap out of the ghetto and onto the TV screens of suburban America, but now in this unfamiliar terrain they stood alone in the limelight with retreat impossible and an uncertain road ahead.

"Walk This Way" provided what they needed—a hall pass into the heartland and a touchstone for the future that both rappers and rockers could follow. Through subtle shifts in attitude and proportion, the track breaks with earlier attempts to graft rap and rock, due in part to Run-D.M.C.'s white producer (and Def Jam founding father) Rick Rubin. A fan of both genres, Rubin helped construct a grudge match between one of rock's most salacious riffs and a hip-hop rhythm track that lashes out like a mean older brother.

The video ratchets up the drama by pitting Run-D.M.C. against Aerosmith's Steven Tyler and Joe Perry, the creators of the original. Together, their collaboration marks the most literal depiction of crossover ever put before a camera, with each group performing its version of "Walk This Way" separated by a brick wall—with Tyler and Perry goading a white crowd on one side while Run-D.M.C. throw down before a black audience on the other. At the climax, the rappers burst through the barrier to win over the (white) Aerosmith fans. Tellingly, Run-D.M.C.'s core audience does not follow. By the time it was all over, *Raising Hell,* the album that included "Walk This Way," became the first rap record to reach the top of the R&B charts; the disc sold some three million copies, and the single topped out in the fall of 1986 at #4 of *Billboard*'s Top 10.

That was the same year another of Rubin's rapping protégés broke through to the mainstream. Unlike Run-D.M.C., the Beastie Boys were white Brooklynites, and their 1986 LP, *Licensed to Ill,* erupted to become Columbia's fastest selling debut ever.

By their own admission, the Beasties—Adam Yauch (MCA), Mike Diamond (Mike D), and Adam Horovitz (Ad-Rock)—were originally more focused on cutting up than cutting records. Although they eventually outgrew their anarchic image, the group originally considered calling their first release *Don't Be a Faggot.* Whether *Licensed to Ill* succeeds despite or because of its juvenilia misses the point. Teens and college kids loved the record's contemporary take on the staples of adolescence. There were anti-authority jams, including the hardcore first hit, "(You Gotta) Fight for Your Right" (#7 pop hit, 1987), drinking songs ("Brass Monkey"), tunes about girls ("Girls"), and the obligatory group history, "Paul Revere." Again, Rubin set the album's tone; this time it's a house party in full effect, complete with a stereo blaring rock riffs, revelers yelling across the room, and the sound of someone seemingly sitting on a TV remote, causing it to change channels— and samples—every few beats. Short on attention span, long on laughs, and with better rhymes and rhythms than anyone expected, *Licensed to Ill* (released by Columbia under a 1985 distribution agreement with Def Jam) became the first rap record to top the pop album charts in 1987, and at last count has sold well over eight million copies.

While the group may have appeared groomed for MTV and the stardom that ensued, the Beastie Boys spent years rapping to whites who didn't care and black audiences who considered their act an affront. They were heckled in the early 1980s at rap's first real home, a Bronx club called Disco Fever, and they dodged debris at the legendary Apollo Theatre in Harlem, where one rapper swears he heard a Beastie yelp, "All you niggers wave your hands in the air!" According to the MC, "I've never seen so many blank stares." When their New York connections scored them an opening slot on Madonna's 1985 tour, they made certain the Material Girl's audience of ingénues left suitably mortified. (At one point, the Beasties' set design included a caged go-go dancer gyrating before a giant inflated phallus, and their souvenir t-shirts announced in big block letters, "Get off My Dick.") Crude humor, chutzpah, and talent would prevail, they insisted. "You must understand one basic fact about the Beastie Boys," MCA told *Creem* reporter Joanne Carnegie at the time, "and that's that we do *anything* we want. Besides that, we've heard the word: 'You white boys are the coolest ever.'"

GETTIN' WIGGY

Consider "Walk This Way" and "Fight for Your Right" as a pair of sonograms—snapshots in the womb of the newest incarnation of the American minstrel, The Wigga. Contemporary slang describes wiggas as young whites who prefer the customs and uniforms of hip-hop to the exclusion of signifying their own cultural inheritance. Just as disaffected black kids adopted the term "nigga" to detoxify and reclaim the word "nigger" and to differentiate themselves from blacks seeking to assimilate, wiggas are in various stages of rebellion against the white-dominated status quo. Many are called to wiggadom at that moment when the pinch of adolescence is most acute; they're kids too old to accept parental authority at face value, and as yet untouched by the financial penalties that nonconformity can bring. Like their great-grandparents who scandalized polite society by Lindy-Hopping to jazz and swilling moonshine, teens of the 21st century envision hip-hop as a backstage of cool just beyond the padlocked doors of propriety.

In fact, the hip-hop code of ethics—to hell with rules, fuck authority, pay me now, get me to the party, get me high, and get me laid—merely updates the lifestyle last espoused by disco, without the social niceties ("Hi, what's your sign?"). Just as *The Godfather* movies glamorized decadence disguised as class in the 1970s, rap reveres the naked hedonism of another Al Pacino film, 1983's *Scarface*, where all that matters is the instant gratification of the next impulse, whether it's sex, drugs, power, the latest gadget or bauble.

In order to maintain its counterculture appeal, hip-hop must try (or appear to try) to thwart white access. Just how badly white kids crave entré into black culture was well illustrated by a group of white rappers who hoped to legitimize themselves by naming their band Young Black Teenagers and including a tune on their debut album called "Proud to Be Black." In a race for self-preservation, hip-hop constantly changes styles and regularly re-encrypts its jargon—which white aspirants just as quickly decode and drop into their conversations. In this donkey-and-carrot scenario, suburban kids scour the malls for knockoffs of rap's latest trinkets of rebellion, and hip-hop is obliged to introduce new elements or lose credibility among its home base of inner city youth. It's an advertising dream come true—a perpetual motion machine of supply and demand.

Following trends and quoting rap stars is no wigga E-ticket to the Magic Kingdom of hip-hop, either. Much like the bebop of the 1940s, rap's posture of resisting white intrusion keeps the music and lifestyle enticing to a segment of white youth, just as it did in eras long since vanished. In a collection of essays called *Everything But the Burden: What White People Are Taking from Black Culture*, Carl Hancock Rux writes that hip-hop is "still an outsider culture, perpetuating its own outsider mythology, and if there are nonblack, economically privileged teenagers who wear their oversized jeans pulled down around their knees and sleep beneath posters of self-proclaimed rapists, gang members, and murderers with record deals, it is because every generation of youth culture since Socrates has identified with outsider/outcast/radicalism, and typically pursued some kind of participation in it."[1]

Madison Avenue richly deserves the enmity of hip-hoppers for diluting black culture into mall fodder, but advertising didn't create that desire. The white itch to affect blackness is an ineffable part of the American experience. Nearly two hundred years ago, Stephen Foster won accolades for his approximations of African American slaves and their music. In the jazz age, Cab Calloway's fans plunked down two bits for a *Hepcat Dic-*

tionary compiled by their zoot-suited idol, and by the 1960s and 1970s white fascination with black jargon had become the stuff of farce. (Recall the 1980 disaster spoof *Airplane!* where a conversation between soul brothers requires subtitles and Barbara Billingsley—Beaver Cleaver's TV Mom—calms a flight attendant with her reassurance, "It's all right, stewardess, I speak jive.")

Wigga wannabes are discouraged not only through freshly minted phrases, but also through a liberal use of household expletives. Certainly raunchy ditties have a rich history that predates records by thousands of years, but once the music industry became a bankrolled enterprise in the 1920s, the vast majority of artists retreated into the shadows of double-entendre to crack their dirty jokes.

"As every book about raising kids will tell you," Lorraine Ali opined in a 2000 *Newsweek* article, "children need limits—in part to protect them, and in part to give them boundaries to smash and trample. Generation after generation of iconoclasts, from Joyce and Picasso to Elvis and Marilyn to punks and gangstas, have gradually pushed the limits a little further."

By the turn of the century, even the ladies were leaving nothing to the imagination. "Pussy don't fail me now, I gotta turn this nigga out," Missy Elliot rhymes on "Pussycat" from 2002's *Under Construction*, "so he don't want nobody else but me and only me." Elliott may rap in the gutter, but her reasons for doing so are grounded in both the First Amendment and the timeless battle of the sexes. The album also includes her justification: "People always say, 'yo, that's too nasty,' and 'why yo' mouth so vulgar?' 'Why you gotta sing all those nasty records and all that?' But I be representin' for the ladies and we got something to say. We been quiet too long; ladylike, very patient. We didn't get mad when Prince had his ass out (on the *MTV Video Music Awards*). We thought he was gonna turn around to the front and have the front out, too. But that didn't happen. We always had to deal with the guys talking about how they gonna wear us out on records. So I had to do records that's strictly representing for my ladies, and how to keep your man, keep his eye from wandering, lookin' around. Sex is not a topic that we should always sweep under the rug."

But according to Ray Charles, "Music ain't never supposed to be filthy, ever. I remember the old blues singers, they'd be talking about pussy and yet you never hear the word. It'd be, 'I wanna play with your poodle,' or something like that. *Mmmm . . .* (sings) *Your little poodle dog!!* You don't have to say 'bitch' or 'whore.' That's too far for me, and maybe I'm too old-fashioned, but I think music ought to be beautiful. And if you wanna talk about sex, there's a thousand ways to say what you wanna say without being filthy."

Here rap and rock part company. In the 1970s, Robert Plant moaned, "squeeze my lemon 'till the juice runs down my leg" on *Led Zeppelin III*, and ZZ Top followed suit a decade later to offer ladies their very own "Pearl Necklace" (gutter slang for the residue of oral sex). But across the color line in hip-hop, 1980s artists often spiked their records with "pussy," "dick," and "motherfucker," while a maverick like Prince might skitter from one to the other. Sometimes the metaphor would suffice, as it did in his vaginal homage, "Sugar Walls." But occasionally he opts for the more direct approach with a title like "Jack U Off," or lets slip in "Let's Pretend We're Married" that he'd "sincerely want to fuck the taste out of your mouth."

When Tipper Gore, the wife of U.S. Senator Al Gore, bought a copy of "Sugar Walls" for their eight-year-old daughter before discovering its sexual nature, she decided that the music industry needed a good housecleaning. In 1985, Democrat Gore founded a cabal of well-heeled women that included Republican Mrs. James Baker, wife to the Secretary of the Treasury, and more than a dozen ladies married to prominent politicos. All that stood between them and the gleaming bastion of morality they sought were America's record companies and the First Amendment to the Constitution of the United States.

PARENTS DON'T UNDERSTAND

By the time Gore's Parents Music Resource Center (PMRC) materialized to scour the smut from contemporary music, rock had little connection to blacks. No matter. By focusing on the offense rather than the offenders, Gore and her group were able to revive the sentiments of the 1950s that claimed that rock 'n' roll was "immoral" and "sexualistic." Since the twin genies of sex and drugs had run free in Western society since the Beatles' heyday, there was no need to place blame on blacks exclusively, anyway—they would become targets on their own when the PMRC began to examine rap.

"Animalistic nigger bop," it had been called in the 1950s. Democrats in the 1980s shrank from such graphic terms about the music's origins. Instead, they retreated into jargon that went well with coffee breaks and commutes to and from the job—where music content could be weighed sensibly according to its "family values."

In 1985, the PMRC rolled onto the network morning shows, afternoon chat-fests, and evening news (more than a hundred appearances in all) in an evangelical blitzkreig. Their opening salvo decried a "growing trend toward lyrics that are sexually explicit, excessively violent, or glorify the use of drugs and alcohol"—the very kinds of accusations once hurled at ragtime, jazz, and the blues. Stating a mission to "educate and inform parents," the PMRC demanded the industry police itself or face the consequences. Financial and in-kind support came from sources ranging from Beach Boy Mike Love (who donated some start-up money) to the rigidly conservative Coors Beer company, which provided office space. For a group with no official power (and no actual members, only "founders"), the PMRC became a formidable adversary overnight. They gathered momentum, credibility, and through a hastily reached alliance with the national Parent/Teacher Association, a vital link to five-and-a-half million concerned adults.

Their suggestions weren't an overture to censorship, they maintained, but rather "guidelines" to help parents better choose the kinds of entertainments most suitable for young and impressionable minds. What the PMRC actually proposed was a top-to-bottom restructuring of the music business—some of which would have countermanded existing copyright law that grants composers control over how lyrics are reprinted. In their view, each song should receive a rating before release, with "O" for occult, "D/A" for drugs and alcohol, "V" for violence, and "X" for explicit content, with warnings affixed to every record sleeve individually. Since rappers gave the impression that they'd go as far as their imaginations would let them no matter how young the listening audience might be, even First Amendment champions took sides against them.

Former CBS anchor Walter Cronkite has heard his share and considers rap content "a lowering of our standards." "It's frighteningly color conscious and highly racist," he says, "racist from their viewpoint. The language is profane and the thoughts suggest that violence is an answer to our problems. I think it's highly objectionable and makes me believe it ought to be labeled. If parents are not aware of what's on the record, then material should be categorized so that it's easily identified. Are you going to ask parents to read everything a kid is going to read, or listen to everything their child is going to hear? That's a full-time job, and I'm not sure that busy parents today have time to devote to their children's cultural development. They probably should, and, ideally, that's the way it should be done. Absent that, when they can't approve of every record or every show, this is a substitute."

In September 1985, the PMRC was able to nudge the Senate Committee on Commerce, Science, and Transportation into hearings to expose what the press now termed "porn rock." (Three committee members also had wives in the PMRC, Al Gore among them.)

Smokey Robinson and Mike Love appeared before the panel to describe the corruption of America's youth at the hands of Prince and a hit list of white co-conspirators that ranged from headbangers Mötley Crüe and Judas Priest to Madonna (whose "Like a Virgin" Mrs. James Baker found particularly detestable). In response, the opposition trotted out its own celebrity parade, including folk singer John Denver, Twisted Sister's Dee Snider, and rock iconoclast Frank Zappa. Record executives remained uncharacteristically quiet. They were happy to stretch obscenity standards to the breaking point in order to maximize counterculture appeal and sales, but became solemn and earnest when talk turned to self-regulation versus government intervention.

Several recording artists recorded public service announcements (PSAs) to denounce the PMRC's McCarthyesque tactics—among them devout Mormon Donny Osmond. The Osmond PSA opened with a tight shot framing his face, then pulled back while the former teen idol spoke forebodingly about artistic expression and the zealots who would restrict it. Practice and protect free speech, he said, or risk looking up one day to realize it's been taken away. As the camera finished panning out, the squeaky clean Osmond stood costumed head-to-toe as an officer of the Nazi SS.

"I guess you could call me adventurous," Osmond said a decade later. "There's a line I won't cross, but I feel so strongly about rating records. Sure, there are CDs in my collection that I wouldn't let my little children listen to. There are some Prince songs from albums like *Controversy*—and I have a great collection of Prince CDs, by the way. I wouldn't let my kids listen to them, but it's great music. So what am I going to do, put a blindfold on? You can't isolate yourself from the world."

Osmond says he taped the spot to suggest that parents who impart their principles to kids early on will find they can make reasonable moral judgments as teens. "My kids know what's right and what's wrong," the singer says, "because my wife and I have taught them. But kids will always want to experience whatever it is that's off-limits to them. That was my whole platform in saying, 'Don't rate the records, 'cause you're just adding fuel to the fire.' And the other reason is that if a record is rated, then you're giving power to a committee to say, 'this deserves the R rating, this deserves a G rating,' whatever the system may be. Then *they* determine what is right or wrong for society. And the image could determine the rating. The example I like to use is that if Donny Osmond recorded 'Little Red Corvette,' that's a G-rated record because it's Donny Osmond singing about a red car. Prince is singing about something else."

The White House joined the fray that fall, when President Reagan opined in a speech October 10 that the framers of the Constitution didn't intend smut to become a form of protected expression. Reagan asserted that the media and the record business shared responsibility for the "glorification of drugs, violence, and perversity" so prevalent in the culture, and that "the First Amendment has been twisted into a pretext for license."

The hearings ended in a compromise between the industry and PMRC that remains in place today, with record companies agreeing to voluntarily advise purchasers of explicit content with a label affixed to the disc jacket. The forecasted pall fell over the industry when retailers Sears and J.C. Penney vowed not to carry stickered product and Wal-Mart outmaneuvered them both by purging itself of releases considered at the fringe of good taste. Smelling blood in the water, the PMRC supervised a video in 1988 called *Rising to the Challenge* to disseminate its beliefs and include suicide in their list of social ills exacerbated by music.

Attempts to muzzle rap's provocateurs finally got traction in June 1988 when an Alabama shop owner was arrested and charged with obscenity for selling a sleazy rap album to an undercover cop. The record was everything prosecutors could hope for—frothing over with sexual content and four-letter words—precisely the reason the merchant kept it behind the counter and refused to sell it to anyone underage. It hardly mattered that the record had the obligatory warning posted on its cover and hadn't been legally found obscene; the judge determined that at the same moment that he fined the offending retailer five hundred dollars. Later, the shop owner was acquitted on appeal, but 2 Live Crew and its leader Luther Campbell were not so lucky.

In 1990, federal district court judge Jose Gonzales ruled their *Nasty As They Wanna Be* an obscene recording—a first in the history of American jurisprudence. Soon after, the group was arrested at an adults-only club for performing their own material. Again the performers fought back. Campbell was protecting his small indie label, Luke Records, and battling for the right to both speak his mind and make a living doing so.

The case became a cause célèbre, with Campbell's defenders claiming his records were no more bawdy or bereft of value than the "party" records of such blue comedians as Redd Foxx, Richard Pryor, or Eddie Murphy. (The controversy also lofted *Nasty* and its signature tune, "Me So Horny" into the Top 30 of both the album and singles charts.) At trial, experts testified how Campbell's graphic approach fit into the black tradition of playing the dozens, and even Bruce Springsteen got into the act by loaning out his "Born in the U.S.A." hook for 2 Live Crew to remake into "Banned in the U.S.A." The track actually out-performed "Me So Horny," landing at #21 on the pop charts in 1990. Campbell disappeared from the headlines as soon as the nightclub conviction was overturned and the obscenity ruling reversed on appeal, but black artists came to believe that they were targets of the right and that juries were more likely to convict rappers than rockers.

Reaction from the hip-hop community was swift and defiant. Just as Spike Lee's alterego Mookie goes aggro to heave a trash can through his employer's window in *Do the Right Thing*, rappers took aim at the authority figures most likely to return fire: the government and the police.

THIS 2 IS CNN

Conventional wisdom among rappers held that America had been waging economic war on blacks since the election of Ronald Reagan. In their view, conservatives never hesitated to bash Cadillac-driving welfare Moms (even if the incidence of such abuse was about as common as stigmata), and their antipathy toward minority concerns coupled with the administration's hardline law enforcement directives led to an underclass mistrustful of anyone wearing a badge. Just as systematic neglect spawned the culture of hip-hop in the 1970s, the crack wars of the 1980s gave rise to black music's most militant offshoot: gangsta rap.

This genre, which began as party music with the occasional message, evolved into message music with lyrics wound tautly into what rapper Ice Cube calls "revenge fantasies." These imaginary confrontations revealed that rap was both elastic and durable, not some momentary hiccup between disco and the next passing fad. Like the blues, rap structure proved dynamic enough to allow for an infinite range of expression. Like the great soul epics *What's Going On, Stand!,* and *Superfly,* hip-hop addressed current events, but looked to past labels and statistics to examine their significance in the black community. So, while the daily paper or cable news might be able to explain what happened when crack arrived in urban America, rappers could convey how it felt to actually be there. MCs began referring to rap as "CNN for black culture."

Philadelphia's Schoolly-D (born Jesse Weaver) struck the first gangsta pose in his 1986 reflection on life as a member of a street gang called the Park Side Killers in "PSK—What Does It Mean?" New York's Boogie Down Productions took a similar path, although MC KRS-One (a.k.a. Lawrence Brown) gave his raps a political spin by addressing the cycles of poverty and violence and the amoral cops whose vow to protect and serve began and ended with self-interest. Boogie Down Productions' other visionary, Scott La Rock (née Sterling), was shot to death while trying to break up a fight in 1987. A year later, KRS-One responded with a spitfire disc that tempered fury with reason and occasionally danced across both sides of an issue. *By All Means Necessary* (#75 pop and #18 R&B hits) used the life and teachings of Malcolm X as a template to revisit the black struggle in America.

So while gangsta rap wasn't invented in the drive-by killing fields of Los Angeles County, the inhabitants had reason to make it their own, paramount among them a mushrooming drug culture. A kilo of crack cost approximately $50,000 in 1980, the year Richard Pryor set himself afire while freebasing and took to the streets shrieking. In less than four years, the price of crack plummeted to $35,000, and by 1992, a mere $12,000 could put a pusher in business.

Dealers justified victimizing the people around them as their best springboard from poverty to the good life. Addicts—and even a first-time user could become one—found their world took on a happy glow when that high kicked in, and that nothing (including friends and family) could stop the craving for that sensation again once it began to wane. Suburbanites who survived the '60s civil rights riots and the urban decay of the 1970s were suddenly caught between law enforcement and the kingpins and crackheads their neighbors had become. What was once a crime scene collapsed into a war zone, and rappers began a discourse on one society besieged inside another.

Helping to set the stage was the first rap group to channel its disaffection into a political battle cry, the Long Island–based Public Enemy. Its logo put a black man in the crosshairs of a rifle; its crew of dancers carried imitation Uzis and executed their moves with paramilitary precision. Their production team was known as the Bomb Squad. During its brief reign (the glory days lasted from 1988 to 1992), Public Enemy became the flagship of hip-hop. Reviewers compared them favorably to the Clash, the English band of half a decade earlier who used reggae-tinged punk to confront the global power elite. Everything about Public Enemy assailed the ear or the eye, and the group found two perfect foils in "prophet of rage" Chuck D (Carlton Ridenhour) and the group's comic relief, Flava Flav (William Drayton), who spiked his update of Louis Jordan with sardonic asides and his signature yelp, "yeah Boy-ee."

Their 1987 debut, *Yo! Bum Rush the Show*, made few creative or commercial inroads, but their 1988 sophomore effort, *It Takes a Nation of Millions to Hold Us Back*, crept onto the airwaves like a toxic spill. The title alone spoke volumes; record buyers felt they were getting the unvarnished truth about bigotry in America—or at least one side of the debate. The disc hit #42 on the pop album chart, and roared to the top of the R&B charts with its shotgun observations on black angst set off by a collage of samples and sirens. "Night of the Living Baseheads," for example, probes the wounds of freebasing by comparing addicts to horror movie zombies. "Don't Believe the Hype" (#18 R&B hit, 1988)

With albums like *Fear of a Black Planet* and *It Takes a Nation of Millions to Hold Us Back*, Public Enemy gave urban blacks an angry but articulate voice. Seemingly impenetrable from without, they were undone from within when one member's antisemitic remarks caught up with them. (Vinnie Zufante/Star File)

takes on white-dominated media, and in "Bring the Noise" (#56 R&B hit, 1988), Chuck D allies himself with Muslim leader Louis Farrakhan. Name checks also went out to Harlem Renaissance leader Marcus Garvey, anti-apartheid crusaders including the Mandelas and Steven Biko, and both Martin Luther King, Jr. and Malcolm X.

Their first national tour was spent opening for Def Jam labelmates the Beastie Boys, and Public Enemy hit it big with hip-hop crowds of every color. The group's integrity was such that they were unassailable without; it took self-sabotage to implode them from within. Concertgoers became accustomed to P.E.'s "minister of information," Professor Griff (Richard Griffin) making bigoted statements onstage, but in May 1989, his views generated a firestorm when he informed a *Washington Times* reporter that Jews were behind "the majority of wickedness that goes on across the globe." In the confusion that followed, Chuck D fired Griff, rehired him, then dissolved and reconstituted the group without Griff, all within a few weeks.

After contributing "Fight the Power" (not to be confused with the Isley Brothers' 1970s funk jam) to Spike Lee's breakthrough film, *Do the Right Thing*, the group issued *Fear of a Black Planet* in 1990. No disc ever issued by black artists ever went further to illustrate how members of the same society could be blind to the chasm between them. It seemed no one in the corridors of power could understand how Chuck D was rapping about *their* country, too. "Get up, get down, 9-1-1 is a joke in your town," Public Enemy said, and many Americans shook their heads at the album's casual profanity, while on the opposite coast, Los Angelinos were nodding in agreement.

STRAIGHT OUTTA COMPTON

Observation, bombast, and Afro-centrism were Public Enemy's calling cards, but in South Central Los Angeles, gangstas saw no reason to separate themselves from the lifestyles they outlined in song. Let Public Enemy talk about overcoming obstacles through solidarity. West Coast gangstas had no orders to uplift the masses. Rapper Eric Wright began his trek to stardom as a drug dealer who invested his profits in a rap label he dubbed Ruthless Records. When one of his groups, HBO, passed on a song called "Boyz-in-the-Hood," Wright agreed to record the song with its composers, Andre Young and O'Shea Jackson. Together, Eazy E (Wright), Young (Dr. Dre), and Jackson (Ice Cube) formed the nucleus of N.W.A.—Niggaz With Attitude. The lineup expanded to include MC Ren (Lorenzo Patterson) and DJ Yella (Antoine Carraby), and in less than two years, N.W.A. revolutionized rap.

Their first full-length album, *Straight Outta Compton* (1988), helped distill gangsta into the formula that would lead it to national prominence—violent lyrics, pared-back beats, and videos extolling the good life (translation: inexhaustible supplies of malt liquor and bitches). Accordingly, the disc registered sales of 75,000 before the group ever left town to promote it. Without loyalties, political agendas, or much chance for airplay to hold them in check, N.W.A. ran amok and made it look like fun. When "Fuck Tha Police" arrived ("a young nigga on a warpath," it seethes, "and when I'm finished, it's gonna be a bloodbath of cops dyin' in L.A."), the group received a warning letter from the F.B.I., prompting a response from N.W.A.'s distributor, Priority Records. Company president Brian Turner told *Billboard* that "N.W.A. and Eazy E . . . lived the things they talk about." He complained that the only viewpoints getting media attention were those of the police and other unnamed "outsiders." Turner said that N.W.A.'s writing impressed him, and that "their side of the story is important to tell."

Whether Turner was being candid or coy, he could likely read a sales report and grasp its import. Kids of all colors were scooping up N.W.A. records because the artists were their antiheroes—real gangstas who answered to no one, carried guns, had done dope, and maybe even slapped a girl occasionally—the kinds of things endorsed as true in numerous label-sanctioned interviews and press releases. But industry watchdogs and would-be censors got a different speech from executives: Yes, it's "real," record flaks would say, fingers tugging the air to emphasize their quotation marks. Gangsta rap represents street poets talking about the vices people face every day in the slums of South Central. But rap artists are taking license. When they claim, "I could just kill a man," or call to "smack my bitch up," it's apocryphal, much the same as Johnny Cash claiming he "shot a man in Reno, just to watch him die."

Still, a disproportionate number of the gangstas who preach lawlessness on disc later found themselves facing charges that run the gamut from traffic violations to assault and murder. So, does the press department not really know its own clients? Are they trying to have it both ways, selling kids a renegade image while appealing to free speech advocates that their clients are artists, not anarchists? Or are these arrests—as the rappers often maintain—based on jealousy and racism? "Any time a cop see a black man in L.A. and he don't look broke down like some Fred or Lamont Sanford shit," said one MC, "they figure a crime been committed somewhere close by."

Gangsta remains a hot commodity today, but its pioneers disintegrated in 1990 when Ice Cube left N.W.A., claiming the group's manager had cheated him out of royalties. Cube's first solo disc, *AmeriKKKa's Most Wanted*, continued the band's commercial streak later that year by going gold in ten days and platinum in ninety, and a short time later he established a solid acting career. His ex-bandmates continued to make headlines true to the gangsta image: Eazy E died a month after discovering he had AIDS in 1995 and Dr. Dre had repeated clashes with the law (one involving a 1991 assault charge from a TV rap show host to which he pleaded no contest) before he resurfaced in 1993 with *The Chronic* (#3 pop and #1 R&B hits). Dre's record wrote a new chapter into the gangsta mythology with its hit singles, "Nothin' But a 'G' Thang" (#2 pop and #1 R&B hits) and "Dre Day" (#8 pop and #6 R&B hits), and introduced fans to the heir apparent gangsta prince, Snoop Doggy Dogg.

Ironically, the same voices of sanctimony that denounced gangsta rap may have helped to legitimize it in the early 1990s. In March 1991, a slumbering volcano of race hatred stirred to life when the arrest of black motorist Rodney King was videotaped by a nearby amateur following a high-speed police chase by the LAPD. Three officers were shown on the tape striking King more than fifty times before wrestling him into handcuffs. The following April, a jury refused to convict any of the indicted officers on charges of racism or incompetence, which triggered a citywide riot resulting in fifty-three deaths, more than $1 billion in property damage, and several thousand arrests.

Following the acquittal of King's assailants and its violent aftermath, strangers of different races in Los Angeles were as approachable as downed power lines, and the 1992 election cycle only cranked up the voltage. Both Democrats and Republicans tongue-lashed rappers to score cheap rhetorical points with voters, and hip-hop became as much a political football as family values, flag burning, or the vanishing social security trust fund.

Rapper Ice-T (Tracy Marrow) was already on the PMRC watch list for such songs as "Girls, L.G.B.N.A.F." ("Girls, Let's Get Buck Naked and Fuck"), but when he recorded "Cop Killer" with his thrash metal band, Body Count, he became a target himself. Written as one man's violent response to police persecution, "Cop Killer" was first singled out by the Combined Law Enforcement Associations of Texas, who demanded that Time Warner (the parent company of Ice-T's record label, Sire) excise the track or face a boycott of all its products. Then-President George H.W. Bush and running mate Dan Quayle latched onto the controversy, calling the track "sick" and "obscene." Ice-T, who had been performing the song for more than a year, was dumbfounded. "Maybe I underestimate my juice," he told Alan Light of *Rolling Stone*, "but there's people out there with nuclear bombs, people with armies, and the president has time to sit up and get into it with me."

Not to be outdone, Arkansas governor Bill Clinton found his own scapegoat in Sister Soulja, a member of Public Enemy's extended family. Soulja made an ill-advised comment to *Washington Post* reporter David Mills that she was aggrieved by the Rodney King verdict and the carnage it inspired, much of it black on black. "If black people kill black people every day," Soulja told Mills, "why not have a week and kill white people?" Out of context as it was, Clinton pounced, condemning her comments as "full of hatred."

Hip-hop became the stuff of media frenzy, with such disparate celebrity pundits as Larry King, Oliver North, and Charleton Heston (a Time Warner board member, who once recited Ice-T's lyrics at a meeting of the board) weighing in on the controversy. Ultimately, Sister Soulja wound up on the cover of *Newsweek*, while Ice-T relented and had "Cop Killer" removed from the *Body Count* album. A year later, he was released from his contract.

THE NEXT EPISODE

The same year that *It Takes a Nation of Millions* and *Straight Outta Compton* strafed the airwaves, MTV finally introduced a program targeting the burgeoning hip-hop market, *Yo! MTV Raps*. For a second time in five years, the channel supposedly most attuned to youth culture was late to its own party. By 1988, the network couldn't have missed the crossover surge toward rap—they were, after all, already programming hugely successful clips by the Beasties, Run-D.M.C., and Def Jam's multiplatinum answer to Otis Redding, L.L. Cool J (Todd Smith). But if MTV programmers were skittish about Michael Jackson and Prince in 1983, what must they have made of Public Enemy and N.W.A.?

Out of ignorance more than fear, the network ceded control to those who could best differentiate what was cutting edge from commercial fad—the people who assembled the show. They had a sense of what makes rap watchable, and with a national series as their power base, the hosts and director could make or break individual performers or entire movements. As a result, viewers got front-row seats to hip-hop's transformation from playing the dozens to toying with guns.

The initial Saturday night episodes with rap legend Fab 5 Freddy Braithwaite earned MTV its highest ratings ever, prompting the network to make room for weeknight installments with hosts Ed Lover, Dr. Dre, and T-Money. Both versions were directed by Ted Demme, the nephew of *Stop Making Sense* director Jonathan Demme. In addition to promoting new personalities, sounds, and styles, the show was also more consumer oriented (many rappers delighted in pitching products they liked, from techno gear and hair care to shoes and soda), which made it an advertiser's dream, since the stars paraded trendy fashions before the viewers most likely to purchase them. A year later Black Entertainment Television (BET) introduced *Rap City*, hoping to lead for a change rather than follow.

On the big screen, the same Hollywood that somehow filmed the Bronx at the dawn of hip-hop culture and missed it entirely made amends in the ensuing years with a string of movies that followed rap into maturity. *Wild Style* captured the colorful tagging craze of early hip-hop; Afrika Bambaataa and Kool Herc weathered a breakdancing storyline in *Beat Street* (produced by Harry Belafonte), while *Breakin', Breakin' 2: Electric Boogaloo*, and *Body Rock* all saw wide screen release in the mid-1980s.

Krush Groove towers above them all in capturing the early spirit of hip-hop. The 1985 docudrama pitches a revisionist history of Def Jam Records' rise to fame through the eyes of up-and-coming talents L.L. Cool J, the Beastie Boys, and Run-D.M.C. Directed on a two-million-dollar shoestring by black filmmaker Michael Schultz, the movie unfolds like a two-hour love letter to the company and its founders—who, after all, underwrote the picture. Nonetheless, *Krush Groove* does for rap what Sinatra did for crooners. By zeroing in on the vocalists, the film relegates all others in the hip-hop hierarchy (in this case, graffiti artists and break-dancers) to permanent supporting role status. Today, the film wears better than most movies of its time because it presented believable characters whose passion is rap, rather than building a rap fable around hitmakers of the moment. In due course, *Krush Groove* became *A Hard Day's Night* for hip-hoppers, the picture that introduced Def Jam's constellation of stars to moviegoers around the world.

The kaleidoscopic rush of hip-hop's formative years gave way to darker visions as the 1990s offered up such gangsta films as John Singleton's *Boyz N the Hood* and *New Jack City*, the vehicles that propelled Ice Cube and Tupac Shakur to fame on a second front in 1991. Granted, their plotlines of families ripped apart by street violence and intragang betrayal occasionally tilt toward melodrama; on the other hand, there's not much depicted in either picture, or in the acclaimed 1993 Hughes Brothers film, *Menace II Society*, that couldn't be found in the news section of any major daily at the time.

But the truest exemplar of hip-hop in film remains Spike Lee. His sharp eye for finding the stories and angles missed by his contemporaries, coupled with his unwavering allegiance to black art (and particularly music), have made him America's honorary hip-hop filmmaker. Particularly in committing the black experience to the screen, Lee not only documents time and place, he promotes black culture across boundaries of race and generation to all who care to embrace it. He's given a boost to jazz (*Mo' Better Blues*), soul (*Crooklyn*, to name but one), rap (*Do the Right Thing*), and two of hip-hop's spiritual godfathers, Malcolm X and Louis Farrakhan. In addition, Lee has directed numerous music videos (check his work for Naughty by Nature, Arrested Development, Miles Davis, and Tracy Chapman), and suffered criticism from the black community in the latest Iraq war for agreeing to participate in a U.S. Navy recruiting campaign. Opinionated and unrepentant? Both describe the director and the community he depicts onscreen.

The press generated by *Yo! MTV Raps* and *Do the Right Thing* confirmed that hip-hop was mainstream recreation by 1988—entering that world where *Entertainment Weekly* and National Public Radio take pains to cover major releases and the celebrities pushing them. And, as had happened so many times before with ragtime, jazz, blues, rock, and soul, a formerly insular and terrifying art form was now a part of the cultural matrix acknowledged (if not appreciated) by the majority. All rap needed now was its own Elvis, "a white man with the negro sound and the negro feel," who could rap and dance his way onto America's cable boxes and then bank, in Sam Phillips' words, "a billion dollars."

ICY RECEPTION

"Walk This Way" and "Fight for Your Right" comprise the media's first wigga sightings, but the phenomenon clearly reached epidemic proportions in the early 1990s when Marky Mark and Vanilla Ice strutted onto MTV. According to suburban Dallas native Robert Van Winkle, his neighborhood was overrun with white rap fans, but only he grew up to become Vanilla Ice.

"Funk, rap, hip-hop, I thought that's what everybody listened to," he says in retrospect. "All my friends on my block were listening to it, and I didn't really travel beyond that neighborhood, so I didn't know. I thought the rest of the world was doing the same thing I was, regardless of what color they were. At fourteen years old, I'd pull out the cardboard and break-dance at the mall or out in the parking lots near where everybody cruised in their cars.

"There was a place called Handy Dan," he recalls, "and in the back when it was closed in the parking lot next to a service road, we could make as much noise as we wanted. So we'd pop the trunks, you know, big fifteen-inch woofers all over the backseat—if there was a backseat. And they'd stop and throw me some change, so I'd make about thirty bucks a day on a good day. Hanging out there or at the mall at thirty bucks a day was more than most kids I knew got for an allowance. I would run around the mall and chase girls and eat pizza, maybe check out a movie."

Ice played some rough clubs as a beginner, but he believes that over time, the crowd, promoters, and acts he met grew to accept him. By the end of the 1980s, he had a CD of his own out on an independent Atlanta label called Ichiban and was a featured opener on the "Stop the Violence" tour, which also featured Stetasonic, Sir Mix-a-Lot, Hammer, and headliner Ice T. Ichiban sold Vanilla Ice's contract to SBK/EMI records, and they released *To the Extreme*, "and," he says, "everybody knows the rest of the story."

Before it was all over, *To the Extreme* dislodged MC Hammer's *Please Hammer Don't Hurt 'Em* from the number one slot on the album charts. "And 'Ice Ice Baby' got to #1 around the country before the video came out," he says. "That's before anyone knew whether I was black or white. Everybody just assumed that since it was rap that I was black. 'Ice Ice Baby' was pretty basic; that's why everyone can relate to it. Simple sells. It's luck, sure. But more than that, it's talent, and applying yourself—getting up and doing something instead of sitting around thinking about it."

Had it only been a successful song, video, or album, Ice might have gotten away as clean as Mark Wahlberg, a.k.a. Marky Mark, who parlayed his physique and modest rapping skills into a movie career. But two things happened to Vanilla Ice: One, "Ice Ice Baby" sold fifteen million records, making him the best-selling rap artist of the day. Two, in order to enhance his image and bolster his credibility, his press materials claimed that he was a street tough from Miami. That was a lie.

"I don't like to point fingers," he says, "but when EMI Records picked me up, they wanted to beef up some kind of story, so they wrote the bio without me even knowing about it. I read it, and I go, 'Who the fuck wrote this?' And here I am doing an interview the next day and they're asking me questions about it, and I go, 'Uh . . . what? Who told you that?' Even all the books—they had five books out on me and said I wrote them. I never wrote a book in my life. Anybody who's on top they're going to try to bring you down, so for me it was a roller coaster. I was very young—sixteen when I did 'Ice Ice Baby,' and nineteen when it started blowing up."

The rappers who applauded his early success vanished from his side. "I guess they take offense when you sell fifteen million records," he shrugs, "more than any rap artist in history, and it's your debut record, and you're white. I don't think I would have gotten any of the criticism if I had done the same exact thing and my skin was black. For me it was a big learning experience, all my dreams, and things beyond my dreams coming true. Fifteen million records sold. I didn't imagine after the first million that it would go to the second million. Every time it went platinum again, it was an amazement to me. But I was also doing a show every night and having to deal with facing all these critics every day."

He became an instant punch line for late-night television comics, and during the dogpile, another group of white rappers dragged him through the dirt. During the video for "Pop Goes the Weasel," the members of 3rd Bass beat him up in absentia, with punk rocker Henry Rollins turning in a cameo as Vanilla Ice. "They were coming at me out of the woodwork like flies," he says. "It got to be too much at once, so I got involved in drugs to escape, because to me reality was a drag. Ecstasy was pretty much my main favorite, and then anything else that would come around when I was on that. Being in the record industry, that was always available to me. I never had to pay for it, or order it, or anything like that, it was just always there."

And when he most wanted to disappear, Vanilla Ice found himself everywhere. He had a movie. He had a doll (okay, "action figure"), and he had a tune that went platinum seven times over. He could score a date with Madonna, but he couldn't buy an ounce of respect. Van Winkle released several follow-ups (one hardcore), became a born-again Christian, got involved in professional auto racing, and now tours the same bar circuits that book Harry (KC) Casey with his Sunshine Band—most of which is made up of backing tracks recorded on DAT. He also returned to television in 2003 as one of the regulars in the WB network's reality show, *The Surreal Life*, which focuses on celebrities whose stars twinkled more brightly in years past.

The hip-hop media (led in print by *The Source, Vibe,* and *XXL* magazines) could also wreak havoc on a career if they felt a performer was "fronting," that is, behaving in a way inauthentic or disrespectful to rap's unwritten code of ethics. KRS-One took his homeboys to a P.M. Dawn show in 1992, and stormed the stage when he satisfied himself that the group wasn't "keeping it real." He ripped the mike from the artist's hand, and called it "the first time a believed-to-be-hardcore artist took a physical reaction to a believed-to-be commercial artist."

Philadelphian Will Smith, on the other hand, rose above the fray. From the moment he and mixmaster Jeffrey Townes hit the airwaves in 1987 as DJ Jazzy Jeff and the Fresh Prince with "Girls Ain't Nothin' But Trouble," rap purists found them irksome. Too processed, too safe, and too damned cheesy with their *I Dream of Jeannie* sample as a melodic hook, they grumbled. According to the arbiters of hip-hop, Smith and Townes walked a fine line between pop and Tomming with an album that explained rap to neophytes (*He's the D.J., I'm the Rapper*) and a video for their innocuous single "Parents Just Don't Understand," which features Smith on camera mugging and popping his eyes.

After rehabilitating themselves with "Summertime" in 1991 (which sampled Kool & the Gang rather than a TV theme), Smith chose to focus on his acting career and solo work. *The Fresh Prince of Bel Air* ran for six full seasons on NBC, launching Smith into film, where he vaulted from the 1995 buddy action picture *Bad Boys* opposite comic Martin Lawrence into the paydays of such blockbusters as *Independence Day* and *Men in Black*. By 1988, he was back on the Hot 100 without Jazzy Jeff, sailing all the way to #1 via "Gettin' Jiggy Wit It," and a year later he rang the bell again with "Wild Wild West," which rented its hook from Stevie Wonder's "I Wish" for a mere $500,000. These days, Smith gets props from the hip-hop community because he conquered Hollywood on his terms (remember, getting paid commands respect) and he has now graduated to "serious actor" status, courtesy of an Oscar-nominated turn in the 2001 biopic *Ali*.

By contrast, Oakland native Stanley Burrell never broke free of the material that launched him. Better known to the public as MC Hammer, Burrell regifted Rick James' "Super Freak" to the video generation as "U Can't Touch This" in 1990. Hammer first hit #8 on the pop charts, then shilled for Pepsi-Cola and showed Vanilla Ice what to do with a pair of harem pants. He had a Saturday morning cartoon called *Hammerman* based on his exploits, and spent millions faster than he made them. In a two-year reign, Hammer took $750,000 from Capitol and recorded *Please Hammer Don't Hurt 'Em*, for less than $10,000. The disc moved some ten million copies, and clung to the #1 position on the album charts for more than twenty weeks. An overblown extravaganza of a tour followed, as did the singles "Pray" (based on "When Doves Cry") and an all-too-faithful reading of the Chi-Lites' 1970s tearjerker, "Have You Seen Her?"

Again, the gatekeepers of rap ridiculed his love to entertain, suggesting that his doing what he most enjoyed—putting the "show" in show business—somehow betrayed the true spirit of hip-hop. Public Enemy's Chuck D disagreed, and he told *Rolling Stone*, "You're supposed to sell out. If you got fifteen tapes on the shelf, your mission is to sell. You ain't giving it away. So I can't be mad at Hammer for doing what he's got to do."

HOOK OR CROOK?

Before he died in the summer of 2004, Rick James maintained that he loathed sampling and had he known about it in advance, he would have denied Hammer the rights to "Super Freak." Which begs the question: What would "U Can't Touch This?" have sounded like without Rick James' unwitting and unwilling participation? Furthermore, is sampling the theft of intellectual property and part of the gangsta take-what-I-want ethos, or is it the hi-tech descendant of centuries-old African traditions?

The technology of sampling progressed quickly from the cut-and-paste process the Sugarhill Gang used to assemble "Rapper's Delight" in 1979. Hip-hoppers considered sampling merely a user-friendly way to find and isolate the hottest elements of a great track and bring them together, a chore simplified over time by advances in recording. Fairlight's Computer Musical Instrument, joined in 1981 by the E-mu Emulator, were the first of many tools that put the history of music at the fingertips of rappers and remixers. Hip-hop artists (who were used to making art from the debris around them) began to create intricate sound collages—audio's answer to those computer-generated portraits comprised of hundreds of smaller photos. Every bit of the source material belongs to someone else, but by incorporating that material, another artist transforms the original into something altogether new.

What goes through Nile Rodgers' mind when he sees his 1970s hits re-ascend the pop charts without his participation? Not only did the Rodgers/Edwards tune "Good Times" yield "Rapper's Delight," and "He's the Greatest Dancer" serve as the foundation of "Gettin' Jiggy Wit It," their "I'm Comin' Out" morphed into the P. Diddy/Notorious B.I.G. hit, "Mo Money Mo Problems." The track vaulted to the top of the pop charts in 1997, while the Diana Ross original stalled out at #5.

"What samplers do is clever," Rodgers said later, "there's no question about that. But they're working from something amazing that's already demonstrated power in the marketplace. Diana Ross is singing. Chic is playing the music. Bob Clearmountain is the session engineer, and it's recorded at the Power Station, one of the most famous studios in the world. All of that is in place before you even begin."

"Sure sounds like a formula for success to me," Donald Fagen concurs. Fagen could stake a claim of his own to hip-hop fame, since Steely Dan's *Aja* tracks have also surfaced in a handful of rap hits. "Because of who we are and the culture we come from, it seems like cheating," he says. "You could never really feel responsible for your own success if you started with a record that was already a hit—something that makes an instant impact by familiarity alone."

Producer Sean "Puffy" Combs (a.k.a. Puff Daddy, Puffy, and, most recently, P. Diddy) is the man most responsible for recycling the hits to get ahead. As the mastermind behind the Bad Boy Records label, he's the one who reduced Diana Ross to singing background and Chic to bit players for "Mo Money, Mo Problems." In 1999, he told *TIME* magazine, "If I learned to play an instrument, it would take away from what I do, which is to listen and let the feelings come and absorb them. Then I can say, 'Put that beat there, do this, do that.'"

"I guess that's one approach to making a hit," Fagen's partner Walter Becker adds sardonically. "Starting with a hit record sure gives you something road tested to work from."

"And it does allow nonmusicians to make records, which is cool," Fagan counters.

Becker agrees: "Putting aside the issues of legality and the fine points of what's being done, that's absolutely correct. The biggest drawback to this very literal sampling is that it's limiting. You're stuck with a lot of repetition and it's very confining as to what you can do with it. You also have the problem that your supposedly new thing has a lot of familiar elements in it, and while that might be a good thing in terms of it being a hit or resonating, if you're trying to do something serious, it's a problem. People have already heard it."

Hip Hop America author Nelson George concedes the point, but arrives at a different conclusion by comparing hip-hop's samples to the day Bob Dylan went electric. He writes, "I long for old familiar sounds to remain in their original context and for younger musicians, with new approaches, to dominate the musical mainstream." But George accepts his logic is antiquated. Therefore, he concludes, "My answer to the question—is or isn't sampling an extension of African American tradition?—is a straightforward no *and* yes." George grants that sampling does nothing to create new chords, notes, or harmonies in the African American musical tradition. "However," he maintains, "if that tradition means embracing new sounds, bending found technology to a creator's will in search of new forms of rhythm made to inspire and please listeners, well then sampling is as black as the blues."[2]

The scope of copyright law was broadened in the late 1980s and into the 1990s to protect artists from having their melodies, voices, and beats lifted without permission or compensation. As things stand now, says David Byrne, "whatever they take from a song, you get paid for a chunk of it. So you don't mind on that level. From my point of view, since I'm being sampled for people who like sampling, part of me thinks that maybe someone will hear more of my stuff, and maybe in some small way I'll reach a wider audience."

That's likely what Natalie Cole had in mind when she abandoned a middling R&B career (which had its stellar moments, including "This Will Be" and a saucy cover of Bruce Springsteen's "Pink Cadillac") to duet with her late father Nat on "Unforgettable." It's sampling taken to the next level, with Natalie's voice technologically comingled with the original until the naked ear would swear the duet was recorded by adults side by side, even though the elder Cole passed away while his daughter was still a child. Hank Williams, Jr. did the same with his legendary father on "Tear in My Beer" in 1988. And in 2000, Jazz rocker Pat Metheny began one of the most vituperative diatribes in the short history of the Internet when he took pap/pop jazzbo Kenny G to task for insinuating himself into Louis Armstrong's "What a Wonderful World," a tune which first reached the charts in the mid-1960s, then enjoyed a second life on the charts when it was included on the *Good Morning Vietnam* soundtrack.

"This type of musical necrophilia," Metheny writes in his posting, "the technique of overdubbing on the preexisting tracks of already dead performers—was weird when Natalie Cole did it with her Dad on 'Unforgettable' a few years ago, but it was her Dad. When Tony Bennett did it with Billie Holiday it was bizarre, but we are talking about two of the greatest singers of the twentieth century who were on roughly the same level of artistic accomplishment . . . but when Kenny G decided that it was appropriate for him to defile the music of the man who is probably the greatest jazz musician that has ever lived by spewing his lame-ass, jive, pseudobluesy out-of-tune, noodling, wimped out, fucked up playing all over one of the great Louis' tracks (even one of his lesser ones) he . . . shit all over the graves of all the musicians past and present who have risked their lives by going out there on the road for years and years developing their own music inspired by the standards of grace that Louis Armstrong brought to every single note he played over an amazing lifetime as a musician."

Although it's easier than ever to create these hybrids of art and commerce, many consider it a point of pride to keep their distance. Maurice Gibb said that the Bee Gees regularly decline sampling requests, but remain open to performers interpreting their songs. In 2001, Destiny's Child covered "Emotion," the Bee Gees tune that clicked in the 1970s for Samantha Sang. "We always get a demo to see how far they've gone with it," Gibb explained. "People like Wyclef (Jean) want to do 'Stayin' Alive,' and tons of rap artists have come looking for other things to sample. They don't need our permission to record it as long as they don't change the melody and the lyrics, but once they do that, yes, they have to get permission. Usually it's done out of respect and we're honored. If they've changed it, done it like crap, or taken the piss—made a joke out of it, then we say no, and the same is true for commercials. A lot of people like to remix and would love to get their hands on the masters of 'Night Fever' or 'You Should Be Dancing.' No way. Nobody touches those, they're sacred."

MISSING YOU

The chasm between dance club hip-hop and gangsta rap grew deeper and wider as the 1990s downshifted from agitprop indictments of George Bush the elder into the touchy-feely idealism of the Clinton years. The trial balloon of tolerance and equality floated by the Native Tongues movement exploded over Los Angeles in May of 1992 when white truck driver Reginald Denney was dragged from his cab after the Rodney King verdict and beaten nearly to death by Los Angeles gang members.

Rap on the West Coast, as Ice-T pointed out, was not about the party; it reflected the crackling tension of existence of life just beneath the Hollywood sign. "Real life had turned darker," Gabriel Alvarez writes in *The Vibe History of Hip Hop.* "The fiery aftermath of the Rodney King beatdown, trial, and subsequent 1992 Los Angeles Rebellion vindicated gangsta rap. Not until King got his ass crowned on videotape did the world witness the extent of police terrorism in the City of Angels."

Not a year later, the violence incited by gangsta began to spin off America's turntables and out into the streets. Sleepy-voiced Snoop Dogg could weave a rhyme about cars, chronic, and bitches, but his raps at least had the ring of parable about them. Tupac Shakur, on the other hand, kept it as real as reality would allow, and during the last years of his life, his name appeared with astonishing regularity on the *Billboard* charts and police blotters across the country.

On Halloween of 1993 in Atlanta, Shakur—then the promising young screen star of *Fresh* and *Poetic Justice*—was arrested in the shooting of two off-duty cops. Less than a month later, a 19-year-old woman filed charges alleging that Tupac and his posse kidnapped and sexually abused her. On March 10, 1994, he was sentenced to fifteen days of jail time in Los Angeles for punching director Allen Hughes, who had dismissed Shakur from the cast of *Menace II Society.*

But by mid-decade, Tupac could also claim three wildly successful albums, *2Pacalypse Now*, *Strictly 4 My N.I.G.G.A.Z.*, and *Me Against the World.* On December 1st, 1994, he beat the accusations of sodomy and weapons possession, but found himself convicted of sexual abuse and sentenced to a four and a half years in a maximum-security prison. He had other troubles to consider as well. A few days earlier, Shakur was shot five times and robbed of $40,000 worth of jewelry by unknown assailants while standing in the lobby of a Times Square high rise.

Shakur had arrived intending to meet with Christopher Wallace, a.k.a. Biggie Smalls, or the Notorious B.I.G., and producer Sean "Puffy" Combs. Combs was an ambitious producer on the verge of breaking out with his label, Bad Boy. Biggie, conversely, made for a study in contrasts with Tupac. Where Shakur was raised as the son of militant Black Panthers and carried the tattoo THUG FOR LIFE on his washboard abs, Biggie clocked in at well over six feet and three hundred pounds. Smalls was a man of the street whose

A rift between California rapper Tupac Shakur (pictured) and New York MC Biggie Smalls mushroomed into the 1990s East Coast/West Coast rap war. What began with Shakur's shooting in 1994 ended three years later with both men murdered and no one convicted for either crime. Hip-hop magazines encouraged their rivalry through inflammatory coverage, and record labels stood by silently as the feud racked up sales. (Al Periera/Star File)

expansive tastes included sexy women, fine clothes, and big meals. He'd sold crack to pregnant girls and could convert a man's monthly welfare check into a couple of rocks that he knew would disappear in a few hours without a twitch of remorse. As adversaries, they were well matched.

Who wanted Tupac Shakur dead? No one knew for certain, but within a few months, Death Row Records chief executive officer Suge Knight had Shakur freed on a $1.4 million bond and back on his home turf in California to record *All Eyez on Me*. The physical wounds healed quickly enough, but mentally, Shakur became consumed by those who tried to take his life. Slowly—and with relentless goading from the national hip-hop press—Tupac grew convinced that Biggie Smalls and Puffy were behind the attempt.

What ensued was a spectacle unlike entertainment has ever seen. It was a trumped-up pulp novel billed as Billy the Kid meets Jesse James, Rubin "Hurricane" Carter squaring off against Mike Tyson, and Alien versus Predator all rolled into one. Awards programs became televised stare-downs, and backstage threats often escalated into parking lot gang bangs. Rap fans raced for each new release from Tupac, Biggie, or Puff Daddy, waiting for the one insult that might push the other rapper over the edge. Many blacks regarded the feud as a fraternal war that demanded a vow of loyalty to one side or another. For wiggas, it was proof that blacks lived by a tribal code of cool that bore no resemblance to America's traditional and antiseptic white courtroom justice.

It's impossible to overestimate the impact of this East Coast/West Coast row on hip-hop fans of every color, and music video channels jockeyed to provide regular updates of their skirmishes. Hip-hop magazines like *Vibe* and *The Source* exacerbated the feud by goading each side to unload on the other in their pages. In turn, laissez-faire record companies did nothing to diffuse the situation because it was good for business. Then again, perhaps no one thought that a pair of adults trading insults in the press might lead to murder.

"I dug the hell out of Tupak and Biggie Smalls," says Morris Day of the Time. "Some of it you may think is over the top, but you can't deny that it's some funky shit, man. I think if you're livin' the streets today, rap is your newspaper. I mean we got into some squabbles with bands on the road and come to a verbal situation and a couple of times it seemed like it might have wanted to get physical. But we all drew the line there, walked away and went home. Now it's gone to a dangerous level with the gang violence and all. I just think it's sad."

The East Coast/West Coast war quickly filtered down into the streets, where rap fans emulated their heroes. In a 2003 article for *Village Voice*, writer Ta-Nehisi Coates reflected on the saturation of gangsta in urban America. "These were the days when fashion became a health risk," she observed. "Mothers started shunning Jordans, Lottos, and Diadoras, fearing their sons would come home in their socks, or not at all. Schools ran damage control, implementing uniforms and banning bookbags for fear of what kids might be packing. And still the crazy reports kept filtering through—young boys attacking their mothers or smoking each other over an accidental footprint on someone's suede Pumas."

In 1996, Puffy and his Bad Boy Records set about prettifying the East Coast wing of rap with samples from Grandmaster Flash, as well as from white artists like Herb Alpert, the Police, and others. Out west, Knight and Death Row's new acquisition, Tupac

Shakur, disparaged anything that bore the scent of Biggie or Bad Boy. Shakur even claimed to have bedded Smalls' estranged wife out of spite. "Already people can't look at Biggie and not laugh," he told *Vibe*. "I took every piece of his power. Anybody who tries to help them, I will destroy."

Tupac's "How Do U Want It/California Love" raced to the top of *Billboard*'s pop charts that July, but the rapper had no time to savor his success. Less than ninety days later, Shakur was shot again by would-be assassins, this time on the Las Vegas strip, and on September 13, 1996 he died from his wounds. Those looking for someone to blame narrowed their eyes eastward at Biggie Smalls and Puffy Combs.

Oftentimes, the death of one combatant signals the end of a feud. Not this time. By March 1997, an eerily quiet pall of hip-hop détente hung in the air. Combs scored a pop hit of his own when "Can't Nobody Hold Me Down" made it to #1 that month, only to be undone six weeks later by the lead single from a new disc called *Life After Death* by the Notorious B.I.G. The album was intended as the middle act of a trilogy, since Biggie's debut was titled *Ready to Die* and the conclusion was to have been called *Born Again*. Two months after their collaboration on "Hypnotize," though, Puffy was back with another chart-topper—"I'll Be Missing You"—a tribute to Smalls, who was slain in a Los Angeles drive-by shooting in the early hours of March 9.

Both executions still haunt the world of hip-hop. Neither murder has been solved. Two talented young men were dead, and urban rap fans and wiggas alike recoiled in shock—although both white and black, East and West, were free to interpret the killings as they saw them. To the outside world, Tupac and Biggie may represent little more than contemporary John Dillingers who finally gave gangsta rap a celebrity body count worthy of its bravado. But to the hip-hop faithful, they were the first rappers to uncover the true power of the spoken word.

R.I.P. FOR R&B

At the end of the first Bush presidency, the tide of violence and crack cocaine receded from urban America, leaving behind the squirming detritus of decimated families and trashed communities. Gangsta faded in kind, although a few rappers clung to its vestiges or tried to make something new from its spare parts. Nas, Master P, and Jay-Z kept reporting from the front lines, while Lil' Kim, Foxy Brown, and Eve kept flipping the script by alternating sexual come-ons with in-your-face demands for respect. Some found it difficult to shake their past thug lives—among them Dr. Dre, whose attempt to break free of the gangsta label with 1997's *The Aftermath* sold a paltry two million copies when he'd become used to selling more than double that. In 2003, rapper 50 Cent used outlaw mystique as his launching pad with a disc called *Get Rich or Die Tryin'*, and any Doubting Thomases in the music media were treated to a firsthand glimpse at his war wounds.

Gangsta may no longer be rap's most popular strain, but it remains one of the sturdiest. From the close of the 1990s to the present, artists have diversified, and audiences have followed many of their detours. Hip-hop mythologists Wu-Tang Clan, for example, followed in the footsteps of George Clinton and Sun Ra. While never able to reduce their stew of martial arts mysticism and Nation of Islam morality into a five-minute single, the nine-man group has built up a steady following through such turn-of-the-century offerings as *Enter the Wu-Tang*, *Wu-Tang Forever*, and *The W*.

Others appeared to bridge the gaps between R&B, rap, and commerce effortlessly without pandering. The Fugees were comprised of Wyclef Jean, a first-generation Brooklynite whose parents immigrated from Haiti, Prakazrel rapper-turned-actor "Pras" Michel, and Lauryn Hill, whose voice boomed low and lovely like a latter-day Etta James. Their first record (*Blunted on Reality*, 1994) got urban airplay, but met a tepid response elsewhere.

While album sales hovered near 130,000 copies, the group honed its approach, assumed their own production, and issued *The Score* in 1996. Was it ska? Reggae? Hip-hop? Certainly it was the record Middle America was waiting for—something with an aura of levity that set its Haitian/street observations in crystalline arrangements. *The Score* overflowed with radio-ready fare, from its catchy choruses of "Fu-Gee-La" and "Ready or Not" to a delicate cover of Bob Marley's "No Woman, No Cry" (Hill also has children with one of Marley's sons, Rohan). Think of the album as Hip-Hop for Dummies, a rare disc that neither alienates nor condescends. But covering Roberta Flack's "Killing Me Softly with His Song"? No you *di'int*. Well, yes they did, and accordingly, *The Score* sailed through the roof, eventually selling in excess of seventeen million copies. After a lengthy world tour, the trio began a sabbatical interrupted by occasional reunions. Most recently, the Fugees appeared unnanounced at a 2004 New York block party hosted by comedian Dave Chapelle.

In 1997, Wyclef went solo with *The Carnival*, featuring what touring artists around the world ought to consider their national anthem, "Gone Until November." Pras issued *Ghetto Superstar* in 1998—the same year that Hill won five of the ten Grammy nominations accorded *The Miseducation of Lauryn Hill*. With more than twelve million records sold, Lauryn Hill was the hottest property in the industry, but having been to the mountaintop, she decided her view wasn't worth the climb.

Hill stepped back from showbiz in 2002 after releasing an album of downbeat tunes on *MTV Unplugged*. She'd already made a name for herself with roles on TV (*As the World Turns*) and in such films as *King of the Hill* and *Sister Act 2*. Now she passed on *Charlie's Angels* and *The Bourne Identity* and declined a part in *The Matrix* trilogy. Instead she took her career off-road, leaving social commentary to the Roots, Erykah Badu, Black Star alumnus Mos Def, and others. "I used to be a performer," she was quoted as saying, "and I really don't consider myself a performer anymore . . . . I had created this public persona, this public illusion, and it held me hostage. I couldn't be a real person, because you're too afraid of what your public will say." One record executive lamented Hill's disappearance to *Rolling Stone*, saying, "She woulda been bigger than J. Lo." Exactly.

In her wake, though, a half dozen singer-songwriters took another run at rhythm and blues from a hip-hop perspective, among them Jill Scott, Angie Stone, and Alicia Keys. In an era where beats predominate and a good melody can be flown in from someone else's hit, the prospect of writing a song as an outlet for personal expression still appeals to Keys. "It's very gratifying to write and create something that comes from inside," she told one journalist, "and I think the audience gets that, too. They feel like they're getting a piece of who you are as an artist, kind of a look inside, and that's special to them."

In 1988, *Billboard* columnist Nelson George wrote a book called *The Death of Rhythm and Blues*, bemoaning the decline of an art form once synonymous with black America and the civil rights struggle. But as the millennium began to turn, R&B showed signs of

Nearly a decade after the Beastie Boys brought rap to the suburbs, the Fugees—
Wyclef Jean, Lauryn Hill, and Pras Michel—became the first black rap act to woo
middle America. Their 1996 album, *The Score*, sold seventeen million copies—soon
to be joined by Hill's solo debut, *The Miseducation of Lauryn Hill*, which sold another
twelve million and earned her ten Grammy nominations. She took home five.
(Dominick Conda/Star File)

After a series of personnel shifts, Destiny's Child settled into a trio featuring Kelly Rowland, Michelle Williams, and budding superstar Beyonce Knowles. What began as a family project in the Motown tradition has become an industry unto itself, with Beyonce successfully branching out into solo work and movie roles. (Danny Chin/Star File)

life after its rumored demise—largely due to young performers who grew up in the hip-hop 1980s and 1990s and missed soul music on the radio and in the marketplace. As producer and multi-instrumentalist Stevie J. explained in 2000 to *USA Today*, R&B and hip-hop are opposite sides of the same coin, just like headbangers have both ballads and rockers in their repertoire. "Young men want to have something to play when their honey comes over," he told the daily. "I guess it's cool to be a lover and a thug at the same time. I can speak for myself. (Rapper) Eve is my honey, and I'll have my CD on, and I'll hear this extra voice on top of it. I'll turn around, and the thug queen is singing my joint."

The British remain preoccupied with American black music, too, as artists ranging from Seal, the Brand New Heavies, Soul II Soul, and Jamiroquai to current seventeen-year-old white singing sensation Joss Stone have returned old-school R&B to the charts intermittently since the 1990s. Back in the States, an entire nation of white kids have grown up listening to the soul greats of yesteryear, with Alabama-bred Shelby Lynne picking up the trail Dusty Springfiled abandoned after *Dusty in Memphis*, and Boston's Susan Tedeschi winning generations X and Y over to the soulful side of the blues with a vocal attack that recalls Janis Joplin at full throttle.

Despite Nelson George's fear, it appears that a changing record industry murdered R&B pretty much the same way that Watergate killed the Republican Party. Not all the singers share Snoop Dogg's effortless flow, and rappers who share Mariah Carey's range are scarce, but popular music still rewards honest emotion over technical proficiency, at least since the days of Billie Holiday and Sinatra. As the lines blur between pop, hip-hop, and R&B, the space between black and white gets harder to identify, too. Consider Christina Aguilera: she's all pop, but with a crew of R&B producers behind her and a voice trained from years of singing every kind of music in competitions, casual listeners could mistake her for Alicia Keys or a member of TLC gone AWOL. And when Aguilera joined Pink, Mya, and Lil' Kim for the 2001 remake of "Lady Marmalade" filmed for *Moulin Rouge*, genre and skin color were blown to smithereens in a blaze of vocal pyrotechnics.

Hip-hop's strain of R&B doesn't exactly sound like its predecessor, either. Destiny's Child may be a stylistic descendant of the Supremes and En Vogue, but today's production is more aggressive, the lyrical flirts are more pointed ("my body's too bootylicious for ya" is *not* how Mary, Flo, and Diana would have put it), and the beats are no longer simplified for mass consumption as they were back in the Motown day. There are marked similarities, however, including Destiny's Child's core belief that theirs is a family business. Beyonce Knowles still writes occasional songs and sings most of the leads, galpals Kelly Rowland and Michelle Williams shore up the roster (this after a series of personnel shake-ups in the 1990s), Mom Tina contributes costume ideas, and Dad Matthew Knowles oversees the group's soaring fortunes. In addition to Beyonce's record contracts as a solo and the leader of Destiny's Child, there are movies (she starred in an adaptation of *Carmen* for MTV and appeared opposite Mike Myers in the most recent Austin Powers caper) and endorsement deals with Tommy Hilfiger and L'Oreal.

Calling it a cottage industry would be like calling the Taj Mahal a Love Shack. Beyonce's solo record, *Dangerously in Love*, practically jumped out of the box to $2 million in sales within ninety days thanks to such crossover singles as "Crazy in Love" and "Baby Boy." Add that to Destiny's Child's four #1 pop hits, "Bills Bills Bills" (1999),

"Say My Name" and "Independent Women" (both 2000) from the *Charlie's Angels* soundtrack, and the 2001 throwdown "Bootylicious," which owes its synthesizer bed to Stevie Nicks' "Edge of Seventeen."

For some, the new millennium may actually offer a glimmer of those "good old days" that black artists say have been historically few and far between. Beyonce, with her caramel nougat complexion, her natural beauty, and her talent as a singer-songwriter, is poised to be a star for decades to come with or without Destiny's Child. While she aligns herself to studios and labels for projects, she is accepted as the steward of her own destiny, giving her the kind of career that performers like Sam Cooke strove to establish.

It's also an era of renewed esteem for the producer-as-artist. The Neptunes—multiethnic Virginia Beach producers Pharrell Williams and Chad Hugo—are a case in point. Future investigations into the music of the 2000s will likely find fingerprints leading back to Virginia Beach. The Neptunes also have a sometime band called N.E.R.D. (an acronym for No One Ever Really Dies), which goes a long way toward explaining why Williams and Hugo are today's svengalis to the stars.

After absorbing the disparate sounds of the rock and soul era, Williams and Hugo use N.E.R.D. as a wormhole to bring it all into real time, smashed together, deconstructed, and reconstituted into something equally fearsome and delightful. There are echoes of the Beatles and P-Funk as well as new jack swing and grunge strewn about everywhere. Their computer files are rumored to be a combination Fort Knox and Smithsonian Institution of bytes borrowed and created. "The Neptunes are where Nile Rodgers and Bernard Edwards were in the 1980s, where Gamble and Huff were in 1975," said one insider. "Right now, they are the ones with the all-access pass to the music industry."

In 2003, the Neptunes were handed the masters to the Rolling Stones' "Sympathy for the Devil," which the duo rebuilt from the vocals up with a cappella passages, finger cymbals, and a sinister sitar darting in and out of the mix. The year before, Williams was called in to perform the hi-tech surgery that would separate Justin Timberlake from his boy band past as an 'N Sync symbiant. "Pharell's someone I look up to musically," Timberlake explained to *Vibe* magazine in launching his 2002 solo debut, *Justified*. "And he's my homeboy. That's a deadly combination for bringing out the artist in you."

Within days, Pharrell Williams offered his own assessment in a conversation with an English periodical called *The Observer*. "Justin could have been raised in the black church," he tells a reporter. "To say he's got soul is something you'd expect me to say, but it's true . . . he's a great singer, a great talent. Justin is my boy." The *Justified* campaign left nothing to chance in establishing Timberlake as the white R&B star of the moment. Videos are crafted to emphasize both his Paul Newman–like baby blues and the Jacksonesque moves he's been perfecting since his days on the *Mickey Mouse Club* in the 1980s.

When an artist like Timberlake or No Doubt's Gwen Stefani goes solo (her 2004 release, *Love, Angel, Music, Baby*, is one long discotheque romp), they're not only making records expected to cross over. They're sent forth as the record label's designated breadwinners. The music *and* the appearances have to be in order. When Timberlake bared Janet Jackson's breast on national television during the 2004 Superbowl, the fracas put him on front pages around the world. An accident? "Wardrobe malfunction?" Don't bet on it, especially since the key phrase Timberlake was singing at the moment said it plain and simple: "Gotta have you naked by the end of this song."

Having outgrown the teen-pop idol image he established as a member of 'N Sync, Justin Timberlake made his solo debut in 2002 with *Justified*. With help from such state-of-the-art black producers as the Neptunes and Timbaland, the album and its videos set Timberlake's new course to become America's preeminent white R&B singer. (VDL/Star File)

In looking for tunes to flesh out *Justified*, Williams and Hugo raided the Neptunes' pantry and salvaged five songs rejected previously by one Michael Jackson. Along with fellow Virginia producer and childhood friend Timbaland (Timothy Mosely), Williams and Justin Timberlake carefully pieced together the nucleus of the album, including "Cry Me a River" and "Rock Your Body," Top 40 smashes that packed dance floors from Brooklyn to Barcelona. Timbaland has been working the rap side of the hip-hop equation, too. Lately he's been helping his producer pal Missy Elliott transition from behind-the-scenes work (she was one of the producers behind the sista summit that yielded "Lady Marmalade") into a household name on her own—a modern twist on Isaac Hayes' rise to fame in the 1970s.

In a 2004 conversation with *The New York Times*, Timbaland spoke about breaking down the barriers between music forms, rap and hip hop from rock and R&B, and black from white. "It's time for me to retire," he said wearily, "because it ain't the same. Music's almost becoming like damn near toys and cars. It's too easy. That's why I want to go over there to that rock side, but it ain't popping like it used to."

Don't tell that to Lenny Kravitz, the mixed-race rocker who's scored hits on both sides of the color line. He had a hand in writing Madonna's sexually charged "Justify My Love," covered the Guess Who's "American Woman" for *Austin Powers: The Spy Who Shagged Me*, and regularly packs rock crowds into arenas and concert halls. Kravitz has also been regularly berated in the press for too closely following the footsteps of his hippie-era forefathers—a list that runs from Curtis Mayfield to Led Zeppelin. In fact, many of the tracks on his "Greatest Hits" album owe something essential to someone else. "Are You Gonna Go My Way" updates Jimi Hendrix, "Always on the Run" takes its inspiration from Sly and the Family Stone, and "It Ain't Over Till It's Over" owes most of its production elements to Earth, Wind & Fire's "That's the Way of the World." It's not sampling, but it might as well be.

Kravitz calls his critics racist. When a British magazine called *Untold* caught up with him in 2000, the guitarist grumbled, "It's only because I'm a black man playing music they believe belongs to them. If I was white, they'd be calling me a fucking genius. The same things they cite that make a group like Oasis genius are the same things they say make me shit. They don't understand that rock 'n' roll is as black as hip-hop."

True enough. But while Kravitz points out that even the Beatles and Rolling Stones have slavishly copied their black predecessors (remember Paul McCartney's rewrite of Little Richard with "I'm Down" and the Stones' jones for blues and soul covers), neither owes their celebrity to a sound that isn't theirs. Kravitz grouses that either way he's damned, because black radio programmers consider him too identified with the rock world. "I could come out with the blackest sounding record on the planet and they wouldn't play it," he says. "I've spoken to program directors who have told me they don't consider me a black artist because I've never catered to a black audience. How ridiculous is that?"

The rap press takes no more kindly to the psuedosoul experiments of a blue-eyed rock auteur like Beck, whose work often blends bits of hip-hop with Mick Jagger and Prince influences to achieve a kind of creamy pop Nutella. His appearance on the 1998 MTV Video Music Awards drew the ire of Hinton Als, whose "No Respect" essay is reprinted in *And It Don't Stop: The Best American Hip-Hop Journalism of the Last 25 Years*. Hinton writes, "Parodying the great James Brown's stage moves, he tossed off his light-gray suit jacket and began to dance in a contrived, funky way that seemed to call attention to his appropriated blackness. Then, as (singer Tori) Amos prepared to announce the winner, Beck whipped out two cell phones. Holding one to each ear, he mock-talked into them simultaneously, as if he were describing the glam goings-on around him to a couple of brothers stuck in the hood." Als goes on to assail the "graceless performance," insisting that it "served only to reinforce Beck's obdurate whiteness."

"I think the best rock performances have that quality of being somewhere between ridiculous and anarchy," Beck said a few months later. "I take what I do very seriously, but I don't take myself within the songs very seriously. I think people creating music are being very careful right now; they don't want to be this or that. I think that attitude goes beyond music, actually. It's kind of pervasive right now. People aren't really inclined to want to offend anybody . . ."

Beck admits that for all his musical adventurism, he's been pigeonholed as "someone who relies on retro or pastiche." But, he insists, it's all in good fun, and he can't resist playing with pop as though it's Play-Doh, no matter who believes it ought to be sacrosanct. "I'm really interested in what's going on—the good, the bad, and the ugly—just all of it," he defends. "The things that seem kind of trashy or tasteless now are going to seem really cool in thirty years. I think a lot of contemporary R&B is overproduced and bad, but if you listen to it for a while, you can start picking out things that are really raw and cool. And they're things you'd never hear in alternative music or pop music. There's naked emotion, but it's not pompous. It's honest, and they can slip in something that's tasteless. You can be sincere and insincere at the same time. We have this demand to have sincerity from our songwriters, but I like how R&B can walk that line."

When white stars like Beck and Justin Timberlake issue records that sound like the sequel to *1999* and *Thriller II* refitted with state-of-the art production, and a black rocker insists that he can't steal something that he owns by heritage, then it's time to ask once again: Whose music is it, anyway?

8 MILE HIGH

"You know it's gone to hell," basketball icon Charles Barkley remarked in 2000, "when the best rapper out there is a white guy and the best golfer is a black guy."

The white artist in question is Marshall Mathers III, a.k.a. Slim Shady, both alter egos of the rapper known as Eminem, undisputed emperor of the Wigga Nation. He actually lived the childhood that a publicist once dreamed up for Vanilla Ice—on the edge of the (Detroit) projects, one foot in the world of underclass whites and another in the struggling black community where rap music ruled.

Just as America was accepting the permanence of hip-hop, Eminem showed up with *The Slim Shady LP* in 2000 to add a new layer of confusion. This kid—who bears the stamp of gangsta approval from his producer, Dr. Dre—sure can rap, and with 20 million records sold in his seven-year career, his audience cuts across the spectrum of class and race. And why not? His perspective is fresh, his flow fearlessly funky, and his aim renowned for its smart-bomb accuracy. Although his distinctly Midwestern twang gives him away as white (much like the Beasties, he's never tried to pass for anything else), his sense of humor suggests he takes nothing seriously—including his image or that of his victims. He once marched an army of Eminem clones onstage in their bleached blond Caesar cuts and hip-hop fashions to perform "The Real Slim Shady" on a television awards show. In 2004, he mocked Michael Jackson by dressing up as the *Thriller*-era Gloved One, catching his hair on fire and watching his nose fall off, then appearing on a bed surrounded by cavorting children.

In 2002, the semi-autobiographical film *8 Mile* fictionalized Mathers' rise from trailer park survivor to hip-hop homeboy. "8 Mile is like the color line for Detroit," he explained to *Blender* magazine before the movie's release. "On one side it's [mostly black] Detroit; the other side it's [mostly white] Warren. I grew up on the Detroit side, but everywhere I lived was on those borderlines." Although the rags-to-rapper flick hugs all the same turns that animate *Purple Rain* (excepting its white star and a rap rather than R&B soundtrack), Eminem earned favorable notices for his gritty performance and won the first Oscar ever accorded a rap tune for the movie's single, "Lose Yourself."

While Eminem takes no prisoners with his raps on celebrity, sex, and revenge, there are topics where return fire penetrates the armor provided by Mathers' stage personas. Reporters find themselves on dangerous ground when asking about race or whether his lyrics incite hate. After *The Marshall Mathers LP* declared, "Hate fags? The answer's yes," gay activists dogged him even after appearing opposite Elton John to perform "Stan" at the 2001 Grammy Awards. But he never recanted and never apologized, other than to remind listeners not to take him seriously. Eminem is a pied piper who relishes dangling his fans over the edge of anarchy just to show them the view.

Skin color, although he's loath to discuss it in interviews, is never too far from his mind. "White America" opens his 2002 disc, *The Eminem Show*. In it, he raps, "look at my sales, let's do the math/ If I was black, I would've sold half." Marshall Mathers is acutely aware that he walks a fine line where his wiggas, like the hooligans of Anthony Burgess' *A Clockwork Orange*, love the fantasy ultraviolence of Eminem slitting his enemies' throats and dumping them in the trunk of his car. "I don't go door to door," he told *Blender*, "but I see that probably eighty percent of my fan base is white, suburban America."

At the same time his legitimacy among blacks hinges on giving back to the same community that boosted him to stardom. He's chief executive officer of his own rap imprint, Shady Records, and has been instrumental in bringing the careers of 50 Cent and the group D-12 to full boil. But in 2003, the Eminem Show nearly closed early when *The Source* magazine unearthed a few tapes of a teenaged rapper referring to blacks as "moon crickets" and "porch monkeys."

Mathers admits that the voice on one track is his. In it, he raps, "All the girls I like to bone have big butts/ No they don't, 'cause I don't like that nigger shit/ I'm just here to make a bigger hit." It was nothing premeditated, he told *Source* competitor *XXL*, just an innocent youngster freestyling (improvising) in a friend's basement. "I was seeing this black girl for a matter of two to three weeks," Mathers tried to explain. "That's how the topic came about." In another public statement, he volunteered, "I'd just broken up with my girlfriend, who was African American, and I reacted like the angry, stupid kid I was."

The "angry, stupid kid" who grew up to become the most famous rapper in the world says that those tapes were made before the beginning of his career, and only go to illustrate how much rap and the world of hip-hop had to teach him. "Racism starts by people being ignorant of each other's cultures," he told *XXL* at the end of 2004, "by not mixing and mingling. Let's say you got a room full of white people. If all you hang around with is white people, and you don't know any black people, and you don't know any Asian people, any Hispanic people, you're more prone to say some shit about a muthafucka that's not in the room, you know what I'm sayin?"

Without knowing it, Eminem identifies exactly why music has been front and center in America's dialogue between the races for nearly four centuries. In traditional stories passed from one generation to the next, in sheet music and films, and in recordings and video, music has provided an unvarnished account of what's been said once the other party leaves the room. Artists can be capricious, either admitting their mistakes or backpedaling in interviews, but music unflinchingly reports what happened at the moment of creation before any spin doctor can work his magic on it.

Music allowed Thomas "Daddy" Rice to jump like Jim Crow for slavers' amusement. It put Louis Armstrong and Duke Ellington in front of crowds that they'd have been taking drink orders from only a few years before. Music gave Al Jolson's "Mammy" meaning, and put the threat in Elvis' pelvis. Songs could speak their truths in code—the way slaves used "Steal Away to Jesus" to call each other to meet in secret—or ring with the clarity of a national address, as Bob Marley did in urging his listeners to "Get up, stand up. Stand up for your rights."

According to a Nielsen BDS poll conducted at the end of 2004, R&B and hip-hop are still gaining in prominence on the American airwaves. Rap or R&B singers accounted for sixty-one percent of radio's top hundred songs of the year, up from fifty-three percent in 2003, according to the survey. Pop is slipping, down 36 percent from the year previous. The message is clear that hip-hop is to the new millennium what swing was to the 1930s and what rock and soul became to the baby boomers. And now that the platform belongs to their children, what will their music tell us about who we've become?

NOTES

1 Tate, Greg. *Everything But the Burden.* New York: Harlem Moon/Broadway Books, 2003, p. 24.

2 George, Nelson. *Hip Hop America.* New York: Viking Penguin, 1998, p. 96.

Epilogue

n *Slaughterhouse-Five*, Kurt Vonnegut's protagonist Billy Pilgrim came unstuck in time, and now I have, too. "He has walked through a door in 1955 and come out another one in 1941," the novel reads, and "gone through that door to find himself in 1963." Vonnegut's hero repeatedly witnesses his own birth and death, and lingers for a time at various moments between.

For me, music is that door. I can't watch Latino roots rockers Los Lonely Boys electrify a crowd without feeling the ghosts of Stevie Ray Vaughan, Jimi Hendrix, and T. Bone Walker reverberate in every chord. Turn-of-the millennium albums by Justin Timberlake and Beck echo Michael Jackson and Prince. For me, the early folk of Tracy Chapman channels Odetta, Alabama's Shelby Lynne knows exactly what Dusty Springfield was aiming for with *Dusty in Memphis*, and Chuck D and Eminem tell us as much about life in America today as Fats Waller and Elvis did about the Great Depression and the baby boom. In my Bible of music, the Supremes begat Honey Cone ("Want Ads"), who begat the Three Degrees ("When Will I See You Again"), who begat the Pointer Sisters, who begat En Vogue, who begat TLC ("Waterfalls"), who begat Destiny's Child. Usher and R. Kelly are the new shamen of sex, just as surely as Al Green, Marvin Gaye, and Sam Cooke were once showered onstage with hotel room keys and panties. "Ain't nothin' new under the sun," as Little Richard likes to say. "Rhythm and blues had a baby, and they called it rock 'n' roll."

When I see Eminem in the rock press, I'm reminded of Elvis sparring with the journalists of the 1950s. Sinatra preceded them both in his black-influenced jazz phrasing and irascibility, and Jolson had a bigger ego and borrowed more from black performers than any of his artistic descendants.

WHAT'D I SAY?

This book wasn't much more than an assortment of random articles and audiotapes when I attended a seminar in 1986 where the speaker insisted that "true communication is the response you get." That struck me as so much New Age–speak at the time, but as the research and interviews accumulated, I found that dictum central to the themes under discussion here.

I'm now convinced that popular music is a unique barometer of trust between the races inflected through time. Innovations in music arise less from a desire to reorganize the same notes and rhythms in new patterns than as the challenge each new generation faces to make itself understood to the outside world. Out of politeness, most people will sugarcoat their truth during a dinner party, in line at the bank, at a church bake sale, or after a little league game. But in music, true communication is the response you get.

Consider that for a moment.

Focusing attention on the person at the receiving end of a conversation to gauge how clearly a message is coming through evenly apportions the responsibilities of information exchange to both sender and recipient. Taken a step further, the same theory sorts every artist, critic, and industry professional according to how he or she approaches the intersection of music and race—to reach out, cash in, or thwart our attempts to unite as one people living diverse lives. And if we can agree that at its best, music promotes a free-flowing exchange between artist and audience, then observing how both parties interact as genres wax and wane in the public consciousness ought to tell us something about who we are, what we want, and how well we understand one another. Accepting that as a premise, though, what do rap and hip-hop culture say about who we are today and where we're headed tomorrow?

Village Voice writer Ta-Nehisi Coates suggests that the reaction to rap from whites reveals as much about them as the music does about those who created it. In an essay titled, "Keepin' It Unreal," Coates describes an America that still fetishizes black males as the personification of white man id run amok—the Hyde side of Dr. Jekyll, irredeemably hard-wired to fight or fuck. "Since the days of *Birth of a Nation* up through *Native Son* and now with gangsta rap," the writer opines, "whites have always been loyal patrons of such imagery, drawn to the visceral fear factor and antisocial fantasies generated by black men. Less appreciated is the extent to which African Americans have bought into this idea. At least since the era of blaxploitation, the African American male has taken pride in his depiction as the quintessential man in the black hat. It is a desperate gambit by a group deprived of real power—even on our worst days, we can still scare the shit out of white suburbanites."

Are we acting out a social pecking order established before the Civil War; do we see in Andre 3000 and Lenny Kravitz what our ancestors saw in Zip Coon? That would mean that 50 Cent—today's Thug-du-Jour—and our current white men in transparent blackface (Justin Timberlake and Eminem), alongside such latter-day multi-culti chanteuses as Mariah Carey, Christina Aguilera, and Alicia Keys are merely the latest apparitions in a shadow play written centuries ago. The jazz plea of "Strange Fruit" changed nothing, civil rights soul music was just a dance party, and rap is an industry boardroom invention rather than evidence of a growing disparity between the haves and the rebellion of the have-nots.

But if our progress is linear rather than cyclic, then rap—like every music preceding it—has a message to deliver. Remember: true communication is the response you get. "I think we should listen to what they have to say," Walter Cronkite says, "and apparently we do. I think rappers are saying something to us quite clearly. This is their soapbox, and they're entitled to it. It's the way that we're living, the very essence of our culture and politics that they're responding to, and it's perfectly acceptable for rappers to do that with their words and in their form."

Rap remains an exaltation of materialism and misogyny, and gangsta violence is nowhere near over, as a knifing at the 2004 *Vibe* Awards clearly demonstrates. Bill Cosby's nuclear black family of Huxtables only exists on TV in reruns. The party line espoused by the current Bush administration holds up outgoing Secretary of State Colin Powell and his replacement, Condoleezza Rice, as exemplars of black success, while according to the Pew Hispanic Center's October 2004 report, the actual distance between the wealthy and the wanting grew along racial lines after the last recession. "White households had a median net worth of greater than $88,000 in 2002, eleven times more than Hispanics and more than fourteen times that of blacks," the organization reported.

Throughout American history, popular music has forecast every societal shift from slavery and emancipation to the civil rights movement and the Rodney King and O.J. Simpson verdicts. Over time, artists moved from coded messages about race into bittersweet candor and, lately, demagoguery. Nostalgia lovers that we are, when we don't like what the current generation is saying to us, we revisit the music of the past and honor its onetime revolutionaries, forgetting that they were once vilified for defying convention, too.

TV GUIDES

In January of 2001, televison documentarian Ken Burns unveiled an ambitious ten-part, nineteen-hour project called *JAZZ*. In it, Burns dug deep into the sociological roots of the music, grappling with slavery, minstrelsy, reconstruction, lynchings, prohibition, segregation, and civil rights.

In launching the series, Burns said, "I am always looking for great stories, which jazz has, but I am also looking for things that tell us about who we are. Jazz not only has this great, joyous music, but it allows me to penetrate in the same way as (his earlier series) *The Civil War* into that larger question: Who are we? My feeling is that the jazz greats are as important to our republic in their own field as the founding fathers were on the political/military end. That means that if you're curious about how our country ticks, you have to know about jazz, just as you have to know what happened on the second day of the battle of Gettysburg."

The sales of classic Armstrong, Ellington, and Coltrane recordings spiked in the months surrounding Burns' series, but have since returned to pre-broadcast levels, estimated as a small fraction of the total annual market. Still, by many accounts, it was a monumental and successful effort, due in part to a gargantuan marketing campaign underwritten by General Motors. An oversized coffee-table book, a ten-disc DVD collection, a CD box set, and more than a dozen related reissues bearing the Burns stamp of quality made *JAZZ* the gift of choice for music aficionados that year.

"It's great that such a series exists," Donald Fagen says, "because the story of jazz has never really been told in such a way before, with that kind of detail in a medium where so many people have access to it. And sure, people are going have problems with their favorite artists who they thought were slighted or should have been included. And for me, from about 1950 on, it seemed like they ran out of money or something because they didn't really take the time to examine it closely. But the stuff from the beginning until then was well represented."

Some disagreed. Critic Terry Teachout scolded in *The New York Times* that the series provides "hour upon hour of garrulous anecdotage and gaseous generalizations." Burns, he wrote, "rarely allows any piece of music to play for more than a few seconds, uninterrupted by the distracting chatter of a talking head (usually Wynton Marsalis)."

Others chafed at the dearth of attention granted white jazz innovators. "Ken Burns," the irascible Artie Shaw opined, "was just doing *The World According to Wynton Marsalis*." Fagen shrugs, "It didn't really bother me that Wynton Marsalis and Stanley Crouch were heavy on the black side of jazz, which obviously there's a lot of justification for; it's just that they're so tiresome in other ways. Stanley was quite funny in the interviews, I thought, and at least he had a sense of humor, which Wynton tends not to have."

The series, popular as it was, seemed to divide those who had any practical experience of jazz as a music or cultural phenomenon. And Marsalis' racially revisionist viewpoint appears to have prevailed, leaving fusion and any jazz-tinged music since stumbling for a historical toehold.

In October of 2004, *Newsweek* devoted a special section to Marsalis' crowning glory: a new, $180-million facility called Frederick P. Rose Hall. It is now officially the permanent home of jazz in New York City. Gotham even held a parade in its honor, with Marsalis leading a grand procession to the dedication. But what will be created there, in environs so far removed from the music's birthplace in time and temperament, especially when its artistic director fears and loathes contemporary music?

The accompanying *Newsweek* interview is not encouraging. "You were very hard on hip-hop early on," the reporter prods. "I'm still hard," Marsalis replies, "but not just on hip-hop. The entire country has been in decline in terms of the arts. A lot of what I said back then was exaggerated, because the media loves to make blacks seem like they're downing other blacks. But in truth, this country is known for putting a lot of trash into the world, and that's not just hip-hop music. I hear my son's music, and it's stuff like 'bitch' this and 'n————' that. Short of being given rituals of initiation into adulthood," he concludes, "and art courses that demand engagement and development of your taste—there is nothing to do but descend."

But true communication is the response you get, here and now. Hands-on courses in hip-hop are conducted around the clock across the nation in nightclubs and teenagers' basements—the same kinds of dingy places that spawned the music Marsalis so fiercely protects. What he still doesn't get is that jazz needs fresh influences as much as it needs living virtuosos.

Should jazz survive as a vital medium, it will not be because Wynton Marsalis has staged another Armstrong/Ellington tribute, or that he's seen to it that the Beiderbeckes, Stan Kentons, and Dave Brubecks have been marginalized into obscurity. Any resurgence of jazz lies in the possibility that it could once again become the people's music—some surely turned onto jazz by Wynton and his pals, to give credit where due. But the advent of the Internet and the ability to make and market records without having to sign a contract with a major label means that there could be thousands of boutique Web sites with any number of potential stars who could incorporate contemporary influences, reinvigorate jazz, and recapture the public imagination.

If the goal of *JAZZ* and an acoustically superior home for jazz was to info-tain generations to come, then plaudits all around. If the intention was, as Burns hoped, to find out "who we are," the conclusion is considerably murkier. It's admirable to recount who we were, but impossible to know who we are when listening with prejudice.

TRUE BLUES

Two years after Ken Burns' film, director Martin Scorcese chose a vastly different approach in a television miniseries called *The Blues: A Musical Journey.* Where Burns presented jazz history as a sequential chronology of cause-and-effect events, Scorcese enlisted filmmakers who approached the blues from their own idiosyncratic perspectives. Some installments were straightforward documentaries; others were deliberately oblique and allegorical. And although the series didn't lumber into the marketplace with the same swagger of the Marsalis/Burns eight-hundred-pound gorilla, it didn't need to. Blues isn't dying. It's everywhere—at the center of rock 'n' roll, rhythm and blues, and hip-hop.

"I'm not really worried about the blues," says Double Trouble drummer Chris Layton, who confesses he's more concerned about how all music is made these days. "The whole process of how music is even made anymore is kind of scary," he says. "You don't even have to play a song to have a song these days. A simple thing of writing a song and playing it, you'll know how good it is and what parts are working when you have to flesh it out organically through the process. But if you sit down at a computer with a bunch of samples and point and click and it all comes together and can do anything you want, then you won't know anything about how you feel about it, because you've cut your humanity out of the process."

Technology surely will revolutionize the way music is created and heard in the next few years. But because the Internet is so egalitarian, anyone with a computer and Web access can take any*one*'s music and do any*thing* with it. When remix artist Brian Burton adopted the pseudonym Danger Mouse and blended Jay-Z's *The Black Album* with samples from *The Beatles* (a.k.a. *The White Album*) in 2004, he created a must-have record that was never sold over the counter. The Beatles' label quickly generated a cease-and-desist order, but not before the project took on a life of its own—and that's the wave of the future. Music has always belonged to the people who create and listen to it first—and to publishers and record labels only secondarily.

Music remains as untamable as the human spirit. Its guardians cannot direct it, and its profiteers can only exercise limited control over its dispersal. Ultimately the burden of moving music forward always falls on those who listen and those who create with the intention to record their lives and times in music—including the culture's embrace of whatever technology exists at the time. A few years ago, synthesizers and samples were considered anathema to the creative process, but now an entirely new generation of creative music makers has shown that when both are used in order to create something entirely new, then it's no different from building a new song on a bass or horn line that's been around for years.

SHUT UP!

Flash forward to March 18, 2004, the first day of the annual South By Southwest music conference, where keynote speaker Little Richard is addressing a capacity crowd at the Austin Convention Center. In a speech punctuated by "Whooo!" and "Shut up," Richard rattles off a litany of retreaded interview lines—many of which were probably well worn when I first heard them in our late-night phone exchanges twenty years earlier. Wasn't no name for this music when Little Richard started out, he tells the audience, because he was the only one making it.

The crowd is smitten, hanging on every word. No one seems to mind that the keynote—billed as a live onstage interview between Richard and rock journalist Dave Marsh—has been left in the dust. Dave doesn't seem to mind either, as he sits nervously stroking the arm of his wicker chair, eyes blazing with delight as Richard does Little Richard in a way that neither Paul McCartney nor John Fogerty could ever approximate.

Richard, remember, is also 70-year-old Richard Penniman, a fellow who hasn't had a recorded hit in generations. But the audience understands exactly what this man in the pancake make-up and multicolored cowboy boots has been through—and he has an inkling of where they are, too. In a stream-of-consciousness ramble, he offers advice in the same evangelical preacher cadence Jesse Jackson has used to good effect over the years—don't fake it to make it, he says. Always sign your own checks, and it's okay to use drum machines and sampled beats, provided they don't take the place of developing your own skills.

It's standing room only in the Austin Convention Center auditorium at this point. As expected, patches of the crowd are decked out in buckskin and cowboy hats. Nose rings, tattoos, and multicolored hair are in evidence, too. Music professionals from around the globe all seem to be wound up in this veteran's reverie. In a business that guarantees no one's survival, this piano-playing peacock has managed not only to survive, but thrive. All of his contemporaries are either dead or settled into an unthreatening complacency. Legions of imitators have come and gone, but Little Richard remains, in his own appraisal, "the emancipator, the originator, and the architect of rock 'n' roll." He isn't bragging, either. He's the genuine article and still wholly intact: the wit, the flash, the outrageousness and the pounding piano are all right there. And as the next generation of Eminems, Beyonces, Shanias, and Stevie Rays sits listening, perhaps they see in Little Richard what drew me to this topic in the first place, the grand procession of time, with each artist performing a unique role that reinvigorates our national debate on coexistence. Little Richard is only one cog in the wheel, but a large one.

When he finally pauses for breath, Marsh asks about those who owe their entire careers to Little Richard. And Marsh uses *the* word: Stolen. "Not financially," the writer stipulates, "but creatively." Richard makes a few short quips on the sex life of onetime sideman Jimi Hendrix, and recalls being offered a percentage of the Beatles early on ("I thought they sounded like four Everly Brothers," the singer shrugged, "and I knew where I could get two"). His brown eyes flash for a moment, and he realizes Marsh is still waiting for an answer. "Black and white, red, brown, and yellow . . . music is the thing that's going to bring us all together."

If Richard is thinking of "Blowin' in the Wind," "A Change Is Gonna Come," or "Lean on Me," he's absolutely right. But music can also measure the distance between us, and "Strange Fruit" and "Fight the Power" represent the flip side of that coin. Populist songs have become the nation's diary, flipped open to a random page—at times wracked with anguish, at other times filled with joy and hope for our future together.

Keep listening. Because either way, true communication is still the response you get.

Index